Anonymous

Farmers' and Country Merchants' Almanac and Ready Reference Book

Anonymous

Farmers' and Country Merchants' Almanac and Ready Reference Book

ISBN/EAN: 9783337235987

Printed in Europe, USA, Canada, Australia, Japan

Cover: Foto ©Suzi / pixelio.de

More available books at **www.hansebooks.com**

PRESERVE THIS BOOK FOR REFERENCE.

FARMERS'
And Country Merchants'
ALMANAC,
1870.

WATKINS HOUSE,
On the European Plan,
No. 100 STATE St., ALBANY, N. Y.

Strangers visiting Albany will find it to their advantage to give this house a call.

Oysters, and all kinds of Game in season,
Served in a superior Manner.

CHARLES A. WATKINS, Prop.

GROVER & BAKER'S

HIGHEST PREMIUM

Shuttle and Elastic Stitch

SEWING MACHINES,

51 North Pearl Street,
ALBANY, N. Y.

AGENTS WANTED.

RIPLEY FEMALE COLLEGE, POULTNEY, VT.

CHARLES S. BELCHER,   E. J. LARRABEE.

BELCHER & LARRABEE,
AGENTS,

Albany Aerated Bread Co.,
MANUFACTURERS OF

AERATED BREAD,

Milk Biscuit,	Wine Biscuit,	Sugar Crackers,
Soda Biscuit,	Boston Crackers,	Pilot Bread,
Lemon Biscuit,	Oyster Crackers,	Ginger Snaps,
Cream Biscuit,	Butter Crackers,	Lemon Snaps.

ORDERS PROMPTLY ATTENDED TO.
193, 195 & 197 North Pearl St., cor. Lumber,
ALBANY, N. Y.

M. LILIENTHAL'S
NEW
MILLINERY AND FANCY STORE,

53 North Pearl Street,

Corner of Steuben,   **ALBANY, N. Y.**

Constantly Supplied with the
LATEST PARISIAN NOVELTIES.

Bonnets and Jockies Altered, Bleached and Pressed.

☞ **ALL ORDERS PROMPTLY ATTENDED TO.** ☜

THE DAVIS EXCELSIOR SEWING MACHINE.

Awarded Twelve First Premiums this Year in Competition with every Machine now in use.

THE VERTICAL FEED BAR

Involves a new feature in Sewing Machines, possessing one of the most valuable working principles ever patented; its operation is positive, enabling it to run over seams, and turn corners, without changing the tension, length of stitch, or stopping the motion of the Machine.

The feed of all ratchet or four-motion and wheel-feed Machines is taken when the needle is up, while "The Davis" differs from all these in this—The Vertical Feed-Bar is close to and in rear of the needle, the feed taking place while the needle down through the cloth moves at the same time, enabling the sewing of any number of thicknesses of any length without basting; entirely preventing the fulling and puckering of one piece while the other remains straight; and at the same time, in a practical manner, will do what no other Machine can, to wit, take all the stretch from the goods, operating with equal facility on the heaviest as well as the lightest fabrics, leaving a seam alike on both sides, beautifully smooth, strong and elastic.

It is especially adapted to the diversified wants of family sewing, and is so simple in construction that it can be used by any one with alacrity. It is one of the largest machines manufactured that is

Adapted to all kinds of Family Sewing, Tailoring and Leather Work.

Its Hemming, Tucking, Cording, Braiding, Binding, Felling and Gathering are superior and more even than done by any other Machine.

MACHINES SOLD ON LIBERAL TERMS. AGENTS WANTED IN EVERY TOWN.

JAMES J. GOODALE,
Traveling Agent for Davis' Sewing Machine.

W. W. SMITH, Whitehall,
General Agent for Washington and Essex Counties.

DEALER IN

FOREIGN AND DOMESTIC
DRY GOODS,
WHITEHALL, N. Y.

We have always on hand the largest and best assorted Stock of Goods north of New York. Also, a large stock of

LADIES' AND MISSES' FURS IN THEIR SEASON, CLOAKING, CLOAKS AND SHAWLS.

A Specialty at our Store—CLOAKS made to order by Experienced Cloakmakers.

W. W. SMITH,
General Dry Goods Store, Whitehall, N. Y.

☞ All kinds of FUR SKINS bought, and highest market price paid.

Wilson Nursery,

Madison Avenue (opposite Parade Ground),
ALBANY, N. Y.

FRED. J. MEECH,

DEALER IN

Trees, Shrubs, VINES,

GREEN and HOT-HOUSE PLANTS.

WREATHS, BOUQUETS, &c., Made to Order.

F. S. GRAVES,

MANUFACTURER OF

SILVER PLATED WARE.

Watches and Chains Plated with Gold.

Old Ware Re-Plated.   Door Plates Made to Order.

608 BROADWAY,

Three Doors above Columbia St.   **ALBANY, N. Y.**

HICKS & WOLFE,
SOLE MANUFACTURERS
OF THE
CELEBRATED IMPERIAL

COOKING STOVE.
WITH CAST IRON RESERVOIR.
FIVE SIZES—Nos. 7, 8, 8 1-2, 9, 9 1-2.

UNSURPASSED
FOR
Economy, Durability, Finish,
AND
PERFECTNESS OF OPERATION.

☞ THOUSANDS IN USE. EVERY STOVE WARRANTED. ☜
Send for "Book of Testimonials."

HICKS & WOLFE,
SALESROOM, No. 263 RIVER STREET,
TROY, N. Y.

WM. RODGERS,

DEALER IN

GENTS'
Silk, Soft & Straw
HATS
OF ALL STYLES.
Boys'
Soft Hats and Caps,
CHILDREN'S
FANCY CAPS,
LADIES FURS,
Silk and Gingham
UMBRELLAS, &C.
No. 406 Broadway,
ALBANY, N. Y.

N. B.—Silk Hats made to order.

Dealer in

Trunks, Valises, Carpet Bags,

And Ladies' French Dress and Hat Boxes, Gents' Sole Leather Trunks and Valises, Packing Trunks of all sizes, at Wholesale and Retail.

406 BROADWAY, ALBANY, N, Y.

N. B.—Trunks covered and repaired at the shortest notice.

BOOT AND SHOE STORE,

646 BROADWAY,
Cor. Orange Street,

ALBANY, N. Y.

THE CHEAPEST IN THE CITY.

FRANK B. RODGERS,

Will offer to the Public a New and Unequalled Stock of

BOOTS, SHOES & GAITERS,

Consisting of all the Latest Styles of

Ladies', Misses', Children's and Gents' Wear,

And everything appertaining to a

First-class Boot and Shoe Store,
At the very

LOWEST CASH PRICES.

Don't Forget—646!

WM. M. ROBERTS & CO.,

FAIR HAVEN, RUTLAND COUNTY, VT.,
MANUFACTURERS OF AND DEALERS IN

ROOFING SLATE,

Keep Constantly on Hand and for Sale a Large Stock of

PURPLE, GREEN AND VARIEGATED SLATE,

Which they will Sell in Large or Small Lots, at the Lowest Prices. Their Slate are of

THE BEST AND MOST DURABLE QUALITY,

TOUGH AND FREE FROM FLINT.

They also have Constantly on Hand a Large Supply of

FLAGGING

FOR WALKS, CELLAR BOTTOMS, &c.

They have in their employ Practical Slaters, and will put on Slate Roofs for parties desiring it. ALL ORDERS PROMPTLY FILLED. GIVE US A CALL BEFORE PURCHASING ELSEWHERE.

THE
Farmers' and Country Merchants'
ALMANAC

AND

READY REFERENCE BOOK.

1870.

CONTAINING

HISTORICAL SKETCHES

OF THE

COUNTIES OF ALBANY, RENSSELAER, WASHINGTON, WARREN, SCHENECTADY, SARATOGA
RUTLAND AND BENNINGTON; TOGETHER WITH FARMERS' NAMES, POSTAL
AND INTERNAL REVENUE MATTERS, VALUABLE RECEIPTS,
MAXIMS, AND INFORMATION USEFUL TO EVERYBODY.

396 BROADWAY.   **ALBANY, N. Y.**

TRADE MARK.

THREE THOUSAND TWO HUNDRED AND FIFTY COPIES
ARE DISTRIBUTED AMONG ADVERTISERS, COUN-
TRY MERCHANTS AND OTHERS.

CHARLES VAN BENTHUYSEN & SONS, PRINTERS AND BINDERS, ALBANY.

Entered according to Act of Congress, in the year 1869, by ANDREW BOYD, in the Clerk's Office
of the District Court of the United States for the Northern District of New York.

Gold Pens, Pencils, Diaries, SCHOOL BOOKS, PHOTOGRAPH ALBUMS, Stereoscopic Views, &c., at BENDER'S, 73 State Street, Albany.

10   FARMERS' ALMANAC.

D. McMASTER,

176 BROADWAY,

Opposite Marvin House,

Saratoga Springs

DEALER IN

BOOTS & SHOES.

Always on hand, a Full Assortment of all the styles of Boots and Shoes, and sold at the Lowest Prices.

FORT EDWARD

MATCH FACTORY,

ESTABLISHED IN 1860.

SPLIT CEDAR,

And all Styles of

Box Matches

OF SUPERIOR QUALITY

CONSTANTLY ON HAND.

Orders solicited. Address

J. H. BROUGHAM,

FORT EDWARD, N. Y.

Look at the New Phaeton at Joubert & White's, Glen's Falls.

Orders for Custom Work promptly attended to at WHITE & PEARSALL'S, Glen's Falls.

TABLE OF CONTENTS.

Agricultural Societies	72,	Middletown	131,	198
Albany City	91,	Milton	105,	
Argyle	117, 178	Moreau	107,	187
Arlington	123,	Mount Holly	133,	200
Ballston	103, 191	Mount Tabor	133,	184
Bennington	123, 179	Nassau	97,	182
Benson	129, 184	New Scotland	93,	204
Berlin	95, 182	Niskayuna	111,	205
Berne	91, 202	North Greenbush	97,	195
Bethlehem	91,	Northumberland	107,	187
Bolton	113, 204	Patents, How to Obtain	177,	
Brandon	129, 196	Pawlet	133,	195
Brunswick	95, 186	Peru	125,	198
Caldwell	113, 182	Petersburgh	99,	186
Cambridge	117, 195	Pittsfield	133,	187
Castleton	129, 197	Pittsford	133,	199
Charlton	103, 188	Pittstown	99,	
Chester	113, 205	Poestenkill	99,	193
Chittenden	131, 188	Postal Rates and Regulations,	153,	
Clarendon	131, 196	Poultney	133,	181
Clifton Park	103, 199	Pownal	125,	186
Coeymans	93, 200	Princetown	111,	205
Corinth	103, 201	Providence	107,	191
Danby	131, 199	Putnam	121,	191
Day	103, 184	Queensbury	115,	
Dorset	125, 194	Readsboro	125,	206
Decimal System of Weight and Measures	165,	Recipes	171,	
		Recipes for Horses	175,	
Dresden	117, 197	Rensselaerville	93, 186,	199
Dunnesburgh	109, 200	Rotterdam	111,	201
East Greenbush	95, 190	Rupert	127,	195
Easton	117, 193	Rutland	135,	202
Edinburgh	103, 183	Salem	121,	180
Fairhaven	131, 188	Sandgate	127,	198
Fort Ann	117, 194	Sandlake	99,	184
Fort Edward	119,	Saratoga	107,	
Galway	103, 183	Saratoga Springs	107,	185
Glastenbury	125, 193	Schaghticoke	99,	179
Glenville	111,	Schenectady	111,	
Government Land Measure	163,	Schodack	99,	
Grafton	97, 189	Searsburg	127,	199
Granville	119, 180	Shaftsbury	127,	189
Greenbush	97, 190	Sherburne	135,	197
Greenfield	105, 206	Shrewsbury	135,	183
Greenwich	119,	Shushan		205
Guilderland	93, 190	Stamford	127,	206
Hadley	105, 188	Stamp Duties	137,	
Hague	113, 197	Stephentown	99,	184
Halfmoon	105,	Stillwater	109,	203
Hampton	119, 191	Stony Creek	115,	195
Hartford	119, 184	Sudbury	135,	186
Hebron	119, 194	Sutherland Falls	135,	
Historical Sketch	73,	Sunderland	127,	186
Hoosick	97, 195	Thurman	115,	
Horicon	113, 192	Tinmouth	155,	198
How to do Business	168,	To Secure Public Lands	157,	
Hubbardtown	131,	Troy City	101,	
Interest Table	39,	United States Government	73,	
Ira	131, 192	Wallingford	135,	188
Jackson	121,	Warrensburgh	115,	187
Johnsburgh	113, 189	Waterford	109,	204
Kingsbury	121,	Watervliet	93,	
Knox	93, 194	Wells	135,	206
Landgrove	125, 190	Westerlo	95,	192
Lansingburgh	97, 193	West Haven	137,	192
Law Maxims	159,	White Creek	121,	181
Luzerne	115, 194	Whitehall	121,	196
Malta	105, 205	Wilton	109,	185
Manchester	125, 206	Winhall	127,	193
Mendon	131, 189	Woodford	127,	191

PIANOS, ORGANS and MELODEONS, for sale by P. H. COREY, GLEN'S FALLS.

WRITING DESKS in Rosewood, PAPIER-MACHE, Plain or Beautifully Inlaid with Pearl, at BENDER'S, 73 State Street, Albany.

VAN DEUSEN BROS.

GO TO
VAN DEUSEN BROTHERS,
AND BUY YOUR
DRY GOODS.

THE CHEAPEST HOUSE
To Buy at North of New York. They have
ONLY ONE PRICE,
AND
Sell Exclusively for Cash.
Don't Fail to Call and Examine their Stock. It will save you
FIFTEEN PER CENT.
On your Purchases. No trouble to show Goods.
Don't fail to call at their Store, at
Nos. 124 & 126 BROADWAY,
Where you will find the Largest Assortment of Dry Goods in Saratoga. A Splendid Assortment of
JEWELRY AND YANKEE NOTIONS,
We are also Importers of
GERMAN AND ENGLISH FANCY GOODS.
We are Sole Agents for the celebrated Harris Seamless Kids; Sole Agents for the best Needles and Pins in the World; the Cylinder Needles, and Patent Pin Books (three sizes in one paper). We make a specialty of Black Silks, Black Alpacas, Shawls, Cloaks, Cloths, and Ladies' and Gents' FURNISHING GOODS, &c., &c.

☞ Please call and examine our stock, and you will be satisfied that we sell the best of goods, and as low as you can find them in the city. ☞ Remember, we have ONE PRICE—SELL FOR CASH. It will pay you to see us before you make your purchases.

124 & 126 BROADWAY,
SARATOGA SPRINGS.
VAN DEUSEN BROS.

WHITE & PEARSALL allows no one to undersell them. Glen's Falls.

GARRETT'S TOOTH PASTE is entirely Vegetable. Glen's Falls.

Heavy SHIRTS and DRAWERS for 62 Cents, at WAIT'S.
For a nice-fitting suit of CLOTHES, go to WAIT'S. (See page 81.)

INDEX TO ADVERTISEMENTS.

SPECIAL NOTICE IS CALLED
TO THE FOLLOWING
INDEX TO ADVERTISEMENTS
OF ENTERPRISING BUSINESS FIRMS,
Whom we Respectfully Recommend to Public Patronage.

Agricultural Implements.
Nutting, Hull & Co., Troy........ 166

Ale, Porter, &c.
Taylor's John, Son, Albany....... 18

Bakers—Crackers, Biscuits and Bread.
Belcher & Larrabee, Albany....... 2

Bitters.
Allen Wm., Fort Edward......... 134

Bookseller and Stationer.
Bender E. H., Albany ....opposite 192

Boots and Shoes.
Engel J., Lansingburgh.......... 98
Gilligan & Kirkland, Whitehall... 116
Lempe G. H., Lansingburgh 104
Gordan P., Salem............... 130
Lucas J. L., Saratoga Springs..... 112
Mabbett T. G., Fort Edward...... 22
McMaster D., Saratoga Springs... 10
Porter & McNish, Cambridge..... 126
Rodgers F. B., Albany........... 7
Spicer J., Waterford............ 102

Brewer and Malster.
Taylor's John, Son, Albany....... 18

Carpenter and Builder.
Loudon J., Fort Edward.......... 148

Carriage and Sleigh Builders.
Babcock, J. C., Troy............ 132
Betts, C. H., Mechanicville...... 26
Joubert & White, Glen's Falls.... 14
Lown & Horton, Troy............ 132
Norris D. G. & Co., Glen's Falls... 152

Carriage Trimmers.
Penfield D. & Son, Whitehall..... 118

Carriage and Saddlery Hardware.
Woodward & Hill, Albany........ 19

Clothiers and Merchant Tailors.
Clark C., Lansingburgh.......... 98
Goldring's, Fort Edward......... 146
Lustig & Cohn, Fort Edward 146
Wait H. R. & W. F., Whitehall... 81
White & Pearsall, Glen's Falls, left-
    hand side lines
Wilkins W. A., Whitehall........ 96
Wright & Cady, Cambridge....... 130

Coffee, Spices, &c.
Dusenberry & Anthony, Troy..... 88

Country Stores.
Porter & McNish, Cambridge..... 126
Powell W., Hoosic Falls.......... 162

Dentists.
Benson J. W. Dr., Glen's Falls.... 156
Carpenter C., Saratoga Springs... 114
Cotton Z. Dr., Cambridge........ 158
Garrett, Glen's Falls, bottom left pages
Stewart J., Cambridge........... 128
Tefft Dr., Cambridge............ 130
Thurston E. P., Salem........... 134

Doors, Sash and Blinds.
Collins Wm., Troy............... 88
Loudon J., Fort Edward......... 148
Woodworth & Co., Cambridge..... 128

Druggists.
Broughton J. R., Whitehall...... 114
Davis F. B., Fort Edward. 136
Manville & Weidman, Whitehall... 15
Whitehouse & Co., Fort Edward... 146

Dry Goods, Carpets, &c.
Carpenter H. & Son, Cambridge... 28
Chapin & Allen, Whitehall....... 118
Hawkins & Porter, Cambridge.... 162
Hayes J. jr., Ballston Spa........ 24
Mabbett T. G., Fort Edward 22
Porter & McNish, Cambridge..... 126
Powell W., Hoosic Falls.......... 162
Schoolhouse & Oppenhimer, Ft. Ed-
    ward 158
Smith W. W., Whitehall.......... 3
Vandeusen Brothers, Sar. Springs.. 12

Fancy Goods and Ladies' Furnishings.
Carpenter H. & Son, Cambridge ... 28
Baker P. A., Fair Haven......... 142
Corey P. H., Glen's Falls, right
    hand side lines
Hayes J. jr., Ballston Spa........ 24
Lilienthal M., Albany........... 2
Mabbett T. G., Fort Edward 22
Prindle M. M. V., Whitehall..... 114

Furniture and Cabinet Ware.
Barton W. P., Cambridge........ 158
De Forest & Irving, Fort Edward .. 140
Doren's Whitehall Furniture Rooms, 120
Lavender J. B., Lansingburgh.... 98
Mason H. J. & Son, Lansingburgh . 100
Nash H. B., Sandy Hill.......... 70

Latest styles Bonnets, Jockeys, and Boys' and Infants' Caps and Hoods, at COREY'S, Glen's Falls.

Ding, dong, bell! WILKINS is bound to sell. (See p. 96.)

Plain and Fancy INKSTANDS, PEN RACKS, SEGAR STANDS and CASES, and Unique WATCH SAFES, at BENDER'S, 73 State Street, Albany.

14 — INDEX TO ADVERTISEMENTS.

We buy for the ready cash. WHITE & PEARSALL, Glen's Falls.

Ouderkirk S. A., Saratoga Springs, 110	Kelso J. S., Waterford 102
Peck O. A., Fair Haven 172	Mills & Williams, Fair Haven 124
Scofield C. A., Waterford 102	Pritchard H. & Co., W. Rutland... 142
Smith, Hotchkin & Co., Troy 80	Thomas W. H., Saratoga Springs.. 70
Viele P. N., Ballston Spa......... 26	Wrangman T. J., Whitehall....... 124
Wilmarth M. L., Glen's Falls 152	**Match Manufacturer.**
Wilson J. C. & Co., Poultney 128	Brougham J. H., Fort Edward..... 10
Groceries.	**Music, Pianos, &c.**
Hayes J. jr., Ballston Spa......... 24	Corey P. H., Glen's Falls, right
Porter & McNish, Cambridge 126	hand side lines
Powell W., Hoosic Falls. 162	Hidley & Moes, Troy............... 92
Wright & Cady, Cambridge 130	**Musical Institute.**
Hardware, Cutlery, &c.	Newman J. Rev., Ripley Female
Hall C. A., Whitehall 118	College, Poultney,........ .....back cover
Martin James & Co., Albany..opp. 144	
Nutting, Hull & Co., Troy 166	**Newspapers.**
Sanford, Smith & Co., Ft. Edward, 134	Saratoga Sentinel, S. Young, Sara-
Thomas J, S., Ballston Spa...... 18	toga 96
Yelverton Thos. Fort Edward...... 144	**Nurseryman, and Florist.**
Harness and Saddle Makers.	Meech F. J., Albany.............. 4
Amer M. W. Glen's Falls.......... 156	**Paper Hangings and Window Shades.**
Brokaw G., Fort Edward. 144	Rickard S. A., Saratoga Springs... 110
Hartwell & Akin, Sar. Springs 106	**Patent Agents.**
Northrup S. A., Waterford 102	Munn & Co., New York 176
Thompson P. & Co., Saratoga Sp'gs, 106	**Photographers.**
Watford's, Waterford 104	Alden A. E., Troy................. 132
Hats, Caps, Furs, &c.	Baker P. A., Fair Haven 142
Barrett A. R., Saratoga Springs,.. 106	Cobden A., Troy 88
Rodgers Wm., Albany 6	Conkey G. W., Glen's Falls 154
Hotels.	Haines, Albany 30
Hazelton J. H., West Rutland 122	Hardy G. R., Lansingburgh....... 100
Watkin's House, Albany . ..front cover	Irish G. S., Glen's Falls 156
Insurance and Real Estate.	Moore T. & C. H., Troy........... 74
Potter T., Glen's Falls 162	Orr A. jr., Glen's Falls 164
Pratt & King, Fort Edward........ 138	Prichard's Gallery, Rutland....... 122
Lawyers.	Sunderlin J. C., Fort Edward 136
Fletcher L., Cambridge 130	**Physician.**
Redfern M., Fort Edward 146	Andrews E. Dr., Albany........... 72
Leather Preservative.	**Railroads.**
Lucas J. L., Saratoga Springs..... 112	Rensselaer & Saratoga RR., Troy.. 17
Marble Works.	Troy and Boston Railroad 16
Grant P., Troy 160	**Restaurant.**
Harrington & Everson, Sar. Springs, 108	Billett R. W., Whitehall........... 124

JOUBERT & WHITE,
Carriage & Sleigh Makers

The business carried on in all of its branches in the most *thorough* manner. All kinds of Open and Top Buggies, Two-Seated, Open and Top Carriages. Phaetons and all kinds of heavy work on hand and made to order on short notice.

None but the best of workmen employed, and the very best of material used.

☞ PRICES REASONABLE AND ALL WORK WARRANTED.☜

Cor. Warren and Jay Sts., Glen's Falls, N. Y.

For a First Class Market Wagon go to Joubert & White's.

The HOWE MACHINE is the Latest Improved, at WAIT'S.
For Tapestry Brussels CARPETING, go to WAIT'S. (See page 84.)

FARMERS' ALMANAC. 15

MANVILLE & WEIDMAN,
Successors to E. W. HALL,

Canal Street, Whitehall, N. Y.

Wholesale and Retail,

DRUGGISTS & APOTHECARIES,

And Dealers in

PAINTS, OILS,
WINDOW GLASS,
BOOKS, STATIONERY,
PERFUMERIES,
FANCY GOODS.

Also Pure Wines and Liquors

For Medicinal Purposes.
Great inducements offered in PAINTS, OILS and WINDOW GLASS. Try us if you don't believe it.

TRY DR. ATHERTON'S WILD CHERRY SYRUP,

FOR THE CURE OF

Bronchitis, Catarrh, Hoarseness, Coughs, Colds, Asthma, Influenza, Croup, Whooping Cough, & all diseases of the Lungs & Throat.
Only 35 Cents per bottle. Send your orders to

MANVILLE & WEIDMAN, Proprietors.

Use Dr. Atherton's Sugar Coated Headache and Cathartic Pills,

For Loss of Appetite, Sick Headache, Indigestion, Costiveness, Fever and Ague, Liver Complaint, Nervous Debility, &c.
Only 25 cents per box. Send your orders to.

MANVILLE & WEIDMAN, Proprietors.

Wholesale Prices of Dr. Atherton's Remedies:

1 Dozen Wild Cherry Syrup,..$2.75
1 Gross   "   "   " 30.00
Retails,..35
1 Dozen Headache and Cathartic Pills,..................................1.75
1 Gross   "   "   " 18.00
Retails,..25

TERMS, NET CASH. FIVE GROSS LOTS, TEN PER CENT. DISCOUNT.

MANVILLE & WEIDMAN, Proprietors,
WHITEHALL, N. Y.

Have your Clothing made at WILKINS'. (See page 96.)

Davis' Sewing Machine, best in market, on account of simplicity, durability, strength and perfection of work. For sale by COREY, Glen's Falls.

BENDER will furnish you any Books Published; also, ENGINEERS' INSTRUMENTS, STATIONERY, FIELD BOOKS, &c., at 73 State Street, Albany.

16   INDEX TO ADVERTISEMENTS.

Roofing Slate.
Roberts W. M. & Co., Fair Haven,   8

Saw and Planing Mills.
Woodworth & Co., Cambridge 128

Seminaries.
Elmwood Seminary, Glen's Falls... 150
Hudson Vale Institute, Lans'gb'gh. 20
Ripley Female College, Poultney,
                                back cover

Sewing Machines.
Benson J. W. Dr.................. 156
Brush O. B., Troy................. 86
Corey P. H., Glen's Falls, right hand
                                side lines
Elliott A. B., Troy................ 74
Fowler A., Troy................... 92
Griswold, H. A., Whitehall....... 122
Grover & Baker's............front cover
Pratt & King, Fort Edward........ 138
Smith O., Albany..........opposite 72
Smith W. W., Whitehall............ 3
Tallmadge J., Troy................ 20
Todd H. D. Dr., Saratoga Springs. 110
White J. C., Ballston Spa......... 16

Silver Plated Ware.
Graves F. S., Albany.............. 4

Sporting Goods.
Martin James & Co., Albany..opp. 144

Spring Beds, Mattresses, &c.
Farrar M., Saratoga Springs...... 114

Steamboats.
N. Y. and Troy Steamboat Co...... 76

Stoves, Tinware, &c.
Brewster A. L., Waterford........ 98
Bussey, McLeod & Co., Troy....... 94
Buswell, Durant & Co., Troy...... 84
Hicks & Wolfe, Troy............... 5
Hilton John & Co., Cohoes....... 104
McGuirk & Gaffney, Cohoes....... 104
Morrison & Colwell, Troy........ 160
Phillips Geo. H. & Co., Troy.... 90
Swett, Quimby & Perry, Troy..... 78
Thomas J. S., Ballston Spa....... 18

Undertakers.
(See also *Furniture*.)
Clute P. S., Saratoga Springs.... 108
Peck O. A., Fair Haven........... 172
Viele P. N., Ballston Spa........ 26

Upholsterers.
Penfield D. & Son, Whitehall..... 118

Watches, Jewelry, &c.
Griswold H. A., Whitehall........ 122
Jones A. O., Cambridge........... 130
Stevenson G. L., Albany.......... 20

(left margin: WHITE & PEARSALL took the First Premium on Clothing.)

Grover & Baker's
HIGHEST PREMIUM,
Shuttle and Elastic Stitch
SEWING MACHINES,
J. C. WHITE, Agent,
BALLSTON SPA, N. Y.

TROY & BOSTON RAIL ROAD.
STATIONS AND DISTANCES.

Troy,.................................
Lansingburgh,................. 3.50
Grant's,....................... 8.60
Schaghticoke,................ 12.50
Valley Falls,................. 14.00
Johnsonville,................. 16.06
Buskirk's,.................... 21.33
Eagle Bridge,................. 23.20
Hoosick Junction,............. 25.66

Hoosick Falls,................ 27.23
Hoosick,...................... 30.28
Petersburgh,.................. 32.75
North Pownal,................. 35.35
Pownal,....................... 38.80
Williamstown,................. 43.33
Blackinton,................... 45.03
North Adams,.................. 47.95

C. W. MOSELEY, Sup't., Troy, N. Y.

GARRETT'S TOOTH PASTE warranted to give satisfaction.

*The HOWE MACHINE is the Latest Improved, at WAIT'S.
For Tapestry Brussels CARPETING, go to WAIT'S. (See page 81.)*

FARMERS' ALMANAC. 17

RENSSELAER & SARATOGA
RAILWAY.

GEO. H. CRAMER, President.
I. V. BAKER, Superintendent.
H. S. MARCY, Gen. Freight Agent.
OTIS N. CRANDALL, Gen. Ticket Agt.
TROY, N. Y.

STATIONS.

Albany, (connects with New York Central, Hudson River, Harlem, Albany & Susquehanna, and Boston & Albany Railways. Also with Steamboats to New York.)
Schenectady,
Troy, (Connects with railways diverging from troy.)
Green Island,
Waterford,
Albany Junction,
Mechanicsville,
East Line,
Ballston, (junction of Saratoga and Schenectady Division.)
Saratoga,
Gansevort,
Moreau,
Fort Edward, (Connects with branch Railway to Glen's Falls, &c.)
Dunham's Basin,
Smith's Basin,
Fort Ann,
Comstock's Landing,

Junction,
L. Champlain, } Whitehall,
Steamboats to Burlington, Plattsburgh & Montreal.
Fairhaven,
Hydeville,
Eagle Bridge, (connects with Troy & Boston Railway.)
Cambridge,
Shushan,
Salem,
Rupert,
Pawlet,
Granville,
Middle Granville,
Poultney,
Castleton,
West Rutland and Clarendon Springs, (connects with Stages for Clar. Sp'gs.)
Center Rutland,
Rutland, (connects with Rutland & Burlington and Bennington & Rutland Railways.)

} The Rutland & Washington Branch

ALBANY DIVISION.
ROBERT MORRIS, Gen. Agent, Albany.

Albany, | West Troy, | Waterford,
Cemetery, | Cohoes, | **Junction,**
Distance 12 miles.

SCHENECTADY DIVISION.
Schenectady, | Half-way House, | Ballston, | **Saratoga.**
Distance, 22 miles.

GLEN'S FALLS, from Fort Edward, 5 miles.

W. A. WILKINS' Cheap Clothing Store, established 1859.

Go to P. H. COREY'S, GLEN'S FALLS, for HOOP SKIRTS, CORSETS, GLOVES, HOSIERY, &c.

The Trade Supplied with STATIONERY and Every Article Used in the Counting Room, at Manufacturer's Prices, at BENDER'S, 73 State Street, Albany.

Always a large stock of fine, ready-made Clothing at WHITE & PEARSALL'S, Glen's Falls.

18   FARMERS' ALMANAC.

JOHN TAYLOR'S SON,

BREWER OF

Draught and Bottled Ales,

DEPOTS:

133 BROADWAY, ALBANY,
334 GREENWICH STREET,
23 AND 25 JAY STREET,
NEW YORK.

117 Commercial Street, BOSTON.

SEND FOR CIRCULAR.

J. S. THOMAS,

(Successor to J. S. & J. B. Thomas,) Dealer in

HARDWARE,

The Conquest and other Stoves,
IRON,
STEEL,
NAILS,

Agricultural Implements, &c., &c.,

MILTON AVENUE,

BALLSTON SPA, N. Y.

CARRIAGES! CARRIAGES! Joubert & White. (See page 14.)

For CARPETS and OIL CLOTHS, go to WAIT'S.
For FINE READY-MADE CLOTHING, go to WAIT'S. (See page 81.)

FARMERS' ALMANAC. 19

Calendar for the Year 1870.

	Sund.	Mon.	Tues.	Wed.	Thur.	Frid.	Satur.
January							1
	2	3	4	5	6	7	8
	9	10	11	12	13	14	15
	16	17	18	19	20	21	22
	23	24	25	26	27	28	29
	30	31					
February			1	2	3	4	5
	6	7	8	9	10	11	12
	13	14	15	16	17	18	19
	20	21	22	23	24	25	26
	27	28					
March			1	2	3	4	5
	6	7	8	9	10	11	12
	13	14	15	16	17	18	19
	20	21	22	23	24	25	26
	27	28	29	30	31		
April						1	2
	3	4	5	6	7	8	9
	10	11	12	13	14	15	16
	17	18	19	20	21	22	23
	24	25	26	27	28	29	30
May	1	2	3	4	5	6	7
	8	9	10	11	12	13	14
	15	16	17	18	19	20	21
	22	23	24	25	26	27	28
	29	30	31				
June				1	2	3	4
	5	6	7	8	9	10	11
	12	13	14	15	16	17	18
	19	20	21	22	23	24	25
	26	27	28	29	30		
July						1	2
	3	4	5	6	7	8	9
	10	11	12	13	14	15	16
	17	18	19	20	21	22	23
	24	25	26	27	28	29	30
	31						
August		1	2	3	4	5	6
	7	8	9	10	11	12	13
	14	15	16	17	18	19	20
	21	22	23	24	25	26	27
	28	29	30	31			
September					1	2	3
	4	5	6	7	8	9	10
	11	12	13	14	15	16	17
	18	19	20	21	22	23	24
	25	26	27	28	29	30	
October							1
	2	3	4	5	6	7	8
	9	10	11	12	13	14	15
	16	17	18	19	20	21	22
	23	24	25	26	27	28	29
	30	31					
November			1	2	3	4	5
	6	7	8	9	10	11	12
	13	14	15	16	17	18	19
	20	21	22	23	24	25	26
	27	28	29	30			
December					1	2	3
	4	5	6	7	8	9	10
	11	12	13	14	15	16	17
	18	19	20	21	22	23	24
	25	26	27	28	29	30	31

PIANOS, ORGANS and MELODEONS, for sale by P. H. COREY, GLEN'S FALLS.

WOODWARD & HILL,

MANUFACTURERS AND IMPORTERS OF

CARRIAGE AND SADDLERY
HARDWARE AND TRIMMINGS,

324 Broadway, corner Hamilton Street,

ALBANY, N. Y.

Would you be happy? Buy your Clothing of WILKINS.

The CHEAP Wholesale and Retail STATIONERY STORE,
is BENDER'S, 73 State Street Albany.

20   *FARMERS' ALMANAC.*

Terms, $50 per *Quarter,* **including Board, Washing and Tuition.
No extras, save for instruction in Music, Painting,
Drawing and the Languages.**

For further particulars, send to the Principal for Circulars.

HUDSON VALE
INSTITUTE.
LANSINGBURGH, N. Y.

Rev. A. B. WHIPPLE, Principal.

The FALL and WINTER TERM of the

HUDSON VALE INSTITUTE
WILL OPEN THE
First Wednesday of September.

SPRING AND SUMMER TERM WILL OPEN FIRST WEDNESDAY OF FEBRUARY.

THE
HOWE
SEWING MACHINE.

JOHN TALLMADGE
Agent,
342 RIVER ST.
(*Up Stairs,*)
TROY, N. Y.

G. L. STEVENSON,
Importer of **WATCHES** and **FINE JEWELRY**,
Diamonds, Watches and Gold Chains a Specialty.
STERLING COIN & PLATED WARE, GOLD-HEADED CANES, &c.
No. 6 Green Street, Albany. N. Y.
Engraving and Repairing of Fine Watches and Jewelry executed in the neatest manner.

GARRETT'S Dental Rooms, Bank Building, Glen's Falls, N. Y.

The most complete stock of Cloths, Cassimeres and Vestings at WHITE & PEARSALL'S.

OVERCOATS from $5 to $30, at WAIT'S CASH STORE.
FROCK COAT SUITS Cheap at WAIT'S. (See page 81.)

1st Month.	JANUARY, 1870.	31 Days.
Satur.	1.	
Sun.	2.	
Mon.	3.	
Tues.	4.	
Wed.	5.	
Thur.	6.	
Fri.	7.	
Satur.	8.	
Sun.	9.	
Mon.	10.	
Tues.	11.	
Wed.	12.	
Thur.	13.	
Fri.	14.	
Satur.	15.	
Sun.	16.	
Mon.	17.	
Tues.	18.	
Wed.	19.	
Thur.	20.	
Fri.	21.	
Sat.	22.	
Sun.	23.	
Mon.	24.	
Tues.	25.	
Wed.	26.	
Thur.	27.	
Fri.	28.	
Satur.	29.	
Sun.	30.	
Mon.	31.	

Latest styles Bonnets, Jockeys, and Boys' and Infants' Caps and Hoods, at COREY'S, Glen's Falls.

Ding, dong, bell! **WILKINS** is bound to sell. (See p. 96.)

PAPER of all Kinds by the Case, Ream or Quire,
at BENDER'S, 73 State Street, Albany.

FARMERS' ALMANAC.

TRUMAN G. MABBETT'S.
NEW STORE,
FORT EDWARD, NEW YORK.

Always on hand a large and extensive assortment of

FANCY
AND
DOMESTIC GOODS.

DRESS TRIMMINGS,
BUTTONS,
LACES, WHITE GOODS,
MILLINERY GOODS,

Bonnets, Hats, Jockies,
CLOAKS, SHAWLS AND FURS.
Cloth, Cassimere & Cloaking
FOR LADIES' CLOAKS,
And for Men and Children.

ALSO
A LARGE VARIETY OF
NOTIONS,
AND
Small Fancy Goods
Too Numerous to Mention.

Ladies and Childrens'
BOOTS AND SHOES,
ALSO, SOLE AGENT AT
Fort Edward, Sandy Hill and Vicinity,
FOR

E. BUTTERICK & CO.'S
CELEBRATED PATTERNS OF GARMENTS.

COME ONE, COME ALL!   GOODS FOR THE MILLION!
Large Sales and Small Profits. No Trust, No Barter.
CHEAP FOR CASH IS THE MOTTO.
TRUMAN G. MABBETT, PROPRIETOR.

Cheapest place to buy your Business Suits, at WHITE & PEARSALL'S, Glen's Falls.

Light and Heavy Wagons at Joubert & White's, Glen's Falls, N. Y.

2d Month.   FEBRUARY, 1870.   28 Days.

Tues. 1.
Wed. 2.
Thur. 3.
Fri. 4.
Satur. 5.
Sun. 6.
Mon. 7.
Tues. 8.
Wed. 9.
Thur. 10.
Fri. 11.
Satur. 12.
Sun. 13.
Mon. 14.
Tues. 15.
Wed. 16.
Thur. 17.
Fri. 18.
Satur. 19.
Sun. 20.
Mon. 21.
Tues. 22.
Wed. 23.
Thur. 24.
Fri. 25.
Satur. 26.
Sun. 27.
Mon. 28.

Have your Clothing made at WILKINS'. (See page 96.)

Davis' Sewing Machine, best in market, on account of simplicity, durability, strength and perfection of work. For sale by COREY, Glen's Falls.

Prices of BOOKS, STATIONERY, FANCY GOODS, &c., &c.,
Reduced at BENDER'S, 73 State Street, Albany.

24   FARMERS' ALMANAC.

NEW
Ready-Pay
STORE,

The Cheapest Place in BALLSTON SPA

TO BUY

Ladies' Dress Goods,

FANCY AND RAW SILKS,

All Kinds of White Goods,

EMBROIDERIES,

Hoop Skirts, Delaines and Prints,

COTTON GOODS,

SHAWLS,

Yankee Notions,

Carpets and Oil Cloths,

PAPER HANGINGS,

Gloves, Mittens, Hosiery, &c.

NOTTINGHAM CURTAINS,

Cloths and Cassimeres,

CHOICE FAMILY GROCERIES.

J. HAYES, JR.

Cor. Washington & Melton Avenues.

We mean what we say—at WHITE & PEARSALL'S, Glen's Falls.

If you have aching teeth, call on GARRETT, Glen's Falls, N. Y.

HATS and CAPS can always be found at WAIT'S.
Get a HOWE MACHINE and be happy, at WAIT'S. (See page 81.)

3d Month. MARCH, 1870. 31 Days.

Tues. 1.
Wed. 2.
Thur. 3.
Fri. 4.
Satur. 5.
Sun. 6.
Mon. 7.
Tues. 8.
Wed. 9.
Thur. 10.
Fri. 11.
Satur. 12.
Sun. 13.
Mon. 14.
Tues. 15.
Wed. 16.
Thur. 17.
Fri. 18.
Satur. 19.
Sun. 20.
Mon. 21.
Tues. 22.
Wed. 23.
Thur. 24.
Fri. 25.
Satur. 26.
Sun. 27.
Mon. 28.
Tues. 29.
Wed. 30.
Thur. 31.

P. H. COREY, dealer in MILLINERY and STRAW GOODS, GLEN'S FALLS.

WILKINS sells Clothing 15 per cent cheaper than others.

E. H. BENDER, 73 State Street, Albany, Manufactures his own BLANK BOOKS, and Sells the CHEAPEST and BEST.

26   *FARMERS' ALMANAC.*

PHILIP N. VIELE,

MANUFACTURER AND DEALER IN EVERY VARIETY OF

CABINET AND UPHOLSTERED FURNITURE,

Matresses, &c.,

Gilt & Rosewood Enameled Looking Glass and Picture Frames

MADE TO ORDER.

SOUTH STREET,

Opposite the Union Hotel,

BALLSTON SPA, N. Y.

COFFINS

Of Black Walnut, Rosewood and Mahogany Grains,

MANUFACTURED.

A First Class HEARSE will be provided, and all work in the General UNDERTAKING line done in a satisfactory manner.

CHARLES H. BETTS,

Manufacturer and Dealer in all kinds of

CARRIAGES,

LUMBER WAGONS,

CUTTERS

AND

SLEIGHS,

A Large Assortment on Hand and Made to Order.

Repairing attended to with neatness & dispatch.

MECHANICSVILLE, N. Y.

For a nice open Buggy go to Joubert & White's, Glen's Falls.

WHITE & PEARSALL'S Clothing Emporium, Glen's Falls.

For WINDOW SHADES, go to WAIT'S.
Kid, Buck and Calf GLOVES and MITTENS, at WAIT'S. (See page 81.)

4th Month.   APRIL, 1870.   30 Days.

Fri.	1.
Satur.	2.
Sun.	3.
Mon.	4.
Tues.	5.
Wed.	6.
Thur.	7.
Fri.	8.
Satur.	9.
Sun.	10.
Mon.	11.
Tues.	12.
Wed.	13.
Thur.	14.
Fri.	15.
Satur.	16.
Sun.	17.
Mon.	18.
Tues.	19.
Wed.	20.
Thur.	21.
Fri.	22.
Satur.	23.
Sun.	24.
Mon.	25.
Tues.	26.
Wed.	27.
Thur.	28.
Fri.	29.
Satur.	30.

Go to COREY'S, GLEN'S FALLS, for RIBBONS, TRIMMINGS, FANCY GOODS, &c.

W. A. Wilkins' Cheap Cash Clothing Store, Whitehall, N.Y.

BLANK BOOKS Made after any Pattern at BENDER'S, 73 State Street, Albany.
LITHOGRAPHING and PRINTING in Every Style done at BENDER'S, 73 State St.

FARMERS' ALMANAC.

DRY GOODS & NOTIONS.

We keep constantly on hand a large and splendid stock of Dress Goods, consisting of all the most

FASHIONABLE STYLES,

and at prices which cannot fail to please. To our stock has been added a line of

The Celebrated Royal Standard Double Warp Black Alpacas,

the most beautiful and perfect Goods ever made. We make DOMESTICS a SPECIALTY, and sell them as low as can be found in any city.

PAISLEY SHAWLS,

Wool Shawls, Square and Double.

SPLENDID PATTERNS OF CHANGEABLE SILK AND HEAVY BLACK SILK.

A LARGE STOCK OF

HOSIERY,

comprising the very best grades than can be found in the city, and at prices that cannot be equalled. Ladies will find every size and quality needed both for themselves and children. British and Iron Frame in abundance.

Fringes, Gimps, Buttons, Loops, and every variety of Trimmings. Stewart's Alexandra Kid Gloves, Courvoisier's Seamless Kid Gloves, all Colors—in fact everything in the Dry Goods line.

ZEPHYR WORSTEDS

IN GREAT ABUNDANCE

Beavers, Cassimeres, Broadcloths, Coatings, Doeskins, Tailors' Trimmings, Repellants and Sackings, all **CHEAP** and **STYLISH.**

HOOP SKIRTS to fit all. Odessa Patent Collapsing Skirt, and Bradley's Duplex Elliptic Skirt.

A splendid line of CORSETS. Glove-Fitting, Gold Ticket and French, in all Sizes.

Carpet Warp, Dexter's Knitting Cotton, Wool Yarns, Flannels, Knit Undershirts, Damask Wool Table Spreads, Traveling Bags, Turkey Morocco Bags, Umbrellas, Cotton Bats, Paper Curtains, Wall Paper, Oil Shades, Floor Oil Cloths, Table Oil Cloths, Stair Carpeting, Hemp Carpeting, Buckskin Gloves, Neck Ties, &c., &c.

An experience of over thirty years in Dry Goods has enabled us to fill our Store with Goods which are of the best quality, and at prices which are right.
☞ Our stock is carefully selected, and **no** store can show a **smaller** amount of **Old Stock.**
Our Goods are bought CHEAP, and we mean to SELL THEM CHEAP! Give us a call, and we will sell you nothing that is not what we represent it to be.

H. CARPENTER & SON,

Cor. Main and Union Sts., Cambridge, N. Y.

Garrett's Dental Establishment is Complete, Glen's Falls, N. Y.

Gents' FURNISHING GOODS, at WAIT'S One Price Store.
Ladies' FURS, in great variety, at WAIT'S. (See page 81.)

5th Month.	MAY, 1870.	31 Days.

Sun. 1.
Mon. 2.
Tues. 3.
Wed. 4.
Thur. 5.
Fri. 6.
Satur. 7.
Sun. 8.
Mon. 9.
Tues. 10.
Wed. 11.
Thur. 12.
Fri. 13.
Satur. 14.
Sun. 15.
Mon. 16.
Tues. 17.
Wed. 18.
Thur. 19.
Fri. 20.
Satur. 21.
Sun. 22.
Mon. 23.
Tues. 24.
Wed. 25.
Thur. 26.
Fri. 27.
Satur. 28.
Sun. 29.
Mon. 30.
Tues. 31.

Ladies' Undergarments and Gored Tucked Skirts, at P. H. COREY'S, GLEN'S FALLS.

Buy your Clothing of W. A. Wilkins, Whitehall, N. Y.

BANKS, INSURANCE COMPANIES, and all other Companies
Supplied at BENDER'S, 73 State Street, Albany.

30   FARMERS' ALMANAC.

"HAINES,"
Photographer,
478 BROADWAY,

(*Opp. Stanwix Hall.*)

PHOTOGRAPHY IN ALL ITS BRANCHES,

PORTRAITS, VIEWS

Enlarging and Finishing
—IN—

Oil, Water Color or Indian Ink,

ON PAPER, CANVAS OR PORCELAIN,

Also Printing for the Trade, of

SCULPTURE, ENGRAVINGS, ETC.,

Both by Contact and Solar Process, at Lowest Market Rates.

PUBLISHER OF

STEREOGRAPHS OF MORBID SPECIMENS

For the Medical Profession.

The best selected stock of fine Clothing is at WHITE & PEARSALL'S, Glen's Falls.

The latest style of Pony Sleighs at Joubert & White's, Glen's Falls.

C. O. D. BOOTS and SHOES are the cheapest, at WAIT'S.
Boots and Shoes, every pair Warranted, at WAIT'S. (See page 81.)

6th Month.	JUNE, 1870.	30 Days.
Wed. 1.		
Thur. 2.		
Fri. 3.		
Satur. 4.		
Sun. 5.		
Mon. 6.		
Tues. 7.		
Wed. 8.		
Thur. 9.		
Fri. 10.		
Satur. 11.		
Sun. 12.		
Mon. 13.		
Tues. 14.		
Wed. 15.		
Thur. 16.		
Fri. 17.		
Satur. 18.		
Sun. 19.		
Mon. 20.		
Tues. 21.		
Wed. 22.		
Thur. 23.		
Fri. 24.		
Satur. 25.		
Sun. 26.		
Mon. 27.		
Tues. 28.		
Wed. 29.		
Thur. 30.		

SASH and BONNET RIBBONS, in great variety, at COREY'S, GLEN'S FALLS.

Bie yer Cloze ov W. A. WILKINS. (See page 96.)

SCRIP, CERTIFICATES, DRAFTS, CHECKS, &c., &c., Gotten up in ALL STYLES, at BENDER'S, 73 State Street, Albany.

7th Month.	JULY, 1870.	31 Days.

Fri. 1.
Satur. 2.
Sun. 3.
Mon. 4.
Tues. 5.
Wed. 6.
Thur. 7.
Fri. 8.
Satur. 9.
Sun. 10.
Mon. 11.
Tues. 12.
Wed. 13.
Thur. 14.
Fri. 15.
Satur. 16.
Sun. 17.
Mon. 18.
Tues. 19.
Wed. 20.
Thur. 21.
Fri. 22.
Satur. 23.
Sun. 24.
Mon. 25.
Tues. 26.
Wed. 27.
Thur. 28.
Fri. 29.
Satur. 30.
Sun. 31.

We defy competition. **WHITE & PEARSALL**, Glen's Falls.

GARRETT, DENTIST, Glen's Falls, N. Y.

Latest Novelties in Ladies' Boots, at WAIT'S.
Romeo and Juliet Walking Boots, at WAIT'S. (See page 81.)

8th Month.	AUGUST, 1870.	31 Days.

Mon. 1.
Tues. 2.
Wed. 3.
Thur. 4.
Fri. 5.
Satur. 6.
Sun. 7.
Mon. 8.
Tues. 9.
Wed. 10.
Thur. 11.
Fri. 12.
Satur. 13.
Sun. 14.
Mon. 15.
Tues. 16.
Wed. 17.
Thur. 18.
Fri. 19.
Satur. 20.
Sun. 21.
Mon. 22.
Tues. 23.
Wed. 24.
Thur. 25.
Fri. 26.
Satur. 27.
Sun. 28.
Mon. 29.
Tues. 30.
Wed. 31.

P. H. COREY, GLEN'S FALLS, furnishes SHEET MUSIC, &c., to Teachers, at a discount.

W. A. Wilkins sells Bully Cloze Cheaper nor anybody elts.

LAW BLANKS of Every Form, by the Single Sheet, Quire or Ream, and ATTORNEY'S STATIONERY, at BENDER'S, 73 State Street, Albany.

Call and examine before purchasing elsewhere. WHITE & PEARSALL, Glen's Falls.

9th Month.	SEPTEMBER, 1870.	30 Days.

Thur. 1.
Fri. 2.
Satur. 3.
Sun. 4.
Mon. 5.
Tues. 6.
Wed. 7.
Thur. 8.
Fri. 9.
Satur. 10.
Sun. 11.
Mon. 12.
Tues. 13.
Wed. 14.
Thur. 15.
Fri. 16.
Satur. 17.
Sun. 18.
Mon. 19.
Tues. 20.
Wed. 21.
Thur. 22.
Fri. 23.
Satur. 24.
Sun. 25.
Mon. 26.
Tues. 27.
Wed. 28.
Thur. 29.
Fri. 30.

Our Stock of open Carriages is Complete. Joubert & White.

Rubber Boots and Overshoes, at WAIT'S.
Mens' and Womens' Artic Overshoes, at WAIT'S. (See page 81.)

10th Month.   OCTOBER, 1870.   31 Days.

Satur.	1.
Sun.	2.
Mon.	3.
Tues.	4.
Wed.	5.
Thur.	6.
Fri.	7.
Satur.	8.
Sun.	9.
Mon.	10.
Tues.	11.
Wed.	12.
Thur.	13.
Fri.	14.
Satur.	15.
Sun.	16.
Mon.	17.
Tues.	18.
Wed.	19.
Thur.	20.
Fri.	21.
Satur.	22.
Sun.	23.
Mon.	24.
Tues.	25.
Wed.	26.
Thur.	27.
Fri.	28.
Satur.	29.
Sun.	30.
Mon.	31.

FRINGES, GIMPS and DRESS TRIMMINGS, of every description, at COREY'S, GLEN'S FALLS.

Custom Work done better at WILKINS' than elsewhere.

County Clerk's RECORD and DEED BOOKS, &c., Made after Special Forms by E. H. BENDER, Dealer in Books and Stationery, 73 State Street, Albany.

11th Month.	NOVEMBER, 1870.	30 Days.

Tues. 1.
Wed. 2.
Thur. 3.
Fri. 4.
Satur. 5.
Sun. 6.
Mon. 7.
Tues. 8.
Wed. 9.
Thur. 10.
Fri. 11.
Satur. 12.
Sun. 13.
Mon. 14.
Tues. 15.
Wed. 16.
Thur. 17.
Fri. 18.
Satur. 19.
Sun. 20.
Mon. 21.
Tues. 22.
Wed. 23.
Thur. 24.
Fri. 25.
Satur. 26.
Sun. 27.
Mon. 28.
Tues. 29.
Wed. 30.

Superior inducements at WHITE & PEARSALL'S, Glen's Falls.

Garrett's Tooth Paste, the best in use. Glen's Falls, N. Y.

Fine and Coarse BOOTS, at WAIT'S One Price Store.
Boys' and Youths' Boots, at WAIT'S One Price Store. (See page 81.)

12th Month.	DECEMBER. 1870.	31 Days.
Thur.	1.	
Fri.	2.	
Satur.	3.	
Sun.	4.	
Mon.	5.	
Tues.	6.	
Wed.	7.	
Thur.	8.	
Fri.	9.	
Satur.	10.	
Sun.	11.	
Mon.	12.	
Tues.	13.	
Wed.	14.	
Thur.	15.	
Fri.	16.	
Satur.	17.	
Sun.	18.	
Mon.	19.	
Tues.	20.	
Wed.	21.	
Thur.	22.	
Fri.	23.	
Satur.	24.	
Sun.	25.	
Mon.	26.	
Tues.	27.	
Wed.	28.	
Thur.	29.	
Fri.	30.	
Satur.	31.	

SATINS, SILKS, VELVETS, FLOWERS and FEATHERS, in variety, at COREY'S, GLEN'S FALLS.

W. A. WILKINS' Cheap Clothing Store, established 1859.

70   FARMERS' ALMANAC.

WILLIAM H. THOMAS,

BROADWAY MARBLE WORKS,
COR. BROADWAY AND GROVE STS.,
SARATOGA SPRINGS, N. Y.

MONUMENTS AND HEADSTONES
FURNISHED TO ORDER AT SHORT NOTICE, in ALL STYLES.

H. B. NASH,
MANUFACTURER AND DEALER IN

HOUSE FURNISHING GOODS,

Cabinet-Ware
Of all kinds, and sells as cheap as can be bought anywhere north of New York. Always on hand, a good assortment of Chairs, Sofas, Looking Glasses, Extension Tables, Picture Frames, Mattresses, Curtains, Fixtures, Pails, Brooms, Wooden-Ware, Children's Carriages, Sleighs, Wheelbarrows, Toys, &c., &c.

COFFINS AND BURIAL CASES,
Trimmed in the best style, may be found at our Warerooms. Entire charge taken of Funerals when desired.

MAIN STREET, SANDY HILL, N. Y.

For a nice two-seated Carriage go to Joubert & White's, G. Falls.

Ready-made Clothing at bargains, at WAIT'S.
For your WEDDING SUITS, go to WAITS. (See page 81.)

Interest Table.

At Seven per Cent. in Dollars and Cents, from $1 to $10,000.

AMOUNT.	1 day.	7 days.	15 days.	1 mo.	3 mos.	6 mos.	12 mos.
$1	$0 00	$0 00	$0 00¼	$0 00½	$0 01¾	$0 03½	$0 07
2	00	00¼	00½	01¼	03½	07	14
3	00	00½	00¾	01¾	05¼	10½	21
4	00	00½	01	02⅜	07	14	28
5	00	00¾	01½	03	08¾	17½	35
6	00	00¾	01¾	03½	10½	21	42
7	00	01	02	04	12¼	24½	49
8	00	01	02¼	04⅔	14	28	56
9	00	01¼	02½	05¼	15¾	31½	63
10	00¼	01¼	03	05¾	17½	35	70
20	00⅜	02¾	06	11⅔	35	70	1 40
30	00½	04	09	17½	52½	1 05	2 10
40	00¾	05½	12	23⅛	70	1 40	2 80
50	01	06¾	15	29¼	87½	1 75	3 50
100	02	13½	29	58⅓	1 75	3 50	7 00
200	04	27¼	58	1 16⅔	3 50	7 00	14 00
300	06	40¾	87½	1 75	5 25	10 50	21 00
400	08	54½	1 17	2 33⅓	7 00	14 00	28 00
500	10	68	1 46	2 91⅔	8 75	17 50	35 00
1,000	19½	1 36	2 92	5 83⅛	17 50	35 00	70 00
2,000	39	2 72¼	5 83	11 66⅔	35 00	70 00	140 00
3,000	58	4 08¼	8 75	17 50	52 50	105 00	210 00
4,000	78	5 44½	11 67	23 33⅛	70 00	140 00	280 00
5,000	97	6 80½	14 58	29 16⅔	87 50	175 00	350 00
10,000	1 94	13 61	29 17	58 33	175 00	350 00	700 00

COMPUTING INTEREST.—The following is a new rule for computing interest:

Six per cent.—Multiply any given number of dollars by the number of days of interest desired, separate the right hand figure and divide by six, the result is the true interest of such for the time required, at six per cent.

Eight per cent.—Multiply any given amount by the number of days upon which it is desired to ascertain the interest, and divide by forty-five, and the result will be the interest of such for the time required, at eight per cent.

Ten per cent.—Multiply the same as above and divide by thirty-six, and the result will show the rate of interest at ten per cent.

PEOPLE'S LINE OF STEAMBOATS,

RUNNING BETWEEN

Albany and New York,

In connection with the various

RAILROADS LEAVING BOTH CITIES.

P. C. SMITH, Agent, New York.

J. W. HARCOURT, Agent, Albany.

Would you be happy? Buy your Clothing of WILKINS.

Go to P. H. COREY'S, GLEN'S FALLS, for HOOP SKIRTS, CORSETS, GLOVES, HOSIERY, &c.

BLANK BOOKS, MEMORANDUM and PASS BOOKS, on hand and made to order,
by BENDER, 73 State Street, Albany.

Town and Union Agricultural Societies.

Afton, Chenango county.
Barton, Tioga county.
Brookfield, Madison county.
Cattaraugus Reservation, Cattaraugus county.
Cazenovia Farmers' and Mechanics' Association, Madison county.
Connewango Valley, Cattaraugus Co.
Constantia, Oswego county.
Danby, Tompkins county.
Delhi Agricultural and Mechanical Society, Delaware county.
Dryden, Tompkins county.
Ellisburgh, Adams and Henderson, Jefferson county.
Farmers' Club, Castle Creek, Broome county.
Farmers' Club, East Maine, Broome Co.
Farmers' Club, Allen's Settlement Broome county.
Farmers' and Gardeners' Club of Pomfret, Chautauqua county.
Galen, Wayne county.
Gorham, Ontario county.
Gowanda, Cattaraugus county.
Gouverneur Agricultural and Mechanical Society, St. Lawrence county.
Hamilton, Madison county.
Hammond Union Agricultural and Mechanical Society, St. Lawrence Co.
Hess Road Farmer's Club, Niagara Co.
Horticultural, Pomological and Floral Society, 1st Assem. Dist., Washington county.

Iroquois Agricultural Association, Cattaraugus county.
Kirkland, Oneida county.
Lenox Farmers' and Mechanics' Club, Madison county.
Lodi, Seneca county.
Maine, Broome county.
Manlius and Pompey Agricultural Association, Onondaga county.
Moravia, Scipio, Venice, Genoa, Locke, Cayuga county.
Moriah, Essex county.
North Bay, Oneida county.
Otisco Farmers' Club, Onondaga county.
Ridgeway Agricultural and Horticultural Club, Orleans county.
Riverhead Town, Suffolk county.
Sandy Creek, Richland, Orwell and Boylston, Oswego county.
Sangersfield and Marshall, Oneida Co.
Schenevus Valley, Otsego county.
Skaneateles Farmers' Club, Onondaga county.
Seneca Falls Union, Seneca county.
Thorn Hill Farmers' Club, Onondaga Co.
Trenton Union, Oneida, county.
Union, Covert, Hector and Ulysses, Seneca and Tompkins counties.
Union, Brockport, Monroe county.
Union, Winfield, Herkimer county.
Vernon, Oneida county.
Vienna, Oneida county.
Yorktown Agricultural and Horticultural Society, Westchester county.

EXTRA SPECIAL NOTICE
TO INVALIDS.

I solicit the very Worst Cases—those that have been given up by the doctors especially. I am curing Hundreds of such Cases every year. DO NOT FAIL to write out the particulars of your cases as soon as you read these lines. I tell you there is Balm in Gilead. You, WHO have been given up, Can be Cured in 17 out of 20 cases. The ONLY Thing required is to find a Physician that knows how to do it. I am often permitted to make Cures that men call wonderful. WRITE ME Immediately; it costs you nothing to do that. Thousands have been saved from Death and the Grave through my treatment, and other Thousands will yet be saved. For is it WRITTEN on the SCROLL of ETERNAL TIME, that the SICK, and the Diseased who are CURABLE, shall Not *Always Perish* through Ignorance, as for long Ages in the past they have done. Address

Dr. E. ANDREWS, M. D.,
Office No. 58 State Street, Albany, N. Y.

GARRETT'S Tooth Paste removes all scurf. Glen's Falls.

NEW NOISELESS

TRIUMPHANT!

THE POPULAR VERDICT DECLARES IT THE BEST.

450,000 Sold.

The Wheeler & Wilson received the **ONLY** GOLD MEDAL at the Paris Exposition, over 82 Competitors, as the Best Sewing Machine in the World.

GENERAL AGENCY:

551 & 553 Broadway;

After May 1st, 1870, at - - - 530 Broadway.

O. SMITH, Agent.

Local Agents Wanted in localities where we are not already represented.

For CARPETS and OIL CLOTHS, go to WAIT'S.
For FINE READY-MADE CLOTHING, go to WAIT'S. (See page 81.)

United States Government.

The twenty-first Presidential Term of four years, commenced on the 4th of March, 1869, and will expire on the 4th of March, 1873.
President—Gen. Ulysses S. Grant, of Illinois, $25,000.
Vice-President—Schuyler Colfax, of Indiana, $8,000.
Secretary of State—Hamilton Fish, of New York, $8,000.
Secretary of the Treasury—George S. Boutwell, of Massachusetts, $8,000.
Secretary of War—Gen. Wm. M. Belknap, of Iowa, $8,000.
Secretary of the Navy—Geo. M. Robeson, of New Jersey, $8,000.
Secretary of the Interior—Jacob D. Cox, of Ohio, $8,000.
Postmaster General—John A. Creswell, of Maryland, $8,000.
Attorney General—E. C. Hoar, of Massachusetts, $8,000.

U. S. CONGRESS.

The Legislative powers of the General Government are vested in the United States Congress, which consists of two houses, Senate and House of Representatives.

SENATE.

The Senate consists of 72 members, two from each State.
President—The Vice-President of the United States, *ex-officio*.
Salary of Senators, $3,000 and mileage, 20 cents per mile.

HOUSE OF REPRESENTATIVES.

This house consists of 241 members.
Salary and mileage of Representatives same as Senators. The salary of the Speaker is $6,000.

JUDICIAL—SUPREME COURT OF THE UNITED STATES.

Chief Justice—Salmon P. Chase, of Ohio. Salary, $6,500.
Associates—Samuel Nelson, Cooperstown, New York; Robert C. Grier, Philadelphia, Pennsylvania; Nathan Clifford, Portland, Maine; Noah M. Swayne, Columbus, Ohio; David Davis, Bloomington, Illinois; Samuel F. Miller, Keokuk, Iowa; Stephen J. Field, California. Salary of each, $6,000.
The Court holds one term annually, at Washington, commencing on the first Monday in December.

The United States.

THE UNITED STATES OF AMERICA, with its TERRITORIES, extends from the Atlantic west to the Pacific Ocean, occupying the middle division of North America; being bounded on the north by the British Possessions, and on the south by the Gulf of Mexico and the Republic of Mexico. It lies between 25 deg. and 49 deg. of north latitude, and between 66 deg. 5 min. and 125 deg. west longitude from Greenwich; or between 10 deg. 1 min. east and 48 deg west longitude from Washington city. Its greatest length from east to west is estimated at 3,000 miles, and its greatest breadth from north to south 1,700 miles; containing an estimated area of 3,250,000 square miles. It has a frontier line of about 10,000 miles, of which 3,500 miles is along the Atlantic coast and Gulf of Mexico, and 1,620 miles on the Pacific Ocean and Straits of Juan de Fuca. Its surface embraces about one-third of North America, including the West India Islands, being about one-twentieth of the land of the whole earth. It was first discovered to the inhabitants of the Old World by John Cabot, A. D., 1497, being five years after the landing of Columbus at St. Salvador.

Buy your Clothing of **W. A. Wilkins**, Whitehall, **N. Y.**

WHEELER & WILSON'S
NEW IMPROVED,
NOISELESS SEWING MACHINES.

A. B. ELLIOTT, General Dealer,   **No. 3 Broadway, TROY, N. Y.**

These world-renowned Sewing Machines took the Highest Premium—a GOLD MEDAL,—at the Paris Exposition, 1867, against 82 competitors. Upwards of 400,000 of these Machines have been manufactured and sold, and the demand is increasing. They are the best Family Sewing Machine in the world.

GENERAL OFFICE, No. 3 Broadway, TROY, N. Y.

A. B. ELLIOTT, Gen'l Agent.

The Old Stand.
T. & C. H. MOORE'S
Photograph, Ambrotype and Bon-Ton Gallery,

No. 2 First St., Opposite Troy House.

Pictures of all kinds

COPIED,

And Finished in

INDIA INK,
WATER OR OIL COLORS,

Being the only Sure Way of Obtaining

Perfect Likenesses from Small Indistinct Pictures.

For CARPETS and OIL CLOTHS, go to WAIT'S.
For FINE READY-MADE CLOTHING, go to WAIT'S. (See page 81.)

United States Government.

The twenty-first Presidential Term of four years, commenced on the 4th of March, 1869, and will expire on the 4th of March, 1873.
President—Gen. Ulysses S. Grant, of Illinois, $25,000.
Vice-President—Schuyler Colfax, of Indiana, $8,000.
Secretary of State—Hamilton Fish, of New York, $8,000.
Secretary of the Treasury—George S. Boutwell, of Massachusetts, $8,000.
Secretary of War—Gen. Wm. M. Belknap, of Iowa, $8,000.
Secretary of the Navy—Geo. M. Robeson, of New Jersey, $8,000.
Secretary of the Interior—Jacob D. Cox, of Ohio, $8,000.
Postmaster General—John A. Cresswell, of Maryland, $8,000.
Attorney General—E. C. Hoar, of Massachusetts, $8,000.

U. S. CONGRESS.

The Legislative powers of the General Government are vested in the United States Congress, which consists of two houses, Senate and House of Representatives.

SENATE.

The Senate consists of 72 members, two from each State.
President—The Vice-President of the United States, *ex-officio*.
Salary of Senators, $3,000 and mileage, 20 cents per mile.

HOUSE OF REPRESENTATIVES.

This house consists of 241 members.
Salary and mileage of Representatives same as Senators. The salary of the Speaker is $6,000.

JUDICIAL—SUPREME COURT OF THE UNITED STATES.

Chief Justice—Salmon P. Chase, of Ohio. Salary, $6,500.
Associates—Samuel Nelson, Cooperstown, New York; Robert C. Grier, Philadelphia, Pennsylvania; Nathan Clifford, Portland, Maine; Noah M. Swayne, Columbus, Ohio; David Davis, Bloomington, Illinois; Samuel F. Miller, Keokuk, Iowa; Stephen J. Field, California. Salary of each, $6,000.
The Court holds one term annually, at Washington, commencing on the first Monday in December.

The United States.

THE UNITED STATES OF AMERICA, with its TERRITORIES, extends from the Atlantic west to the Pacific Ocean, occupying the middle division of North America; being bounded on the north by the British Possessions, and on the south by the Gulf of Mexico and the Republic of Mexico. It lies between 25 deg. and 49 deg. of north latitude, and between 66 deg. 5 min. and 125 deg. west longitude from Greenwich; or between 10 deg. 1 min. east and 48 deg west longitude from Washington city. Its greatest length from east to west is estimated at 3,000 miles, and its greatest breadth from north to south 1,700 miles; containing an estimated area of 3,250,000 square miles. It has a frontier line of about 10,000 miles, of which 3,500 miles is along the Atlantic coast and Gulf of Mexico, and 1,620 miles on the Pacific Ocean and Straits of Juan de Fuca. Its surface embraces about one-third of North America, including the West India Islands, being about one-twentieth of the land of the whole earth. It was first discovered to the inhabitants of the Old World by John Cabot, A. D., 1497, being five years after the landing of Columbus at St. Salvador.

Buy your Clothing of **W. A. Wilkins, Whitehall, N. Y.**

WHEELER & WILSON'S
NEW IMPROVED,
NOISELESS SEWING MACHINES.

A. B. ELLIOTT, General Dealer,

No. 3 Broadway, TROY, N. Y.

These world-renowned Sewing Machines took the Highest Premium—a GOLD MEDAL—at the Paris Exposition, 1867, against 82 competitors. Upwards of 400,000 of these Machines have been manufactured and sold, and the demand is increasing. They are the best Family Sewing Machine in the world.

GENERAL OFFICE, No. 3 Broadway, TROY, N. Y.

A. B. ELLIOTT, Gen'l Agent.

The Old Stand.
T. & C. H. MOORE'S
Photograph, Ambrotype and Bon-Ton Gallery,

No. 2 First St., Opposite Troy House.

Pictures of all kinds

COPIED,

And Finished in

INDIA INK,
WATER OR OIL COLORS,

Being the only Sure Way of Obtaining

Perfect Likenesses from Small Indistinct Pictures.

OVERCOATS from $5 to $30, at WAIT'S CASH STORE.
FROCK COAT SUITS Cheap at WAIT'S. (See page 81.)

UNITED STATES AND TERRITORIES. 75

The first permanent English settlement in the United States was at Jamestown, Virginia, in 1607,* which continued an English colony till the Declaration of Independence, July 4, 1776. After a war of seven years' duration, peace was made, and independence acknowledged by treaty with England in 1783. The Articles of Confederation were entered into in 1777. The present United States Constitution, framed in 1787, went into operation March 1st, 1789, after being approved of by the thirteen original States of the Union. Louisiana, comprising the States and Territories now belonging to the United States west of the Mississippi, was purchased of France in 1803, and Florida of Spain, in 1819. Texas was admitted into the Union by "Joint Resolutions" of Congress, passed March 1st, 1845. New Mexico and Upper California, including Utah, were acquired by treaty with Mexico, ratified in 1848. Arizona was acquired by treaty with Mexico, ratified in June, 1854.

In the DISTRICT OF COLUMBIA, originally formed by cessions from Maryland and Virginia,† is situated WASHINGTON CITY, the United States seat of government, being first occupied in 1800. The District and Capital are exclusively under the jurisdiction of the Federal Government. Congress meets on the first Monday of December in every year, unless otherwise directed by law.

The population of the United States at the time of taking the first Census in 1790, was 3,929,328; in 1800, 5,309,758; in 1810, 7,239,903; in 1820, 9,638,166; in 1830, 12,866,020; in 1840, 17,068,666; in 1850, 23,191,876; in 1860, 31,443,321; of the latter number, 3,953,760 were slaves of African descent.

The slave trade was prohibited by act of Congress, after January 1. 1808. In 1818, Congress declared the traffic to be piracy. Slavery was abolished in the District of Columbia in 1862, by act of Congress; in the United States, by Proclamation of Abraham Lincoln, January 1, 1863.

Maine, Vermont, Louisiana, Kentucky, Tennessee, Florida, Texas, and fourteen Territorial Governments, have been organized and converted into States since the Revolution, making in all (in 1867), thirty-seven States,‡ together with nine organized territories.

ALASKA, or NORTHWESTERN AMERICA, ceded to the United Stats by the Emperor of Russia, in consideration of $7,200,000, was taken possession of October 18, 1867. It contains an estimated area of 400,000 square miles. Population about 75,000. Capital, NEW ARCHANGEL.

STATES.

MAINE.—Settled in 1625 by the English; belonged to Massachusetts till 1820, when it was admitted into the Union as a State; capital AUGUSTA. The elective franchise rests on a residence in the State of three months next preceding any election, for any citizen of the United States, except paupers and persons under guardianship. Area, 35,000 square miles. Population in 1850, 583,169; in 1860, 628,279.

NEW HAMPSHIRE.—Settled in 1623 by the English; acceded to the Union, June, 1788, being one of the original thirteen States; capital, CONCORD. Every male citizen of 21 years of age, except paupers, has the right to vote. Area, 9,280 square miles. Population in 1850, 317,876; in 1860, 326,073.

VERMONT.—Settled in 1763 by English, chiefly from Connecticut, under grants from New Hampshire, admitted into the Union in 1791; capital MONTPELIER. One year's residence gives the right to vote to any citizen of the United States who will take an oath of allegiance. Area, 10,212 square miles. Population in 1850, 314,120; in 1860, 315,098.

MASSACHUSETTS.—Settled in 1620 by English Puritans, who landed at Plymouth; acceded to the Union in February, 1788; capital, BOSTON. One year's residence in the State, and payment of a State or county tax, gives the right to vote to every male citizen of 21 years and upward, excepting paupers and persons

---

* St. Augustine, Florida, was settled in 1565, by the Spaniards.

† The Virginia part, constituting the County of Alexandria, has been re-annexed to the above State.

‡ West Virginia was organized by act of Congress, approved December 31, 1862.

Bie yer Cloze ov W. A. WILKINS. (See page 96.)

Gold Pens, Pencils, Diaries, SCHOOL BOOKS, PHOTOGRAPH ALBUMS, Stereoscopic Views, &c., at BENDER'S, 73 State Street, Albany.

1870.   1870.
NEW YORK AND TROY STEAMBOAT CO.

STEAMERS VANDERBILT & CONNECTICUT,
RUNNING BETWEEN
TROY, ALBANY AND NEW YORK,
IN CONNECTION WITH THE
Rensselaer & Saratoga, Albany & Susquehanna,
Troy & Boston, and New York Central Railroads,
DAILY—SATURDAYS EXCEPTED.
TICKETS SOLD ON THESE STEAMERS, AND BAGGAGE CHECKED TO ALL POINTS ON THE LINE OF THE ABOVE ROADS.

GENERAL OFFICE, 308 WEST STREET, NEW YORK.

J. W. HANCOX, Esq., Pres't.   M. D. HANCOX, Vice Pres't.

The steamers of this Line are furnished with neat and elegant Family and State Rooms, and Berths, and are replete with all the comforts and conveniences that can be desired by the traveler. Baggage taken free to and from the Cars and Boats at Troy. This route offers special inducements to parties of pleasure, as well as business men, traveling between the North and New York in the heat of summer, by which the monotony of a long railroad ride and the annoyance of dust in crowded and noisy cars, are all exchanged for a quiet, pleasant and expeditious steamboat ride.

Leaving New York from Pier No. 44, N. R., foot of Spring St., at 6 p. m., stopping at Albany, and arriving at Troy to take the Morning Trains West, East and North, Saratoga Springs, and the Lakes.

Leave Troy and Albany from Steamboat Landing on arrival of P. M. Trains from the North, arriving in New York in time to reach the Morning Trains for Philadelphia and ALL POINTS SOUTH AND EAST.

ALL FREIGHT HANDLED WITH CARE,
And Forwarded with Safety and Despatch.

For Passage or Freight, apply on Board, or at the Office,
FOOT OF BROADWAY.

RUSSELL P. CLAPP, Agent, Troy, N. Y.
HOWARD HOLDRIDGE, Agent, Albany, N. Y.

OVERCOATS from $5 to $30, at WAIT'S CASH STORE.
FROCK COAT SUITS Cheap at WAIT'S. (See page 81.)

UNITED STATES AND TERRITORIES. 75

The first permanent English settlement in the United States was at Jamestown, Virginia, in 1607,* which continued an English colony till the Declaration of Independence, July 4, 1776. After a war of seven years' duration, peace was made, and independence acknowledged by treaty with England in 1783.
The Articles of Confederation were entered into in 1777. The present United States Constitution, framed in 1787, went into operation March 1st, 1789, after being approved of by the thirteen original States of the Union. Louisiana, comprising the States and Territories now belonging to the United States west of the Mississippi, was purchased of France in 1803, and Florida of Spain, in 1819. Texas was admitted into the Union by " Joint Resolutions " of Congress, passed March 1st, 1845. New Mexico and Upper California, including Utah, were acquired by treaty with Mexico, ratified in 1848. Arizona was acquired by treaty with Mexico, ratified in June, 1854.
In the DISTRICT OF COLUMBIA, originally formed by cessions from Maryland and Virginia,† is situated WASHINGTON CITY, the United States seat of government, being first occupied in 1800. The District and Capital are exclusively under the jurisdiction of the Federal Government. Congress meets on the first Monday of December in every year, unless otherwise directed by law.
The population of the United States at the time of taking the first Census in 1790, was 3,929,328; in 1800, 5,309,758; in 1810, 7,239,903; in 1820, 9,638,160; in 1830, 12,866,020; in 1840, 17,068,666; in 1850, 23,191,876; in 1860, 31,443,321; of the latter number, 3,953,760 were slaves of African descent.
The slave trade was prohibited by act of Congress, after January 1. 1808. In 1818, Congress declared the traffic to be piracy. Slavery was abolished in the District of Columbia in 1862, by act of Congress; in the United States, by Proclamation of Abraham Lincoln, January 1, 1863.
Maine, Vermont, Louisiana, Kentucky, Tennessee, Florida, Texas, and fourteen Territorial Governments, have been organized and converted into States since the Revolution, making in all (in 1867), thirty-seven States,‡ together with nine organized territories.
ALASKA, or NORTHWESTERN AMERICA, ceded to the United Stats by the Emporor of Russia, in consideration of $7,200,000, was taken possession of October 18, 1867. It contains an estimated area of 400,000 square miles. Population about 75,000. Capital, NEW ARCHANGEL.

STATES.

MAINE.—Settled in 1625 by the English; belonged to Massachusetts till 1820, when it was admitted into the Union as a State; capital AUGUSTA. The elective franchise rests on a residence in the State of three months next preceding any election, for any citizen of the United States, except paupers and persons under guardianship. Area, 35,000 square miles. Population in 1850, 583,169; in 1860, 628,279.
NEW HAMPSHIRE.—Settled in 1623 by the English; acceded to the Union, June, 1788, being one of the original thirteen States; capital, CONCORD. Every male citizen of 21 years of age, except paupers, has the right to vote. Area, 9,280 square miles. Population in 1850, 317,876; in 1860, 326,073.
VERMONT.—Settled in 1763 by English, chiefly from Connecticut, under grants from New Hampshire, admitted into the Union in 1791; capital MONTPELIER. One year's residence gives the right to vote to any citizen of the United States who will take an oath of allegiance. Area, 10,212 square miles. Population in 1850, 314,120; in 1860, 315,098.
MASSACHUSETTS.—Settled in 1620 by English Puritans, who landed at Plymouth; acceded to the Union in February, 1788; capital, BOSTON. One year's residence in the State, and payment of a State or county tax, gives the right to vote to every male citizen of 21 years and upward, excepting paupers and persons

---

* St. Augustine, Florida, was settled in 1565, by the Spaniards.

† The Virginia part, constituting the County of Alexandria, has been re-annexed to the above State.

‡ West Virginia was organized by act of Congress, approved December 31, 1862.

Bie yer Cloze ov W. A. WILKINS. (See page 96.)

Gold Pens, Pencils, Diaries, SCHOOL BOOKS, PHOTOGRAPH ALBUMS, Stereoscopic Views, &c., at BENDER'S, 73 State Street, Albany.

76 FARMERS' ALMANAC.

1870. **1870.**

NEW YORK AND TROY STEAMBOAT CO.

STEAMERS VANDERBILT & CONNECTICUT,

RUNNING BETWEEN

TROY, ALBANY AND NEW YORK,

IN CONNECTION WITH THE

Rensselaer & Saratoga, Albany & Susquehanna, Troy & Boston, and New York Central Railroads,

DAILY—SATURDAYS EXCEPTED.

TICKETS SOLD ON THESE STEAMERS, AND BAGGAGE CHECKED TO ALL POINTS ON THE LINE OF THE ABOVE ROADS.

GENERAL OFFICE, 308 WEST STREET, NEW YORK.

J. W. HANCOX, Esq., Pres't.   M. D. HANCOX, Vice Pres't.

The steamers of this Line are furnished with neat and elegant Family and State Rooms, and Berths, and are replete with all the comforts and conveniences that can be desired by the traveler. Baggage taken free to and from the Cars and Boats at Troy. This route offers special inducements to parties of pleasure, as well as business men, traveling between the North and New York in the heat of summer, by which the monotony of a long railroad ride and the annoyance of dust in crowded and noisy cars, are all exchanged for a quiet, pleasant and expeditious steamboat ride.

Leaving New York from Pier No. 44, N. R., foot of Spring St., at 6 p. m., stopping at Albany, and arriving at Troy to take the Morning Trains West, East and North, Saratoga Springs, and the Lakes.

Leave Troy and Albany from Steamboat Landing on arrival of P. M. Trains from the North, arriving in New York in time to reach the Morning Trains for Philadelphia and ALL POINTS SOUTH AND EAST.

ALL FREIGHT HANDLED WITH CARE,

And Forwarded with Safety and Despatch.

For Passage or Freight, apply on Board, or at the Office, **FOOT OF BROADWAY.**

RUSSELL P. CLAPP, Agent, Troy, N. Y.
HOWARD HOLDRIDGE, Agent, Albany, N. Y.

under guardianship. Area, 7,800 square miles, being the chief manufacturing and most densely populated State in the Union. Population in 1850, 994,514; in 1860, 1,231,066.

RHODE ISLAND.—Settled in 1631 by English from Massachusetts; acceded to the Union in May, 1790; capitals, PROVIDENCE and NEWPORT. By the constitution recently adopted, the qualifications for voting may be stated, omitting details, to be a freehold possession of $13; or, if in reversion, renting for $7, together with a year's residence in the State and six months in the town; or, if no freehold, then two years' residence in the State and six months in the town, and payment of a dollar tax, or militia service instead. Area, 1,306 square miles. Population in 1850, 147,545; in 1860, 174,620.

CONNECTICUT.—Settled in 1633 by English from Massachusetts; acceded to the Union in January, 1788; capitals, NEW HAVEN and HARTFORD. Residence for six months, or militia duty for the year, or payment of State tax, or a freehold of the yearly value of $7, gives the right to vote. Area, 4,750 square miles. Population in 1850, 370,792; in 1860, 460,147.

NEW YORK.—Settled in 1613 by Dutch; submitted to the English in 1664; retaken by the Dutch in 1673; restored to the English in 1674; acceded to the Union in July, 1788; being the most populous, wealthy, and commercial State of the Union; capital, ALBANY. One year's residence in the State and six months in the county gives the right to vote; but every man of color must have a residence of three years, and have owned and paid taxes, on a freehold assessed $250 for a year. Area, 46,000 square miles. Population in 1850, 3,097,394; in 1860, 3,880,735.

NEW JERSEY.—Settled in 1627 by Swedes; conquered by the Dutch in 1665; submitted to the English in 1664; acceded to the Union in December, 1787; capital, TRENTON. One year's residence in the State gives the right to vote, except to paupers, etc. Area, 8,320 square miles. Population in 1850, 489,555; in 1860, 672,035.

PENNSYLVANIA.—Settled in 1682 by English; acceded to the Union in December, 1787; capital, HARRISBURGH. One year's residence in the State and ten days in the election district, and payment of a State or county tax, assessed ten days prior to an election, gives the right to vote; except that citizens between 21 and 22 years of age need not have paid a tax. Area, 47,000 square miles. Population in 1850, 2,311,786; in 1860, 2,906,115, ranking as the second State in wealth and population.

DELAWARE.—Settled in 1627 by Swedes; granted to William Penn in 1682; separated in 1703; acceded to the Union in December, 1787; capital, DOVER. Qualifications of voters same as in Pennsylvania. Area, 2,120 square miles. Population in 1850, 91,532; in 1860, 112,216, of whom 1,798 were slaves.

MARYLAND.—Settled in 1634 by English; acceded to the Union in April, 1788; capital, ANNAPOLIS. One year's residence in the State and six months in the county gives the right to vote to every white male citizen. Area, 11,124 square miles. Population in 1850, 583,034; in 1860, 687,049, of whom 77,188 were slaves. Slavery abolished Nov. 1, 1864.

WEST VIRGINIA.—This new State, detached from the old State of Virginia by popular will, was admitted into the Union by act of Congress, approved December 31, 1862, "upon the condition that certain changes should be duly made in the proposed constitution for that State," which changes being approved by popular vote of the people, the President of the United States, by proclamation, dated the 20th of April, 1863, in pursuance of the act of Congress aforesaid, declared and proclaimed that the said act shall take effect and be in force on the 20th day of June, 1863. An election for State officers was held on Thursday, May 28th, and on the 20th of June following the Governor and State officers were duly inaugurated. Capital, WHEELING. The new State comprises forty-eight counties, lying west of the Allegany mountains; having an estimated area of 24,000 square miles, and a population, according to the census of 1860, of 350,599, of whom 12,754 were slaves. It is rich in iron, coal, salt springs, etc., and has a large amount of fertile and arable lands lying on the east bank of the Ohio river, and in the valleys of the Allegany mountains, together with a mild and salubrious climate, well adapted to free white labor.

VIRGINIA.—Settled in 1607 by English, being one of the most important of the thirteen original States; acceded to the Union in June, 1788; capital, RICHMOND. A freehold in possession, or in the occupancy of only a tenant at will or sufferance,

WRITING DESKS in Rosewood, PAPIER-MACHE, Plain or Beautifully Inlaid with Pearl, at BENDER'S, 73 State Street, Albany.

THE NEW EMPIRE
HOT-AIR, GAS AND BASE-BURNING
Cooking Stove,

WITH
COPPER OR CAST IRON
RESERVOIR.

FOR
WOOD OR COAL.

THE NEW EMPIRE
IS THE ONLY
First-Class Cooking Stove
WHICH HAS THE
HAWKS AUXILIARY AIR CHAMBER ATTACHED.

Patented..................April 23, 1867.
Re-issued.................August 3, 1869.

BY MEANS OF THIS ATTACHMENT WE GUARANTEE:

First. A saving of 50 per cent. in Fuel.
Second. A fire may be maintained throughout an entire season, with either wood or coal, without rekindling, and not become dull by the accumulation of slag or ashes in the fire-box.
Third. A perfect consumption of gas and smoke, so that the damper in the smoke-pipe may be kept closed the most of the time (thereby retaining the heat in the stove), without any escape of gas or smoke into the room.
Fourth. It makes perfect Base Burners of stoves to which it is applied. The fire being at all times bright on the grate, no clinkers form, and the slate in the coal is reduced to ashes, and passes through the grate, instead of remaining in the fire-box as cinders, as is the case in other stoves.
Fifth. The heat being retained in the stove to a very great extent, the temperature of the room is kept very uniform, there seldom being more than two degrees difference in temperature between the floor and ceiling.
Sixth. These Stoves are easily managed; the fire can be perfectly controlled, so that there is no difficulty in making them the most comfortable stoves for summer as well as winter use.
Sixth. THE BEST BAKING STOVE IN THE WORLD!
Besides the above advantages, this Stove has the best Cast-Iron Reservoir that has yet been produced, in which water can be boiled in 30 minutes or kept at a moderate degree of heat as may be desired. This stove has been before the public but little more than one year, and is now having a larger sale than *any Cooking Stove* in the market. It has taken the *First Premium* at every County Fair at which it has been exhibited up to the present time.

Manufactured and for Sale by
SWETT, QUIMBY & PERRY, No. 221 RIVER ST., TROY, N. Y.

worth $25; or the reversion of a freehold to vest on the termination of a life estate, and worth $50; or a leasehold of the yearly value of $20, for a term of not less than five years; or the payment of State tax within the year by a housekeeper who is the head of a family, and has a year's residence, gives the right of voting to every citizen, except paupers, felons and persons in the army and navy not having commissions. Area, 61,352 square miles, including West Virginia. Population in 1850, 1,421,661; in 1860, 1,596,318, of whom 490,887 were slaves. (See West Virginia.)

NORTH CAROLINA.*—Settled in 1650 by English; acceded to the Union, November 21, 1789; capital, RALEIGH. Every freeman of the age of 21 years and upwards, who has resided one year in any county within the State, may vote for a member of the House of Commons, but must own fifty acres of land to vote for a Senator. Area, 50,700 square miles. Population in 1850, 869,039; in 1860, 992,-622, of whom 331,081 were slaves.

SOUTH CAROLINA.*—Settled in 1689 by English; acceded to the Union, May 23, 1788; capital, COLUMBIA. Voters, residents of the State two years, who have paid a State tax, and resided six months in the district where voting. Area, 34,000 square miles. Population in 1850, 668,507; in 1860, 703,708, of whom 402,541 were slaves, being an excess of 101,270 over the whites.

GEORGIA.*—Settled 1733 by English; acceded to the Union, January 2, 1788; capital, MILLEDGEVILLE. Voters, citizens of the State and six months' resident of the county where voting, and have paid taxes for the year preceding the election. Area, 58,000 square miles. Population in 1850, 906,185; in 1860, 1,057,286, of whom 462,230 were slaves.

FLORIDA.*—(East and West.)—Settled early by the Spaniards, being more than 200 years under Spain; was ceded to the United States in 1819; it was admitted into the Union March 3, 1845; capital, TALLAHASSE. Area, 59,268 square miles. Population in 1850, 87,445; in 1860, 140,425, of whom 61,753 were slaves. This State is tropical in its climate and products.

ALABAMA.*—Settled in 1713 by French; admitted into the Union in 1819, and is the chief cotton growing State of the country; capital, MONTGOMERY. Voters, white male citizens of the United States, one year resident of the State, and three months in the county where they shall offer to vote. Area, 50,722 square miles. Population in 1850, 771,623; in 1860, 964,201, of whom 435,132 were slaves.

MISSISSIPPI.*—Settled in 1716 by French; admitted into the Union in 1817. Voters, citizens of the United States, one year resident of the State, and in the county four months, and have done military duty, or paid taxes; capital, JACKSON. Area, 47,156 square miles. Population in 1850, 606,526; in 1860, 791,305, of whom 436,696 were slaves.

LOUISIANA.*—Settled in 1699 by French; purchased of France in 1803; admitted into the Union in 1812. This is the greatest sugar producing region of the country. Voters to reside two years in the State and one in the parish where they offer to vote; capital, BATON ROUGE. Area, 41,346 square miles. Population in 1850, 517,762; in 1860, 708,002, of whom 331,726 were slaves.

TEXAS.*—Early settled by Spaniards, and more recently by emigrants from the United States; formed a part of the Republic of Mexico until 1836, when declared its independence, and existed as a separate government until 1845, when it was admitted into the Union by "joint resolution for annexing Texas with the United States." Every free white male, 21 years old, a citizen of the United States or Texas, who has resided in the State one year, and six months in the district where he offers to vote, shall have the right to suffrage; capital, AUSTIN. Area, 274,356 square miles. Population in 1850, 212,592; in 1860, 604,215, of whom 182,566 were slaves. According to the late act of Congress, "the boundary of Texas on the North shall commence at the point at which the meridian of 100 deg. west from Greenwich is intersected by the parallel of 36 deg. 30 min. north, and shall run from said point due west to the meridian of 103 deg. west from Greenwich; thence her boundary shall run due south to the 32 deg. north latitude; thence, on the said parallel of 32 deg. north, to the Rio Bravo del Norte; and thence with the channel of said river to the Gulf of Mexico."

* The States of Virginia, North Carolina, South Carolina, Georgia, Florida, Alabama, Mississippi, Louisiana, Arkansas, Texas and Tennessee, seceded from the Union, by resolution of their respective conventions, during the years 1860 and '61. Rebellion ceased April, 1865.

Custom Work done better at WILKINS' than elsewhere.

Plain and Fancy INKSTANDS, PEN RACKS, SEGAR STANDS and CASES, and Unique WATCH SAFES, at BENDER'S, 73 State Street, Albany.

SMITH, HOTCHKIN & CO.

SUCCESSORS TO LEONARD SMITH,

Manufacturers and Dealers in all Kinds of

CABINET FURNITURE,

329 & 331 River Street,

TROY, N. Y.

OTIS SMITH,   A. L. HOTCHKIN,   GEO. D. SMITH.

UNITED STATES AND TERRITORIES. 79

worth $25; or the reversion of a freehold to vest on the termination of a life estate, and worth $50; or a leasehold of the yearly value of $20, for a term of not less than five years; or the payment of State tax within the year by a housekeeper who is the head of a family, and has a year's residence, gives the right of voting to every citizen, except paupers, felons and persons in the army and navy not having commissions. Area, 61,352 square miles, including West Virginia. Population in 1850, 1,421,661; in 1860, 1,596,318, of whom 490,887 were slaves. (See West Virginia.)

NORTH CAROLINA.*—Settled in 1650 by English; acceded to the Union, November 21, 1789; capital, RALEIGH. Every freeman of the age of 21 years and upwards, who has resided one year in any county within the State, may vote for a member of the House of Commons, but must own fifty acres of land to vote for a Senator. Area, 50,700 square miles. Population in 1850, 869,039; in 1860, 992,-622, of whom 331,081 were slav s.

SOUTH CAROLINA.*—Settled in 1689 by English; acceded to the Union, May 23, 1788; capital, COLUMBIA. Voters, residents of the State two years, who have paid a State tax, and resided six months in the district where voting. Area, 34,000 square miles. Population in 1850, 668,507; in 1860, 703,708, of whom 402,541 were slaves, being an excess of 101,270 over the whites.

GEORGIA.*—Settled 1733 by English; acceded to the Union, January 2, 1788; capital, MILLEDGEVILLE. Voters, citizens of the State and six months' resident of the county where voting, and have paid taxes for the year preceding the election. Area, 58,000 square miles. Population in 1850, 906,185; in 1860, 1,057,286, of whom 462,230 were slaves.

FLORIDA.*—(East and West.)—Settled early by the Spaniards, being more than 200 years under Spain; was ceded to the United States in 1819; it was admitted into the Union March 3, 1845; capital, TALLAHASSE. Area, 59,268 square miles. Population in 1850, 87,445; in 1860, 140,425, of whom 61,753 were slaves. This State is tropical in its climate and products.

ALABAMA.*—Settled in 1713 by French; admitted into the Union in 1819, and is the chief cotton growing State of the country; capital, MONTGOMERY. Voters, white male citizens of the United States, one year resident of the State, and three months in the county where they shall offer to vote. Area, 50,722 square miles. Population in 1850, 771,623; in 1860, 964,201, of whom 435,132 were slaves.

MISSISSIPPI.*—Settled in 1716 by French; admitted into the Union in 1817. Voters, citizens of the United States, one year resident of the State, and in the county four months, and have done military duty, or paid taxes; capital, JACKSON. Area, 47,156 square miles. Population in 1850, 606,526; in 1860, 791,305, of whom 436,696 were slaves.

LOUISIANA.*—Settled in 1699 by French; purchased of France in 1803; admitted into the Union in 1812. This is the greatest sugar producing region of the country. Voters to reside two years in the State and one in the parish where they offer to vote; capital, BATON ROUGE. Area, 41,346 square miles. Population in 1850, 517,762; in 1860, 708,002, of whom 331,726 were slaves.

TEXAS.*—Early settled by Spaniards, and more recently by emigrants from the United States; formed a part of the Republic of Mexico until 1836, when declared its independence, and existed as a separate government until 1845, when it was admitted into the Union by "joint resolution for annexing Texas with the United States." Every free white male, 21 years old, a citizen of the United States or Texas, who has resided in the State one year, and six months in the district where he offers to vote, shall have the right to suffrage; capital, AUSTIN. Area, 274,356 square miles. Population in 1850, 212,592; in 1860, 604,215, of whom 182,566 were slaves. According to the late act of Congress, "the boundary of Texas on the North shall commence at the point at which the meridian of 100 deg. west from Greenwich is intersected by the parallel of 36 deg. 30 min. north, and shall run from said point due west to the meridian of 103 deg. west from Greenwich; thence her boundary shall run due south to the 32 deg. north latitude; thence, on the said parallel of 32 deg. north, to the Rio Bravo del Norte; and thence with the channel of said river to the Gulf of Mexico."

* The States of Virginia, North Carolina, South Carolina, Georgia, Florida, Alabama, Mississippi, Louisiana, Arkansas, Texas and Tennessee, seceded from the Union, by resolution of their respective conventions, during the years 1860 and '61. Rebellion ceased April, 1865.

Plain and Fancy INKSTANDS, PEN RACKS, SEGAR STANDS and CASES, and Unique WATCH SAFES, at BENDER'S, 73 State Street, Albany.

SMITH, HOTCHKIN & CO.

SUCCESSORS TO LEONARD SMITH,

Manufacturers and Dealers in all Kinds of

CABINET FURNITURE,

329 & 331 River Street,

TROY, N. Y.

OTIS SMITH,   A. L. HOTCHKIN,   GEO. D. SMITH.

1841. Established 1841.

H. R. & W. F. WAIT,
WHITEHALL, N. Y.

Offer great Inducements to CASH BUYERS at Wholesale or Retail in

CARPETS & OIL CLOTHS.

We keep constantly on hand a full line of

THE NEWEST AND MOST DESIRABLE STYLES IN

Brussels, Three Plys, Ingrains and Hemp

CARPETING,

Also OIL CLOTHS of all Widths,

From 5-8 to 16-4—Enameled Cloths.

WINDOW SHADES,
Elegant Styles.

BUFF, WHITE AND GREEN HOLLANDS,

Rugs, Mats, Cord, Tassels, &c., &c.

Why can we offer great inducements to CASH BUYERS in the above lines of Goods?
  1st. We have the advantage of twenty-nine years' experience.
  2d. We buy of manufacturers in large lots, for cash.
  3d. You do not have to pay anything for bad debts, as we always sell for CASH.
  4th. We have but ONE PRICE, and that is always made as low as the lowest New York Prices.

H. R. & W. F. WAIT,
MERCHANT TAILORS,
WHITEHALL, N. Y.,

Do the LARGEST Custom Clothing Business in Washington County.

Parties in want of Clothing will find it for their interest to examine their
LARGE AND ELEGANT STOCK OF
Cloths, Cassimeres and Beavers,
COMPRISING THE FOLLOWING:

French Cloths, Cassimeres and Beavers; German Cloths, Cassimeres and Beavers; English Cloths, Cassimeres and Beavers, Scotch Suitings,

AND LARGE LINE OF:
LADIES CLOAKINGS.
ALSO,

American Cloths, Cassimeres, (Plaid, Striped and Plain,) Melton Beavers and Doeskins, Velvet, Silk and Duck Vestings.

Our Master Cutter is a Man of Experience and is sure to give
A PERFECT FIT.

You will also find the largest Stock of
GENT'S FURNISHING GOODS
To be found in Northern New York.

TERMS CASH. ONE PRICE.

N. B.—We have also on hand some Custom Made Clothing, that we will sell as cheap as ready made can be found.

For **WINDOW SHADES**, go to **WAIT'S**.
Kid, Buck and Calf **GLOVES** and **MITTENS**, at **WAIT'S**. (See page 81.)

UNITED STATES AND TERRITORIES. 83

ARKANSAS.*—Settled by French emigrants from Louisiana; admitted into the Union in 1836. Voters, citizens of the United States and resident in the State for six months are entitled to vote in the county or district where they reside; capital, LITLLE ROCK. Area, 52,198 square miles. Population in 1850, 209,897; in 1860, 435,450, of whom 111,104 were slaves. Slavery abolished March, 1864.

TENNESSEE.*—Settled in 1765, by emigrants from North Carolina and Virginia; admitted into the Union in 1796. Voters, citizens of the United States, and six months resident in the county where voting; Capital, NASHVILLE. Area, 45,000 square miles. Population in 1850, 1,002,717; in 1860, 1,109,801, of whom 275,784 were slaves.

KENTUCKY.—Settled in 1775 by Virginians; admitted into the Union in 1792. Voters, two years resident in the State, and in the county where offering to vote one year preceding the election; capital, FRANKFORT. Area, 37,680 square miles. Population in 1850, 982,405; in 1860, 1,155,684, of whom 225,400 were slaves.

OHIO.—Settled in 1788 by emigrants from Virginia and New England, being formed out of the Northwestern Territory ceded to the United States by Virginia; admitted into the Union 1802. Voters, one year resident in the State preceding the election, having paid or been charged with State or county tax; capital, COLUMBUS. Area, 39,954 square miles. Population in 1850, 1,980,329; in 1860, 2,339,502.

INDIANA.—Settled in 1730 by French; admitted into the Union in 1816. Voters, one year resident of the State preceding the election, entitled to vote in county of residence; capital, INDIANAPOLIS. Area, 33,809 square miles. Population in 1850, 988,416; in 1860, 1,350,423.

ILLINOIS.—Settled in 1749 by French; admitted into the Union in 1818, having rapidly increased in wealth and population. Voters, all white male inhabitants resident in the State six months, but can only vote in the county where actually residing; capital, SPRINGFIELD. Area, 55,409 square miles. Population in 1850, 851,470; in 1860, 1,711,951.

MISSOURI.—Settled in 1763 by French; admitted into the Union in 1821. Voters, citizens of the United States, one year resident in the State next preceding the election, and three months in the county; capital, JEFFERSON CITY. Area, 65,037 square miles. Population in 1850, 682,044; in 1860, 1,182,012—114,965 were slaves. Slavery abolished in 1864.

MICHIGAN.—Settled in 1670, by French; admitted into the Union in 1837. Voters, all white male citizens 21 years of age, and resident in the State six months preceding election; capital, LANSING. Area, 56,243 square miles, including the Upper Peninsula, bounded by Lakes Michigan and Superior, where are extensive mines of copper and iron. Population in 1850, 397,654; in 1860, 740,113.

IOWA.—Settled by emigrants chiefly from the Northern and Eastern States; was formed into a territorial government by act of Congress in June, 1838, and admitted into the Union in December, 1846. Every white male citizen of the United States, 21 years old, having resided in the State six months, and in the county where he claims to vote twenty days, shall have the right of suffrage; capital, DES MOINES. Area, 55,000 square miles. Population in 1850, 192,214; in 1860, 674,948.

WISCONSIN.—First settled by emigrants chiefly from the Northern and Eastern States, since largely augmented by emigrants from Europe; it was formed into a territorial government in 1836, and admitted into the Union in 1848. All males, 21 years old, residents of the State for one year next before the election, who are white citizens of the United States, or white foreigners who have declared their intention to become citizens, or persons of Indian blood, once declared by the laws of the United States to be citizens, subsequent laws to the contrary notwithstanding, may vote; capital, MADISON. Area, 53,924 square miles. Population in 1850, 305,391; in 1860, 775,881.

MINNESOTA.—Organized as a territory by act of Congress, passed March 3, 1849; was settled by emigrants chiefly from the Northern and Western States; also inhabited by several tribes of Indians of a warlike character. Admitted into the Union February 26, 1857. Voters, every male person, aged 21, of either of the

---

* The States of Virginia, North Carolina, South Carolina, Georgia, Florida, Alabama, Mississippi, Louisiana, Arkansas, Texas and Tennessee, seceded from the Union, by resolution of their respective conventions, during the years of 1860 and '61. Rebellion ceased April, 1865.

W. A. WILKINS' Cheap Clothing Store, established **1859**.

BENDER will furnish you any Books Published; also, ENGINEERS' INSTRUMENTS, STATIONERY, FIELD BOOKS, &c., at 73 State Street, Albany.

FARMERS' ALMANAC.

THE NEW LIGHT.
A STRICTLY FIRST-CLASS STOVE.
In Economy of Fuel,

Keeping Fire,   **and Baking Well,**

THE NEW LIGHT IS UNEXCELLED.

THE VENTILATOR.

SELF-FEEDER.   **BASE-BURNER.**

BUSWELL, DURANT & CO.,
MANUFACTURERS,
OFFICE, 283 RIVER STREET, TROY, N. Y.

UNITED STATES AND TERRITORIES.

following classes, to wit: white citizens of the United States; white persons of foreign birth, who have duly declared their intentions to become citizens; persons of mixed white and Indian blood, who have adopted the customs and habits of civilization; and persons of Indian blood residing in the State, who have adopted the language, customs, and habits of civilization, when pronounced capable by any District Court in the State, may vote, if they have resided in the United States one year, in the State four months, and in the election district ten days next preceding the election. Capital, ST. PAUL. Area, 83,531 square miles. Population in 1860, 172,023 whites, and about 25,000 Indians.

KANSAS.—Organized as a territory by act of Congress, passed May, 1854, settled by emigrants from the Eastern, Northern and Southern States. Admitted into the Union January 29, 1861. It lies between 37 deg. and 40. deg. north latitude, being bounded on the east by the State of Missouri, and on the west by the twenty-fifth meridian of longitude west from Washington. For several years a fierce contest raged in this territory on the subject of slavery, but the strife was finally adjusted by its being admitted as a free State, that being the declared will of the majority of its inhabitants. Capital, TOPEKA. Area, 83,000 square miles. Population in 1860, 107,206.

CALIFORNIA.—Settled by Spaniards in 1769, the early establishments being of a missionary and military character. The boundary of this large region of country was considered rather indefinite while under Mexican authority, in regard to its eastern limits. By treaty of peace with Mexico, ratified March 16, 1848, this territory, together with New Mexico, was ceded to the United States. Admitted into the Union September, 1850. Its area is 169,000 square miles, lying between the 32d deg. and 42d deg. of north latitude. The gold mines of this State are the most valuable and extensive of the known world. Every white male citizen of the United States, and every white male citizen of Mexico, who shall have elected to become a citizen of the United States, under the treaty of peace exchanged and ratified at Queretaro on the 30th of May, 1848, of the age of 21 years, who shall have been a resident of the State six months next preceding the election, and the county or district in which he claims his vote, thirty days, shall be entitled to vote at all elections which are now, or hereafter may be, authorized by law. Capital, SACRAMENTO. Population in 1852, from official returns, 262,435; in 1860, 305,430.

OREGON.—This extensive region, including Washington Territory, was discovered by Captain Robert Gray, May 7, 1762, who entered the Columbia river, to which he gave the name of his vessel. Settled by British, belonging to the Hudson Bay Company, and American emigrants; also inhabited by numerous tribes of Indians. Organized as a territory August 4, 1848; admitted into the Union February 14, 1859. This is a fertile and healthy region of country. Capital, EUGENE CITY. Area, 100,000 square miles. Population, 1860, 52,464.

NEBRASKA.—Organized by act of Congress, May, 1854; admitted into the Union, 1866; was mostly settled by emigrants from the Northern and Western States. It lies between 40 deg. and 43 deg. north latitude, being bounded on the east by the Missouri river, which separates it from the State of Iowa, and on the west by the 104th parallel of longitude, dividing it from the territory of Idaho. The Nebraska or Platte River runs centrally nearly its entire length from east to west, its head waters rising near the South Pass of the Rocky Mountains. Capital, OMAHA CITY. Est. area, 70,000 square miles. Pop. in 1860, 28,842. The Union Pacific Railroad extends from Omaha City, westward, along the north bank of the Platte River, to the base of the Rocky Mountains, a distance of 530 miles.

NEVADA.—Organized March 2, 1861; was admitted into the Union Oct. 3, 1864, by act of Congress. It lies east of the Sierra Nevada range of mountains, and mostly within the Great Basin of North America. Gold and silver mines of great value are found along the western slope of the Sierra Nevada, while the climate and soil produce grasses, cereals, and vegetables of almost every description, when properly cultivated. Capital, CARSON CITY. Est. area, 90,000 square miles. Population in 1860, 6,857.

TERRITORIES.

NEW MEXICO.—This large Territory, as defined by Spanish or American authority, extended from 32 deg. 30 min. to 42 deg. north latitude, and from 23 deg. to about 33 deg. longitude west of the city of Washington. It was early settled by

E. H. BENDER, Wholesale and Retail Dealer in every Variety of BOOKS, STATIONERY, &c., 73 State Street, Albany.

WILLCOX & GIBBS
NOISELESS
SEWING MACHINE.

The following points we claim and can sustain over any other Machine now offered to the public:

In simplicity of construction, parts and movements.
In non-liability to get out of order, either by use or standing.
In perfection of workmanship; it is the best made of all Sewing Machines.
In quietness of operation; it is almost entirely silent.
In ease of working; no other Sewing Machine is so light running.
In ease of management; it requires far less skill to operate it than any other.
In non-liability to miss stitches, or break the thread.
In requiring the least time and patience to learn it.
In rapidity of execution; may be run at twice the speed of any other.
In having a patent rubber break—prevents the wheel turning backward.
In its needle, which is straight, being the shortest and least liable to break.
In its self-adjusting needle, requiring neither skill nor experience to set it.
In the simplicity of its tension, and the ease of managing it.
In having a guard, which protects the dress from rubbing against the wheel.
In its more perfect adaptation to all capacities.
In its being more easily and speedily changed to different kinds of work.
In its more perfect adaptation to all kinds of sewing.
In its capacity for making beautiful embroidery, by a mere change of spools.
In making the BEST STITCH, especially for family use.
In its stitch being the most even and beautiful.
In its seam being the strongest and most elastic.
In its seam being automatically fastened by the machine.
In its seam being the least liable to rip in use or wear.
In its seam being more easily taken out when desired.
In having the best hemmers; no others have the ELASTIC BLADE, OT TURN THE HEM UNDER.
In having the best feller, the only one that works with the goods right side up.
In having the best braider, one always adjusted and ready for use.

AND IN MANY OTHER POINTS OF EXCELLENCE.

Each Machine Warranted three Years from the Date of Sale. Call and see them for yourself at the Salesrooms,

455 FULTON STREET, TROY, N. Y.
O. B. BRUSH, Agent.

Spaniards, and formed a territory of the Republic of Mexico until 1848, when it was ceded to the United States. In September, 1850, this territory was defined by act of Congress, and provision made for its organization. *Right of Suffrage.*— Every free white male inhabitant, above the age of 21 years, who shall have been a resident of said territory at the time of the passage of this act, shall be entitled to vote at the first election, and shall be eligible to any office within said territory; but the qualifications of voters and of holding office, at all subsequent elections, shall be such as shall be prescribed by the Legislative Assembly. Capital, SANTA FE. Est. area, 110,000 square miles. Population in 1850, 61,517; in 1860, 93,516. Within the bounds of this territory and Arizona, are residing large tribes of Indians, many of a warlike character, roaming over this region and western Texas, as well as the northern part of Mexico.

UTAH.—Organized by act of Congress, passed Sept. 9, 1850, comprises a large extent of country in the "Great Basin of North America," west of the Rocky Mountains. It originally included a portion of the new Territories of Colorado on the east, and Nevada on the west. Capital, GREAT SALT LAKE CITY, situated about two miles due east of the river Jordan or Utah, near the base of a mountain, in north latitude 40 deg. 45 min.; west longitude from Greenwich, 111 deg. 36 min.; altitude, 4,300 feet above the level of the sea, being in the valley of the Great Salt Lake. Est. area, 121,000 square miles. Population in 1850, 11,380; in 1860, 40,273, being mostly Mormons, or "Latter Day Saints."

WASHINGTON TERRITORY.—Organized by act of Congress, passed March 2, 1853, settled by emigrants from the Northern and Western States. It was taken from the northern part of Oregon, "being all that portion of territory lying and being south of the 49th degree of north latitude, and north of the middle of the main channel of the Columbia river, from its mouth to where the 46th degree of north latitude crosses said river, near Fort Wallah Wallah; thence east to Snake river; thence north to the 49th parallel of latitude, being bounded on the east by the Territory of Idaho, and on the north by the British Possessions." Capital, OLYMPIA, lying on Puget's sound in north latitude 47 deg.; west longitude from Greenwich, 122 deg. 25 min., having a mean annual temperature of 51 Fahrenheit.* Est. area, 71,000 square miles. Population in 1860, 11,594.

DAKOTAH TERRITORY.—Organized by act of Congress, passed March 2, 1861; comprises a large extent of country, being bounded on the east by Minnesota, south by Nebraska, west by the 27th degree of longitude west of Washington, separating it from the territory of Idaho, and on the north by the British Possessions, running along the 49th parallel of latitude. It is drained by the Missouri river on the south, and by the Red river of the north emptying into Hudson Bay, possessing, for the most part, a fine healthy climate and good soil; first settled on the north by emigrants in the employ of the Hudson Bay Company, and now being peopled by a hardy race of men from Northern and Western States. Capital, YANKTON. Est. area, 220,000 square miles. Population in 1860, 4,837 whites, and a large number of Indians of different tribes. In this territory the buffalo and other wild animals are found in great abundance.

COLORADO TERRITORY.—Organized March 2, 1861, is included within the following limits, viz.: "Commencing on the 37th parallel of north latitude where the 25th meridian of longitude west from Washington crosses the same; thence north on said meridian to the 41st parallel of north latitude; thence along said parallel west to the 32d meridian of longitude west from Washington; thence south on said meridian to the northern line of New Mexico; thence along the 37th parallel of north latitude to the place of beginning," embracing "Pike's Peak and the gold regions in the vicinity of the Rocky Mountains." Capital, GOLDEN CITY. Est. area, 104,000 square miles. Population in 1860, 34,277, also many tribes of Indians. The climate of this elevated country is remarkably healthy and invigorating, while "the soil is rich and productive, being capable of producing corn, wheat, barley, potatoes, oats, turnips, and every kind of vegetable in profusion, and of most superior quality. The climate of the South Platte Valley, and of the mountain region is mild and regular, and from its altitude very dry and of surprising purity.

* The climate of Washington Territory is much milder than in the same parallels of latitude east of the Rocky Mountains, while the soil is mostly rich and very fertile, producing a large growth of forest trees. Gold and other valuable minerals also abound in many parts of the territory.

Fancy NOTE PAPER and ENVELOPES, Stamped with Initials or Monograms, at E. H. BENDER'S, 73 State Street, Albany.

88   FARMERS' ALMANAC.

A. COBDEN,
PHOTOGRAPHS AND AMBROTYPES,

In Every Style of the Art.

AMBROTYPES,
Daguerreotypes,
PHOTOGRAPHS, &C.

Copied at the shortest notice.

Corner of Fourth and River Streets,
(FRANKLIN SQUARE,)

TROY, N. Y.

USE
DUSENBERRY & ANTHONY'S
Ground Coffee,
SPICES, CREAM TARTAR,
SALERATUS, &c.
"UNION MILLS," No. 363 River Street,
TROY, N. Y.

WILLIAM COLLINS,
MANUFACTURER OF
Sash Doors, Blinds
AND MOULDINGS,
Office and Salesrooms, 124 CONGRESS STREET,
MANUFACTORY AT MT. IDA,
Troy, N. Y.

UNITED STATES AND TERRITORIES.

ARIZONA.—Organized by act of Congress, approved Feb. 24, 1863; embraces "all that part of the present Territory of New Mexico situate west of a line running due south from the point where the southwest corner of the territory of Colorado joins the northern boundary of the territory of New Mexico, to the southern boundary of said territory," containing an estimated area of 131,000 square miles. It is thinly settled by natives of Mexico and emigrants from different States of the Union, besides containing a large number of Indians of a warlike character. The right of suffrage and territorial organization is similar to that of New Mexico, with the provision, "that there shall neither be slaves or involuntary servitude in said Territory." Capital, PRESCOTT, situated north of the Gila river, in a fertile valley. This Territory is rich in gold, silver, copper, and other minerals, while the soil is mostly sterile, except in a few valleys susceptible of irrigation. Arizona proper, was acquired by treaty with Mexico known as the "Gadsden treaty," and ratified in June, 1854, the estimated area being 39,000 square miles, lying south of the Rio Gila.

IDAHO.—This new territory, lying on the west side of the Rocky mountains, was organized by act of Congress, approved March 3, 1863. Its boundary is as follows: "Beginning at a point in the middle channel of Snake river where the northern boundary of Oregon intersects the same; then follow down the said channel of Snake river to a point opposite the mouth of the Kooskooskia, or Clearwater river; thence due north to the forty-ninth parallel of latitude; thence east to the new territory of Montana; thence west along the 42d parallel of latitude to the eastern boundary of the State of Oregon; thence north along said boundary to the place of beginning." Capital, LEWISTON, situated on the western confines of the territory. Est. area, 100,000 square miles. A great portion of this extensive region is susceptible of cultivation, the climate being comparatively mild and healthy. Gold is found in numerous localities along the different ranges of mountains, as well as in the beds of streams flowing into the Columbia river, by which this territory is drained. By late authority, the territory is found to contain 60,000 white inhabitants. The delegate to Congress and members of the Legislature are elected in October.

MONTANA.—This new territory, lying between the 45th and 49th degrees of north latitude, and the 27th and 39th degrees of longitude west from Washington, was organized by act of Congress, approved May 26th, 1864. It may be said to form the northern half of the territory of Idaho, as organized March 3, 1862. Est. area of Montana, 150,000 square miles. This extensive territory embraces the head sources of the Missouri river, lying east of the Rocky Mountains, and the head sources of the north branch of the Columbia river, lying west of the above mountains and north of the Bitter Root mountains. A great portion of this region is susceptible of cultivation, although forming in part the northern limit of the United States, the climate being comparatively mild and remarkably healthy. Gold is found in numerous localities along the different ranges of mountains, as well as in the beds of streams flowing into the Columbia and Missouri rivers, by which this territory is drained. The Indian tribes are numerous, but generally peaceably inclined. Capital, BANNOCK CITY. Fort Benton, situated on the Upper Missouri river, north latitude 47 deg. 50 min., lies near the center of the territory, favored with a mean annual temperature of 48 deg. Fahrenheit. The proposed line of the Northern Pacific Railroad will, no doubt, pass Fort Benton, and cross the Rocky Mountains through one of the several mountain passes explored by authority of the United States Government.

INDIAN TERRITORY.—Situated west of the States of Arkansas and Missouri, and south of the 37th deg. of north latitude, is bounded on the south and west by the State of Texas. This is a fruitful region, inhabited by many tribes of civilized Indians, mostly Cherokees, Creeks, Choctaws and Seminoles, amounting to 60,000 or 70,000 souls. Capital, TAU-LE-QUAH. Est. area, 70,000 square miles.—
U. S. Register, or Blue Book.

E. H. BENDER, Wholesale and Retail Dealer in every Variety of
BOOKS, STATIONERY, &c., 73 State Street, Albany.

FARMERS' ALMANAC.

GEO. H. PHILLIPS & CO.,
TROY, N. Y.

VINDICATOR,

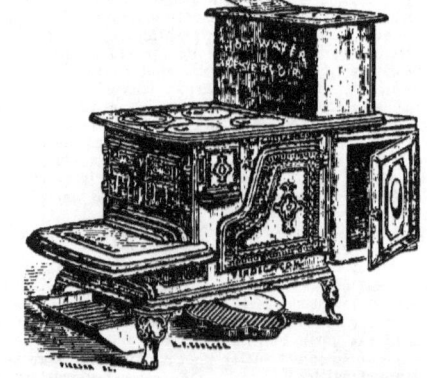

A New and Beautiful Cook Stove, for Wood or Coal, with Reservoir and Warming Closet, Six Boiler Holes, Large and Well Ventilated Oven, Ash Pan, Sifter, and all modern improvements.

Will soon offer this Stove, with our New and Perfect CAST IRON RESERVOIR, which we have used on other stoves, and has been so well received by the trade that we have been crowded to fill our orders. It is easily managed, and any family desiring a First Class Stove in every particular should purchase the "VINDICATOR."

We make a full line of Stoves, both Parlor and Cook.
SEND FOR CIRCULAR AND CUT.

Manufactured and for sale by

GEO. H. PHILLIPS & CO.,
No. 249 RIVER STREET, TROY N. Y.

Albany County, N. Y.

This county was formed Nov. 1, 1683. Montgomery and Washington counties were taken off in 1772; Columbia in 1786; Rensalaer and Saratoga in 1791; part of Schoharie in 1795; part of Greene in 1800, and Schenectady in 1809. The county lies on the west bank of the Hudson River, about 150 miles from its mouth, and contains an area of 544 square miles. Its surface is undulating and hilly, and it has a general inclination toward the southeast. Population over 115,500.

ALBANY CITY is the County seat and Capital of the State. It is 144 miles from New York city, 200 from Boston, 298 from Buffalo, and 257 from Montreal. It was incorporated by patent July 22, 1686, and has been known by the names of *Bereruick*, *William Stadt*, *New Orange* and *Albany*. It was made the capital of the State in 1798. The city lies upon the west bank of the Hudson river, near the head of navigation and at the eastern terminus of the Erie canal. The Capitol stands on a high hill at the head of State street, and is surrounded by a park or public square, ornamented with trees and walks, and commands a fine view of the city and adjacent country. The old capitol, however, is to be replaced with a building which, for beauty and magnificence, will outrival everything of the kind in the country. Ground has been broken and the work fairly commenced. The city contains many public institutions of learning and benevolence. There are 5 agricultural implement manufactories, 6 brass foundries, 16 iron foundries, 12 machine shops, 16 malt houses and breweries, 18 carriage builders, 18 book and job printers, 9 newspapers, 56 churches, 18 stove manufactories, about 50 lumber dealers, 67 flour and grain dealers, 1 saw manufactory, besides numerous other large works. Albany, Troy and West Troy are the largest lumber markets in the State Albany is finely built up with magnificent stores, handsome residences, public buildings and institutions. The New York Central, the Albany, Vermont, Albany and Susquehanna, and Canada railroads either commence or terminate in Albany. Connecting with these lines and terminating at Greenbush, directly opposite, are the Hudson River, Harlem, Troy and Greenbush, and Albany and Boston railroads. Steamboats ply morning and evening between Albany and New York. The People's Line of evening boats, with their magnificent furnishings, are called "floating palaces." Troy line of steamers also touch at Albany.

TOWN OF BERNE was formed March 17, 1795. Knox was taken off in 1822. It lies near the centre of the western border of the county. The soil is a sandy and gravelly loam interspersed with clay. Bernville; E. Berne; S. Berne, Reidsville and Peoria, are small villages. Population of town, 2,851.

TOWN OF BETHLEHEM was formed from Watervliet, March 12, 1793. New Scotland was taken off in 1832. It lies on the bank of the Hudson east of the centre of the county. Its surface consists of a rolling upland

BIBLES, PRAYER and HYMN BOOKS, SUNDAY SCHOOL BOOKS,
Merit Cards, &c., at E. H. BENDER'S, 73 State Street, Albany.

HIDLEY & MOCS,

AGENTS FOR THE FOLLOWING

FIRST CLASS

Piano Fortes:

CHICKERING, STECK, WEBER, GRAY (formerly BOARDMAN & GRAY), EMERSON, and the beautiful little COLIBRI, only four feet ten inches long, and two feet ten inches wide, with great power and sweetness of tone;

Also the Mason & Hamlin Cabinet and Metropolitan Organs,
With greatly reduced prices.

Our Stock is the Best and Largest in the City; our motto—
"Quick sales and small profits."

MUSIC SENT BY MAIL FREE OF POSTAGE.

Tuning and Repairing done and warranted.

Direct to

HIDLEY & MOCS,
12 Mansion House Block, Broadway, TROY, N. Y.

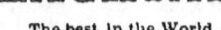

SEWING

MACHINES

The best in the World.

HIGHEST PREMIUM:
New York and Pennsylvania State Fairs, 1866.

GOLD MEDALS:
Maryland Institute, 1866; American Institute, 1867.

This machine makes the lock-stich that cannot be raveled out, and that presents the same appearance upon each side of the seam. This is the only stitch that has commended itself fully to public favor, forming a beautiful, firm and elastic seam. It is so light to run that scarcely any exertion is required to use it. It is almost noiseless in its operation, and the durability of the machine is such as to wear an ordinary lifetime, and to run for years without repairs.

Circulars furnished free upon application. Principal Office and Salesrooms—

9 Mansion House Block, Broadway, Troy, N. Y.

AMBROSE FOWLER,
Gen'l Ag't for Northern N. Y. and Vermont.

ending upon the river in steep bluffs. The soil is sand and clay. Groesbeck, (a suburb of Albany) and Kenwood, Upper Hollow, Adamsville, Normanskill, Bethlehem Centre, Becker's Corners, Cedar Hill, S. Bethlehem, and Callanan's Corners, are small villages. Population of town, 5,928.

Town of Coeymans was formed from Watervliet, March 18, 1791. A part of Westerlo was taken off in 1815. It is the S. E. corner town in the county. Its surface consists of an upland 200 to 400 feet above the river, broken by ridges and hills rising 100 to 400 feet higher. The principal streams are the Coeymans and Hanakrois creeks. Lawson's Lake is in the N. W. part of the town. Coeymans' Landing, Coeymans' Hollow, Stephensville, Indian Fields and Keefer's Corners, are small villages. Population of town, 3,264.

Town of Guilderland was formed from Watervliet, Feb. 26, 1803. It lies near the centre of the Northern border of the county. The Normanskill, with its branches, the Bozens Kill (from "Boos," angry, because of its rapid descent and severe freshets). The soil is light and sandy in the east; and gravelly loam mixed with clay in the west. Knowersville is an important village on the A. & S. Railroad, seventeen miles from Albany. Hamiltonville, Guilderland Centre, Dunnsville and French's Mills, are also villages in this town. Population of town, 3,207.

Town of Knox was formed from Berne, Feb. 28, 1822. It is the N. W. corner town in the county. Its surface consists of a high plateau region broken by a few small hills. The soil is principally gravel and clay, with hard pan underneath. Knoxville—formerly known as Union street; E. and W. Township, and Peoria (on the line of Berne) are small villages. Sam'l Abbot and Andrew Brown, from Conn. settled in this town in 1789. Population of town, 1,809.

Town of New Scotland was formed from Bethlehem, April 25, 1832. It is the central town of the county, and the soil is a gravelly loam mixed with clay. Clarksville, New Salem, New Scotland, Unionville, Fleuribush and Oniskethau, are villages. Population of town, 3,311.

Town of Rensselaerville was formed from Watervliet, March 8, 1790. Berne was taken off in 1795, and a part of Westerlo in 1815. It is the S. W. corner town of the county. The soil is clay and gravel underlaid by hard pan. Rensselaerville, Williamsburgh, Preston Hollow, Medusa, Potter's Hollow and Cooksburg, are small villages. The town was mostly settled by emigrants from New England soon after the Revolution. Population of town, 2,745.

Town of Watervliet was formed March 7, 1788. Rensselaerville was taken off in 1790, Coeymans in 1791, Bethlehem in 1793, Guilderland in 1803, and Niskayuna in 1809. West Troy was incorporated April 30, 1836. It is a commercial and manufacturing city opposite the city of Troy, and is especially noted for the extent of its lumber trade, and for being the seat of an extensive United States Arsenal. It contains a bank ; a printing office and weekly newspaper, extensive manufacturers of woolen goods, bells, carriages, &c. Green Island is situated upon an island in the Hudson directly opposite Troy. It was incorporated Oct. 14, 1853. It contains

E. H. BENDER, BINDER and PRINTER, and Wholesale and Retail
BOOKSELLER and STATIONER, 73 State Street, Albany.

FARMERS' ALMANAC.

ESTABLISHED 1859.
BUSSEY, McLEOD & CO.,
STOVE FOUNDERS,
311 RIVER ST., TROY N. Y.

COSMOPOLITAN,

The People's Stove, with Patent Galvanized Cast Iron Reservoir, on a level with the top of the Stove. Convenient Durable, Economical, and with or without the Auxiliary Hot Air Chamber, Warranted to be the best Cooking Stove in the world. Made by
BUSSEY, McLEOD, & Co., 311 River St., Troy, N. Y.,
And For Sale by one Stove Dealer in nearly every town in New York.

extensive iron foundries and machine shops, car factory, &c. It is also the seat of considerable lumber trade. Cohoes is a manufacturing city upon the Mohawk, nine miles from Albany. A dam is here erected across the Mohawk, and the water is conducted by canals to convenient places for factories. The whole fall is one hundred and three feet, and the water is used five times from canals of different levels. The annual aggregate of manufactured products is nearly $3,000,000. The village contains two banks, six churches, and a large number of stores, shops, &c. Ireland Corners; Tivoli Hollow; North Albany; Spencerville or West Albany; Shaker Settlement; Town House Corners; Watervliet Centre; Newtonville; Lishas Kil. Boght and Londonville are villages in this town. Population of town, 27,279.

Town of Westerlo was formed from Coeymans and Rensselaerville, March 16, 1815. It lies upon the centre of the southern border of the county. Chesterville; Dormansville; South Westerlo; Lamb's Corners and Van Leuven's Corners. Settlement commenced in the town before the Revolution. Population of town, 2,497.

Rensselaer County, N. Y.

This county was formed from Albany, Feb. 7, 1791. Its surface is very broken and hilly. The Hudson river is on the west boundary of the county. It contains an area of 690 square miles. Population about 100,000.

Town of Berlin was formed from Petersburgh, Schodack and Stephentown, March 21, 1806. A portion of Sand Lake was taken off in 1812. It lies near the center of the east border of the county. The principal streams are Kinderhook creek and Little Hoosick river. The west part of the town is covered with forest, in which are several fine lakes. Berlin, South Berlin, Center Berlin and West Berlin, are small villages. Population over 2,149.

Town of Brunswick was formed from Troy, March 20, 1807. A part of the town was re-annexed April 15, 1814. It lies a little N. W. of the center of the county, upon the hilly region west of the summits of the Petersburgh mountains. The soil in the valleys and lowlands consists of a fertile gravelly loam, intermixed with clay. The people are largely engaged in furnishing milk, vegetables, hay, &c., to the Troy market. The first settlements were by Germans, in 1760. Brunswick Center, East Brunswick, Millville and Cropseyville, are small villages. Population of the town 3,300.

Town of East Greenwich was formed from Greenbush, as "Clinton," Feb. 23, 1855; changed April 14, 1858. It lies on the bank of the Hudson, S. W. of the center of the county. The soil is sand, gravel and clay, and is very fertile. East Greenbush is a village opposite Albany. During the

CHANTS OF THE MUSES.

Who sells clothing so very cheap,
And buys to sell, not to keep,
Is never known to sell goods steep?
     W. A. WILKINS.

Who keeps the largest stock of Caps,
And Hats to suit all kinds of chaps,
To fit hard heads and soft, "perhaps?"
     W. A. WILKINS.

Who keeps all kinds of Scarfs and Ties,
Bows, Ribbons, Tubulars and Butterflies,
The latest style he always buys?
     W. A. WILKINS.

Who makes Garments to fit so nice,
Always at a reasonable price,
The seams are strong as any vice?
     W. A. WILKINS.

Who keeps Gloves, Hosiery, Collars,
Suspenders and Shirts of all colors,
And sells them cheap? Bring on your dollars,
     W. A. WILKINS.

Who keeps all kinds for men to wear,
Boys' clothing you will find there,
The price so low you sure will stare?
     W. A. WILKINS.

WHITEHALL, N. Y.

The Saratoga Sentinel,

A DEMOCRATIC PAPER,

Published Friday's at Saratoga Springs, N. Y.

BY SAMUEL YOUNG.

Terms, - - - - - $2.00 per year.

Every Description of

Book and Job Printing

Executed with Neatness and Despatch. Advertisements Solicited.

Heavy SHIRTS and DRAWERS for 62 Cents, at WAIT'S.
For a nice-fitting suit of CLOTHES, go to WAIT'S. (See page 81.)

war of 1812, extensive barracks were erected on the hills, and for several years the place was the center of active military preparation, and the rendezvous of large bodies of troops. Settlements were made here in 1630. Population of town, 1,663.

TOWN OF GRAFTON was formed from Troy and Petersburgh, March 20, 1807. It lies N. of the center of the county. Among the hills are about twenty-five ponds, which are noted for the wild beauty of their locality; they are favorite resorts of sportsmen. Grafton, East Grafton and Quackenkill, are small villages. Population of town over 1,673.

TOWN OF GREENBUSH was formed from "Rennselaerwyck," April 10, 1792. A part of Sand Lake was set off in 1812, and "Clinton"—now called E. Greenbush—and N. Greenbush, in 1855. Greenbush was incorporated April 14, 1815. It is locally known as East Albany, and contains the depots, freight houses and machine shops of the several railroads which terminate opposite Albany, and is a place of considerable business. It is connected by ferry and railroad bridge. The first settlement was made before 1631. Population about 5,000.

TOWN OF HOOSICK was formed March 7, 1788. It lies in the N. E. corner of the county. The soil in the valleys is principally clay mixed with disintegrated slate. Hoosick Falls was incorporated April 14, 1827. It is on the Troy and Boston Railroad, twenty-seven miles from Troy. It contains a seminary, two cotton factories, two mowing machine factories, and an establishment for the manufacture of machinery for cotton and woolen factories. North Hoosick, Buskirk's Bridge, Hoosick Corners, Eagle Bridge, Walloomsac, West Hoosick and Potter Hill, are small villages. Population of town, near 5,000.

TOWN OF LANSINGBURGH was formed from Troy and Petersburgh, March 20, 1807. A tract was annexed from Schaghticoke in 1819. A part of Troy was taken off in 1836, and a part of Brunswick in 1839. Lansingburgh village was formed in 1770. In 1869 it was consolidated with Troy, under which heading it will receive mention. Speigletown is a small village in the town. Population of town, including Lansingburgh, over 6,000.

TOWN OF NASSAU was formed from Petersburgh, Stephentown and Schodack, March 31, 1806, by the name of "Phillipstown," but was changed April 6, 1808. It lies near the center of the S. border of the county. Its surface is very broken. The soil is clay and gravel underlaid by hardpan. Considerable manufacturing is carried on in the town. Nassau village was incorporated March 12, 1819. East Nassau, Hoag's Corner, Alps, North Nassau, Miller's Corners, Slab City and Brainards, are small villages. Population of town, about 3,000.

TOWN OF NORTH GREENBUSH was formed from Greenbush, Feb. 23, 1855. It lies upon the Hudson, west of the center of the county. The people are extensively engaged in supplying the markets of Albany and Troy with garden vegetables, milk, &c. Bath is a small village opposite the upper part of Albany. Defriestville—or Blooming Grove—and Wynantskill are settlements. Population of town about 2,600.

Bie yer Cloze ov W. A. WILKINS. (See page 96.)

BENDER will furnish you any Books Published; also, ENGINEERS' INSTRUMENTS, STATIONERY, FIELD BOOKS, &c., at 73 State Street, Albany.

98   FARMERS' ALMANAC.

J. B. LAVENDER,
CABINET WARE,

Coffins, Shrouds and Metallic Burial Cases,
GRAVE CAPS, &c., ALL QUALITIES,
WINDOW SHADES, AND FIXTURES,
Extension, Dining and Tea Tables, Feathers, Looking Glasses, &c.,
Walnut Chestnut & Grained Chamber Setts.
No. 219 STATE ST., LANSINGBURGH, N. Y.
Orders for Upholstering, Repairing and Undertaking promptly attended to.

CHARLES CLARK,
DRAPER AND
MERCHANT TAILOR,

No. 246 State St., Lansingburgh, N. Y.

Dealer in Gents' Furnishing Goods.

SHIRTS,   CANES,   NECK-TIES,   UMBRELLAS.

JOHN ENGEL,

Manufacturer of and Dealer in

BOOTS AND SHOES,

No. 224 State Street,

LANSINGBURGH, N. Y.

A. L. BREWSTER,

Manufacturer and Dealer in

TIN WARE, STOVES, PIPE, &c.

Also, Dealer in Hardware, Glassware, Kerosene Oil and Lamps, House Furnishing Goods, &c.
Agent for the Oriental and Morning Glory Base-Burner Stoves, and Littlefield's Heaters.

No. 66 Broad St., Waterford, N. Y.

N. B.—All Kinds of Paper Stock Taken in Exchange.

TOWN OF PETERSBURGH was formed from Stephentown March 18, 1791. Its boundary on the line of Berlin was changed Jan. 4, 1793; parts of Berlin and Lansingburgh were taken off in 1806, and parts of Nassau and Grafton in 1807. It lies upon the east border of the county, north of the center. The soil in the valley is a gravelly loam. Petersburgh—formerly "Rennselaer Mills"—and Petersburgh Four Corners, are small places. The first settlers were Dutch, who came in about 1750. Subsequently many families came in from Rhode Island. Population, 1,670.

TOWN OF PITTSTOWN was formed March 7, 1788. Its boundary was changed Feb. 14, 1793, (township originally erected July 23, 1761). It lies in the center of north part of the county. Flax is extensively cultivated, and there are several manufactories in town. Johnsonville; Tomhannock; Raymertown; Pittstown; Boynton; Valley Falls; N. Pittstown; Cooksborough and Sherman's Mills, are small villages. Settlement was commenced in 1650. Population of town, 3,831.

TOWN OF POESTENKILL was formed from Sand Lake, March 2, 1848. It lies near the center of the county, upon the western declivities of the Petersburgh mountains. One mile west of the falls of the Poestenkill is a medicinal spring of some local celebrity. Poestenkill, East Poestenkill and Barberville, are small villages. Population of town, 1,952.

TOWN OF SAND LAKE was formed from Greenbush and Berlin, June 19, 1812. A part of Greenbush was taken off in 1843, and Poestenkill in 1848. It lies a little south of the centre of the county. Its surface is mountainous in the east, and hilly in the west. There are several lakes in the town. Sand Lake and West Sand Lake are villages of some importance. Sliter's Corners, Glass House and South Sand Lake, are villages. Settlement commenced before the Revolution. Population of town, 2,606.

TOWN OF SCHAGHTICOKE was formed as a district, March 24, 1772, and as a town, March 7, 1788. Pittstown was taken off March 7, 1788, and a part of Lansingburgh, in 1819. It lies on the Hudson in the N. W. corner of the county. The soil is generally a fertile, sandy or gravelly loam. Schaghticoke, recently changed to Hart's Falls, is a place of considerable business. The Hoosick river runs through the village. It is thirteen miles from Troy. Schaghticoke Hill, the Borough, Junction and Old Schaghticoke, are villages. About 1670, Governor Andros settled a remnant of the Pequots and other Eastern tribes, under the name of "Schaghticokes," in this town. Population of town, 3,054.

TOWN OF SCODACK was formed March 17, 1795. Parts of Berlin and Nassau were taken off in 1806. It lies upon the Hudson in the S. W. corner of the county. The soil in the east is clay, and in the west a fertile, sandy and gravelly loam. Castleton is a fine village upon the Hudson, fifteen miles from Troy. Schodack is three miles below Castleton. East Schodack, Schodack Centre, South Schodack, Muitzes Kill, &c., are small villages. This vicinity was thickly inhabited by native tribes at the time of Hudson's visit in 1609. Population of town, 4,015.

TOWN OF STEPHENTOWN was formed from "Rennselaerwyck," March 29, 1784. Petersburgh was taken off in 1791, and parts of Berlin and

The STATIONERY Department Replete with every variety of STATIONER'S ARTICLES, at BENDER'S, 73 State Street, Albany.

FARMERS' ALMANAC.

GEORGE R. HARDY'S
PHOTOGRAPH AND AMBROTYPE
GALLERY,
266 STATE STREET, LANSINGBURGH.

Mr. HARDY would respectfully inform the citizens of Lansingburgh and vicinity that he has purchased the GALLERY formerly occupied by E. S STERRY, where he intends to pay personal attention to every branch known to the Art. An experience of many years with Brady of New York, Haines & Wicks of Albany, and Cobden of Troy, will enable him to give entire satisfaction to all who may favor him with a call.

H. J. MASON & SON,

No. 241 State St.,
3d Door Below Phœnix Hotel,

LANSINGBURGH, N. Y.

Manufacturers of

CABINET FURNITURE,
AND
PICTURE FRAMES OF ALL KINDS.
Constantly on hand a Large Assortment of all kinds of
COFFINS.
Hearse, Carriages and everything in the Undertaking Line Furnished at the Shortest Notice.
ALL KINDS OF PACKING AND JOBBING DONE TO ORDER.

Nassau in 1806. It lies in the S. E. corner of the county. The soil is hard and sterile among the mountains, but a gravelly loam in the valleys. Stephentown, Stephentown Flats, North, South and West Stephentown, are small villages. Population of town, 2,026.

TROY was formed as a town, March 18, 1791. The city charter was granted April 12, 1816. It is a city and capital of Rensselaer county, and is situated on the Hudson river, at the mouth of the Poestenkill creek, and at the head of steamboat navigation, six miles above Albany, and 150 miles north of New York. Troy is favorably situated for commerce. It has lines of tow-boats to New York city, of propellers and barges to Philadelphia, and of sail packets to Boston. Many here discharge their cargoes on board of large barges to be towed down the river, and receive, in exchange, cargoes passing North or West. This transhipment constitutes the principal commercial business of the place. Four railroads meet at this point, viz.: The Hudson River, the Troy and Boston, the Schenectady and Troy, and the Rensselaer Railroads, which, with their several extensions, connect it with New York, Boston, Montreal, Buffalo, &c. A dam across the river here renders it navigable for sloops to Lansingburgh. The New York and Troy Steamboat Company, with a superior class of steamboats, ply daily between Troy and New York, touching at Albany both ways. Its manufactures reach all parts of the Union. Green Island village, on an island of that name above West Troy, and also in Albany county, is properly a suburb of Troy and mainly dependent upon it, with a population of about 3,000. It contains the largest railroad-car and stage-coach factory in the State. The following are prominent establishments in Troy: 2 extensive nail factories, 21 iron foundries, 26 paper and cloth collar factories, extensive manufactories of knitted goods, 1 large manufactory of slate mantels, 18 stove factories, 2 varnish factories, 10 breweries, 1 extensive car manufactory, 3 distilleries, 1 paper mill, 1 large cotton mill, 1 large flouring mill, 1 extensive chemical factory, 3 manufactories of hosiery, and 1 extensive woolen mill, besides a large number of smaller concerns. It has five newspapers. Lansingburgh, recently consolidated with Troy, is a place of extensive manufactories. Brushes, oil cloths, flax, cordage, &c., &c. A bridge here crosses the Hudson to Waterford. The Troy and Boston Railroad passes through the town. There are two banks and one newspaper.

The Troy Female Seminary, so long and so favorably known, is one of the most prominent objects in Troy. The educational institutions, besides the public schools, are the Troy Academy, incorporated in 1834. The Rensselaer Polytechnic Institute, organized in 1824. The Troy Lyceum of Natural History was incorporated in 1820. St. Peter's College is built on Mount St. Vincent. St. Joseph's Academy was founded in 1842. The Troy Hospital, in the care of the Sisters of Charity, was incorporated in 1851. The Marshall Infirmary, incorporated in 1851. The Troy Orphan Asylum, incorporated in 1835. St. Mary's Orphan Asylum, connected with St. Mary's Church, is under the care of the Christian Brothers and Sisters of Charity. The Warren Free Institute, a school for indigent female children, was incorporated in 1846.

Competition Defied in Quality, Quantity and Prices of STATIONERY,
at BENDER'S, 73 State Street, Albany.

FURNITURE STORE.

AN EXTENSIVE ASSORTMENT OF

FURNITURE OF EVERY DESCRIPTION.

A FULL SUPPLY OF

COFFINS

IN DIFFERENT STYLES AND PRICES.

MATTRASSES MADE AND RE-STUFFED.

CHAS. A. SCOFIELD, WATERFORD, N.Y.

JESSE SPICER,

MANUFACTURER AND DEALER IN

BOOTS, SHOES,

RUBBERS, &c.,

Broad Street, Waterford, N. Y.

All Kinds of Custom Work Done with Neatness and Dispatch.

S. A. NORTHRUP,

HARNESS MAKER,

ALSO, DEALER IN

Hats, Caps, Trunks, Valises, Traveling Bags, Umbrellas, &c. Whips, Gloves, Mittens, Robes and Horse Blankets of all kinds.

No. 55 Broad Street, Waterford, N. Y.

J. S. KELSO.

WATERFORD MARBLE WORKS,

1 door north of the corner of 3d and Broad sts.,

WATERFORD, N. Y.

VERMONT AND ITALIAN MARBLE,
MONUMENTS, TOMB-STONES,
TABLE-TOPS, PIER-SLABS,

And ALL KINDS OF MARBLE WORK.

All Work Delivered Free of Charge.

Saratoga County, N. Y.

This county was formed from Albany, Feb. 7, 1791. It lies in the north angle formed by the junction of the Hudson and Mohawk rivers, centrally distant thirty-one miles from Albany, and contains 862 square miles. Population 50,000.

TOWN OF BALLSTON was formed from Saratoga as a district, April 1, 1775; organized as a town March 7, 1788. Charlton, Galway and Milton were taken off in 1792. It lies upon the border of the county S. W. of the center. Ballston is on the line of Milton, a small portion only of the village is within this town. Burnt Hills, Ballston Centre, Academy Hill, East Line and South Ballston, are small villages. Population of town, 2,089.

TOWN OF CHARLTON was formed from Ballston, March 17, 1792. It is the S. W. corner town of the county. The soil is an excellent quality of sandy, gravelly and clayey loam. Charlton and West Charlton are villages. The first settlement in this town was made in 1774. Population of town, 1,589.

TOWN OF CLIFTON PARK was formed from Halfmoon, March 3, 1828, as "Clifton," and changed March 31, 1829. Clifton Park is on the border of Halfmoon. Amity and Rexford Flats are canal villages; Jonesville, Groom's Corners, Dry Dock and Forts Ferry, are small places. Settlements were made in the Mohawk valley previous to 1700. Population of town, 2,712.

TOWN OF CORINTH was formed from Hadley, April 20, 1818. A part of Moreau was annexed Jan. 28, 1848. It lies upon the Hudson in the N. E. part of the county. The soil is a clayey and sandy loam. Jessup's Landing and South Corinth are small villages. The first settlement was made near South Corinth, in 1790. Population of town, 1,491.

TOWN OF DAY was formed from Edinburgh and Hadley, as "Concord," April 17, 1819; its name was changed Dec. 3, 1827. It is the N. W. corner town of the county. The soil is a moderately fertile, sandy and clayey loam. Huntsville and Day are small places. Population of the town, 1,185.

TOWN OF EDINBURGH was formed from Providence, March 13, 1801, as "Northfield," but changed April 6, 1808. A part of Day was taken off in 1819. It lies upon the west border of the county, north of the center. The soil on the river flats is a good quality of clayey and gravelly loam. Batchelorville, on the east bank of the Sacondaga, and Beecher's Hollow, on the west side of the river, are small villages. Population of town, 1,357.

TOWN OF GALWAY was formed from Ballston, March 7, 1792. Providence was taken off in 1796. It lies on the west border of the county, S. of the center. The soil is generally a heavy clay, intermixed in places

The Trade Supplied with STATIONERY and Every Article Used in the Counting Room, at Manufacturer's Prices, at BENDER'S, 73 State Street, Albany.

104   FARMERS' ALMANAC.

1870.   1870.

WATFORD'S
Harness Establishment
BROAD STREET, WATERFORD, N. Y.
(TWO DOORS BELOW CITY HOTEL),

A complete variety of all Goods pertaining to the Trade. Sole Proprietors of

The Improved Scotch Collar & Neck Pad,
Warranted not to gall

Repairing a Specialty.

GEORGE H. LEMPE,
Manufacturer of and Dealer in

BOOTS AND SHOES,
Rubbers, Gaiters, Slippers, &c.

264 State St., Lansingburgh, N. Y.

NEW HARDWARE STORE.
McGUIRK & GAFFNEY,
DEALERS IN

Copper, Tin and Sheet Iron Ware,
THE IMPROVED "AMERICA" COOK STOVE,
Also "Fire Light" Parlor Stove,
Also Dealers in Old Barter of all kinds,

No. 100 Remsen St.   -   Cohoes, N. Y.
JAMES McGUIRK.   THOMAS GAFFNEY.

STOVES AND
Hardware.
JOHN HILTON & CO.
COHOES, N. N.
Agents for the celebrated new

Empire Cooking Stove,
Also Dealers in all kinds of
Tin, Sheet Iron & Copper Ware,
Steam and Gas Fitters
and Plumbers.

with sand and gravel. Galway is near the center of the town, and was incorporated April 18, 1838. West Galway is on the border of Fulton county. York's Corners, North and South Galway, Mosherville and Whiteside Corners, are small villages. The first settlers from Galway, Scotland, located in the town in 1774. Population of town, 2,202.

TOWN OF GREENFIELD was formed from Saratoga and Milton, March 12, 1793. A part of Hadley was taken off in 1801. It lies a little N. W. of the center of the county. The soil is generally a gravelly loam, intermixed with clay. Iron ore has been found in the east part. Greenfield Centre, Jamesville, Mount Pleasant, Porter's Corners, North and West Greenfield, and Page's Corners, are in this town. Settlements were made in 1784. Population of town, 2,891.

TOWN OF HADLEY was formed from Greenfield and Northumberland, Feb. 27, 1801. Its boundaries were amended Feb. 28, 1808. Corinth was taken off in 1818, and a part of Day in 1819. It lies upon the Hudson, in the N. E. corner of the county. The soil generally is a coarse, yellowish, unproductive sand and gravel. Conklingville is in the west part, Hadley is a hamlet. Population of town, 1,067.

TOWN OF HALFMOON was formed as a district March 24, 1772, and as a town, March 7, 1788. Its name was changed to "Orange," April 17, 1816, and the original name was restored Jan. 16, 1820. Waterford was taken off in 1816, and Clifton Park in 1828. The soil is a clayey and gravelly loam upland, and a fine quality of alluvium in the intervales. Crescent is a canal village. Newtown, Smithtown, Gray's Corners, are small villages. Mechanicsville lies mostly in Stillwater. Clifton Park is on the west line. Settlements were made about 1680.

TOWN OF MALTA was formed from Stillwater, March 3, 1802; part of Saratoga was annexed March 28, 1805. It lies upon the west bank of Saratoga lake, S. E. of the center of the county. The soil is principally a light, sandy loam, with clay and muck in the lowlands. Dunning Street is near the center of the town. Maltaville, Malta Ridge and Hall's Corners, are in the town. Settlements were made before the Revolution. Population of town, 1,190.

TOWN OF MILTON was formed from Ballston, March 7, 1792, and a part of Greenfield was taken off in 1793. It lies a little S. of the center of the county. The Saratoga mineral spring region extends through the S. E. part. There are several establishments for the manufacture of cotton, oil cloths, edge tools, sash and blinds, paper, &c.; a knitting factory, &c. Ballston is the County Seat, and was incorporated March 21, 1807. It contains the county buildings, several churches, two weekly newspapers, and printing offices; a bank, &c. Its mineral waters, which were discovered in 1769, are celebrated for their medicinal qualities. It is a place of considerable summer resort, being preferred by many for the beauty and quiet of the place. It is twenty-five miles from Troy, and seven from Saratoga. Rock City Mills, West Milton, Bloodville, Factory Village, Milton Centre and Crane's Village, are in this town. Settlements were made before the Revolution. The grandfather of Stephen A. Douglas (Benajah Douglas), built a log house near the spring for the accommodation of visitors in 1792. Population of town, over 5,000.

Would you be happy? Buy your Clothing of WILKINS.

HARTWELL & AKIN,

MANUFACTURERS OF

SADDLES, HARNESS & TRUNKS,

No. 172 Broadway, opp. Marvin House.

SARATOGA SPRINGS, N. Y.

A. R. BARRETT,

Dealer in

HATS, CAPS, FURS,

Gents' Furnishing Goods,

UMBRELLAS, &c.,

148 BROADWAY, SARATOGA SPRINGS.

P. THOMPSON & CO.,

Next to Post Office, Phila St., Saratoga Springs,

MANUFACTURERS AND DEALERS IN

HARNESS,

Whips, Trunks,

TRAVELING BAGS, &c.

P. THOMPSON,   J. O. WINCHESTER.

**HATS and CAPS can always be found at WAIT'S.
Get a HOWE MACHINE and be happy, at WAIT'S.** (See page 81.)

HISTORY OF SARATOGA COUNTY. 107

TOWN OF MOREAU was taken from Northumberland, March 28, 1805; a part was annexed to Corinth in 1848. It lies in the great bend of the Hudson, in the N. E. corner of the county. The soil is generally a light, yellow, sandy loam, but in the S. and W. are tracts of clay and gravel. South Glen's Falls—opposite Glen's Falls—contains several manufacturing establishments, and a population of seven or eight hundred. Fortsville is in the central part. Clark's Corners, Reynold's Corners, State Dam and Moreau Station, are in this town; the latter is a station on the Rens. & Saratoga R. R., sixteen miles north of Saratoga. Here take stages for Lake George, Glen's Falls and Chester. Population of town, 2,279.

TOWN OF NORTHUMBERLAND was formed from Saratoga, March 16, 1798. A part of Hadley was taken off in 1801, Moreau in 1805, and Wilton in 1818. It lies upon the Hudson, N. of the center of the county. The soil is generally a light, sandy loam. Gansevoort is a station on the R. & S. R. R. Northumberland is in the S. E. part of the town. Bacon Hill is a hamlet. Population of town, 1,705.

TOWN OF PROVIDENCE was formed from Galway, Feb. 5, 1796, and Edinburgh was taken off in 1801. It lies near the center of the W. border of the county. The soil is chiefly a coarse, yellow sand or gravel. Barkersville, Hagidorn, Hollow, Providence and W. Providence, are in this town. Settlements were made previous to the Revolution. Population of town, 1,295.

TOWN OF SARATOGA was formed as a district, March 24, 1772, and as a town, March 7, 1788. Easton (Washington county), was taken off in 1789. A part of Greenfield in 1793; Northumberland in 1798; a part of Malta in 1805, and Saratoga Springs in 1819. It lies upon the Hudson, near the center of the E. border of the county. Schuylerville, situated on the river, at the mouth of Fish Creek, was incorporated April 16, 1831. Gen'l Philip Schuyler resided here previous to the Revolution. It is a place of some manufacturing; contains an academy, &c. Victory Mills is on Fish Creek; it contains a machine shop, cotton mill, &c. Quaker Springs, Grangerville, Dean's Corners and Coveville, are in this town. Population of town, 3,730.

TOWN OF SARATOGA SPRINGS was formed from Saratoga, April 9, 1819. It is located nearly central in the county. Saratoga Lake is a pleasant drive, and much frequented by Saratogians in the summer season. Saratoga Springs was incorporated April 17, 1826. It is upon the Rensselaer & Saratoga Railroad, thirty-two miles from Troy, twenty-two from Schenectady, and sixty-three from Rutland. It contains three banks, three newspapers, and many large, fine stores. This tract of country abounds in mineral springs, justly the most celebrated in the United States, and vying with the famous Spas of Continental Europe. At an early a date as 1767, the waters were used for medicinal purposes. The beauty of the surrounding country, and the well known remedial quality of its waters, greatly diversified as to their mineral combinations, and varying in their efficacy as medicinal agents, renders Saratoga Springs the most popular resort of fashion and pleasure. While the invalid from all portions of this continent, and foreign tourists from all climates, seek the healing and invigorating water so bountifully supplied by nature, and adapted to all the complaints that " flesh

Ding, dong, bell! WILKINS is bound to sell. (See p. 96.)
14

PAPER of all Kinds, by the Case, Ream or Quire,
at BENDER'S, 73 State Street, Albany.

108   FARMERS' ALMANAC.

VERMONT AND SARATOGA

MARBLE WORKS.

The Cheapest Place in Northern New York to buy

Marble and Granite Monuments, Headstones,
AND ALL KINDS OF MARBLE WORK.

HARRINGTON & EVERSON,
Front Street (near Van Dam,)
SARATOGA SPRINGS, N. Y.

A Complete Stock, and Orders Promptly Answered.

PLATT S. CLUTE,

Successor to LOWELL HOWE,

DEALER IN

MAHOGANY, ROSEWOOD, BLACK WALNUT, PINE AND CHERRY

COFFINS AND CASKETS,
ROOMS, 191 BROADWAY,
SARATOGA SPRINGS, N. Y.

A First-Class Hearse Furnished if Desired.

Light and Heavy Wagons at Joubert & White's, Glen's Falls.

is heir to." Ample accommodations are provided for all who, in search of health or pleasure, flock to the springs. Hotels, which are the resort of wealth and fashion, and minor places of entertainment, and boarding-houses for such as prefer the quiet of private residences.

TOWN OF STILLWATER was formed March 7, 1788. A part of Easton (Washington county), was taken off in 1789, and Malta in 1802. It lies upon the Hudson, S. E. of the center of the county. Stillwater (village) was incorporated April 17, 1816; it is situated on the Hudson, and contains manufactories of lumber, paper, &c. Mechanicsville, incorporated July 16, 1859, situated on the Hudson, at the mouth of Anthony's Kill, on the line of Halfmoon, is a station on the Rensselaer and Saratoga Railroad, eighteen miles from Albany. It contains five churches, a printing office, the Mechanicsville Academy, carriage manufactory, hotel, and an extensive linen thread manufactory. Bemis Heights and Ketchum's Corners, are in this town. Settlements were commenced about 1750. Population of town, over 3,000.

TOWN OF WATERFORD was formed from Halfmoon, April 17, 1816. It lies at the junction of the Hudson and Mohawk rivers, in the S. E. corner of the county. The falls in the Mohawk furnish a valuable water power. Waterford was formed April 17, 1816. In 1784 the site of the present village was purchased by Colonel Jacobus Van Schoon, Ezra Hickok, Judge White, and others, mostly from Connecticut. The village was incorporated April 6, 1801; is situated on the Champlain canal, near the confluence of the Hudson and Mohawk rivers; is distant from Troy four miles, from Albany ten miles; on the Rensselaer & Saratoga Railroad. The facilities for manufacturing are only second to one or two places in the State, and the village contains several large factories. Settlement was commenced by the Dutch at a very early day. Population of town, about 4,000.

TOWN OF WILTON was formed from Northumberland, April 20, 1818. It lies a little N. E. of the center of the county. Wilton and Emerson's Corners, are in the town. The first settlement was made in 1774. Population of the town, 1,362.

Schenectady County, N. Y.

This county was formed from Albany, March 7, 1809. It is centrally distant from Albany twenty miles, and contains 221 square miles. The greater part lies between Mohawk river and Schoharie creek. The principal streams are Mohawk river, Schoharie creek, and Normans Kill, and their branches. Settlement by white people was made in 1661. Population about 21,000.

TOWN OF DUANESBURGH was erected as a township by patent, March 13, 1765. It lies in the S. W. corner of the county. The soil is principally a stiff, clay loam, with a slight intermixture of gravel. Duanesburgh, Qua-

Prices of BOOKS, STATIONERY, FANCY GOODS, &c., &c.,
Reduced at BENDER'S, 73 State Street, Albany.

FARMERS' ALMANAC.

S. A. RICKARD,
DEALER IN
WALL PAPER, WINDOW SHADES,
Window Cornices, Looking Glasses, Pictures, Stationery and Fancy Articles,
ALSO MANUFACTURER OF ALL KINDS OF PICTURE FRAMES,
179 Broadway, Saratoga Springs, N. Y.

☞ Paper Hanging Done to Order. ☜

E. W. OUDERKIRK,
Furniture Manufacturer
And Dealer in
Tete-a-Tetes, Sofas, Chairs,
Tables, Stands, Bureaus,
BEDSTEADS, MATRESSES, FEATHERS,
Lounges, Cushions, Hall Stands, Looking Glasses, Window Shades, Picture Cords,
Tassels, Oval and Square Frames, Looking Glass Plates, &c.
183 Broadway, Saratoga Springs.

FLORENCE SEWING MACHINES.

THE SIMPLEST
AND THE BEST.

ONLY NINE WORKING PARTS in each Machine.
300 Sold in Saratoga and vicinity.
EVERY ONE GIVING UNBOUNDED SATISFACTION,
They are very still, run very easy, carry the work either way, make a beautiful stitch, which never puckers after washing, and never skip stitches.
SALE ROOM AT
JENNINGS BROTHERS' STORE,
Saratoga Springs.
BY DR. H. D. TODD,
Also an assortment of all the different kinds of Machines in market, very cheap.

We have a fine stock of Imported Cloths. **WHITE & PEARSALL,** *Glen's Falls.*

Garrett, Dentist, Glen's Falls, N. Y.

ker Street, Mariaville, Braman's Corners and Eaton's Corners, are in this town. Population of town, 3,099.

Town of Glenville was formed from Schenectady, April 14, 1820. It lies north of the Mohawk. The soil among the hills is a stiff clay, underlaid by hardpan, with an occasional outcrop of slate; and in the east part, it is a sandy and gravelly loam. The Mohawk intervales are very fertile, and are chiefly devoted to the culture of broom-corn. Glenville, Scotia Reesville, High Mills, Hoffman's Ferry (a station on the N. Y C. R. R), East Glenville and Town Centre, are in this town. Population of town, 3,038.

Town of Niskayuna was formed from Watervliet (Albany Co.), March 7, 1809. A part of Schenectady was annexed in 1853. It lies upon the Mohawk in the east part of the county. Watervliet Centre and Niskayuna, are small places. The first settlements were made about 1640. Population of town, 845.

Town of Princetown was formed from Schenectady, March 26, 1798. It lies a little W. of the center of the county. The soil is a heavy clay loam, underlaid by hard pan, and is best adapted to grazing. Princetown is a small place. Upon the Kantzeekil stream is a cascade sixty feet high, and from this point to the Mohawk are numerous rapids and cascades. Population of town, 931.

Town of Rotterdam was formed from Schenectady, April 14, 1820. A part of the city was annexed in 1853. It lies near the center of the county, upon the S. bank of the Mohawk. Rotterdam, Mohawkville and Factoryville, are hamlets. Settlements were first made about 1661. Population of town, 2,290.

Schenectady City was patented Nov. 4, 1684; chartered as a borough, Oct. 23, 1765; incorporated as a district, March 24, 1772; as a town, March 7, 1788, and as a city, March 26, 1798. Princetown was set off in 1798; Rotterdam and Glenville in 1820, and parts of Niskayuna and Rotterdam in 1853. It is on the N. Y. C. R. R., distant from Albany seventeen miles. The railway from Troy strikes the main trunk of the Central at this point; so does the Rensselaer and Saratoga R. R. It lies on the beautiful Mohawk, with the Erie Canal running through its centre. The distinguishing feature of Schenectady is Union College. This celebrated seat of science and literature was incorporated nearly seventy years ago. The manufacturing interest is quite an extensive one; and it is the centre of a considerable agricultural district. The settlement of the place was commenced more than two centuries ago, and in 1690 it contained eighty houses. The growth of Schenectady has been gradual, but slow, for many years past. It is an opulent town, and contains many families distinguished for cultivation and refinement. The inhabitants are social in their habits, and dispense a liberal hospitality in admirable taste. About the middle of the last century an extensive fur trade was prosecuted from Schenectady, and this lucrative enterprise brought much treasure to the town. In 1795 it was the mart of the "Western Navigation Company," which traded with the West by means of the Mohawk, Wood Creek, and lakes Oneida and Ontario. It is now a great market for broom corn, one of the staple products of the fertile bottom lands of the Mohawk. Population, about 12,000.

WILKINS sells Clothing 15 per cent cheaper than others.

E. H. BENDER, 73 State Street, Albany, Manufactures his own
BLANK BOOKS, and Sells the CHEAPEST and BEST.

112 *FARMERS' ALMANAC.*

IRGOOT,

GREAT RUSSIAN — **LEATHER PRESERVATIVE**

Go to White & Pearsall's for a Complete Outfit in Clothing at a Bargain.

AND WATER PROOF DRESSING,

Sold by all Boot and Shoe Dealers.

J. L. LUCAS,

BOOT & SHOE STORE,

No. 102 Broadway, Saratoga Springs.

For a nice open Buggy, go to Joubert & White's, Glen's Falls.

Warren County, N. Y.

This county was formed from Washington, March 12, 1813, and named in honor of Gen'l Joseph Warren, of Revolutionary fame. It lies S. and W. of Lake George, near the east border of the State. It is centrally distant sixty-five miles from Albany, and contains 968 square miles. Lake George ("The Lake of Silver Water,") has long been celebrated for its wild and picturesque beauty. It is almost surrounded by precipitous and rocky mountains, and is studded with little green islands. Each mountain, precipice, and cape, has its own tales and reminiscences of historic interest of the olden time. Population, 21,128.

TOWN OF BOLTON was formed from Thurman, March 25, 1799. Hague was taken off in 1807, a part of Caldwell in 1810, and a part of Horicon in 1838. It lies east of the center of the county. The soil is a thin, sandy loam. Bolton (village) is on Lake George, opposite Green Island. The settlement of the town commenced in 1792. Population of town, 1,221.

TOWN OF CALDWELL was formed from Queensbury, Bolton and Thurman, March 2, 1810. It lies around the south extremity of Lake George. The soil is a sandy loam among the hills, and a dark, rich, sandy and clayey loam on the lowlands. Caldwell is the county seat, and is near the head of Lake George. This place is the annual resort of great numbers of tourists and pleasure seekers, attracted here by the beautiful scenery of the lake and surrounding region. Population of town, 979.

TOWN OF CHESTER was formed from Thurman, March 25, 1799. It lies upon the north border of the county. The soil is generally light and sandy. The settlement of this town commenced toward the close of the last century. Chestertown and Pottersville, are in this town. Population of town, 2,274.

TOWN OF HAGUE was formed from Bolton, Feb. 28, 1807, as Rochester; its name was changed, April 6, 1808, and a part of Horicon was taken off in 1838. It lies upon the shore of Lake George, in the N. E. corner of the county. The beauty of the lake and the solitary grandeur of the mountain scenery of this town, render it a favorite resort for hunting and fishing parties, and the lovers of the beautiful in nature. Hague and Wardboro, are small places in this town. Population of town, 684.

TOWN OF HORICON was formed from Bolton and Hague, March 29, 1838. It lies upon the N. border of the county, east of Schroon lake. The soil is a sandy loam. Horicon village is on Schroon river, in the S. W. part of the town. Mill Brook is on Schroon Lake. Population of town, 1,398.

TOWN OF JOHNSBURGH was formed from Thurman, April 6, 1805. It lies upon the bank of the Hudson, and is the N. W. corner of the county. The soil is a sandy and gravelly loam. Johnsburgh and Noble's Corners, are on Mill Creek. North Creek and the Glen are on the Hudson. The first settlement was made soon after the close of the Revolutionary War. Population of town, 2,286.

BLANK BOOKS Made after any Pattern at BENDER'S, 73 State Street, Albany.
LITHOGRAPHING and PRINTING in Every Style done at BENDER'S, 73 State St.

For Sale—a large lot of Clothing, Cloths and Cassimeres at White & Pearsall's.

FARMERS' ALMANAC.

M. FARRAR,
Manufacturer of and Dealer in
TOLMAN'S PATENT SELF VENTILATING
SPRING BEDS.

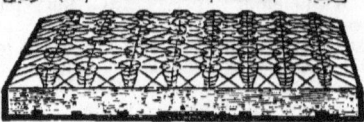

Manufacturer of
Hair, Moss & Husk Matresses & Bolsters.
ALSO DEALER IN FEATHERS.
Other kinds of Beds kept constantly on hand and made to order.

No. 8 Caroline Street, Saratoga Springs, N. Y.

DENTISTRY.
CHARLES CARPENTER,
DENTIST,

Office in Commercial Bank Building

PHILA STREET,
Opposite Post Office,

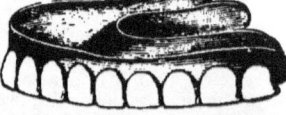

SARATOGA SPRINGS.

New Goods—Winter and Spring Fashions,
AT
M. V. PRINDLE'S,

Just returned from market with the following new Dress Goods, Laces, Embroideries, Ribbons, French Flowers, Feathers, Magnificent in Quality, New Shades, Round Hats, Dress Bonnets, French Frames, Silks and Satins, Felt Hats, Fancy Goods, Hair Nets, Fine Jet Jewelry, Chains, Bracelets, &c., &c.
Real Hair, our Imitation Hair is complete. The latest Novelties of Japan and Chinese Coils, Handkerchiefs, Collars and Cuffs, Corsets, Hosiery, Gloves, Perfumery, Trimmings, Buttons, Fringes, Kid Gloves, Underwear, Small Wear, Neck Ties, Bows, Lace Collars, Princess Alice Crinoline. Agent in Whitehall for E. Butterick & Co.'s Celebrated Patterns of Garments for Ladies, Misses, Boys and Little Children of both sexes. Great Reduction in Prices for Cash.

M. V. PRINDLE,
Over Manville & Weidman's Store, Canal St., Whitehall, N. Y.

JAMES R. BROUGHTON,
WHITEHALL, N. Y.,
DRUGGIST & APOTHECARY,

Keeps constantly on hand a large and well selected assortment of
Drugs, Medicines, Paints, Oils and Window Glass,
Patent Medicines, Perfumery & Toilet Articles.
BOOKS & STATIONERY,
AND CHOICE FAMILY GROCERIES.

Physicians Prescriptions Carefully prepared.   Particular attention given to School Books.

Teeth Extracted without Pain at GARRETT'S, Glen's Falls, N. Y.

Latest Novelties in Ladies' Boots, at WAIT'S.
Romeo and Juliet Walking Boots, at WAIT'S. (See page 81.)

HISTORY OF WARREN COUNTY.

TOWN OF LUZERNE was formed from Queensbury, April 10, 1792, as Fairfield, and changed April 6, 1808. A portion was taken off by Queensbury, March 30, 1802. It lies upon the east bank of the Hudson river, in the southern extremity of the county. The soil is a light, sandy loam. Luzerne is situated upon the Hudson, above its confluence with Sacandaga river. The first settlements were made about 1770. Population of town, 1,136.

TOWN OF QUEENSBURY was incorporated by patent, May 20, 1762, and recognized as a town, March 13, 1786. Luzerne was taken off in 1792, and a part of Caldwell in 1810. A part was added from Luzerne in 1802. It lies between Lake George and the Hudson, and is the S. E. corner town of the county. Glen's Falls is on the branch railroad, five miles from Fort Edward, where it connects with the Rens. and Saratoga Railroad. It is fifty-four miles from Troy, and contains two weekly newspaper offices, two banks, an insurance company, and several extensive manufactories; and it is also a great lumbering district. The fall in the Hudson at this place is about fifty feet high, and affords very valuable mill privileges. The summit level of the Champlain canal is fed through the Glen's Falls navigable feeder with water taken from the Hudson above the Falls. This is a spot trebly interesting, from its natural, its poetical, and its historical character. The passage of the river is through a rude ravine, in a mad descent of seventy-five feet over a rocky precipice 900 feet in length. Within the roar of these cataracts were laid some of the scenes in Cooper's story of the "Last of the Mohicans." They are gently associated with our romantic memories of Uncas and Hawk's Eye, David, Duncan Haywood, and his sweet wards, Alice and Cora Monroe. Glen's Falls was incorporated April 12, 1839. Population, over 5,000. West Glen's Falls, Queensbury and French Mountain, are in this town. Population of town, 8,000.

TOWN OF STONY CREEK was formed from "Athol," Nov. 3, 1852. It lies upon the W. bank of the Hudson river, and is the S. W. corner town of the county. The soil is a light, sandy loam. Creek Centre and Stony Creek are small places, and are situated on Stony creek. The first settlements were made about 1795. Population of town, 935.

TOWN OF THURMAN was formed April 10, 1792. Bolton and Chester were taken off in 1799; Johnsburgh in 1805, and a part of Caldwell in 1810. The town was divided into Athol and Warrensburgh, Feb. 12, 1813, and Athol was divided into Thurman and Stony Creek, Nov. 3, 1852. It lies upon the W. bank of the Hudson, S. W. of the center of the county. The soil is a light, sandy loam. Athol and Thurman are in the east part. Population of town, 1,007.

TOWN OF WARRENSBURGH was formed from Thurman, Feb. 12, 1813. It lies between the two branches of the Hudson, near the center of the county, and upon the ridges south of the junction. Warrensburgh village is upon Schroom river, three miles from its junction with the Hudson. Population, about 1,000. The first settlement was made soon after close of the Revolution. Population of town, 1,585.

Buy your Clothing of W. A. Wilkins, Whitehall, N. Y.

BANKS, INSURANCE COMPANIES, and all other Companies
Supplied at BENDER'S, 73 State Street, Albany.

FARMERS' ALMANAC.

Fine Business Suits of Carr's English Meltons at White & Pearsall's.

E. KIRKLAND,

EXCELSIOR

BOOT MAKER,

GILLIGAN & KIRKLAND'S

ONE PRICE CASH

BOOT AND SHOE STORE,

AT THEIR OLD STAND ON

Canal St., Whitehall, N. Y.

The subscribers would return thanks for the liberal patronage heretofore received, and hope by a strict attention to business to merit a continuance of the same.

We have constantly on hand a fine assortment of

Men's Boots, Shoes, Slippers and Rubbers,
Of the first quality.

LADIES' BOOTS, SLIPPERS, GAITERS AND OVERSHOES,

Children's Boots and Shoes,
In great variety.

Trunks, Traveling Bags, Valises, Umbrellas, Socks, Gloves and Mittens, of various qualities.

We keep constantly on hand the Latest Style of

HATS AND CAPS.

This store is under the direct superintendence of Mr. E. KIRKLAND, who has been a practical Boot Maker for the last twenty years. Having been in the business since he was eleven years of age, he is a competent judge of the qualities of Boots and Shoes.

Those wishing a good article will do well to call here before purchasing elsewhere; for **we will not be undersold,** as our motto is "quick sales and small profits."

GILLIGAN & KIRKLAND.

The Latest Style of Poney Sleighs at JOUBERT & WHITE'S.

Washington County, N. Y.

This county was formed from Albany, as Charlotte county, March 12, 1772, and was changed April 2, 1784. Clinton county was taken off in 1788; the east portion was ceded to Vermont in 1790; a piece was annexed from Albany, Feb. 7, 1791. Warren county was taken off in 1813. It lies on the east border of the State, is centrally distant from Albany forty-five miles, and contains an area of 850 square miles. Population, 46,244.

TOWN OF ARGYLE was granted by patent, March 13, 1764, and formed as a town, March 23, 1786. Greenwich was taken off in 1803, and Fort Edward in 1818. Cossayuna lake is a beautiful sheet of water, three miles long, situated in a narrow valley in the S. E. part of the town. It is everywhere surrounded by steep hill slopes, and contains several beautiful green islands. Argyle village was incorporated March 27, 1838. North Argyle, South Argyle and the Hook, are in this town. Population of town, 3,056.

TOWN OF CAMBRIDGE was incorporated by patent, July 21, 1761. It was formed as a town, in Albany county, March 7, 1788, and annexed to Washington county, Feb. 7, 1791. White Creek and Jackson were taken off in 1815. The soil is generally a gravelly and sandy loam. Cambridge is on the Washington and Rutland Railroad, twenty-nine miles from Troy, and has a population of about 1,500. It contains four hotels, a weekly newspaper office, a bank, an iron foundry and machine shops, a sash and blind factory, furniture manufactory, and several fine stores. Center Cambridge, North Cambridge and Buskirk's Bridge, are in this town. Population of town, 2,458.

TOWN OF DRESDEN was formed from Putnam, as "South Bay," March 15, 1822, and changed April 17, 1822. It lies between Lake George and the southern extremity of Lake Champlain. Settlements were begun about 1784. Population of town, 765.

TOWN OF EASTON was formed from Stillwater and Saratoga, March 3, 1789, while a part of Albany county. It was annexed to Washington county, Feb. 7, 1791. It lies upon the east bank of the Hudson. The town contains several manufacturing establishments. Easton Corners, Easton, South Easton and Crandall's Corners, and parts of Union Village and Galesville, are in this town. Population of town, 2,929.

TOWN OF FORT ANN was formed as Westfield, March 23, 1786. Hartford was taken off in 1793, and Putnam in 1806. It received its present name, April 6, 1808, from the old fort erected here in 1709. It lies south of the southern extremity of Lake Champlain, and S. E. of Lake George. Fort Ann is on the Rensselaer & Saratoga R. R., sixty-one miles from Troy, and twenty-six from Saratoga. It contains near 1,000 inhabitants, two churches, a sash and blind factory, hotel, &c., &c. Comstock's Landing is seven miles from Whitehall, on the line of the Rensselaer and Saratoga rail-

118   FARMERS' ALMANAC.

D. PENFIELD & SON,
WHITEHALL, N. Y.

We would respectfully inform our friends and the public generally that we have opened an

UPHOLSTERY

And CARRIAGE TRIMMING

Establisement in D. P. Nye & Co.'s Building, on William street, where can be found a general assortment of Upholstery Goods. We also keep Spring Beds, Lounges, Mattresses, &c.

☞ Long experience as an Upholsterer places Mr. PENFIELD beyond competition.

☞ All work warranted. Repairing done at short notice.

CHAPIN & ALLEN,
DEALERS IN

STAPLE AND FANCY
DRY GOODS,
PAPER HANGINGS, &c.,

CANAL STREET, WHITEHALL, N. Y.

C. A. HALL,
DEALER IN

Hardware and Crockery, Stoves,

Iron, Steel, Nails, &c.,

Agricultural Implements,

Canal Street, Whitehall, N. Y.

White & Pearsall are Agents for the new Howe Machine, Glen's Falls.

road. It is the home of I. V. Baker, Esq., the popular and efficient railroad superintendent; this residence is one of the finest in the country. Griswold's Mills, West Fort Ann, South Bay, and Cane's Falls, are small villages. Population of town, 3,155.

TOWN OF FORT EDWARD was formed from Argyle, April 10, 1818. It lies upon the east bank of the Hudson, near the center of the W. border of the county. Fort Edward is an important station on the Rensselaer and Saratoga railroad, distant from Troy forty-nine miles, and from Whitehall twenty-four. It contains a large seminary, a newspaper, two banks, a paper mill, brewery and establishments for the manufacture of pottery, wheel stock, iron, sash and blinds, brooms, plaster, matches, Congress Bitters, furniture, &c., and several fine stores. Population, about 2,000. It possesses much historic interest; the tale of the melancholy fate of Jane McCrea, so cruelly murdered by the Indians, belongs here. Fort Miller is on the Hudson, seven miles below Fort Edward. Durkeltown and Fort Edward Centre, are small places. Population of town, 3,997.

TOWN OF GRANVILLE was formed March 23, 1786. It is situated upon the east border of the county, north of the center. Granville is on the Washington and Rutland R. R., fifty-nine miles from Troy. It contains a weekly newspaper office, woolen goods manufactory, &c. Quarries of excellent roofing slate have been opened in different parts of the town. North Granville, Middle Granville (on railroad, sixty-one miles from Troy,) and South Granville, are in this town. Population of town, 3,670.

TOWN OF GREENWICH was formed from Argyle, March 4, 1803. It lies on the west border of the county, in the north angle formed by the junction of the Hudson and Batten Kil. The town is extensively engaged in manufacturing. Union Village is a place of considerable importance. Bald Mountain, East Greenwich, Centre Falls, North Greenwich, Galesville, Battenville and Lakeville, are in this town. Settlements were made previous to the French war. Population of town, 3,959.

TOWN OF HAMPTON was formed March 3, 1786. It lies upon the east border of the county, N. of the center. The soil is a gravelly loam, interspersed with clay. Hampton Corners and Low Hampton are in the town. The first settlements were made some time before the Revolution. Population of town, 985.

TOWN OF HARTFORD was formed from Westfield (now Fort Ann), March 12, 1793. It lies near the center of the county. There are several chalybeate springs in this town. North Hartford, South Hartford and Log Village, are small places. Settlement was made soon after the Revolution. The first church was built in 1789. Population of town, 2,088.

TOWN OF HEBRON was formed March 23, 1786. It lies near the center of the east border of the county. The soil is a sandy and slaty loam, of a light, porous nature, easy of cultivation, and well adapted to resist the extremes of wet and drouth. North Hebron, East Hebron, West Hebron, Belcher and Slateville, are in the town. The first settlements were made before the Revolution. Population of town, 2,590.

LAW BLANKS of Every Form, by the Single Sheet, Quire or Ream, and ATTORNEY'S STATIONERY, at BENDER'S, 73 State Street, Albany.

120   *FARMERS' ALMANAC.*

1870.   FURNITURE.   1870.

DOREN
OF THE
WHITEHALL FURNITURE WAREROOMS,
WHITEHALL, N. Y.,

Is manufacturing and constantly receiving from city and country manufacturers.

CABINET WARE,

In great variety, consisting of Parlor Suits in Plush, Kersey, Reps, and Hair Cloth; Tete-a-Tetes, Sofas, Lounges, Settees, Divans, Ottomans, Mirrors, Marble-top Tables, Etageres, Pier Tables, Side Tables, Tea Tables, Extension Tables, Work Tables, Wood-top Tables, Easy Chairs, Rocking Chairs, Spring-seat Chair Brackets, Cane-seat Chairs, Wood-seat Chairs, Picture Cord, Picture Tassels, Oval Frames, La Pays, Square Frames, Gilt Frames, Foot Stools, Reception Chairs, Rosewood Frames, Children's Chairs, Walnut Frames, Bible Stands, Secretaries and Book-Cases, Flower Stands, What-Nots, Wardrobes, Piano Stools, Music Racks, Book Racks, Bedsteads, Bureaus, Cradles, Walnut Chamber Suits, Chestnut Chamber Suits, Work Boxes, Towel Racks, Wash Stands, Hat Racks and Hall Stands, Cribs, Camp Chairs, Trundle Beds, Iron Chairs, Cots, Looking Glasses, &c., &c.

Also, a constant supply of Hair Mattresses, Cotton and Extra Mattresses, Hair Pillows, Bolsters, Feathers, Feather Pillows, Allen's Patent Spring Bed, Tucker's Patent Spring Bed, The People's Spring Bed, Doren's Spring Bed, which are all warranted to do good service and give entire satisfaction. Also,

CASKETS, BURIAL CASES & COFFINS

Of every style and price, from the most elaborate silver-plated metallic Casket to the plain pine Coffin, constantly on hand.

Rooms open at all hours of the day. Call and see if the above are facts.

The best Sewing Machine in the World is at White & Pearsall's, Glen's Falls.

Our Stock of Open Carriages is complete.   JOUBERT & WHITE.

Ready-made Clothing at bargains, at WAIT'S.
For your WEDDING SUITS, go to WAITS. (See page 81.)

Town of Jackson was formed from Cambridge, April 17, 1815. It lies on the east border of the county, south of the center. The soil is a slaty loam and very productive. Jackson Centre, Coila and Anaquassacook, are in the town. Population of town, 1,757.

Town of Kingsbury was incorporated by patent, May 18, 1762, and recognized as a town by the State Government, March 23, 1786. It lies on the W. border of the county, north of the center. Sandy Hill is on the branch railroad between Fort Edward and Glen's Falls. It contains a population of about 1,500. The dam at this place, across the Hudson, 1,200 feet long and ten feet high, furnishes water power for several mills. Gov. Wright received his legal education at Sandy Hill, and Lieut.-Gov. Pitcher was a citizen of the town. It has a bank, a weekly newspaper, paper mill, sash and blinds, and establishments for the manufacture of pianos, steam engines, portable saw mills, water wheels, and paper machinery, carriages, &c. The Park is a first class hotel. At Baker's Falls is located Wait's turbine water wheel manufactory, and Cornell & Co.'s water wheel and paper machinery works. Moss Street, Kingsbury, Patten's Mills, Dunham's Basin, Vaughn's Corners, Adamsville, Langdon's Corners and Smith's Basin (on the railroad, fifty-seven miles from Troy), are in the town. Population of town, 3,751.

Town of Putnam (named in honor of Gen. Israel Putnam), was formed from Westfield (now Fort Ann), Feb. 28, 1806. Dresden was set off in 1822. It lies in the extreme north end of the county, upon the mountainous peninsula between Lakes George and Champlain. Putnam's Corners is a small village. Settlements were made before the Revolution. Population of town, 746.

Town of Salem was formed by patent, Aug. 7, 1764, and was recognized by Statute, March 23, 1786. It lies on the east border of the county, S. of the center. Salem is on the Washington and Rutland Railroad, forty-one miles from Troy. It contains a weekly newspaper office, a bank, the Washington Academy, a plaster and planing mill, &c. Population about 1,000. A new court house is now being erected. The repair shops of the railroad are located here. Shushan is on the same railroad, thirty-four miles from Troy. Eagleville, Clapp's Mills and Fitch's Point, are in the town. Population of town, 3,239.

Town of White Creek was formed from Cambridge, April 17, 1815. It is the S. E. corner town of the county. The soil is a fine quality of gravelly loam. Sheep and garden seeds are largely raised. North White Creek, White Creek, Post's Corners, Centre White Creek, Ash Grove, Dorr's Corners, Pumpkin Hook and Martindale Corners are small places. Population of town, 2,682.

Town of Whitehall was incorporated by patent, March 31, 1765, as Skenesborough, and changed March 23, 1786. It lies at the southern extremity of Lake Champlain. Whitehall is situated near the mouth of Wood creek, on Lake Champlain. The railroad, canal, and lake trade, give this place commercial importance. A railroad is being constructed to Plattsburgh. The manufactures consist of lumber, machinery, vessels, boats, carpets, sash and blinds, ax and hammer's handles, steam boilers,

P. H. COREY, FANCY GOODS, Warren Street, Glen's Falls.

Custom Work done better at WILKINS' than elsewhere.

122 FARMERS' ALMANAC.

BARNES HOUSE
West Rutland, Vt.,

Three miles from Clarendon Springs, and ten miles from Middletown Springs.

LIVERY ATTACHED.
J. H. HAZELTON, Proprietor.

White & Pearsall's Extensive Clothing Establishment, Glen's Falls.

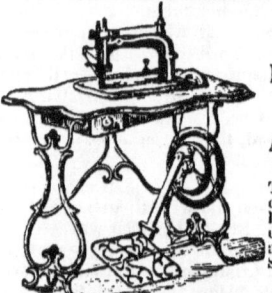

H. A. GRISWOLD,
WHITEHALL, N. Y.

Dealer in Watches, Clocks, Jewelry, Solid Silver and Plated Ware, American Watches at reduced prices. Agent for the American Combination Button-hole Overseaming and Sewing Machine.

The first and only Button-hole and Sewing Machine combined in the World that can do all kinds of sewing needed in the family. It has no equal. Examine all other Machines, then call and see this, the greatest novelty of the age. Send for Circular and samples of work.

H. A. GRISWOLD, Agt. for Co.

Photographs and Ambrotypes
MADE IN ALL STYLES,
And Equally as good on Cloudy as on Clear Days.

I have all of the Negatives of F. MOWERY, formerly on Main Street. Persons wishing Duplicates can have them at any time. Do not forget to call and try the man that
PLEASES EVERYBODY IN MAKING PICTURES.

Nitrous Oxide Gas, PERFECTLY HARMLESS, at Garrett's.

&c., and many large stores. An extensive lumber trade is carried on with Canada and with ports on the Hudson, through Lake Champlain and the Champlain canal. Population about 5,000. A line of steamers run in connection with the R. & S. Railroad to all points on Lake Champlain. The village contains five churches, five free schools, one lodge and chapter of Masons, one lodge and encampment of Odd Fellows, two societies of temperance, five hotels, two newspapers, and two banks. Population of town, 6,000.

Bennington County, Vt.

This county is in the southwest part of the State, and contains an area of 610 square miles. The surface is mountainous, a large portion of it being unfit for cultivation. It is well watered by tributaries of the Deerfield, Hoosic, Battenkill, Otter Creek and West rivers.

ARLINGTON is in the western part of the county, on the boundary line dividing Vermont from New York, and forty miles from Rutland, and contains 24,960 acres. It was chartered by the government of New Hampshire, July 28, 1761, to a number of persons, most of whom belonged to Litchfield, Conn. The first settlement was made in 1763. Granular limestone abounds here; several quarries have been opened, and are successfully wrought. Arlington is on the Bennington and Rutland Railroad, thirty-nine miles from Rutland, and sixteen from Bennington.

BENNINGTON is near the southwest corner of the State. The settlement was begun in the spring of 1761, by emigrants from Massachusetts. It became the head-quarters of the opposition in the New York controversy, as well as of the Green Mountain Boys, during the eventful period of the Revolution. Here Allen, Warner, and others, planned the expedition to Ticonderoga; and here also were deposited the provisions and military stores for the American army, in the attempted capture of which the forces of General Burgoyne met with such a disastrous defeat. Bennington is situated on an eminence commanding an extensive prospect over a most delightful country, intersected by a large number of rivulets that pass through finely cultivated fields and ample meadows. About one-quarter of the surface is mountainous; the remainder being upland, with a considerable quantity of interval. The soil is excellent. The low-lands are well watered by the Walloomscoik and its branches. The principal productions are corn, rye, oats, hay, butter, cheese, beef, pork and poultry, which generally find a ready market. The town is connected with Troy, the head of the Hudson steamboat navigation, by a good macadamized road; the distance being thirty miles. Iron ore is found in several places; also the oxide of manganese and yellow ochre in abundance, the last only of which is at present manufactured. Marble, argillaceous, slate, and hornstone, are also found. The marble is worked, but not to a large extent. Mount Anthony, a considerable elevation in the south-west part, has on its east side a cavern, which is somewhat of a curiosity. The town contains three villages—Bennington, (upon which corporate powers were conferred Nov. 3, 1849,) Centre Bennington,

Surrogate's BLANKS and BLANK BOOKS Prepared by BENDER, 73 State St., Albany.
Engineer's Instruments, Stationery, FIELD BOOKS, &c., at BENDER'S, 73 State St.

124   FARMERS' ALMANAC.

WHITE & PEARSALL. Best stock of fine, ready-made Clothing ever offered in Glen's Falls.

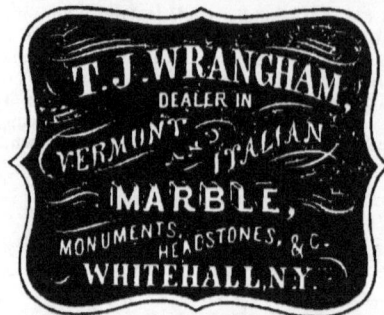

I would inform the public generally that I am prepared to furnish all kinds of

Marble and Monuments,

and all kinds of

CEMETERY
and
FURNITURE WORK.

I will give satisfaction in Price and Workmanship, or no sale.

T. J. WRANGHAM,
WHITEHALL, N. Y.

RESTAURANT
AND
DINING SALOON,
AT
RAILROAD DEPOT, WHITEHALL, N. Y.

Meals at all hours, and on the European plan.

R. W. BILLETT.

MILLS & WILLIAMS,

UNION SLATE MILLS, FAIR HAVEN, VT.,
MANUFACTURERS OF
Marble and Marbleized Slate Mantles,
TABLE AND BUREAU TOPS,
Chess Tables, Bracket Shelves, &c.

For a first-class Market Wagon go to Joubert & White's, G. Falls.

and North Bennington. Bennington is on the Rutland, Bennington and Lebanon Springs, about forty miles from Troy. It has a bank, newspaper, and several manufacturing establishments.

DORSET is in the north part of the county, 190 miles from Montpelier, twenty-two from Rutland, and eighty-nine from Burlington. It was chartered Aug. 20, 1761. Considerable quantities of marble, lumber and iron, are manufactured. It is on the Rutland and Bennington railroad. South Dorset, East Dorset and North Dorset, are in the same town.

GLASTENBURY is in the central part of the county. It is a mountainous, broken township, organized March 31, 1834. It was chartered by New Hampshire, August 20, 1761. It contains about 25,000 acres.

LANDGROVE is in the northeast corner of the county, seventy miles from Montpelier. It was granted on the 6th and chartered on the 8th of Nov. 1780; settlements were made in 1769. The town was organized March 25, 1800, and contains 4,646 acres. It is watered by several of the head branches of West river. The villages are Landsgrove and Clarksville.

MANCHESTER is in the northern part of the county, and is a half shire town; it is eighty miles from Montpelier, thirty from Rutland, and ninety-seven from Burlington. It was chartered August 11, 1761. The town was organized in 1776. The habitable parts of this township lie between the Green Mountains on the east and the Equinox Mountain on the west. The latter is the highest summit in this section of the State, being 2,915 feet above the site of the court house in Manchester south village, and 3,706 feet above tide water. There is a bank, a newspaper, academy, &c. Factory Point is a thriving and pleasant village, in which is located the railroad depot of the Bennington and Rutland Railway Company. There is a variety of manufacturing in this place; a woolen factory, tannery and marble and granite works are also located here, and do a large business; having the advantage of being located at the quarries.

PERU is in the northeastern corner of the county, on the summit of the Green Mountains, eighty miles from Montpelier. It was chartered by New Hampshire, Oct. 13, 1761. Settlement was commenced about 1773. The town was organized March 1, 1802, and contains by charter 23,040 acres. A portion was annexed to Mount Tabor, in Oct., 1805.

POWNAL is the southwest corner town of the county. It was chartered by New Hampshire, January 8, 1760, and under that charter settlement commenced 1762. There were, however, a few Dutch families within the township at the time, who claimed their land under the Hoosic Patent. Along Hoosic river are some rich and beautiful tracts of interval. The soil is well adapted to the production of grain and grass. There are three villages in the town—Pownal, Pownal Centre and North Pownal.

READSBOROUGH is in the southeast corner of the county, adjoining Massachusetts. It contains 20,480 acres. The surface is exceedingly mountainous, and much of it is unsuitable for settlement. The streams are Deerfield river, which runs along the eastern boundary into Massachusetts, and a branch of this river, which runs diagonally through the town, from north-

BLANK BOOKS, MEMORANDUM and PASS BOOKS, on hand and made to order, by BENDER, 73 State Street, Albany.

FARMERS' ALMANAC.

☞ **What a mistake I have made, getting this wrong side up!**

DON'T FAIL TO READ IT.

PORTER & McNISH.

So that any person or persons wishing to build a house, or furnish one, could find almost everything (in our line) to do it with; and to all we would extend a cordial invitation to come and see us and see our Goods, as it costs nothing to show them. To those who pay cash, for Goods we will offer special inducements.

Hardware and Nails,

We also have a complete stock of

GROCERIES, DRY & CANNED FRUIT,

Of every description to be found in the State, also a full line of

Crockery and Glass Ware.

In our basement we have the best assorted and cheapest stock of

BOOTS AND SHOES

Also a full line of

WALL PAPER and SHADES of all kinds.

Tapestry, Ingrain, Brussels, Valentia and other Carpets.

And in fact almost everything to make a complete assortment. We have a room on our second floor 30 x 40, always filled with the most approved patterns of

Dress Goods, Black and Fancy Silks,

The largest and most varied stock of

MOSCOW AND CASTER BEAVER AND CLOAKINGS,

Fancy and Domestic Cassimeres,

SUCH AS

DRY GOODS,

Have the largest Store and the most extensive stock of Goods to be found in Washington County. Their stock comprises a large and attractive assortment of Staple and Fancy

PORTER & McNISH,

—OF—

CAMBRIDGE, N. Y.

Always the newest styles of Hats, Caps and Furnishing Goods at WHITE & PEARSALL'S.

GARRETT, the Dentist, Glen's Falls.

west to southeast. These streams afford several mill privileges, which have been improved. Readsboro City and Hartwellville, are in this town. Manufactures of broom handles, staves, &c., is carried on; there are also saw and grist mills.

RUPERT is a station and post office on the Rutland and Washington Railroad, forty-nine miles from Troy, and thirty-six from Rutland. It was chartered Aug. 20, 1761. Settlement was commenced 1767. There are three villages in the town, East and West Rupert. The inhabitants of the town are mostly engaged in agricultural pursuits.

SANDGATE is in the western part of the county. It was chartered by New Hampshire, Aug. 11, 1761. Settlement was begun in 1771. The surface is very broken and mountainous. The streams are all small, consisting of several branches of the Battenkill and of White Creek. East and West Sandgate, are villages in the town.

SEARSBURGH, a small town in the southeasterly part of the county. It was chartered Feb. 23, 1781, and was organized March 18, 1833. The town lies mostly on the Green Mountains, and contains 10,240 acres.

SHAFTSBURY, in the western part of the county, ninety-seven miles from Montpelier, forty-four miles from Rutland, 111 miles from Burlington, was chartered Aug. 20, 1761. Shaftsbury was organized some time before the Revolution. The soil is generally good. Iron ore, of excellent quality, is found here, and a beautiful white marble has been extensively quarried. South Shaftsbury, is in the same town.

STAMFORD is the center of the south tier of towns in the county. It was chartered by New Hampshire, March 6, 1753, and rechartered June 9, 1754. It contains 23,040 acres, the surface being very uneven. The south part is watered by some of the head branches of Hoosic river; in the north part are several natural ponds.

SUNDERLAND is in the eastern part of the county. It was chartered by New Hampshire, July 30, 1761. Settlement commenced in 1766. This was the home of Ethan Allen during the Revolution. Sunderland was organized in 1769. The surface is very uneven; but on the Battenkill river are some fine alluvial flats. The soil consists of alluvium, loam and marl. Sulphate of iron and lead ore.

WINHALL is in the northeastern part of Bennington county, and was chartered by New Hampshire, Sept. 15, 1761. The town was organized in March, 1796, and contains 23,040 acres. Winhall river furnishes a great number of good mill privileges. There are saw mills, grist mills and tanneries, in town. Bondville, is a village in the town.

WOODFORD is in the southerly part of the county, and was chartered by New Hampshire, March 6, 1753. There are several saw mills, planing mill, powder mill, &c., in the town. Woodford City and Woodford Hollow, are small villages in the town.

Ding, dong, bell! WILKINS is bound to sell. (See p. 96.)

Gold Pens, Pencils, Diaries, SCHOOL BOOKS, PHOTOGRAPH ALBUMS, Stereoscopic Views, &c., at BENDER'S, 73 State Street, Albany.

WHITE & PEARSALL make a specialty of Fine Custom Clothing.

J. C. WILSON & CO.,
MANUFACTURERS OF AND DEALERS IN

POULTNEY,  **VERMONT.**

FURNITURE
OF EVERY DESCRIPTION.

SOFAS, PARLOR CHAIRS, MARBLE-TOP TABLES, A GREAT VARIETY OF CANE-SEAT CHAIRS, BUREAUS, BEDSTEADS, TABLES, CARPET SWEEPERS, STANDS, WHAT-NOTS, SPRING BEDS, MATTRESSES, MIRRORS, PICTURE FRAMES, &c.

Coffins, Caskets and Shrouds Constantly on Hand.

JOB WORK, in all its branches, attended to. ☞ Customers will find it to their advantage by calling on us before purchasing elsewhere.

JOSEPH STEWART,
SURGEON DENTIST,
CAMBRIDGE, N. Y.

WOODWORTH & CO.,
PROPRIETORS OF
CAMBRIDGE STEAM SAW & PLANING MILL,
MANUFACTURERS OF
Sash, Blinds, Doors, Door and Window Frames, Casings, Battens, Brackets, Pickets, Mouldings, Stair Newels, Balusters, &c.

Also, Dealers in Nova Scotia Plaster.
CAMBRIDGE, N. Y.

Blacksmithing of all kinds at Joubert & White's, Glen's Falls.

Rutland County, Vt.

This county is on the west side of the Green mountains, it was incorporated from Bennington county, in Feb. 1781, and embraced all of the State north of the parent county, and west of the mountains, until Addison county was taken from it in 1785, which reduced it to its present, less than one-third of its original size. It contains 958 square miles. Quarries containing marble from the finest to the coarsest qualities, and of all colors as well of purest white, are inexhaustible; very fine slate, too, is found; also, iron ore.

BENSON lies in the northwest part of the county, on the eastern shore of Lake Champlain, and was granted by the State, Oct. 27, 1779, and chartered May 5, 1780. A part was annexed to Orwell, Nov. 8, 1847. The settlement of the town was commenced in 1783. It contains carriage and marble manufactories, &c.

BRANDON is in the north part of the county, sixteen miles from Rutland and fifty-one from Burlington, in the valley of the Otter creek, and was chartered by the name of Neshobe, October 20, 1761; was altered to Brandon, October 20, 1784. The settlement was commenced in 1774; Brandon was organized about the year 1784, and contains 22,750 acres. Territory was taken from it and annexed to Goshen, Nov. 11, 1854, and to Chittenden, Nov. 14, 1855. Stephen A. Douglas was born in this town, on the 23d of April, 1813. After learning the trade of a cabinet maker, he spent some time here as a student in the academy. Lake Dunmore, a great summer resort, is distant about eight miles, and thousands from the great metropolis visit it annually.

The great frozen well, which contains ice the year round, is distant from the village about one-half mile. Brandon contains a large academy, several churches, two banks and many excellent stores; also, one or two marble quarries and paint factories.

CASTLETON is situated near the center of the county. The town was chartered September 22, 1761. The village of Castleton was organized in March 1777. Jesse Belknap was the first town clerk and justice of the peace. The first church was built in 1833. It is pleasantly situated on the southern bank of Castleton river. The dwellings are remarkable for their uniform neatness and convenience. In the village are five churches, also State Normal School, one academy and one bank, and has a population of about 1,000. Hydeville is a small but important manufacturing village in the town of Castleton and midway between the villages of Castleton and Fairhaven. It is situated at the outlet of Lake Bomoseen and on the Rutland and Whitehall Railroad, and hence possesses uncommon business facilities. Lake Bomoseen is nine miles long by two broad, and has as tributaries Glen lake and the chain of lakes extending through the town of Hubbardton. Stone and lumber for building, to an unlimited extent, are waiting to be used; Hydeville must speedily become a very important manufacturing place.

Have your Clothing made at WILKINS'. (See page 96.)

WRITING DESKS in Rosewood, PAPIER-MACHE, Plain or Beautifully Inlaid with Pearl, at BENDER'S, 73 State Street, Albany.

We guarantee perfect fitting Suits at WHITE & PEARSALL'S, Glen's Falls.

LEONARD FLETCHER
ATTORNEY AND COUNSELLOR AT LAW.
CAMBRIDGE, N. Y.

ARTHUR O. JONES,
WATCHMAKER & JEWELER
CAMBRIDGE, N. Y.
Repairing promptly attended to and warranted.

PETER GORDAN,
BOOT & SHOE MAKER,
SALEM, N. Y.
Repairing neatly and promptly done. Shop near the Depot.

WRIGHT & CADY,
CLOTHING & GROCERIES.
Men and Boys Clothing of every variety and price.
FRESH GROCERIES CONSTANTLY ON HAND.
CAMBRIDGE, N. Y.

DR. TEFFT,
OF CAMBRIDGE,
Has a license for the use of Rubber, and will furnish
Sets of the Best Gum Teeth for $15,
PLAIN, $10.00.
Also will Extract Teeth Without Pain, by using a benumbing agent.
Teeth filled with Gold for $1.00, Cement filling 50 cts.

GARRETT Extracts Teeth without Pain at Glen's Falls.

CHITTENDEN is in the northeast part of the county. It was granted on the 14th and chartered on the 16th of March, 1780. Part of Philadelphia was annexed Nov. 2, 1816, and a part taken off Oct. 29, 1829, and added to Sherburne. The first settlement was made soon after the Revolution. The town was organized March 30, 1789. Iron ore is found in abundance. North and South Chittenden.

CLARENDON, in the central part of the county, fifty miles from Montpelier, six miles from Rutland, and seventy miles from Burlington, was chartered by New Hampshire, Sept. 5, 1761, to Caleb Willard and others, embracing in its limits a part or the whole of two former grants from New York. There are four villages in the town, North Flats, South Flats, Chippenhoy and Clarendon Springs. East and North Clarendon, Clarendon and Clarendon Springs, are post offices.

DANBY is in the south part of the county. It was chartered Aug. 27, 1761, and the first settlements were made in 1765. It was organized March 14, 1769, and contains about thirty-nine square miles, a part was annexed from Mount Tabor, Nov. 13, 1848. There are several marble quarries in the town. Danby and Danby Four Corners are the villages. The former is eighteen miles from Rutland, and sixty-seven from Burlington.

FAIRHAVEN is one of the most thriving villages in the county. It is situated on the Rutland and Whitehall Railroad, sixteen miles from Rutland, eighty-three from Burlington, and six from Poultney; it contains about 2,000 inhabitants. It has a weekly newspaper, a bank, a fine hotel, &c. The Castleton river runs through it, and by a succession of rapids furnishes one of the best water powers in this part of the State. Standing on the Green at Fairhaven, and looking eastward through a gorge in the Taconic range of mountains, one gets a distinct view of Mt. Killington, the third highest peak of the Green mountains, rising majestically fifteen miles distant, and furnishing the background to a landscape worthy the pencil of any artist. The manufacture of slate is the principal business, and is carried on extensively. It has a weekly newspaper, a bank, a fine hotel, &c.

HUBBARDTON is in the northwestern part of the county. It was chartered by New Hampshire, June 15, 1764. A part was annexed to Sudbury, Nov. 7, 1806. Its area is about 18,000 acres. Settlement was made in 1774. Hubbardton, East Hubbardton and Hortonville, are post offices.

IRA is in the central part of the county. It was organized May 31, 1779. A part was taken off for Middletown, Oct. 28, 1784, and a part of Clarendon was annexed to Ira, Nov. 9, 1854. Its area is about 12,000 acres.

MENDON is in the eastern part of the county. It was chartered Feb. 23, 1781, by the name of Medway. Parker's Gore was annexed, and the name changed to Parkerstown, Nov. 7, 1804, which name was altered Nov. 6, 1827, to the present one. It was organized March 11, 1806. It lies mostly on the Green Mountains.

MIDDLETOWN is in the south westerly part of the county. It was formed from Tinmouth, Wells, Ira and Poultney. It was incorporated Oct. 28, 1784. The town was organized in 1786.

Plain and Fancy INKSTANDS, PEN RACKS, SEGAR STANDS and CASES, and Unique WATCH SAFES, at BENDER'S, 73 State Street, Albany.

FARMERS' ALMANAC.

A. E. ALDEN'S
PREMIUM PICTURES

ALL WORK EXECUTED IN THE BEST STYLE OF THE ART.

ROOMS:
Cor. Grand, Division and Fourth Streets, Troy, N. Y.;
954 BROADWAY, NEW YORK;
Broadway, Saratoga Springs, N. Y.;
ARCADE, PROVIDENCE, R. I.;
SPRINGFIELD, MASS.

A. E. ALDEN, Proprietor.

J. C. BABCOCK,
19 Grand Division Street, TROY, N. Y.
MANUFACTURER OF

No. 1 Single and Double
CARRIAGES & SLEIGHS
Of all styles.
Repairs of all kinds done at short notice; also Horses and Carriages and Saddle Horses to Let. Horses Boarded by the day or week. Carriages and Sleighs for Sale.

LOWN & HORTON,
CARRIAGE

AND SLEIGH MAKERS,
Cor. of Broadway and Seventh St., - TROY, N. Y.
WM. LOWN.   D. S. HORTON.

JOUBERT & WHITE has the Carriage Trimmer, at Glen's Falls.

The best Custom Cutter at White & Pearsall's, Glen's Falls.

HATS and CAPS can always be found at WAIT'S.
Get a HOWE MACHINE and be happy, at WAIT'S. (See page 81.)

HISTORY OF RUTLAND COUNTY. 133

MOUNT HOLLY is in the southeasterly part of the county. It was made up from Jackson's Gore, Wallingford and Ludlow, and was incorporated Oct. 31, 1792. The settlement was commenced in 1781. The town was organized Nov. 19, 1792. Mount Holly, Mechanicsville, Healdville and Bowlville, are post offices.

MOUNT TABOR is in the southeast corner of the county, thirty-six miles from Bennington, and was chartered by New Hampshire, Aug. 28, 1761, under the name of Harwich. It was organized March 13, 1788. A part of Peru was annexed Oct. 25, 1805, and a part was set off to Dorset, Nov. 17, 1825, and a small part of Danby was annexed Nov. 13, 1848, making its area 23,376 acres. A large portion of the town is on the summit of the Green Mountains, and incapable of cultivation.

PAWLET is a station and post office on the Rutland and Washington railway, fifty-six miles from Troy, and twenty-nine miles from Rutland. The town was chartered Aug. 26, 1761. The soil is dry and warm, easily cultivated, and produces good crops of grain and grass. Settlements were commenced in the town in 1761. Pawlet and West Pawlet, are post offices.

PITTSFIELD is in the extreme northeast corner of the county. It was granted Nov. 8, 1780, chartered July 29, 1781, and organized March 26, 1793. A part was taken off and added to Rochester, Oct. 29, 1806, and Nov. 15, 1824. Portions of Stockbridge were annexed Nov. 15, 1813, and Oct. 22, 1822. The surface is mountainous.

PITTSFORD is in the northerly part of the county, and was granted by New Hampshire, Oct. 12, 1761. It was organized as early as 1770. It has an area of 25,950 acres. The surface is generally level. The soil mostly loam. Iron ore and marble, of excellent quality, is found. Pittsford, Mill, Furnace and Hitchcockville. Pittsford is nine miles from Rutland, and fifty-eight from Burlington. It contains a sash and blind factory, &c.

POULTNEY is on the Rutland and Washington R. R., sixty-seven miles from Troy. It is the point of departure for the celebrated Mineral Springs of Middletown, eight miles distant, and is not behind the most attractive resorts in this attractive portion of the Green Mountain State. Including East Poultney, it contains about 2,000 inhabitants. The various localities which it is interesting to visit, are Lake St. Catherine, Lake Bomoseen, The Bowl, The Gorge and Carver's Falls, only far enough away for a pleasant morning ride, while in the immediate neighborhood are points of historic interest and of a national reputation. Ethan Allen was one of the first settlers of Poultney. It is the native place of Rollin C. Mallory, the author of the Tariff of 1828. Jared Sparks, the Biographer of Washington, learned his trade of carpenter here, and the house in which the Tribune Philosopher served a three years' apprenticeship, is still standing at East Poultney. Ripley Female College, of deservedly high reputation, gives to the place a widely extended fame. Rev. John Newman is president. Those who wish a residence where they can educate their children at a high Institution, and, at the same time live in a healthful region, and have ready access to Mineral Springs of marvelous efficacy, need not look any further than Poultney. The Poultney Bulletin is published here.

W. A. Wilkins' Cheap Cash Clothing Store, Whitehall, N.Y.

BENDER will furnish you any Books Published; also, ENGINEERS' INSTRUMENTS, STATIONERY, FIELD BOOKS, &c., at 73 State Street, Albany.

ALLEN'S CONGRESS BITTERS,

A SUPERIOR TONIC AND UNSURPASSED REMEDY FOR

DYSPEPSIA, HEARTBURN, LOSS OF APPETITE, GENERAL DEBILITY.

Sold by all Druggists, Store and Hotel Keepers.

All Orders Addressed to

WILLIAM ALLEN,
FORT EDWARD, N. Y.,

Or to **BURR & PERRY,**
26 Tremont st., BOSTON,

WILL RECEIVE PROMPT ATTENTION.

SANFORD SMITH & CO.,

DEALERS IN

Hardware, Iron, Stoves, Tinware, Whips, Horse Blankets,

AND ALL KINDS OF

HOUSE FURNISHING GOODS,

FORT EDWARD, N. Y.

ASTRINGENT, - - - - 50 Cents per Bottle.

USE

THURSTON'S VEGETABLE ASTRINGENT

FOR THE TEETH AND GUMS,

Prepared only by

E. P. THURSTON,

SURGEON DENTIST, SALEM, N. Y.

☞ All branches of Operative and Mechanical Dentistry receive most careful attention. ARTIFICIAL PLATES inserted at moderate prices.

Garrett guarantees the "Gas" PERFECTLY HARMLESS.

Buy your Clothing at White & Pearsall's, Glen' Falls, and save money.

HISTORY OF RUTLAND COUNTY. 135

RUTLAND is situated about the center of the county, and was chartered to John Murray and sixty-three others, Sept. 7, 1761. Settlements were scarcely made, however, before 1770. Quarrying marble is the principal branch of business about Rutland; many parts of the United States depend upon this section for supplies. Large quantities are exported to Europe. Rutland was the birthplace of the late Rufus W. Griswold, of literary fame, and the home of the late distinguished Solomon Foot, member of Congress, &c. The Rutland and Burlington, the Western Vermont, the Rutland and Washington, and the Saratoga and Whitehall railroads, all centre here. There are three villages; Rutland, Centre Rutland and West Rutland. The mercantile business is very large. Rutland contains many large and handsome stores, fine hotels and beautiful residences. It is eighty-five miles from Troy.

SHERBURNE is in the eastern part of the county, and was chartered by New Hampshire, July 7, 1761, by the name of Killington, but was changed Nov. 4, 1800. It was organized in 1794. Parker's Gore was annexed Nov. 4, 1822. The celebrated summit of the Green Mountains, called Killington peak, is situated in the south part. Sherburne and North Sherburne are post offices.

SHREWSBURY is in the eastern part of the county, and was chartered Sept. 4, 1761; organized March 20, 1781. It contains forty-four square miles. It lies mostly on the Green Mountains; in the eastern part is situated Shrewsbury Peak. Shrewsbury and Cuttingsville, are post offices.

SUDBURY is in the north part of the county, and was chartered by New Hampshire, Aug. 6, 1763. The first settlement was made about 1780. The town was organized March 16, 1789. North and Centre Sudbury, are in the town. Marble is quarried to some extent.

SUTHERLAND FALLS, celebrated for its beautiful "water-fall," is situated about six miles from Rutland, and ten miles from Brandon, on the Rutland and Burlington railroad, celebrated also for its marble quarries; slate has also been found here in great abundance. There are two quarries, one mill, one store. Population about 450.

TINMOUTH is in the southerly part of the county, and was chartered by New Hampshire, Sept. 15, 1761. It was organized March 8, 1774. Portions were taken off and annexed to Middletown, Oct. 28, 1784, and to Wallingford, Oct. 21, 1793. Several quarries of fine marble have been opened, and iron ore has been found.

WALLINGFORD, in the southeasterly part of Rutland county, on the Bennington and Rutland railroad, nine miles from Rutland, and seventy-six miles from Burlington, was chartered Nov. 27, 1761. The settlement was commenced in 1783. The town was organized March 10, 1778. A portion was taken off from Mount Holly in Oct., 1792, and in Oct., 1793, a part of Tinmouth was annexed. The eastern part lies on the Green Mountains. North, South and East Wallingford, are post offices.

WELLS is in the western part of the county, and was chartered by New Hampshire, Sept. 15, 1761. It was organized March 9, 1773. Parts were

E. H. BENDER, Wholesale and Retail Dealer in every Variety of BOOKS, STATIONERY, &c., 73 State Street, Albany.

136 *FARMERS' ALMANAC.*

FRANCIS B. DAVIS,
Wholesale and Retail Dealer in
CHEMICALS,
Drugs, Medicines, Paints, Oils, Dye-Stuffs,
WINDOW GLASS, BRUSHES,
FANCY ARTICLES,
&c., &c., &c.,

Wing's Exchange, Fort Edward, N. Y.

All Patent Medicines at 20 per cent. less than Retail Price. Proprietor of "Wing's Cough Remedy," and "American Diarrhœa Cure."

J. C. SUNDERLIN,
PHOTOGRAPHER,

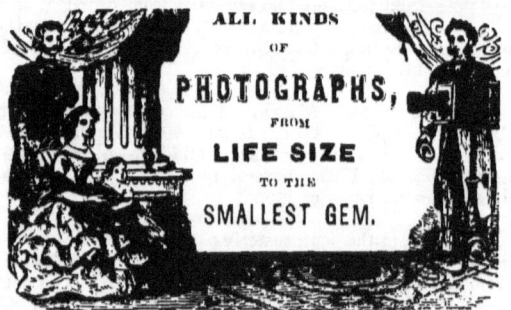

ALL KINDS OF PHOTOGRAPHS, FROM LIFE SIZE TO THE SMALLEST GEM.

WING'S EXCHANGE,
BROADWAY, FORT EDWARD, N. Y.,
Makes Good Work Cheap, and tries to please.

Repairing done neatly at JOUBERT & WHITE'S, Glen's Falls.

WHITE & PEARSALL. Remember, we give the Best Bargains in Glen's Falls.

taken off and annexed to Poultney and Middletown. The western part is generally level, and the eastern part mountainous and broken. The soil is generally good.

WEST HAVEN is in the western part of the county, at the lower extremity of Lake Champlain, and formerly comprised a part of Fairhaven, from which it was set off and incorporated, Oct. 20, 1792. The town has an area of 14,191 acres, and possesses a clayey soil, with an abundance of limestone.

Stamp Duties.

SCHEDULE OF DUTIES.

Accidental injuries to persons, tickets, or contracts for insurance against, exempt.
Affidavits, exempt.
Agreement or contract not otherwise specified—for every sheet or piece of paper upon which either of the same shall be written, 5 cts.
Agreement, renewal of, same stamp as original instrument.
Appraisement of value or damage, or for any other purpose—for each sheet of paper on which it is written, 5 cts.
Assignment of a lease, same stamp as original, and additional stamp upon the value or consideration of transfer, according to the rates of stamps on deeds. (See Conveyance.)
Assignment of policy of insurance, same stamp as original instrument. (See Insurance.)
Assignment of mortgage, same stamp as that required upon a mortgage for the amount remaining unpaid. (See Mortgage.)
Bank check, draft or order for any sum of money drawn upon any bank, banker or trust company at sight or on demand, 2 cts.: when drawn upon any other person or persons, companies or corporations, for any sum exceeding $10, at sight or on demand, 2 cts.
Bill of exchange, (inland,) draft or order for the payment of any sum of money not exceeding $100, otherwise than at sight or on demand, or any promissory note, or any memorandum, check, receipt, or other written or printed evidence of an amount of money to be paid on demand or at a time designated—for a sum not exceeding $100, 5 cts.: and for every additional $100 or fractional part thereof in excess of $100, 5 cts.
Bill of exchange, (foreign,) or letter of credit drawn in, but payable out of, the United States—if drawn singly same rates of duty as inland bills of exchange or promissory notes: if drawn in sets of three or more, for every bill of each set, where the sum made payable shall not exceed $100 or the equivalent thereof in any foreign currency, 2 cts.; and for every additional $100, or fractional part thereof in excess of $100, 2 cts.
Bill of lading or receipt (other than charter party) for any goods, merchandise, or effects to be exported from a port or place in the United States to any foreign port or place, 10 cts.
Bill of lading to any port in British North America, exempt.

Fancy NOTE PAPER and ENVELOPES, Stamped with Initials or Monograms, at E. H. BENDER'S, 73 State Street, Albany.

FARMERS' ALMANAC.

PRATT & KING'S
And Real Estate
Insurance Agency,

Fort Edward, N. Y.

Capital Represented:
OVER THIRTY MILLION DOLLARS.

Life, Fire, Inland, Navigation and Accidental Insurance, in first-class Companies and on the most favorable terms. Buildings Rented and Sales of Real Estate attended to for a small Commission.

Good News to Mothers, Wives, Daughters and Sisters

Get the Best and Cheapest,
The Only Perfect Machine.

The American Button-hole, Overseaming and Sewing Machine is the most simple, perfect and noiseless labor-saving Sewing Machine of modern times. It is warranted to do any kind of sewing that can be done by any Machine now before the public. We have them with or without the Button-hole Attachment, and at a price within the reach of all.

PRATT & KING, Agents.

R. W. PRATT. D. H. KING

Go to White & Pearsall's, Glen's Falls, for the best Improved Sewing Machine.

Dr. JAS. S. GARRETT, Surgeon Dentist, Glen's Falls, N. Y.

C. O. D. BOOTS and SHOES are the cheapest, at WAIT'S.
Boots and Shoes, every pair Warranted, at WAIT'S. (See page 81.)

STAMP DUTIES. 139

Bill of lading, domestic or inland, exempt.
Bill of sale by which any ship or vessel, or any part thereof, shall be conveyed to or vested in any other person or persons: when the consideration shall not exceed $500, 50 cts.; exceeding $500, and not exceeding $1,000, $1; exceeding $1,000, for every additional $500, or fractional part thereof, 50 cts.
Bond for indemnifying any person for the payment of any sum of money—when the money ultimately recoverable thereupon is $1,000 or less, 50 cts.; when in excess of $1,000, for each $1,000 or fraction, 50 cts.
Bond-administrator or guardian, when the value of the estate and effects, real and personal, does not exceed $1,000, exempt; exceeding $1,000, $1.
Bond for due execution or performance of duties of office, $1.
Bond, personal, for security for the payment of money. (See Mortgage.)
Bond of any description, other than such as may be required in legal proceedings, or used in connection with mortgage deeds, and not otherwise charged in this schedule, 25 cts.
Broker's notes. (See Contract.)
Certificates of measurement or weight of animals, wood, coal or hay, exempt.
Certificates of measurement of other articles, 5 cts.
Certificates of stock in any incorporated company, 25 cts.
Certificates of profits, or any certificate or memorandum showing an interest in the property or accumulations of any incorporated company—i for a sum not less than $10 and not exceeding $50, 10 cts.; exceeding $50 and not exceeding $1,000, 25 cts.; exceeding $1,000, for every additional $1,000 or fractional part thereof, 25 cts.
Certificate—any certificate of damage or otherwise, and all other certificates or documents issued by any port warden, marine surveyor, or other person acting as such, 25 cts.
Certificate of deposit of any sum of money in any bank or trust company, or with any banker or person acting as such—if for a sum not exceeding $100, 2 cts.; for a sum exceeding $100, 5 cts.
Certificate of any other description than those specified, 5 cts.
Charter, renewal of, same stamp as an original instrument.
Charter party for the charter of any ship or vessel, or steamer, or any letter, memorandum, or other writing relating to the charter, or any renewal or transfer thereof—if the registered tonnage of such ship, or vessel, or steamer does not exceed 150 tons, $1; exceeding 150 tons, and not exceeding 300 tons, $3; exceeding 300 tons, and not exceeding 600 tons, $5; exceeding 600 tons, $10.
Check—bank check, 2 cts.
Contract—broker's note, or memorandum of sale of any goods or merchandise, exchange, real estate, or property of any kind or description issued by brokers or persons acting as such, for each note or memorandum of sale, 10 cts.; bill or memorandum of the sale or contract for the sale of stocks, bonds, gold or silver bullion, coin, promissory notes, or other securities made by brokers, banks, or bankers, either for the benefit of others or on their own account, for each hundred dollars, or fractional part thereof, of the amount of such sale or contract, 1 ct.; bill or memorandum of the sale or contract for the sale of stocks, bonds, gold or silver bullion, coin, promissory notes, or other securities, not his or their own property, made by any person, firm, or company not paying a special tax as broker, bank or

PIANOS, ORGANS and MELODEONS, for sale by P. H. COREY, GLEN'S FALLS.

W. A. Wilkins sells Bully Cloze Cheaper nor anybody elts.
18

E. H. BENDER, Wholesale and Retail Dealer in every Variety of
BOOKS, STATIONERY &c., 73 State Street, Albany.

Always a large stock of fine, ready-made Clothing at WHITE & PEARSALL'S, Glen's Falls.

140   *FARMERS' ALMANAC.*

FORT EDWARD
FURNITURE STORE.

DE FOREST & IRVING

Are Constantly Making New Additions to their Stock of

FURNITURE AND UPHOLSTERY GOODS,

CONSISTING OF

Chamber Suits in Walnut, Chestnut, and Ornamental of all kinds; Parlor Suits of all kinds, and Parlor and Extension Dining Tables, Looking Glasses, Couches, Stands, What-Nots, Chairs, Bureaus, Bedsteads, Book Cases, Spring Beds, and Mattresses.

Children's Cabs, Wagons, Sleighs, Rocking Horses, &c., &c.

METALLIC, ROSEWOOD AND WALNUT BURIAL CASES;

TOGETHER WITH A GENERAL ASSORTMENT OF

COFFINS

Of every Description, Trimmed in the Best Style, may be found at our Warerooms.

ENTIRE CHARGE TAKEN OF FUNERALS WHEN DESIRED.

BROADWAY, FORT EDWARD.

Repairing done with neatness and despatch at Joubert & White's.

Latest Novelties in Ladies' Boots, at WAIT'S.
Romeo and Juliet Walking Boots, at WAIT'S. (See page 81.)

STAMP DUTIES. 141

banker, for each hundred dollars, or fractional part thereof, of the amount of such sale or contract, 5 cts.

Contract. (See Agreement.)

Contract, renewal of, same stamp as original instrument.

Conveyance, deed, instrument or writing, whereby any lands, tenements, or other realty sold shall be granted, assigned, transferred, or otherwise conveyed to or vested in the purchaser or purchasers, or any other person or persons, by his, her or their direction, when the consideration or value does not exceed $500, 50 cts.; when the consideration exceeds $500, and does not exceed $1,000, $1; and for every additional $500, or fractional part thereof, in excess of $1,000, 50 cts.

Conveyance. The acknowledgment of a deed, or proof by a witness, exempt.

Conveyance. Certificate of record of a deed, exempt.

Credit, letter of. Same as foreign bill of exchange.

Custom-house entry. (See Entry.)

Custom-house withdrawals. (See Entry.)

Deed. (See Conveyance—Trust deed.)

Draft. Same as inland bill of exchange.

Endorsement of any negotiable instrument, exempt.

Entry of any goods, wares or merchandise at any custom-house, either for consumption or warehousing, not exceeding $100 in value, 25 cts.; exceeding $100, and not exceeding $500 in value, 50 cts.; exceeding $500 in value, $1.

Entry for the withdrawal of any goods or merchandise from bonded warehouse, 50 cts.

Gauger's returns, exempt.

Indorsement upon a stamped obligation in acknowledgment of its fulfillment, exempt.

Insurance (life) policy, when the amount insured shall not exceed $1,000, 25 cts.; exceeding $1,000, and not exceeding $5,000, 50 cts.; exceeding $5,000, $1.

Insurance (marine, inland, and fire,) policies, or renewal of the same, if the premium does not exceed $10, 10 cts.; exceeding $10, and not exceeding $50, 25 cts.; exceeding $50, 50 cts.

Insurance contracts or tickets against accidental injuries to persons, exempt.

Lease, agreement, memorandum, or contract for the hire, use, or rent of any land, tenement, or portion thereof, where the rent or rental value is $300 per annum or less, 50 cts.; where the rent or rental value exceeds the sum of $300 per annum, for each additional $200, or fractional part thereof in excess of $300, 50 cts.

Legal documents. Writ, or other original process, by which any suit, either criminal or civil, is commenced in any court, either of law or equity, exempt; confession of judgment or cognovit, exempt; writs or other process on appeals from justice courts or other courts of inferior jurisdiction to a court of record, exempt.

Warrant of distress, exempt.

Letters of administration. (See Probate of will.)

Letters testamentary, when the value of the estate and effects, real and personal, does not exceed $1,000, exempt; exceeding $1,000, 5 cts.

Letters of credit. Same as bill of exchange, (foreign.)

Manifest for custom-house entry or clearance of the cargo of any ship,

Latest styles Bonnets, Jockeys, and Boys' and Infants' Caps and Hoods, at COREY'S, Glen's Falls.

Custom Work done better at WILKINS' than elsewhere.

BIBLES, PRAYER and HYMN BOOKS, SUNDAY SCHOOL BOOKS,
Merit Cards, &c., at E. H. BENDER'S, 73 State Street, Albany.

142 FARMERS' ALMANAC.

P. A. BAKER,
First Door South of the Post Office, Dealer in

FANCY GOODS AND MILLINERY,
INCLUDING

Berlin Zephyrs Fringes, Gimps, Laces.

☞ Hats and Bonnets on hand and Made to Order.

P. A. BAKER'S
PHOTOGRAPH AND GEM GALLERY,
FAIR HAVEN, VT.

☞ *Stereoscopes, Views, Chromos, and Oil Paintings, Oval, Archtop and Square Frames, kept constantly on hand and made to order.*

"STATUARY MANTLES," "STATUARY MANTLES."

If you want first class Statuary, or any other quality of

MARBLE MANTLES,
Send for Designs and Prices to the

West Rutland Marble Mantle Company,
WEST RUTLAND, VERMONT.

Being in the vicinity of the best Marble Quarries in Rutland, it is the cheapest place in the United States to buy first class Marble Mantles. Manufacturers of

Pier and Labratory Slabs,

Bureau, Table and Counter Tops,
BRACKET SHELVES,

Soda Water Fountains,

And every description of Marble Work executed in the best possible manner, and at the Lowest Prices for Cash.

H. PRITCHARD.   H. McNEILL.   R. LANE.

Go to GARRETT'S for improved Dental Rubber Work, G. Falls.

STAMP DUTIES. 143

vessel, or steamer, for a foreign port, if the registered tonnage of such ship, vessel, or steamer does not exceed 300 tons, $1; exceeding 300 tons, and not exceeding 600 tons, $3; exceeding 600 tons, $5. [These provisions do not apply to vessels or steamboats plying between ports of the United States and British North America.]

Measurers' returns, exempt.

Memorandum of sale, or broker's note. (See Contract.)

Mortgage of lands, estate, or property, real or personal, heritable or movable, whatsoever, a trust deed in the nature of a mortgage, or any personal bond given as security for the payment of any definite or certain sum of money, exceeding $100, and not exceeding $500, 50 cts.; exceeding $500, and not exceeding $1,000, $1; and for every additional $500, or fractional part thereof, in excess of $1,000, 50 cts.

Order for payment of money, if the amount is $10, or over, 2 cts.

Passage ticket on any vessel from a port in the United States to a foreign port, not exceeding $35, 50 cts.; exceeding $35, and not exceeding $50, $1; and for every additional $50, or fractional part thereof, in excess of $50, $1; passage tickets to ports in British North America, exempt.

Pawner's checks, 5 cts.

Power of attorney for the sale or transfer of any stock, bonds or scrip, or for the collection of any dividends or interest thereon, 25 cts.

Power of attorney, or proxy, for voting at any election for officers of any incorporated company or society, except religious, charitable, or literary societies or public cemeteries, 10 cts.

Power of attorney to receive or collect rent, 25 cts.

Power of attorney to sell and and convey real estate, or to rent or lease the same, $1.

Power of attorney for any other purpose, 50 cts.

Probate of will or letters of administration; where the estate and effects for or in respect of which such probate or letters of administration applied for shall be sworn or declared not to exceed the value of $1,000, exempt; exceeding $1,000, and not exceeding $2,000, $1; exceeding $2,000, for every additional $1,000, or fractional part thereof, in excess of $2,000, 50 cts.

Promissory note. (See Bill of exchange, inland.) Deposit note to mutual insurance companies, when policy is subject to duty, exempt; renewal of a note, subject to the same duty as an original note.

Protest of note, bill of exchange, acceptance, check, or draft, or any marine protest, 25 cts.

Quit-claim deed to be stamped as a conveyance, except when given as a release of a mortgage by the mortgagee to the mortgagor, in which case it is exempt; but if it contains covenants may be subject as an agreement or contract.

Receipts for satisfaction of any mortgage or judgment or decree of any court, exempt.

Receipts for any sum of money or debt due, or for a draft or other instrument given for the payment of money—exceeding $20, not being for satisfaction of any mortgage or judgment or decree of court, 2 cts. (See Indorsement.)

Receipts for the delivery of property, exempt.

Renewal of agreement, contract or charter, by letter or otherwise, same stamp as original instrument.

Sheriff's return on writ or other process, exempt.

W. A. WILKINS' Cheap Clothing Store, established 1859.

E. H. BENDER, BINDER and PRINTER, and Wholesale and Retail
BOOKSELLER and STATIONER, 73 State Street, Albany.

FARMERS' ALMANAC.

G. BROKAW,
SADDLER
AND
HARNESS MAKER,
FORT EDWARD, N. Y.

HARNESS OF ALL KINDS
ON HAND and MADE TO ORDER, of the Best Materials and Workmanship. Horse Blankets, Whips, Halters, Brushes, &c. Also, a Fine Assortment of Sole Leather and other Trunks, Valises, Traveling Bags, Ladies' Satchels, &c., &c., &c.

All Work Warranted, and at the Lowest Cash Price.

THOMAS YELVERTON,
DEALER IN
HARDWARE, FARMING UTENSILS, TIN-WARE, STOVES, &c.

Agent for the CELEBRATED NEW EMPIRE COOKING STOVE. Also, a Large Variety of other Cooking and Parlor Stoves.

COR. BROADWAY AND EAST STREET, FORT EDWARD, N.Y.

All Carriage and Sleigh Work Warranted at Joubert & White's.

Cheapest place to buy your Business Suits, at WHITE & PEARSALL'S, Glen's Falls.

JAMES MARTIN & CO.

(Successors to R. P. LATHROP,)

IMPORTERS OF AND DEALERS IN

GUNS,
Rifles & Pistols,

SPORTING APPARATUS,

FISHING TACKLE, &c.

DEPOT FOR

Smith & Wesson's and National Revolvers, Hall & Hubbard's Metallic Cartridges, Eley's Caps and Wads, Dixon's Flasks and Pouches, Tatham's Shot, Hazard's Powder, &c.

Also Manufacturers of

SURGICAL AND DENTAL INSTRUMENTS AND APPARATUS,

TRUSSES,

Tailors', Barbers' and Family Shears, Scissors, Razors, &c.

No. 52 STATE ST. and 20 BEAVER ST.

ALBANY, N. Y.

STAMP DUTIES. 145

Trust deed, made to secure a debt, to be stamped as a mortgage.

Warehouse receipts, exempt.

Warrant of attorney accompanying a bond or note, if the bond or note is stamped, exempt.

Weigher's returns, exempt; official documents, instruments, and papers issued by officers of the United States Government, exempt; official instruments, documents, and papers issued by the officers of any State, county, town, or other municipal corporation, in the exercise of functions strictly belonging to them in their ordinary governmental or municipal capacity, exempt; papers necessary to be used for the collection from the United States Government of claims by soldiers, or their legal representatives, for pensions, back pay, bounty, or for property lost in the service, exempt.

CANCELLATION.—In all cases where an *adhesive* stamp is used for denoting the stamp duty upon an instrument, the person using or affixing the same must write or imprint thereupon *in ink* the initials of his name, and the date (the year, month, and day) on which the same is attached or used. Each stamp should be separately cancelled.

It is not lawful to record any instrument, document, or paper required by law to be stamped, or any copy thereof, unless a stamp or stamps of the proper amount have been affixed and cancelled in the manner required by law; and such instrument or copy and the record thereof are utterly null and void, and cannot be used or admitted as evidence in any court until the defect has been cured as provided in section 158.

All willful violations of the law should be reported to the United States District Attorney within and for the district where they are committed.

GENERAL REMARKS.—Revenue stamps may be used indiscriminately upon any of the matters or things enumerated in Schedule B, except proprietary and playing card stamps, for which a special use has been provided.

Postage stamps cannot be used in payment of the duty chargeable on instruments.

The law does not designate which of the parties to an instrument shall furnish the necessary stamp, nor does the Commissioner of Internal Revenue assume to determine that it shall be supplied by one party rather than by another; but if an instrument subject to stamp duty is issued without having the necessary stamps affixed thereto, it cannot be recorded, or admitted, or used in evidence, in any court, until a legal stamp or stamps, denoting the amount of tax, shall have been affixed as prescribed by law, and the person who thus issues it is liable to a penalty, if he omits the stamps with an intent to evade the provisions of the internal revenue act.

The first act imposing a stamp tax upon certain specified instruments took effect, so far as said tax is concerned, October 1, 1862. The impression which seems to prevail to some extent, that no stamps are required upon any instruments issued in the States lately in insurrection, prior to the surrender, or prior to the establishment of collection districts there, is erroneous.

Instruments issued in those States since October 1, 1862, are subject to the same taxes as similar ones issued at the same time in the other States.

No stamp is necessary upon an instrument executed prior to October 1, 1862, to make it admissible in evidence, or to entitle it to record.

Certificates of loan in which there shall appear any written or printed evidence of an amount of money to be paid on demand, or at a time designated, are subject to stamp duty as "promissory notes."

When two or more persons join in the execution of an instrument, the

BENDER will furnish you any Books Published; also, ENGINEERS' INSTRUMENTS, STATIONERY, FIELD BOOKS, &c., at 73 State Street, Albany.

146   FARMERS' ALMANAC.

WHITEHOUSE & CO.
CHEMISTS AND DRUGGISTS,
AND DEALERS IN
Paints, Oils, Glass, &c.
(Next door to Farmers' Bank.)   **FORT EDWARD, N. Y.**

Proprietors of Wing's Cough Remedy and the Great American Diarrhœa Cure.

MATTHEW REDFERN,
Attorney at Law.

Prompt attention given to Collections, and success insured, or no charge.

Office, Over the Farmers' National Bank,

FORT EDWARD, N. Y.

Attention, Fort Edward!

GOLDRING'S
Old-Established Store is RE-OPENED With a Large and Well-selected Stock of

READY-MADE
CLOTHING,
—AND—
Gents' Furnishing Goods.

The Proprietor has just returned from New York, where he has purchased largely for cash, and having much experience in the business, has made a judicious selection of the newest and most fashionable Goods to be found in the market. He can offer great Inducements to purchasers, as he is determined to sell his Goods at the lowest possible prices, and thus secure a large and permanent trade. We respectfully ask the former patrons of this establishment to call on us and examine our

CHOICE ASSORTMENT OF GOODS
Before purchasing elsewhere.

We mean what we say—at WHITE & PEARSALL'S, Glen's Falls.

Artificial Teeth, best style, warranted, at GARRETT'S, Glen's Falls.

STAMP DUTIES. 147

stamp to which the instrument is liable under the law, may be affixed and cancelled by either of them; and " when more than one signature is affixed to the same paper, one or more stamps may be affixed thereto, representing the whole amount of the stamp required for such signatures."

No stamp is required on any warrant of attorney accompanying a bond or note, when such bond or note has affixed thereto the stamp or stamps denoting the duty required; and, whenever any bond or note is secured by mortgage, but one stamp duty is required on such papers—such stamp duty being the highest rate required for such instruments, or either of them. In such case a note or memorandum of the value or denomination of the stamp affixed should be made upon the margin or in the acknowledgement of the instrument which is not stamped.

Particular attention is called to the change in section 154, by striking out the words "or used;" the exemption thereunder is thus restricted to documents, &c., *issued* by the officers therein named. Also to the changes in sections 152 and 158, by inserting the words " and cancelled in the manner required by law."

The acceptor or acceptors of any bill of exchange, or order for the payment of any sum of money, drawn or purporting to be drawn in any foreign country, but payable in the United States, must, before paying or accepting the same, place thereupon a stamp indicating the duty.

It is only upon conveyances of realty *sold* that conveyance stamps are necessary. A deed of real estate made without valuable consideration need not be stamped as a conveyance; but if it contains covenants, such, for instance, as a covenant to warrant and defend the title, it should be stamped as an agreement or contract.

When a deed purporting to be a conveyance of realty sold, and stamped accordingly, is inoperative, a deed of confirmation, made simply to cure the defect, requires no stamp. In such case, the second deed should contain a recital of the facts, and should show the reasons for its execution.

Partition deeds between tenants in common, need not be stamped as conveyances, inasmuch as there is no sale of realty, but merely a marking out, or a defining, of the boundaries of the part belonging to each; but where money or other valuable consideration is paid by one co-tenant to another for equality of partition, there is a sale to the extent of such consideration, and the conveyance, by the party receiving it, should be stamped accordingly.

A conveyance of lands sold for unpaid taxes, issued since August 1, 1866, by the officers of any county, town, or other municipal corporation in the discharge of their strictly official duties, is exempt from stamp tax.

A conveyance of realty sold, subject to a mortgage, should be stamped according to the consideration, or the value of the property *unincumbered*. The consideration in such case is to be found by adding the amount paid for the equity of redemption to the mortgage debt. The fact that one part of the consideration is paid to the mortgagor and the other part to the mortgagee does not change the liability of the conveyance.

The stamp tax upon a mortgage is based upon the amount it is given to secure. The fact that the value of the property mortgaged is less than that amount, and that consequently the security is only partial, does not change the liability of the instrument. When, therefore, a second mortgage is given to secure the payment of a sum of money partially secured by a prior mortgage upon other property, or when two mortgages upon separate property are given at the same time to secure the payment of the same sum, each should be stamped as though it were the only one.

Ding, dong, bell! **WILKINS is bound to sell.** (See p. 96.)

The Largest, the Cheapest and Best BOOK and STATIONERY STORE in Albany is BENDER'S, 73 State Street, Albany.

148   FARMERS' ALMANAC.

JOHN LOUDON,

BUILDER,

MANUFACTURER AND DEALER IN

SASH, DOORS, BLINDS,

WINDOW AND DOOR FRAMES,

CASINGS, AND CORNICE MATERIALS;

Moldings of all kinds and shapes, Planing and Sawing to Order, Pickets Planed and Pointed ready for use, Material Worked to Order for Verandahs, Piazzas, Porches, Vestibules, Observatories, in short,

ANYTHING AND EVERYTHING BELONGING TO HOUSE BUILDING.

All orders promptly attended to. Builders are respectfully invited to call and examine before purchasing elsewhere.

Office and Shop in Second Story of Machine Shop Building,

FORT EDWARD,
Washington Co., N. Y.

Heavy and Light Carriages at Joubert & White's, Glen's Falls.

WHITE & PEARSALL'S Clothing Emporium, Glen's Falls.

STAMP DUTIES. 149

A mortgage given to secure a surety from loss, or given for any purpose whatever, other than as security for the payment of a definite and certain sum of money, is taxable only as an agreement or contract.

The stamp duty upon a lease, agreement, memorandum, or contract for the hire, use, or rent of any land, tenement, or portion thereof, is based upon the *annual* rent or rental value of the property leased, and the duty is the same whether the lease be for one year, for a term of years, or for the fractional part of a year only.

Upon every assignment or transfer of a mortgage, a stamp tax is required equal to that imposed upon a mortgage for the amount remaining unpaid; this tax is required upon every such transfer in writing, whether there is a *sale* of the mortgage or not; but no stamp is necessary upon the endorsement of a negotiable instrument, even though the legal effect of such indorsement is to to transfer a mortgage by which the instrument is secured.

An assignment of a lease within the meaning and intent of Schedule B, is an assignment of the *leasehold*, or of some portion thereof, by the *lessee*, or by some person claiming by, from, or under him; such an assignment as subrogates the assignee to the rights, or some portion of the rights, of the *lessee*, or of the person standing in his place. A transfer by the *lessor* of his part of a lease, neither giving nor purporting to give a claim to the leasehold, or to any part thereof, but simply a right to the rents, &c., is subject to stamp tax as a contract or agreement only.

The stamp tax upon a fire insurance policy is based upon the *premium*.

Deposit notes taken by a mutual fire insurance company, not as payment of premium nor as evidence of indebtedness therefor, but to be used simply as a basis upon which to make ratable assessments to meet the losses incurred by the company, should not be reckoned as premium in determining the amount of stamp taxes upon the policies.

When a policy of insurance properly stamped has been issued and lost, no stamp is necessary upon another issued by the same company to the same party, covering the same property, time, &c., and designed simply to supply the loss. The second policy should recite the loss of the first.

An instrument which operates as the renewal of a policy of insurance, is subject to the same stamp tax as the policy.

When a policy of insurance is issued for a certain time, whether it be for one year only or for a term of years, a receipt for premium or any other instrument which has the legal effect to continue the contract and extend its operation *beyond that time*, requires the same amount of revenue stamps as the policy itself; but such a receipt as is usually given for the payment of the monthly, quarterly, or annual premium, is not a renewal within the meaning of the statute. The payment simply prevents the policy from expiring, by reason of non-performance of its conditions; a receipt given for such a payment requires a two-cent stamp, if the amount received exceeds twenty dollars, and a two-cent stamp only. When, however, the time of payment has passed, and a tender of the premium is not sufficient to bind the company, but a new policy or a new contract in some form, with the mutuality essential to every contract, becomes necessary between the insurer and the insured, the same amount of stamps should be used as that required upon the original policy.

A permit issued by a life insurance company changing the terms of a policy as to travel, residence, occupation, &c., should be stamped as a contract or agreement.

Have your Clothing made at WILKINS'. (See page 96.)

The STATIONERY Department Replete with every variety of STATIONER'S ARTICLES, at BENDER'S, 73 State Street, Albany.

FARMERS' ALMANAC.

ELMWOOD SEMINARY,
FOR YOUNG LADIES,
GLEN'S FALLS, N. Y.

MISS A. TAYLOR,
Principal, and Teacher of Languages, Mental Science and Elocution.

MISS MARY L. SMITH,
Assistant, and Teacher of Mathematics.

MISS MARIA E. COLES,
Assistant Teacher of Music.

MISS MARTHA S. WILSON,
Teacher of Drawing and Painting.

MISS CARILE BEVERLY,
MISS HANNAH SUYDAM,
Graduates, and Assistants in Preparatory Department.

PROF. W. J. HOLDING,
Piano, Melodeon and Vocalization.

SAMUEL TAYLOR, ESQ.,
Treasurer and General Business Superintendent.

MRS. H. J. TAYLOR,
Matron.

REV. M. E. ELLISON,
Chancellor.

EXAMINING COMMITTEE.

REV. C. H. NASH,
REV. M. E. ELLISON,
REV. R. M. LITTLE,

REV. J. I. MORROW,
REV. B. HAWLEY, D. D.,
REV. E. E. BUTLER.

This Institution is a Boarding and Day School, under the direction of MISS A. TAYLOR, graduate of the Oakland Female Institute, Norristown, Pa.; for nine years Principal of the University Female Institute at Lewisburg, Pa., and for five years connected with the first Institutions of New York City.

The Seminary is commodious, and beautifully located in the midst of well shaded grounds. The rooms are airy and well furnished. All the surroundings are such as to render it an attractive home for young ladies of culture and refinement. Glen's Falls is readily accessible from all points by railroads. It is fifteen miles from Saratoga, and nine miles from Lake George. It is in direct communication by telegraph with all important places.

The course of study comprises all the branches taught in a thorough finished English education. To young ladies who complete the course, and sustain a creditable examination, a Diploma will be awarded; and all graduates who become proficient in at least one foreign language, and piano music, will receive a Gold Medal—the highest honor of the Institution. The Principal will be assisted by a full corps of competent and experienced Professors and Teachers. Expenses very moderate. No charge will be made for the education of the daughters of clergymen or missionaries who board in the Institution.

☞ Any questions pertaining to the School or expenses will be promptly answered by addressing the Principal.

Fine fitting Suits—satisfaction given—at WHITE & PEARSALL'S, Glen's Falls.

Garrett's Dental Rooms, Glen's Falls, N. Y.

STAMP DUTIES.   151

A bill single or a bill obligatory, *i. e.*, an instrument in the form of a promissory note, *under seal*, is subject to stamp duty as written or printed evidence of an amount of money to be paid on demand or at a time designated, at the rate of five cents for each one hundred dollars or fractional part thereof.

A waiver of protest, or of demand and notice, written upon negotiable paper and signed by the indorser, is an agreement, and requires a five-cent stamp.

A stamp duty of twenty-five cents is imposed upon the "protest of every note, bill of exchange, check or draft," and upon every marine protest. If several notes, bills of exchange, drafts, &c., are protested at the same time and all attached to one and the same certificate, stamps should be affixed to the amount of twenty-five cents for each note, bill, draft, &c., thus protested.

When a subscription is for a purpose in which there is a community of interest among the subscribers, the list should be stamped as a contract, or agreement, at the rate of five cents for each sheet or piece of paper upon which it is written.

When there is no community of interest, and the subscription is conditional, each signer executes a separate contract, requiring its appropriate amount of stamps; this amount depends upon the number of sheets or pieces of paper upon which the contract is written.

When each of the subscribers contracts to pay a certain and definite sum of money on demand, or at a time designated, the separate contract of each should be stamped at the same rate as a promissory note.

When, as is generally the case, the caption to a deposition contains other certificates in addition to the jurat to the affidavit of the deponent, such as a certificate that the parties were or were not notified, that they did or did not appear, that they did or did not object, &c., it is subject to a stamp duty of five cents.

When an attested copy of a writ or other process is used by a sheriff or other person in making personal service, or in attaching property, a five-cent stamp should be affixed to the certificate of attestation.

A marriage certificate issued by the officiating clergyman or magistrate, to be returned to any officer of a State, county, city, town, or other municipal corporation, to constitute part of a public record, requires no stamp; but if it is to be retained by the parties, a five-cent stamp should be affixed.

The stamp tax upon a bill of sale, by which any ship or vessel, or any part thereof, is conveyed to or vested in any other person or persons, is at the same rate as that imposed upon conveyances of realty sold; a bill of sale of any other personal property should be stamped as a contract or agreement.

An assignment of real or personal property, or of both, for the benefit of creditors, should be stamped as an agreement or contract.

Written or printed assignments of agreements, bonds, notes not negotiable, and of all other instruments, the assignments of which are not particularly specified in the foregoing schedule, should be stamped as agreements.

No stamp is necessary upon the registry of a judgment, even though the registry is such in its legal effect as to create a lien which operates as a mortgage upon the property of the judgment debtor.

When a "power of attorney or proxy for voting at any election for officers of any incorporated company or society, except religious, charitable, or literary societies, or public cemeteries," is signed by several stock-

Competition Defied in Quality, Quantity and Prices of STATIONERY, at BENDER'S, 73 State Street, Albany.

152   FARMERS' ALMANAC.

M. L. WILMARTH,
DEALER IN

FURNITURE,
LOOKING GLASSES, LOOKING GLASS PLATES,
MATTRESSES, GEESE FEATHERS, &c., &c.
ALSO,
COFFINS AND COFFIN TRIMMINGS.
RIDGE STREET, GLEN'S FALLS. N. Y.

D. G. NORRIS & CO.,

BLACKSMITHS AND WAGON MAKERS,
Keep constantly on hand and Manufacture to order all kinds of
Heavy and Light Wagons and Sleighs.
PAINTING AND ORNAMENTING.
Particular attention given to this department.
Cor. LIME AND WARREN STREETS,
GLEN'S FALLS, N. Y.

Our Work is done by Competent Men only.   Joubert & White.

The best selected stock of fine Clothing is at WHITE & PEARSALL'S, Glen's Falls.

For **CARPETS** and **OIL CLOTHS**, go to **WAIT'S.**
For **FINE READY-MADE CLOTHING**, go to **WAIT'S.** (See page 81.)

POSTAL RATES AND REGULATIONS. 153

holders, owning separate and distinct shares, it is, in its legal effect, the separate instrument of each, and requires stamps to the amount of ten cents for each and every signature; one or more stamps may be used representing the whole amount required.

A notice from landlord to tenant to quit possession of premises requires no stamp.

A stamp tax is imposed upon every "manifest for custom-house entry or clearance of the *cargo* of any ship, vessel, or steamer for a foreign port." The amount of this tax in each case depends upon the registered tonnage of the vessel.

If a vessel clears in ballast and has no cargo whatever, no stamp is necessary; but if she has any—however small the amount—a stamp should be used.

A bond to convey real estate requires stamps to the amount of twenty-five cents.

The stamp duty upon the probate of a will, or upon letters of administration, is based upon the sworn or declared value of all the estate and effects, real, personal, and mixed, undiminished by the debts of the estate for or in respect of which such probate or letters are applied for.

When the property belonging to the estate of a person deceased, lies under different jurisdictions and it becomes necessary to take out letters in two or more places, the letters should be stamped according to the value of all the property, real, personal, and mixed, for or in respect of which the particular letters in each case are issued.

Letters *de bonis non* should be stamped according to the amount of property remaining to be administered upon thereunder, regardless of the stamps upon the original letters.

A mere *copy* of an instrument is not subject to stamp duty unless it is a certified one, in which case a five-cent stamp should be affixed to the certificate of the person attesting it; but when an instrument is executed and issued in duplicate, triplicate, &c., as in the case of a lease of two or more parts, each part has the same legal effect as the other, and each should be stamped as an original.

Postal Rates and Regulations.

LETTERS.—The law requires postage on all letters (including those to foreign countries when prepaid), excepting those written to the President or Vice-President, or members of Congress, or (on official business) to the chiefs of the executive departments of the Government, and the heads of bureaux and chief clerks, and others invested with the franking privilege, to be prepaid by stamps or stamped envelopes, prepayment in money being prohibited.

All drop-letters must be prepaid. The rate of postage on drop-letters, at offices where free delivery by carrier is established, is two cents per half ounce or fraction of a half ounce; at offices where such free delivery is NOT established the rate is one cent.

The single rate of postage on all domestic mail letters throughout the United States, is three cents per half ounce, with an additional rate of three

W. A. Wilkins' Cheap Cash Clothing Store, Whitehall, N.Y.

P. H. COREY, GLEN'S FALLS, furnishes SHEET MUSIC, &c., to Teachers, at a discount.

CONKEY'S
PHOTOGRAPH AND FINE ART GALLERY,

Warren Street, over the New York Store,

GLEN'S FALLS, N. Y.

IMPERIAL CARDS, AND PORCELAIN PICTURES,

Cartes-de-Visite, Vignettes, Bon-Tons,
And all kinds of Pictures known to the Art.

We would call especial attention to

Pictures of Children.
WE CAN CATCH A BIRD FOR THEM EVERY TIME.

Particular attention given to

Copying and Enlarging Old Pictures.

A large assortment of Gilt, Rosewood, Black Walnut,
Oval and Square Frames; Albums, Cord,
Tassels, and every kind of goods
kept in a first-class Gallery.

Having been at the picture business for the past nineteen years, we will Warrant the Best Work in the County, or ask no pay. Give as a call; WE WILL USE YOU WELL. ☞ Remember the place:

WARREN ST., OVER THE NEW YORK STORE,

GLEN'S FALLS, N. Y,

GEORGE W. CONKEY, Artist.

P. S. We have no connection with any other Gallery. All Negatives preserved.

We defy competition. WHITE & PEARSALL, Glen's Falls.

All of Garrett's Dental Work is WARRANTED. Glen's Falls.

OVERCOATS from $5 to $30, at WAIT'S CASH STORE.
FROCK COAT SUITS Cheap at WAIT'S. (See page 81.)

POSTAL RATES AND REGULATIONS. 155

cents for each additional half ounce or fraction of a half ounce. The ten cent (Pacific) rate is abolished.

To and from Canada and New Brunswick 10 cents per half ounce, irrespective of distance.

To and from other British North American Provinces, for distance not over 3,000 miles, 10 cents. Over 3,000, 15 cents.

For every additional half ounce, or fraction of a half ounce, an additional rate is charged. Prepayment is optional on all letters for the British North American Provinces except Newfoundland, to which prepayment is compulsory.

NEWSPAPERS, ETC.—Letter postage is to be charged on all handbills, circulars, or other printed matter which shall contain any manuscript writing whatever.

Daguerreotypes, when sent in the mail, are to be charged with letter postage by weight.

Photographs on cards, paper, and other flexible material (not in cases), can be sent at the same rate as miscellaneous printed matter, viz: two cents for each four ounces or fraction thereof.

Photograph Albums are chargeable with book postage—four cents for each four ounces or fraction thereof.

NEWSPAPER POSTAGE.—Postage on daily papers to subscribers when prepaid quarterly or yearly in advance, either at the mailing office or office of delivery, per quarter (three months), 35 cts.; six times per week, per quarter, 30 cts.; for tri-weekly, per quarter, 15 cts.; for semi-weekly, per quarter, 10 cts.; for weekly, per quarter, 5 cents.

Weekly newspapers (one copy only) sent by the publisher to actual subscribers within the county where printed and published, FREE.

Postage per quarter (to be paid quarterly or yearly in advance) on newspapers and periodicals issued less frequently than once a week, sent to actual subscribers in any part of the United States: Semi-monthly, not over 4 oz., 6 cts.; over 4 oz. and not over 8 oz., 12 cts.; over 8 oz. and not over 12 oz., 18 cts.; monthly, not over 4 oz., 3 cts.; over 4 oz. and not over 8 oz., 6 cts.; over 8 oz. and not over 12 oz., 9 cts.; quarterly, not over 4 oz., 1 cent; over 4 oz. and not over 8 oz., 2 cts.; over 8 oz. and not over 12 oz., 3 cts.

TRANSIENT MATTER.—Books not over 4 oz. in weight, to one address, 4 cts.; over 4 oz. and not over 8 oz., 8 cts.; over 8 oz. and not over 12 oz., 12 cts.; over 12 oz. and not over 16 oz., 16 cts.

Circulars not exceeding three in number to one address, 2 cts.; over 3 and not over 6, 4 cts.; over 6 and not over 9, 6 cts.; over 9 and not exceeding 12, 8 cts.

On miscellaneous mailable matter, (embracing all pamphlets, occasional publications, transient newspapers, hand-bills and posters, book manuscripts and proof-sheets, whether corrected or not, maps, prints, engravings, sheet music, blanks, flexible patterns, samples, and sample cards, phonographic paper, letter envelopes, postal envelopes or wrappers, cards, paper, plain or ornamental, photographic representations of different types, seeds, cuttings, bulbs, roots and scions,) the postage to be prepaid by stamps, is on one package, to one address, not over 4 oz. in weight, 2 cts.; over 4 oz. and not over 8 oz., 4 cts.; over 8 oz. and not over 12 oz., 6 cts.; over 12 oz. and not over 16 oz., 8 cts. The weight of packages of seeds, cuttings, roots and scions, to be franked, is limited to thirty-two ounces.

Buy your Clothing of W. A. Wilkins, Whitehall, N. Y.

The CHEAP Wholesale and Retail STATIONERY STORE,
Is BENDER'S, 73 State Street Albany.

FARMERS' ALMANAC.

Dr. J. W. BENSON,
DENTIST,
And Agent for
WEED'S SEWING MACHINE.
Office in Mabbett's Building, Glen St.,

Glen's Falls, N. Y.

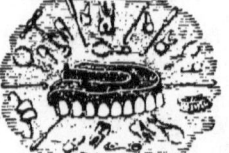

This first-class Machine is offered on favorable terms, and a trial of 30 days given any one wishing to purchase. Equally good for fine or heavy work. ☞ DENTISTRY in all its branches skillfully attended to, and satisfaction guaranteed.

GEORGE S. IRISH,
PHOTOGRAPHER,
MAKES ALL KINDS OF PHOTOGRAPHS FROM
Cartes-de-Visite to Life-Size Portraits,
AMBROTYPES, &c.
PORCELAIN PICTURES and Copies of all kinds, and a full assortment of PICTURE FRAMES. All work WARRANTED. Don't forget the place,
Cor. GLEN and EXCHANGE Sts.,
(Over Coolidge's store,)
GLEN'S FALLS.

M. W. AMER,
Under Cosgrove's Opera House,
GLEN STREET,
GLEN'S FALLS, N. Y.,
MANUFACTURER OF

HARNESS
OF EVERY DESCRIPTION. ALSO, DEALER IN
TRUNKS, BAGS, BLANKETS,
WHIPS, ROBES, &c.
A good assortment of the above goods constantly on hand, to be sold cheap for Cash.

Go to JOUBERT & WHITE'S for the latest styles of Open Buggies.

Call and examine before purchasing elsewhere. WHITE & PEARSALL, Glen's Falls.

The Place to buy Clothing Cheap is at WAIT'S.
The Latest Styles of HATS and CAPS at WAIT'S. (See page 81.)

TO SECURE PUBLIC LANDS. 157

[ALL-printed matter (except single copies of newspapers, magazines, and periodicals to regular subscribers,) sent via overland mail, is to be charged at LETTER POSTAGE rates.]

Any word or communication, whether by printing, writing, marks, or signs upon the cover or wrapper of a newspaper, pamphlet, magazine, or other printed matter, other than the name or address of the person to whom it is to be sent, and the date when the subscription expires, subjects the package to letter postage.

LETTER POSTAGE TO FOREIGN COUNTRIES.—For each half ounce: To England, Ireland and Scotland, 6 cts.; to France and Algeria, by French mails, 15 cts., quarter ounce. By the Bremen or Hamburg mails, the postage to Bremen and Hamburg is 10 cts.; to Frankfort and Wurtemburg, 15 cts.; to the German States, Prussia, Austria, and its States, and Lombardy, 15 cts.; to the Sardinian States, 23 cts.; to Papal States, 28 cts; to the Two Sicilies, 22 cts.; to Denmark, 20 cts.; to Sweden, 33 cts.; to Norway, 38 cts.; to Russia, 29 cts. By the Prussian closed mails, or by French mail, the postage to these countries is higher. The prepayment of letters to them, excepting to the Two Sicilies, is optional; as also to Canada and the British North American States, where the postage is 10 cts. under 3,000 miles, and 15 cts. over. To the following, postage must be prepaid: To British West Indies, Aspinwall, Panama, and Mexico, 10 cts. under 2,500 miles, 20 cts. over; to New Granada, 18 cts.; to Peru, 22 cts.; to Ecuador, Bolivia, and Chili, 34 cts.; to Sandwich Islands, New South Wales, and China, by mail to San Francisco, thence by private ship, 10 cts.; to China and Australia via England, 33 and 45 cts., via Marseilles, 35 and 57 cts.

To Secure Public Lands.

In order to acquire title to public lands, the following steps must be taken:

1. Application must be made to the Register of the district land office in which the land desired may be situated.

A list of all the land offices in the United States is furnished by the Department, with the seats of the different offices, where it is the duty of the Register and Receiver to be in attendance, and give proper facilities and information to persons desirous of obtaining lands.

The minimum price of ordinary public lands is $1.25 per acre. The even or reserved sections falling within railroad grants are increased to double the minimum price, being $2.50 per acre.

Lands once offered at public sale, and not afterwards kept out of market by reservation, or otherwise, so as to prevent free competition, may be entered or located.

2. By the applicant filing with the Register his written application describing the tract, with its area; the Register will then certify to the Receiver whether the land is vacant, with its price; and when found to be so, the applicant must pay that price per acre, or may locate the same with land warrant, and thereafter the Receiver will give him a "duplicate receipt," which he is required to surrender previous to the delivery to him

Bic yer Cloze ov W. A. WILKINS. (See page 96.)

PAPER of all Kinds, by the Case, Ream or Quire, at BENDER'S, 73 State Street, Albany.

158   FARMERS' ALMANAC.

DR. Z. COTTON,
Surgeon Dentist
Corner Pearl and Main Sts.
CAMBRIDGE, WASHINGTON CO., N. Y.

NEW YORK STORE.
SCHOOLHOUSE & OPPENHIMER,
FORT EDWARD, N. Y.
WHOLESALE AND RETAIL DEALERS IN
Fancy and Staple
DRY GOODS.
Cloaks and Shawls, Black and Fancy Silks, Furs, Trimmings, Fancy Goods, Carpets, Hats and Caps, Boots and Shoes, Ready-made Clothing, &c.
Our Motto—Not to be Undersold.

W. P. BARTON,
MANUFACTURER AND DEALER IN

Rosewood, Mahogany, Walnut, Oak, Chestnut and Painted

Furniture,
In Large Variety and Cheap as the Cheapest.

ALSO CONSTANTLY ON HAND,

PATENT METALLIC BURIAL CASES & CASKETS,
Wood Caskets and Coffins, all Sizes and Prices,

PLATES, HANDLES, ROBES, SHROUDS,
And everything needed in the Undertaking Business.

GOODS DELIVERED FREE OF CHARGE.

W. P. BARTON, Cambridge, N. Y.

Superior inducements at WHITE & PEARSALL'S, Glen's Falls.

GARRETT, Dentist, Bank Building, Glen's Falls, N. Y.

HATS and CAPS can always be found at WAIT'S.
Get a HOWE MACHINE and be happy, at WAIT'S. (See page 81.)

LAW MAXIMS. 159

of the patent, which may be had either by application for it to the Register or to the General Land Office.

3. If the tract has not been offered at public sale, it is not liable to ordinary private entry, but may be secured by a party legally qualified, upon his compliance with the requirements of the pre-emption laws of the 4th September, 1841, and 3d March, 1843; and after such party shall have made actual settlement for such a length of time as will show he designs it for his permanent home, and is acting in good faith, building a house and residing therein, he may proceed to the district land office, establish his pre-emption claim according to law, by proving his actual residence and cultivation, and showing that he is otherwise within the purview of these acts. Then he can enter the land at $1.25, either in cash or with bounty land warrant, unless the premises should be $2.50 acre lands. In that case the whole purchase-money can be paid in cash, or one-half in cash, the residue with a bounty land warrant.

4. But if parties legally qualified desire to obtain title under the Homestead Act of 20th May, 1862, they can do so on complying with the Department Circular, dated 30th October, 1862.

5. The law confines Homestead entries to surveyed lands; and although, in certain States and Territories noted in the subjoined list, pre-emptors may go on land before survey, yet they can only establish their claim after return of survey, but must file their pre-emption declaration within three months after receipt of official plat, at the local land-office where the settlement was made before survey. Where, however, it was made after survey, the claimant must file within three months after date of settlement; and where actual residence and cultivation have been long enough to show that the claimant has made the land his permanent home, he can establish his claim and pay for the same at any time before the date of the public sale of lands within the range in which his settlement may fall.

6. All unoffered surveyed lands not acquired under pre-emption, homestead, or otherwise, under express legal sanction, must be offered at public sale under the President's Proclamation, and struck off to the highest bidder, as required by act of April 24, 1820.

Law Maxims.

Any person who voluntarily becomes an agent for another, and in that capacity obtains information to which as a stranger he could have had no access, is bound in subsequent dealing with his principal, as purchaser of the property that formed the subject of his agency, to communicate such information.

When a house is rendered untenantable in consequence of improvements made on the adjoining lot, the owner of such cannot recover damages, because it is presumed that he had knowledge of the approaching danger in time to protect himself from it.

A person who has been led to sell goods by means of false pretenses, cannot recover them from one who has purchased them in good faith from the fraudulent vendor.

W. A. Wilkins sells Bully Cloze Cheaper nor anybody elts.

Go to P. H. COREY'S, GLEN'S FALLS, for HOOP SKIRTS, CORSETS, GLOVES, HOSIERY, &c.

A Full Line of Hats, Caps and Umbrellas at WHITE & PEARSALL'S, Glen' Falls.

FEDERAL STREET MARBLE WORKS,

Cor. N. SECOND ST., Nearly opp. Railroad Bridge.

TROY, N. Y.

PETER GRANT.

Mantles of Italian and American Marble.
GRATES FOR HARD OR SOFT COAL.
MONUMENTS AND HEADSTONES,
Of Marble, Granite, and Free-Stone.
PLAIN AND ORNAMENTAL TILING, CABINET AND PLUMBERS' SLABS, SOAP STONES, &c.
CALCINED PLASTER AND MARBLE DUST.

THE NEW HOME COMFORT.

MANUFACTURED AND FOR SALE BY MORRISON & COLWELL,

No. 269 RIVER STREET, TROY, N. Y.

PATENT HOT-AIR DRAFT COOKING STOVE,

The Best Baking Stove in the World. It is very Economical in Fuel and keeps a Continuous Fire. It is adapted for either Wood or Coal, and has a Patent Dump Grate.

For Lumber Wagons go to JOUBERT & WHITE'S, Glen's Falls.

LAW MAXIMS. 161

An agreement by the holder of a note to give the principal debtor time for payment, without depriving himself of the right to sue, does not discharge the surety.

A seller of goods who accepts, at the time of sale, the note of a third party, not endorsed by the buyer, in payment, cannot in case the note is not paid, hold the buyer responsible for the value of the goods.

A day-book copied from a "blotter" in which charges are first made, will not be received in evidence as a book of original entries.

A bidder at a Sheriff's sale may retract his bid at any time before the property is knocked down to him, whatever may be the conditions of the sale.

Acknowledgment of debt to a stranger does not preclude the operation of the statute.

The fruits and grass on the farm or garden of an intestate descend to the heir.

A deposit of money in bank by a husband, in the name of his wife, survives to her.

Money paid on Sunday contracts may be recovered.

A debtor may give preference to one creditor over another, unless fraud or special legislation can be proved.

When A consigns goods to B to sell on commission, and B delivers them to C, in payment of his own antecedent debts, A can recover their value.

A finder of property is compelled to make diligent inquiry for the owner thereof, and to restore the same. If, on finding such property, he attempts to conceal such fact, he may be prosecuted for larceny.

A discharge under the insolvent laws of one State will not discharge the insolvent from a contract made with a citizen of another State.

When a person contracts to build a house, and is prevented by sickness from finishing it, he can recover for the part performed, if such part is beneficial to the other party.

Permanent erections and fixtures, made by a mortgagor after the execution of the mortgage upon land conveyed by it, become a part of the mortgaged premises.

If any person puts a fence on or plows the land of another, he is liable for trespass whether the owner has sustained injury or not.

When land trespassed upon is occupied by a tenant, he alone can bring the action.

The liability of an innkeeper is not confined to personal baggage, but extends to all the property of the guest that he consents to receive.

The deed of a minor is not absolutely void. The court is authorized to judge, from the instrument, whether it is void or not, according to its terms being favorable or unfavorable to the interests of the minor.

Money paid voluntarily in any transaction, with a knowlege of the facts, cannot be recovered.

In all cases of special contract for services, except in the case of a minor, the plaintiff can recover only the amount stipulated in the contract.

Insurance against fire, by lightning or otherwise, does not cover loss by lightning when there is no combustion.

A person entitling himself to a reward offered for lost property, has a lien upon the property for the reward; but only when a definite reward is offered.

The defendant in a suit must be served with process; but service of such process upon his wife, even in his absence from the State, is not, in the absence of statutory provisions, sufficient.

Custom Work done better at WILKINS' than elsewhere.

E. H. BENDER, 73 State Street, Albany, Manufactures his own
BLANK BOOKS, and Sells the CHEAPEST and BEST.

FARMERS' ALMANAC.

ALL READ AND REMEMBER!
That you can find, at

HAWKINS & PORTER'S,
As complete an assortment of

DRY GOODS
As can be found north of the city.

DON'T PURCHASE UNTIL YOU SEE THEIR STOCK!

They have Bleached and Brown Muslins, Denims, Tickings, Table Linens, Napkins, Counterpanes, Flannels, Cassimeres, Coatings, Beavers, Broadcloths, Tailors' Trimmings; everything in Dress Goods, from ten cent Calicos to French and Irish Poplins; Velveteens, Paisley and Woolen Shawls; Hand-Knit Hoods, Shawls, Scarfs, Waists, &c.; Laces and Embroideries, Lace Collars and Handkerchiefs, Ladies' and Gents' Wrappers and Drawers, Harris' Seamless Kids, and Winter Gloves for Ladies, Gents and Children; Buckskin Mittens and Gloves, Oil Shades, Lace and Embroidered Curtains, Gilt Cornice, Wall Papers, Stationery, a large stock of Notions, Ribbons and Dress Trimmings, Zephyr Worsteds at wholesale and retail, and many goods not here mentioned. Also, AGENTS FOR THE HOWE SEWING MACHINE.

EAST MAIN STREET,
CAMBRIDGE, N. Y.

WILLIAM POWELL,
DEALER IN

DRY GOODS, NOTIONS, GROCERIES,
CROCKERY, &c.
CHURCH ST., HOOSIC FALLS, N. Y.

INSURANCE.
By T. POTTER, Agent,
GLEN'S FALLS, N. Y.
(*Office over the Post Office.*)

In any of the following-named first-class Companies, to any amount desired, at as low rate as any responsible Companies. All losses promptly and liberally adjusted at this Agency.

Company		CAPITAL.	ASSETS.
Ætna Fire Insurance Co. of Hartford, Conn.		$3,000,000 00	$5,500,000 00
Niagara " New York		1,000,000 00	1,400,000 00
North American Fire Insurance Co. of New York		500,000 00	800,000 00
Hanover " "		400,000 00	720,000 00
Republic " "		300,000 00	700,000 00
Germania " "		500,000 00	1,000,000 00
Commerce " Albany		400,000 00	700,000 00
Springfield " Springfield, Mass.		500,000 00	1,000,000 00
Western Fire and Canal Insurance " Buffalo		300,000 00	700,000 00
Continental Fire Insurance Co. of New York		500,000 00	2,250,000 00
Policies issued in this Co. with participation in the profits of the Co., which gives the insured their insurance at about one-half the usual cost.			
Travelers Life and Accidental Insurance Co.		500,000 00	1,300,000 00
Charter Oak Life Insurance Co.		200,000 00	7,000,000 00
Railway Passengers Assurance Co.		300,000 00	400,000 00

Teeth inserted on Rubber Plate at GARRETT'S, Glen's Falls.

For Satchels, Rubber and Oil Clothing go to WHITE & PEARSALL'S, Glen's Falls.

Gents' FURNISHING GOODS, at WAIT'S One Price Store.
Ladies' FURS, in great variety, at WAIT'S. (See page 81.)

GOVERNMENT LAND MEASURE.

The measure of damages in trespass for cutting timber, is its value as a chattel on the land where it was felled, and not the market price of the lumber manufactured.

All cattle found at large upon any public road, can be driven by any person to the public pound.

Any dog chasing, barking, or otherwise threatening a passer-by in any street, lane, road, or other public thoroughfare, may be lawfully killed for the same.

A contract negotiated by mail is formed when notice of acceptance of the offer is duly deposited in the post-office, properly addressed. This rule applies, although the party making the offer expressly requires that if it is accepted, speedy notice of acceptance shall be given him.

The date of an instrument is so far a material part of it, that an alteration of the date by the holder after execution, makes the instrument void.

A person may contract to labor for another during life, in consideration of receiving his support; but his creditors have the right to inquire into the intention with which such arrangement is made, and it will be set aside if entered into to deprive them of his future earnings.

A watch will not pass under a bequest of "wearing apparel," nor of "household furniture and articles for family use."

An innkeeper is liable for the death of an animal in his possession, but may free himself from liability by showing that the death was not occasioned by negligence on his part.

Notice to the agent of a company is notice to the company.

When notice of protest is properly sent by mail, it may be sent by the mail of the day of the dishonor, if not, it must be mailed for the mail of the next day; except that if there is none, or it closes at an unseasonably early hour, then notice must be mailed in season for the next possible mail.

When the seller of goods accepts at the time of the sale, the note of a third person, unindorsed by the purchaser, in payment, the presumption is that the payment was intended to be absolute; and though the note should be dishonored, the purchaser will not be liable for the value of the goods.

When one has been induced to sell goods by means of false pretences, he cannot recover them from one who has bona fide purchased and obtained possession of them from the fraudulent vendor.

If a party bound to make a payment use due diligence to make a tender, but through the payee's absence from home is unable to find him or any agent authorized to take payment for him, no forfeiture will be incurred through his failure to make a tender.

GOVERNMENT LAND MEASURE.—A township, 36 sections, each a mile square.

A section, 640 acres.

A quarter section, half a mile square, 160 acres.

An eighth section, half a mile long, north and south, and a quarter of a mile wide, 80 acres.

A sixteenth section, a quarter of a mile square, 40 acres.

The sections are numbered from one to thirty-six, commencing at the northeast corner.

The sections are all divided in quarters, which are named by the cardinal points, as in section one. The quarters are divided in the same way. The description of a 40 acre lot would read: The south half of the west half of

W. A. WILKINS' Cheap Clothing Store, established 1859.

Latest styles Bonnets, Jockeys, and Boys' and Infants' Caps and Hoods, at COREY'S, Glen's Falls.

164   *FARMERS' ALMANAC.*

A. ORR, JR.
PHOTOGRAPH GALLERY.

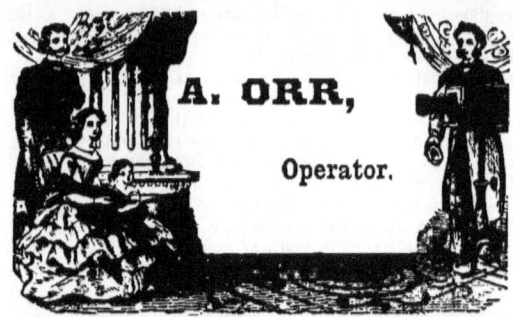

A. ORR, Operator.

LARGE IMPERIAL PHOTOGRAPHS

Finished in Iuk or Colors, and satisfaction guaranteed.

The Card Imperial,

Latest style of Picture, and calculated to display the most elaborate dress

THE PORCELAIN PICTURES

Are superb, and words cannot be found to express their delicacy.

Enlarged Copies from Old Pictures

Are done in Ink or Colors, and made equal to those sat for.

Pictures executed EQUALLY AS WELL in cloudy weather, except of Children.

Paticular attention given to taking **BABIES' PICTURES** without their getting cross.

The Negatives from which your Picture is taken will be preserved.

A large assortment of Photograph Frames always on hand.

Traphagan's Buildings, Ridge Street,
GLEN'S FALLS, N. Y.

Orders for Custom Work promptly attended to at WHITE & PEARSALL'S, Glen's Falls.

Who got the First Premium on Carriages? Joubert & White.

DECIMAL SYSTEM OF WEIGHTS AND MEASURES. 165

the southwest quarter of section 1 in township 24, north of range 7 west, or as the case might be; and sometimes will fall short, and sometimes over-run the number of acres it is supposed to contain.

DISCOUNT AND PREMIUM.—When a person buys an article for $1,00—20 per cent off, (or discount,) and sells it again for $1,00, he makes a profit of 25 per cent. on his investment. Thus: He pays 80 cents and sells for $1,00—a gain of 20 cents, or 25 per cent. of 80 cents. And for any transaction where the sale or purchase of gold, silver, or currency is concerned, the following rules will apply in all cases:

Rule 1st.—To find premium when discount is given: Multiply 100 by rate of discount and divide by 100, less rate of discount.

Rule 2d.—To find discount when premium is given. Multiply the rate of interest by 100, and divide by 100, plus the rate of premium.

Suppose A has $140 in currency, which he wishes to exchange for gold, when gold is 27 per cent. premium, how much gold should he receive? In this case the premium is given, consequently we must find the discount on A's currency and subtract it from the $140, as per rule 2d, showing the discount to be a trifle more than 21 per cent., and that he should receive $110,00 in gold.

5 per cent. Discount allows			†5¼ per ct. Premium or profit.		
10 " "	"	"	†11 "	"	"
15 " "	"	"	†17½ "	"	"
20 " "	"	"	25 "	"	"
25 " "	"	"	33⅓ "	"	"
30 " "	"	"	*43 "	"	"
40 " "	"	"	66⅔ "	"	"
50 " "	"	"	100 "	"	"

☞ A dagger (†) denotes the profits to be a fraction more than specified. A (*) denotes profits to be a fraction less than specified.

The Decimal System of Weights and Measures.

STANDARDS.—In every system of Weights and Measures, it is necessary to have what are called *"Standards,"* as the pound, yard, gallon, &c., to be divided and multiplied into smaller and larger parts and denominations. The definition and construction of these Standards involve philosophical and scientific principles of a somewhat abstruse character, and are made and procured by the legislative department of the government. The nominal Standards in the new system are the METER, the ARE, the LITER, and the GRAM. The only *real* Standard, the one by which all the other Standards are measured, and from which the system derives its name of "Metric" is the METER.

THE METER.—Is used for all measures of length, distance, breadth, depth, height, &c., and was intended to be, and is very nearly, one ten-

BANKS, INSURANCE COMPANIES, and all other Companies
Supplied at BENDER'S, 73 State Street, Albany.

166   FARMERS' ALMANAC.

NUTTING, HULL & CO.
AGRICULTURAL IMPLEMENTS,
MACHINES,
SEEDS & FERTILIZERS.

357 & 359 RIVER ST.,   TROY, N. Y.

WHITE & PEARSALL allows no one to undersell them.   Glen's Falls.

AGENTS FOR THE
Buckeye Mower and Reaper,
AMERICAN HAY TEDDER,
EDDY'S PLOWS, CULTIVATORS, &c.
A FULL LINE OF
AMERICAN AND FOREIGN HARDWARE,
House Trimmings, Cutlery, &c.
MANUFACTURERS OF
Wire Cloth, Sieves, Coal & Sand Screens,
Moulders' Riddles, &c., &c.

Teeth inserted on Gold Plate at Garrett's, Glen's Falls.

WEIGHTS AND MEASURES. 167

millionth of the distance on the earth's surface from the equator to the pole. It is about 39⅜ inches, or 3 feet, 3 inches and 3 eighths, and is to be substituted for the yard.

THE ARE.—Is a surface whose side is ten Meters, and is equal to 100 square Meters or about 4 square rods.

THE LITER.—Is the unit for measuring solids and capacity, and is equal to the contents of a cube whose edge is one-tenth of a Meter. It is about equal to one quart, and is a standard in cubic, dry and liquid measures.

☞ A cubic Meter (or Kiloliter) is called a *stere*, and is also used as a standard in certain cubic measures.

THE GRAM.—Is the unit of *weight*, and is the weight of a cube of pure water, each edge of the cube being one one-hundreth of a Meter. It is about equal to 15½ grains. It is intended as the standard in *all* weights, and with its divisions and multiples, to supersede the use of what are now called Avoirdupois, Apothecaries and Troy weights.

Each of the foregoing Standards is divided decimally, and larger units are also formed by multiples of 10, 100, &c. The successive subordinate parts are designated by the prefixes Deci, Centi and Milli, the successive multiples by Deka, Hecto, Kilo and Myria, each having its own numerical signification.

The terms used may, at first sight, have a formidable appearance, seem difficult to pronounce, and to retain in memory, and to be, therefore, objectionable; but with a little attention and use, the apprehended difficulty will be found more apparent than real, as has been abundantly proved by experience. The importance, also, of conformity in the use of commercial terms, on the part of the United States, with the practice of the many nations in which the system, *with its present nomenclature*, has already been adopted, must greatly overbalance the comparatively slight objection alluded to.

TABLE OF WEIGHTS OF GRAIN, SEEDS, &C.—*According to the Laws of New York:*

Barley weighs................................	48 lbs.	per bushel.
Beans "	62 "	"
Buckwheat weighs............................	48 "	"
Clover Seed "	60 "	"
Corn "	58 "	"
Flax Seed* "	55 "	"
Oats "	32 "	"
Peas "	60 "	"
Potatoes "	60 "	"
Rye "	56 "	"
Timothy Seed "	44 "	"
Wheat "	60 "	"

* Flax Seed, by custom, weighs 56 lbs. per bushel.

TO MEASURE GRAIN IN A BIN.—Find the number of cubic feet, from which deduct *one-fifth*. The remainder is the number of bushels—allowing, however, one bushel extra to every 224. Thus in a remainder of 224 there would be 225 bushels. In a remainder of 448 there would be 450 bushels, &c.

Ding, dong, bell! WILKINS is bound to sell. (See p. 96.)

CAPACITY OF CISTERNS OR WELLS.—Tabular view of the number of gallons contained in the clear, between the brick work for each ten inches of depth:

Diameter		Gallons	Diameter		Gallons
2	feet equals	19	8	feet equals	313
2½	"	30	8½	"	353
3	"	44	9	"	396
3½	"	60	9½	"	461
4	"	78	10	"	489
4½	"	97	11	"	592
5	"	122	12	"	705
5½	"	148	13	"	827
6	"	176	14	"	959
6½	"	207	15	"	1101
7	"	240	20	"	1958
7½	"	275	25	"	3059

How to do Business.

Give us the straightforward, fearless, enterprising man for business—one who is worth a dozen of those who, when any thing is to be done, stop, falter, and hesitate, and are never ready to take a decided stand! * * * * * Make up your mind to be firm, resolute, and industrious, if you desire prosperity. There is good in the saying of the Apostle: Whatsoever thy hand findeth to do, do it with all thy might.—*Merchant's Magazine.*

Truth and equity are the foundations of legitimate trade. Any business structure not based on these principles, totters to its fall; and it deserves to fall. There is a good deal of loose morality abroad in reference to trade. Duplicity is supposed to be necessary, and therefore justifiable. "A fair business transaction," as it is called, is not always a moral or a just transaction. It means a bargain in which there are no grounds for an action at law, but not always an honorable bargain. This is entirely wrong. We do not believe that a dishonest or dishonorable trader is ever permanently successful. Honesty is not only a moral duty, but it is also "the best policy." It is one of the elements of all true success. And it is not enough that you are honest, you must also be honorable. "Although a man cannot be an honorable man without being an honest man, yet a man may be strictly honest without being honorable. Honesty refers to pecuniary affairs; honor refers to principles and feelings. You may defraud no man, you may pay your debts punctually, and yet act dishonorably. You act dishonorably when you give your correspondents a worse opinion of your rivals in trade than you know they deserve. You act dishonorably when you sell your commodities at less than their real value, in order to get away your neighbor's customers. You act dishonorably when you purchase at higher than the market price, in order that you may raise the market on another buyer. You act dishonorably in every case wherein your external conduct is at variance with your real opinions."—*J. W. Gillart.*

HOW TO DO BUSINESS.

"'The tricks of trade,' whatever may be their apparent advantages," truly remarks the *Evening Bulletin*, "impair confidence, and, in the end, injure those who practice them far more than they benefit them. It is a short-sighted, as well as a guilty policy to swerve, under any circumstances, from those great principles which are of universal and everlasting obligation. Let a man maintain his integrity at all times, and he will be satisfied that there is a blessing in it, and a blessing flowing from it, and a blessing all around it."

Without diligence, or a steady application to whatever is undertaken, it is vain to hope for any decided success. Mere fitful activity accomplishes little. To well-directed and persevering industry nothing is denied. The man of business must be a worker.

1. The most trifling actions that affect a man's credit are to be regarded. The sound of your hammer at five in the morning, or nine at night, heard by a creditor, makes him easy six months longer; but if he sees you at the billiard-table, or hears your voice at a tavern, when you should be at work, he sends for his money the next day, demands it before he can receive it in a lump.—*Franklin.*

2. The skill of a merchant or tradesman is exhibited in the combination of the greatest profit with the least expense; and he will make the most money who calmly looks from the "beginning to the end," rather than to be attracted by any intermediate point, however profitable it may appear. —*Hunt.*

3. As a first and leading principle, let every transaction be of that pure and honest character that you would not be ashamed to have appear before the whole world as clearly as to yourself. It is of the highest consequence that you should not only cultivate correct principles, but that you should place your standard so high as to require great vigilance in living up to it.— *Lawrence.*

4. During the first seven years of my business, I never allowed a bill against me to stand unsettled over the Sabbath. If the purchase of goods was made at auction on Saturday, and delivered to me, I always examined and settled the bill by note or credit, so that in case I was not on duty on Monday, there would be no trouble for my boys; thus keeping my business *before* me, instead of allowing it to drive me.—*Lawrence.*

5. Your duty as tradesmen is so to frame your method of business that it shall serve the interests of the public in the highest possible degree; and then, as to gaining the public eye, why, trust to sterling industry, to the intrinsic excellence of your system, and, above all, to the blessing of Providence for as much "custom" as will suffice for your legitimate ends. In competing with others for public favor, no expedient should be permitted that will not bear close examination. Better fail of success, than fall into improper rivalry.—*Rev. William Arthur.*

6. Undertake not what you can not perform, but be careful to keep your promise —*Washington.*

7. John Wesley, in his powerful sermon on the use of money, lays down these three rules—Make all you can; save all you can; give all you can. To make without saving, is useless and absurd. To save without giving, is covetousness and idolatry. To make and then save, is wise. To save and then give, is Christian.—*Rev. William Arthur.*

8. In the first place, make up your mind to accomplish whatever you undertake; decide upon some particular employment, and persevere in it. All difficulties are overcome by diligence and assiduity. Be not afraid to

Have your Clothing made at WILKINS'. (See page 96.)

work with your own hands, and diligently too. "A cat in gloves catches no mice." Attend to your own business, and never trust it to another. "A pot that belongs to many is ill stirred and worse boiled." Be frugal. "That which will not make a pot will make a pot lid. Be abstemious. "Who dainties love shall beggars prove." Arise early. "The sleeping fox catches no poultry." Treat every one with respect and civility. "Every thing is gained and nothing lost by courtesy." "Good manners insure success." Never anticipate wealth from any other source than labor. "He who waits for dead men's shoes may have to go for a long time barefoot." And, above all things, "*Nil desperandum;*" for "Heaven helps those who help themselves." If you implicitly follow these precepts, nothing can hinder you from accumulating.—*Hunt.*

9. I made fifteen hundred dollars the first year, and more than four thousand the second. Probably had I made four thousand the first year, I should have failed the second or third year. I practiced a system of rigid economy, and never allowed myself to spend a fourpence for unnecessary objects until I had acquired it.—*Lawrence.*

10. "Commerce is a dirty thing," we have heard literary lips say. Yes, in dirty hands, it is a dirty thing; and in rude hands, a rude thing; and in covetous hands, a paltry, pelfy thing. Nevertheless, it is a thing on which those who despise it are largely dependent.—*Arthur.*

The following, from 11 to 17 inclusive, are from Hunt's "Worth and Wealth:"

11. Be industrious. Everybody knows that industry is the fundamental virtue in the man of business. But it is not every sort of industry which tends to wealth. Many men work hard to do a great deal of business, and after all, make less money than they would if they did less. Industry should be expended in seeing to all the details of business—in the careful finishing up of each separate undertaking, and in the maintenance of such a system as will keep every thing under control.

12. Be economical. This rule, also, is familiar to everybody. Economy is a virtue to be practiced every hour in a great city. It is to be practiced in pence as much as in pounds. A shilling a day saved amounts to an estate in the course of a life. Economy is especially important in the outset of life, until the foundations of an estate are laid. Many men are poor all their days, because, when their necessary expenses were small, they did not seize the opportunity to save a small capital, which would have changed their fortunes for the whole of their lives.

13. Stick to the business in which you are regularly employed. Let speculators make their thousands in a year or day; mind your own regular trade, never turning from it to the right hand or the left. If you are a merchant, a professional man, or a mechanic, never buy lots or stocks unless you have surplus money which you wish to invest. Your own business you understand as well as other men; but other people's business you do not understand. Let your business be some one which is useful to the community. All such occupations possess the elements of profits in themselves, while mere speculation has no such element.

14. Never take great hazards. Such hazards are seldom well balanced by the prospects of profit; and if they were, the habit of mind which is induced is unfavorable, and generally the result is bad. To keep what you have, should be the first rule; to get what you can fairly, the second.

15. Do not be in a hurry to get rich. Gradual gains are the only natural gains; and they who are in haste to be rich, break over sound rules, fall

into temptations and distress of various sorts, and generally fail of their object. There is no use in getting rich suddenly. The man who keeps his business under his control, and saves something from year to year, is always rich. At any rate, he possesses the highest enjoyment which riches are able to afford.

16. Never do business for the sake of doing it, and being counted a great merchant. There is often more money to be made by a small business than a large one; and that business will in the end be most respectable which is most successful. Do not get deeply in debt; but so manage as always, if possible, to have your financial position easy, so that you can turn any way you please.

17. Do not love money extravagantly. We speak here merely with reference to getting rich. In morals, the inordinate love of money is one of the most degrading vices. But the extravagant desire of accumulation induces an eagerness, many times, which is imprudent and so misses its object from too much haste to grasp it.

18. Any business you may have to transact should be done the first opportunity, and finished, if possible, without interruption. Business must not be sauntered and trifled with, and you must not say to it as Felix did to Paul, "At a more convenient season I will speak to thee." The most convenient season for business is the first; but study and business, in some measure, point out their own times, to a man of sense. Business, of any kind, should never be done by halves, but every part of it should be well attended to, for he that does business ill had better not do it at all.—*Chesterfield.*

Valuable Receipts.

CHEMICAL SOAP.—Take 2 pounds sal soda and 1 pound good stone lime (or 2 pounds slacked lime) and boil in 10 quarts of soft water; let it settle; pour off the clear fluid and add 2 pounds of tallow (or its equivalent in soap-grease, ¼ pound borax and ¼ pound of resin, and boil together till the grease is all taken up, then pour into a shallow box, and, when cool, cut into bars. Two hours' boiling will generally be sufficient.

WASHING FLUID.—Take 2 pounds of sal soda, 1 pound good stone lime, and 2½ gallons soft water, and bring to a boil; when settled, pour off the clear fluid into a stone jug, and add 1 ounce of hartshorn and 1 ounce of borax, and keep it tightly corked. After boiling the lime and soda, for either the soap or washing-fluid, pour on water the second time; let it settle, and again pour off for scrubbing, &c.

CEMENT FOR GLASS, CHINA, WOOD, LEATHER, &c.—Take ¼ pound white glue, 1 ounce white lead, dry, and ½ pint soft water; put these in a tin dish, inside an iron kettle filled with water, and boil, stirring with a stick till all is dissolved; then add ¼ pint alcohol, and boil again till well mixed. Put in a bottle, and keep tightly corked. When required for use, set the bottle in a dish of water on the stove, and gradually heat until the cement is dissolved and of the consistency of cream; then apply a thin coating to one edge, put the parts immediately together, pressing firmly for a few moments, and set the article away a day or so to dry. The cement must be quite warm and thin when used; and, in cold weather, slightly warm the article to be mended, enough to take off the chill; otherwise it will get cold before you can get the parts together, and form a thin coating like paper between the joints, in which case it will not stick. In mending wood, and articles that are porous, don't press hard too soon, or you will press all out, except what the pores of the wood will absorb, leaving none to unite the broken surfaces, but press slightly at first, then hard, after a few moments.

FOR WHITENING THE SKIN, AND REMOVING FRECKLES AND TAN.—Take one ounce of borax, two ounces of cologne, one quart of alcohol, and three quarts of rain water. Bathe three times a day in a solution of two teaspoonfuls in two table-spoonfuls of water.

CURE FOR BUNIONS AND CORNS.—The tincture of iodine applied to bunions is said to afford great relief. A strong solution of pearlash, applied to corns, will soften them so that they may be easily drawn out.

TO REMOVE WARTS.—Take ashes made from burnt willow bark, and mix with sweet cider, and apply several times, and they will soon disappear.

CURE FOR CHILBLAINS.—Apply a wash made of 1 part of muriatic acid and 7 parts of water.

TO REMOVE STAINS FROM BROADCLOTH.—Take 1 ounce of pipe-clay, that has been ground fine, and mix it with 12 drops of alcohol, and the same quantity of spirits of turpentine. Whenever you wish to remove any stains from cloth, moisten a little of this mixture and rub it on the spots. Let it remain till dry, then rub it off with a woolen cloth, and the spots will disappear.

O. A. PECK,

PRACTICAL

Cabinet Maker, Upholsterer and Undertaker.

DEALER IN

FURNITURE & CROCKERY,

Spring Beds, Mattresses and Feathers,

CHILDREN'S CARRIAGES, WILLOW WARE, MIRRORS, GLASS,

PICTURE FRAMES, CORD, &C.

ALSO A LARGE ASSORTMENT OF

COFFINS AND CASKETS,

SHROUDS, CAPS, PLATES, &c.

Brick Block, opp. Vermont Hotel, Main St.

FAIRHAVEN, VERMONT.

Joubert & White employs seventeen men at Glen's Falls.

Ready-made Clothing at bargains, at WAIT'S.
For your WEDDING SUITS, go to WAITS. (See page 81.)

VALUABLE RECEIPTS. 173

TO EXTRACT GREASE FROM SILKS, WOOLEN GOODS, PAPER, AND FLOORS.—Grate on them very thick French chalk, (common will answer, but it is not so good,) cover the spots with brown paper, and set on a moderately warm iron, and let it remain till cool. Care must be taken not to have the iron so hot as to scorch or change the color of the cloth. If the grease does not appear to be out, on removing the iron, grate on more chalk, heat the iron again, and put it on. Repeat the process till the grease is entirely out. Strong pearlash water, mixed with sand, or the washing fluid used in washing, will remove grease spots from floors, if well scrubbed.

TO CLEAN PAINT.—Smear a piece of flannel in common whiting, mixed to the consistency of common paste, in warm water. Rub the surface to be cleaned quite briskly, and wash off with pure cold water. Grease spots will, in this way, be almost instantly removed, as well as other filth, and the paint will retain its brilliancy and beauty unimpaired.

TO REMOVE INK STAINS.—As soon as the ink is spilled, take a little milk and saturate the stain, soak it up with a rag, and apply a little more milk, rubbing it well. In a few minutes the ink will be completely removed.

TO REMOVE MILDEW.—Wet the cloth which contains the mildew with soft water; rub it well with white soap, then scrape some fine chalk to powder, and rub it well into the cloth; lay it out on the grass in the sunshine, watching it, to keep it damp with soft water. Repeat the process the next day, and in a few hours the mildew will all disappear.

CURING RANCID BUTTER.—A correspondent of the *Rural Register* gives the following recipe for curing rancid butter : For 100 pounds rancid butter, take 2 pounds fine white powdered sugar ; 2 ounces saltpeter, finely pulverized, and as much fine dairy salt as you wish to add to the butter to make it to your taste. The butter has to be thoroughly washed in cold water before working in the above ingredients. The amount used should be in proportion to the strongness of the butter.

TO MAKE BUTTER YELLOW IN WINTER.—Just before the termination of churning, put in the yolk of eggs, and your butter will be as yellow as gold.

POLISH FOR OLD FURNITURE.—Take 1 pint alcohol; 1 pint linseed oil; 1 ounce powdered gum arabic ; ¼ ounce tincture red saunders ; ¼ ounce bergamot. Put it on with cotton flannel, then rub it hard with another dry piece.

BREAD.—No one thing is of more importance in making bread than thoroughly kneading it. When bread is taken out of the oven hot, never set flat on a table, as it sweats the bottom, and acquires a bad taste from the wood. Take it out of the tins, wrap it in clean linen, and set it up on the end till cool. If it has a thick, hard crust, first wrap it with a wet cloth, then a dry one over it, and let it sweat till it becomes soft.

COMMON PASTE FOR PIES.—Take a quantity of flour proportioned to the number of pies you wish to make, then rub in some lard and salt, and stir it with cold water; then roll it out, and spread on some lard, and scatter over some dry flour, then double it together and cut it to pieces, and roll it to the thickness you wish to use it.

CREAM CRUST.—This is the most healthy pie crust that is made. Take cream, sour or sweet, add salt, and stir in flour to make it stiff; if the cream is sour, add saleratus in proportion of one tea-spoonful to a pint ; if sweet, use very littly saleratus. Mold it as little as you can.

CUSTARDS.—In making custards always avoid stale eggs. Never put

SASH and BONNET RIBBONS, in great variety, at COREY'S, GLEN'S FALLS.

W. A. Wilkins' Cheap Cash Clothing Store, Whitehall, N.Y.

eggs in very hot milk as it will poach them. Always boil custards in a vessel set in boiling water.

PRESERVES, JELLIES, JAMS, AND PICKLES—Brass, iron, and copper kettles should never be used for making preserves. Iron-ware, lined with porcelain or tin, is far preferable, and not subject to the verdigris which acids produce on the others. If obliged to use a brass or copper kettle, scour it perfectly clean, and don't let your preserves stand in it one minute after they are done. It is bad economy to use too little sugar in the preservation of fruit. When it once begins to spoil, it can never be reinstated. Jellies, without sufficient sugar, will not congeal. Preserves, to look clear and handsome, should be made with loaf sugar. Small jars are preferable to large ones in putting away preserves, as frequent exposure to the air is not good. After pouring the preserves into jars, cut several round pieces of paper made to fit the mouth of the jar, and after laying one or two of them over the fruit, pour upon it a tea-spoonful of good brandy; then cover the jar closely with some paper, or bladder-skin, and tie it down in a manner which will entirely exclude the air. If the preserves candy, after being kept a short time, the jar should be placed in a kettle of water, and permitted to boil from half to three-quarters of an hour.

HINTS TO HOUSEKEEPERS.—If your flat-irons are rough and smoky, lay a little fine salt on a flat surface and rub them well; it will prevent them from sticking to anything starched, and make them smooth.

Rub your griddle with fine salt before you grease it, and your cake will not stick.

When walnuts have been kept until the meat is too much dried to be good, let them stand in milk and water eight hours, and dry them, and they will be as fresh as when new.

It is a good plan to keep your different kinds of pieces tape, thread, &c., in separate bags, and there is no time lost in looking for them.

Oats straw is best for filling of beds, and it is well to change it as often as once a year.

Cedar chests are best to keep flannels, for cloth moths are never found in them. Red cedar chips are good to keep in drawers, wardrobes, closets, trunks, &c., to keep out moths.

When cloths have acquired an unpleasant odor by being kept from the air, charcoal, laid in the folds, will soon remove it.

If black dresses have been stained, boil a handful of fig-leaves in a quart of water, and reduce it to a pint. A sponge dipped in this liquid and rubbed upon them will entirely remove stains from crapes, bombazines, &c.

In laying up furs for summer, lay a tallow candle in or near them, and danger from worms will be obviated.

To prevent metals from rusting, melt together three parts of lard and one of resin, and apply a very thin coating. It will preserve Russia iron stoves and grates from rusting during summer, even in damp situations. The effect is equally good on brass, copper, steel, &c.

POISONS AND THEIR ANTIDOTES.—It not unfrequently happens that serious and distressing results are occasioned by the accidental employment of poisons; and we herewith submit a compendious list of the more common poisons, and the remedies for them most likely to be at hand:

Acids.—These cause great heat and sensation of burning pain, from the mouth down to the stomach. Remedies: Magnesia, soda, pearlash or soap dissolved in water; then use stomach-pump or emetics.

Alkalies.—The best remedy is ginger.

Teeth inserted on Silver Plate at Garrett's, Glen's Falls.

Ammonia.—Remedy : Lemon-juice or ginger ; afterward milk and water, or flaxseed tea.
Arsenic.—Remedies : In the first place evacuate the stomach ; then give the white of eggs, lime-water, or chalk and water, charcoal, and the preparations of iron, particularly hydrate.
Lead.—White lead and sugar of lead. Remedies : Alum, cathartic, such as castor oil and Epsom salts especially.
Creosote.—White of eggs and emetics.
Mushrooms, when Poisonous.—Give emetics, and then plenty of vinegar and water, with dose of either, if handy.
Laudanum.—Same as opium.
Nitrate of Potash, or Saltpeter.—Give emetics, then copious draughts of flaxseed tea, milk and water, and other soothing drinks.
Prussic Acid.—When there is time, administer chlorine in the shape of soda or lime ; hot brandy and water. Hartshorn and turpentine are also useful.
Snake-bites, etc.—Apply, immediately, strong hartshorn, and take it internally. Also give sweet oil and stimulants freely. Apply a ligature tight above the part bitten, and then apply a cupping glass.
Tobacco.—First an emetic, then a stringent tea, then stimulants.
In almost all cases of poisons, emetics are highly useful, and of these one of the very best, because most prompt and ready, is the common mustard flour or powder, one tea-spoonful of which, stirred up in warm water, may be given every five minutes, until free vomiting can be obtained.
Emetics and warm demulcent drinks, such as milk and water, flaxseed or slippery-elm tea, chalk-water, etc., should be administered without delay. The subsequent management of the case will, of course, be left to a physician.

Receipts for Horses.

COUGH BALLS FOR HORSES.—Pulverized ipecac, three-fourths ounce ; camphor, two ounces ; squills, one-half ounce. Mix with honey to form into mass, and divide into eight balls. Give one every morning.
FEVER BALL.—Emetic tartar and camphor, each one-half ounce ; nitre, two ounces. Mix with linseed meal and molasses to make eight balls. Give one twice a day.
WORM BALL.—Assafœtida, four ounces ; gentian, two ounces ; strong mercurial ointment, one ounce. Make into mass with honey. Divide into sixteen balls. Give one or more every morning.
PURGATIVE BALL.—Aloes, one ounce ; cream tartar, and castile soap one-quarter ounce. Mix with molasses to make a ball.
DIURETIC BALLS.—Castile soap scraped fine, powdered rosin, each three teaspoonfuls ; powdered nitre, four teaspoonfuls ; oil of juniper, one small teaspoonful ; honey, a sufficient quantity to make into a ball.
CATHARTIC POWDER.—To cleanse out horses in the spring, making them sleek and healthy—black sulphuret of antimony, nitre and sulphur, each equal parts. Mix well together, and give a tablespoonful every morning.
LINIMENT FOR SPRAINS, SWELLINGS, ETC.—Aqua ammonia, spirits camphor, each two ounces ; oil origanum and laudanum, each one-half ounce. Mix.
LOTION FOR MANGE.—Boil two ounces tobacco in one quart water ; strain ; add sulphur and soft soap, each two ounces.

Buy your Clothing of W. A. Wilkins, Whitehall, N. Y.

BLANK BOOKS, MEMORANDUM and PASS BOOKS, on hand and made to order, by BENDER, 73 State Street, Albany.

American and Foreign Patent Offices.

MUNN & CO., 37 Park row, have been established as Solicitors of American and European Patents nearly a quarter of a century, and during that time they have taken out nearly one-third of all the patents issued by the United States Patent Office, and fully three-fourths of all the patents taken by American inventors in Europe. According to a careful register, MUNN & CO. have made 30,000 preliminary examinations at the Patent Office into the novelty of alleged new inventions. This great experience is of vast importance to all inventors who contemplate to apply for patents, and who need counsel in matters connected with patents.

There is no branch of professional business connected with the Patent Office which MUNN & CO. are not prepared by long experience to attend to promptly and efficiently.

We could refer, if necessary, to thousands of patentees who have had the benefit of their advice and assistance, also to many of the principal business men in this and other cities, also to members of Congress and prominent citizens throughout the country; but they will simply append the testimonial letters addressed to them by Judges Mason and Holt, and the Hon. Mr. Bishop, who successively filled the office of Commissioner of Patents with much acceptance:

Messrs. MUNN & CO.: I take pleasure in stating that while I held the office of Commissioner of Patents, more than one-fourth of all the business of the office came through your hands. I have no doubt that the public confidence thus indicated has been fully deserved, as I have always observed, in all your intercourse with the office, a marked degree of promptness, skill, and fidelity to the interests of your employers.

Yours, very truly,
CHAS. MASON.

Messrs. MUNN & CO.: It affords me much pleasure to bear testimony to the able and efficient manner in which you discharged your duties as Solicitors of Patents, while I had the honor of holding the office of Commissioner. Your business was very large, and you sustained (and I doubt not justly deserved) the reputation of energy, marked ability, and uncompromising fidelity in performing your professional engagements.

Very respectfully, your obedient servant,
J. HOLT.

Messrs. MUNN & CO.: Gentlemen—It gives me much pleasure to say that, during the time of my holding the office of Commissioner of Patents, a very large proportion of the business of inventors before the Patent Office was transacted through your agency, and that I have ever found you faithful and devoted to the interests of your clients, as well as eminently qualified to perform the duties of Patent Attorneys with skill and accuracy.

Very respectfully, your obedient servant,
WM. D. BISHOP.

In order to apply for a Patent, send a model by express to MUNN & CO., 37 Park row, New York, with the first installment of Government and Stamp fees, $16, with full particulars of the invention. Send for pamphlet containing Law and full instructions, free. Opinions free. SCIENTIFIC AMERICAN—the best Illustrated Weekly Mechanical paper, $3 a year. Specimen copies of the paper sent free.

Don't buy your Buggies till you see Joubert & White.

Go to WHITE & PEARSALL'S for a Complete Outfit in Clothing at a Bargain, Glen's Falls.

How to Obtain Patents.

The first inquiry that presents itself to one who has made any improvement or discovery is: "Can I obtain a Patent?" A *positive* answer can only be had by presenting a complete application for a Patent to the Commissioner of Patents. An application consists of a Model, Drawings, Petition, Oath, and full Specification. Various official rules and formalities must also be observed. The efforts of the inventor to do all this business himself are generally without success. After a season of great perplexity and delay, he is usually glad to seek the aid of persons experienced in patent business, and have all the work done over again. The best plan is to solicit proper advice at the beginning.

If the parties consulted are honorable men, the inventor may safely confide his ideas to them; they will advise whether the improvement is probably patentable, and will give him all the directions needful to protect his rights.

In many cases it will be advisable, as a measure of prudence, to order a PRELIMINARY EXAMINATION. This consists of a *special search*, made at the U. S. Patent Office, Washington, to ascertain whether, among all the thousands of patents and models there stored, any invention can be found which is similar in character to that of the applicant. On the completion of this special search we send a *written report* of the result to the party concerned, with suitable advice.

If the device has been patented, the time and expense of constructing models, preparing documents, etc., will, in most cases, be saved by means of this search; if the invention has been in part patented, the applicant will be enabled to modify his claims and expectations accordingly.

Many other obvious advantages attend Preliminary Examination, although the strictest search does not always enable the applicant to know absolutely whether a patent will be granted.

For example, applications for patents are sometimes rejected because the Examining Officer finds a description of the alleged invention in some foreign publication; or some other person has been previously rejected on an analogous device; or some other invention, for a similar purpose, partially resembles the applicant's in its construction; or the Government makes an unjust or uncommon decision. Against none of these contingencies does the Preliminary Examination provide.

It will, however, generally inform the applicant whether an improvement similar to his, and used for the same purpose, *has ever been patented in this country.—Munn & Co.*, 37 *Park Row, N. Y.*

Bie yer Cloze ov **W. A. WILKINS.** (See page 96.)

FARMERS

IN THE COUNTIES OF ALBANY, RENSSELAER, WASHINGTON, WARREN, SARATOGA AND SCHENECTADY, N. Y.; AND BENNINGTON AND RUTLAND COUNTIES, VT.

TOWN OF ARGYLE, N. Y.—A. Armstrong, Wm. J. Armitage, J. Armitage, Wm. J. Armstrong, S. Armstrong, Wm. J. Black, A. Bardin, D. Bardin, J. and P. Bryson, Asa and Alex. Bristol, Alex. and G. Bristol, J. and T. Brennon, G. Burgess, Wm. McBani, Danl. Bani, J. Bani, A. Bani, P. J. Bani, W Boyd, P. Bani, David Bani, A. Barkley, J. B. Bani, C. E. Bani, J. McBani, Wm. H. and Christie Bani, H. W. Bardin, J. Beattie, A. Bevereage, H. Barkley, H. Bani, J. H. Bani, J. D. Barkley, W. Black, J. L. Boyd, J. H. Beattie, D. Black, J. F. Bani, J. Bell, J. B. Barkley, W. Chapman, W. Clapp O. Callahan, H. Crawford, B. Carswell, G. Carswell, R. G. Clark, L. Carl, J. S. Crawford, J. S. Craig, W. Christie, W. Congdon, E. Campbell, D. Curtis, W. Cook, W. J. Copeland, D. Conklin, J. Conway, R. Cuthbert, A. Crosier, S. Cornell, J. S. Cornell, J. Duncan, W. H. Dennis, T. M. Dennis, C. Durkee, J. Dennis, M. Durkee, J. Doyle, S. Donaldson jr., J. Donaldson, J. De Wire, E. Dodd, E. Dunn, G. C. Dennis, M. Donivan, B. Donaldson, M. Dorsey, J. and A. Dings, H. Dixon, W. Edgar, W. Ellis, Forsythe, D. Fowler, A. Furgeson, J. Ford, C. F. Fullerton, A. Ferguson, J. H. Ferguson, J. H. France, J. H. Flack, P. French, G. Fenton, A. Foster jr., J. Foster, D. and W. Foster, S. Ferguson, G. Flack, J. Fenton, S. Guthrie, W. Guthrie, A. Gilchrist, W. Gibson, R. Grant, A. Graham, A. Green, J. Guthrie, J. A. Gillis, D. C. Gilchrist, J. L. Gilchrist, A. Gavitt A. Gifford, A. Gilchrist, C. W. Green, W. Gilchrist, T. Gilchrist, J. Gilchrist, B. Gillis, P. Griffin, J. Gillis, J. Graham, J. G. Hall, D. M. Harsha, William Heath, Henry Hughes, W. Hutchinson, T. W. Hopkins, C. M. Hopkins, M. W. Hopkins, J. B. Hopkins, J. M. Hall, J. Henry, P. C. Hitchcock, J. C. Harsha, J. M. Harsha, T. Henry, G. Henry, W. Henry, J. Hall, J. Hall, M. Hall, D. Hall, P. Higgins, J. Harper, R. Hall, G. Hall, C. Hoyer, W. Hawkins, J. Hall, R. Hamilton, R. G. Hall, A. Haggart, J. Hill, W. D. Hall, J. Huggins, R. Huggins, G. M. Hunt, J. R. Harsha, D. Harsha, A. Hanna, W. Hale, J. M. Henry, S. Irvin, J. Irvin, H. Irvin, J. D. Irvin, J. Irvin, J. Kee, A. Ketchum, H. Knickerbacker, J. Knickerbacker, A. Kilmer, S. Kilmer, G. Kilmer, P. Kilmer, and W. Kays, J. Kinney, Jas. King, Jos. King, M. Kinney, T. H. King, J. N. Kenyon, J. Liddle, G. Laumont, J. Lardon, J. Larkin, W. Lendrum, G. Lester, J. L. Lester, S. Lester, D. Lester, W. C. Lant, W. and J. Livingston, J. A. Lasher, G. Lindsay, J. Lilly, H. G. Laut, J. Livingston, J. Lasher, J. S. Lindsey, W. Lindsay, W. A. Laut, A. Lester, J. H. McDougall, R. McKerrow, A. McNeil, G. McKeachie, J. Moore, D. D. Moshier, G. Moshier, D. H. McDougall, D. S. McDougall, J. Murray, P. and J. McKenna, J. McNeil, J. A. McCoy, T. A. McCoy, J. McDonald, L. B. Morris, V. Mix, J. McNeil, A. McMullen, J. McMillen, J. S. McMillen, G. McMillen, J. and R. McGeoch, T. B. McMillen, M. B. Milliman, J. McMurray, D. McQuarie, N. McConnolee, W. T. McCoy, J. W. McNeil, Rev. G. Mairs, J. McCollum, R. McMurray, J. McMullen, J. McEachron, W. H. McDougall, J. B. McDougall, M. L. McNeil, A. B. McKallor, M. G. McNaughton, W. McNeil, D. McNeil, S. McCandlass, W. J. McMurray, T. Mairs, M. M. McNeil, J. A. McCollum, D. S. McCollum, W. McCollum, J. McGeoch, E. McCall, J. Miller, J. R. McNeil, S. Matthews, A. McDougall, D. Maxwell, F. McMillen, B. Madden, G. McMurray, J. McKercher, J. McCollam, R. McKernan, J. McLain, J. McEachron, C. A. McEachron, A. Mahaffy, J. McNeil, J. R. McEachron, A. McIntyre, F. A. McEachron, D. R. McDougall, W. Moore, R. McAuley, D. McThomas, J. S. McDougall, D. McDougall, D. M. McDougall, J. H. McNeil, W. McAuley, W. McEachron, W. J. McEachron, H. McQuerie, F. McIntyre, A. McEachron, J. McCormick, J. B. McNaughton, A. S. McNeil, J. Moore, L. Milliman, P. S. Milliman, W. D. McDougall, J. Nelson, R. Nichols, S. Nichols, A. Neeson, D. Osgood, W. Patten, W. Pollock, Jas. Pendergrass, Jos. Pendergrass, J. and R. Piester, A. W. Potter, A. Pollock, J. Patterson, J. H. Pendergrass, J. C. Rouse, A. Rowan, A. P. Robinson, J. Rice, N. Robertson, J. Robertson, D. Robertson, W. Robertson, J. Robertson, O. C. Robinson, J. J. Robinson, E. L. Richards, W. Rogers, E. Rogers, A. Reid, W. J. Reid, J. W. Reid, W. D. Robertson, Duncan Robertson, E. Riggs, W. and J. Riddle, C. C. Rouse, T. Reid, D. Reid, J. Ross, P. Reynolds, A. Reid, J. E. Rexstraw, D. G. Randles, R. Randles, A. Randles, G. B. Rouse, R. S. Selfridge, J. C. Stewart, R. Smith, J. D. Stevenson, M. Stack, J. T. Selfridge, D. Stalker, A. C. Sill, G. O. Safford, H. Smith, J. B. Snyder, G. F. Simpson, W. Skellie, W. C. Skellie, G. Shannon, D. Stevenson, H. Shipherd, Dr. J. Savage, J. Shaw, J. H. Savage, S. Stewart, J. D. Smith, J. L. Safford, W. Stewart, A. Stewart, H. B. Sybrant, J. Stevenson, J. B. Shields, J. Stewart, J. Shaw, R. Shannon, W. Sanders, W. Skinner, A. Stewart, Dr. J. C. Sill, J. M. Warren, J. Stott, J. H. Sloan, J. Shankland, E. Scriver, J. Shannon, J. and W. Shannon, A. Streaver, D. Streaver, J. Scott, A. Shields, P. Savage, I. G. Thompson, H. Turnay, D. J. Thompson, J. C. and J. A. Taylor, J. Taylor, J. Timmerman, J. Tompane, S. Terrence, D. C. Todd, T. M. Todd, G. M. Todd, T.

For CARPETS and OIL CLOTHS, go to WAIT'S.
For FINE READY-MADE CLOTHING, go to WAIT'S. (See page 81.)

SEE INDEX, PAGE ELEVEN. 179

Tilford, W. M. Tilford, S. H. Terry, J. Tilford, D. Taylor, R. Tefft, S. Tinkey, D. Tinkey, Daniel Tinkey, James Tilford, J. D. Williams, W. A. White, A. White, J. White, D. M. White, J. and C. White, N. Williams, A. Williamson, A. Weaver, D. Williamson, N. Wilson, J. Williamson, A. Williamson 2d, D. H. Williams, R. Wiggaus, J. W. Wakely, E. Williams. S. Willet, A. Young.

TOWN OF BENNINGTON, VT.—L. Armstrong, R. Armstron, H. Armstron, W. B. Arnold, L. E. Atwater, S. L. Atwater, J. Ayers, C. A. Austin, D. H. and E. H. Austin, L. D. Austin, H. Avery, Armstrong and Richmond, J. Bahan, J. H. Bahan, H. Baker, C. Barnes, M. Barnes, G. Benton, M. Benjamin, F. Blackman, H. Bingham, S. Bingham, J. Bignot, J. H. Burt, W. E. Burt, J. Bugbee, H. Burdan and Son, Burns and Madden, R. Burgess, W. Burgess, Y. H. Brownell, W. S. and W. E. Bronson, O. E. Brown, A. A. and D. Brimmer, G. Brimmer, J. Y. Brickinridge, C. Brewer, W. Camp, J. L. Carpenter, P. Casey, M. Casey, S. Chandler, H. Chandler, B. Chase, S. P. Chase, H. F. Clark, L. Cleveland, H. Cole, S. Calvin, C. Colvin, Mrs. D. H. Conkling, E. Conover, A. Collard, S. B. Cotton, W. Corcoran, A. Crawford, J. Crawford, C. P. Cromack, W. C. Cromack, J. H. Davis, R. Day, G. H. Day, H. Denio, E. E. Dewey, A. Denio, F. Dignon, J. Dowus, L. Down, J. Dowd, C. E. Dewey and Bro., A. R. Dickinson, A. Dunham, D. Dunham, J. Dunham, W. D. Dutcher, H. N. Elwell, L. Ellsworth, J. Essex, P. W. Eldredge, J. Fasett, C. Fay, A. R. Fay, E. D. Fillamone, J. D. Fish, J. H. Fillamone, A. Gage, S. W. Gardner, S. M. Gardner, J. H. Gardner, C. Gilson, R. O. Gone, Graves and Root, Thad. Graves, M. C. Hall, M. Halloran, T. Handershaw, A. H. Harrison, N. Harrington, H. Harrington, M. Hawks, A. Hawks, J. G. Harwood, G. Harwood, H. H. Harwood, L. and M. Harwood, L. B. Harwood, P. Harwood, A. W. Harwood, J. P. Harwood, H. M. Harwood, D. C. Harwood, M. D. and W. H. Harwood, A. Hathaway, Hathaway Bros., B. Hathaway, Martin Hathaway, Marsh Hathaway, H. Hathaway, T. Harlon J. Hilling, A. Henny, E. B. Henny, R. W. Henny, G. and E. Hinsdill, E. Hinsdill, C. Hicks, H. H. Hill, P. Hill, C. Horan, M. Houghton, J. Hollenbeck, C. Huling, A. L. Hubbell, P. T. Hubbell, W. L. Hurley, S. B. Hunt, E. and S. Jewett, G. Jewett, T. Jewett, Jewett, Mrs. I. Judd, T. Kinney, M. Kam, K. Ketchum, E. Kingsley, H. Keraf, J. Lawrence, M Lawrence, J. Lee, D. Lillie, A. Lowry, A. E. Lampman, D. H. Loveland, G. Lyman, P. Lynch, L. Lyon, T. Madden, A. J. Mattison, P. McGuire, H. W. Moores, M. Morgan, A D. Morse, C. Morse, A. Moulds, Merrill and Fay, H. Myers, L. Michols, R. Northrup, H. S. Norton, Mrs. J. Norton, L. Northouse, M. Ogden, C. O'Keefe, N. F. Ovitt, D. Paddock, J. F. Paddock, Paddock and Gardner, M. Page, L. S. Patchin, H. Patchin, T. W. Park, L. J. Potter, H. C. W. Potter, Mrs. A. Potter, A. Potter, I. Y. Pratt, S. S. Pratt, A. Prentice, M. H. Putnam, J. Quackenbush, H. Ray, H. Raymon, E. Rise, I. Rise jr., N. Rise, W. Rise, D. Rise, D. A. Rider, E. Robinson, D. Robinson, G. Robinson, S. F. Robinson, S. Robinson, J. S. Robinson, U. M. Robinson, J. Robinson, Sam'l. Robinson, M. Robinson, P. L. Robinson, D. Rockwood, S. Rockwood, H. Rockwood, J. Rockwood, C. Rockwood, J. E. Root, H. G. Root, A. and R. Rudd, E. F. Rudd, M. F, and B. E. Rudd, S. H. Rudd, E. B. Rudd, H. R. Russell, W. M. Russell, P. M. Sanders, J. Seary, J. Scully, H. Scott, Mrs. S. Scott, R. R. Sears, L. Sherwood, S. B. and A. Sherwood, H. L. Shields, L. Sibley, T. Sibley, Mrs. N. Slade, J. B. and M. Smith, K. J. and H. E. Smith, A. Stetson, A. Stratton, Mrs. E. Stratton, G. B. Stratton, E. F. Stratton, P. Stratton, P. H. Sumner, R. Swift, N. Swift, N. Thayer, S. Townsend, L. L. Upham, J. H. Vail, L. Van Buskirk, F. A. Vandercook, E. Walbridge, B. Webb, J. Walton, M. Walton, Mrs. L. Weeks, W. S. Weeks, T. Wilcox, C. Wilson, H Winslow, J. Winslow, Salem White, Susan White, M. K. Whitney, A. Wood, H. R. Wood, R. Woodward, M. Woodward, W. B. Wright, E. R. Yale.

TOWN OF SCHAGHTICOKE, N. Y.—D. Ackert, Jacob Ackert, John Ackert, P. B. Ackert, Ackert and Herrick, N. G. Aiken, Wm. Allen, H. Buckley, J. D. Buckley, C. Buckley, S. Buckley, W. Brownell, A. Brownell, M. Burch, T. Barton, I. Brett, Banker and Bryan, W. H. Buckley, J. H. Burch, H. Baker, E. Buckley, C. Brown, W. H. Bonesteel, E. S. Baucus, A. Button, J. Bulsom, M. L. Blanchard, J. W. Bauens, J. A. Baucus, G. W. Baucus, D. M. Button, J. H. Bonesteel, A. Bryan, J. Brundage, J. N. Bonesteel, Bellmore and Tibbetts, I. Bretton, D. Brynes, W. P. Button, Button and Mall, W. P. Button, A. Bryant, A. Bratt, W. P. Bratt, N. Bryant, H. Bratt, L. Baker, A. and S. Briggs, H. Bryant, L. Buffett, G. Brewster, A. and B. Briggs, E. P. Chase, S. Corben, E. Curtis, T. Case, F. Carpenter, W. Calkins, P. Collier, W. H. Clapper, Mrs. R. Clapper, W. Connor, Mrs. E. Congdon, J. Dater, H. K. Diver, P. Doty, S. Dennis, J. L. Doty, Dater and Baker, J. Denire, F. Dickinson, W. Durphey, M. Durphey, Mrs. John Downs, E. Edmons, L. Freeman, M. Fellows, I. G. Fleck, J. I. Fort, J. G. H. Fake, H. Fort, M. Fish, J. Fort, J. Gifford, D. Gifford, H. Garrison, W H. Gage, N. and M. Groesbeck, N. Groesbeck, H. Green, T. Gifford, D. Gifford, Mrs. R. Groesbeck, D. Geddis, M. Gleason, J. V. A. Hemstreet, Hoag and Sweet, F. Henniman, D. C. Halstead, C. Hermans, S. Herrie, J. Herrie, J. Hogan, J. W. Haynor, A. Ham, C. A. Hemstreet, R. M. Husbrook H. A. Hemstreet, W. Ham, M. J. Haynor, G. Haynor, C. Hurlike, Dr. Johnson, A. Kenyon, J. Kenyon, C. J. Kenny, Mrs. A. Knickerbacker, S. W. Knickerbacker, W. Knickerbacker, S. G. Lavans, J. Lane, C. W. Larabeg, M. Marhier, I. E. Moshier, P. Murray, L. C. Miller, J. McMahon, A. Morse, E. Masters, R. Masters, A. Myers, S. McGuire, J. W. Miller, L. J. Miller, S. V. R. Miller, Miller and Simmons, F. Miller, L. Myers, Jas. McBride, John McBride, M. L. Overocker, N. S. Overocker, O. H. Perry, H. E. Purdy, Pierson and Myers, Pruyn and Gray, T. N. Phillips, J. A. Quackenbush, J. Rolston, D. Ragan, P. and W. Reed, J. Reed, J. Searls, J. V. Smith, S. D. Starks, C. Starks, J. Sipperley, J. J. Sipperley, Sipperley and Vandenburgh, M. Smyder, J. Smith, 2d, L. Sheldon, J. Snyder,

W. A. Wilkins sells Bully Cloze Cheaper nor anybody elts.
23

SATINS, SILKS, VELVETS, FLOWERS and FEATHERS, in variety, at COREY'S, GLEN'S FALLS.

WRITING DESKS in Rosewood, PAPIER-MACHE, Plain or Beautifully Inlaid with Pearl, at BENDER'S, 73 State Street, Albany.

180 FARMERS' ALMANAC.

Snyder and Moon, Mrs. G. Sipperley, J. L. Simmons, Schaghticoke Powder Co., M. H. Turner, A. Thompson, E. Turner, D. H. Vail, W. Van Vechton, Van Vechton and Hull, W. W. Van Vechton, J. Van Vechton, G. Van Vechton, J. A. Van Vechton, W. Vernon, A. Vandenburgh, Van Vechton and Bratt, J. Verbeck, A. Wicks, M. K. Wicks, M. Welling, F. Wyley, J. H. Wyley, P. Wattsell, A. Wyman, J. Webster, S. Webster, C. Waldron, P. W. Waldron, G. H. and J. Wetsell, J. and D. Wetsell, J. Wyland, G. L. and J. Wetsell, N. Yates, S. F. Yates.

TOWN OF SALEM, N. Y.—W. Austin, W. Ashton, M. Ashton, J. Allen, J. Anglin, E. R. Allen, C. H. Allen, A. Armstrong, S. Archer, E. Austin, G. Austin, Allen and Tearney, S. Bealy, J. H. Beatice, D. R. Beatice, B. Blair, C. Billings, P. Baker, S. Brown, E. Beaty, W. Burch, W. J. Beatie, J. H. Brown, H. Barkley, J. Burnett, J. S. Burnett, N. H. Beebe, S. Bruce, R. Brady, B. Barnes, W. Barnsey, J. F. Beatice, J. M. Beatice, S. H. Brownell, I. Binninger, A. M. Binninger, J. Binninger, H. Bruce, W. Beattie, R. Beattle, A. Crowl, T. Coggshall, Cleveland and Co., C. Colton, T. P. Coon, E. Clough, A. Carswell, W. and D. Creighton, J. M. Clark, R. Coon, J. Croiser, A. Cherry, J. and S. Clark, J. H. Cowan, L. H. Cleveland, J. Cleveland, P. Cruikshank, J. Cruikshank, R. Cruikshank, A. Craig, M. Carter, M Collins, H. Collins, J. Collins, M. Collins, J. H Carswell, G. Currans, J. Dillon, J. Dillon, W. Dillon, A. Dennison, J. Dennison, V. Dorr, J. Dudgeon, B. Dunnigan, J. Dunnigan, D. Duncan, J. Dundon, J. Dundon, T. Dundon, W. Egery, W. Edgar, W. Edie, J. Edgar, W. F. Foster, J. Foster, J. S. Foster, A. Foster, J. Foster, E. and F. Flemming, J. Fairley, J. Ferguson, J. Ferguson, W. Ferguson, B. Fowler, A. Fitch, D. Frasier, J. Frasier, J. B. and S. Fanley, H. E. Fanley, J. and J. Fanley, W. D. Fanley, P. Flemming, M. Flemming, J. G. Gillis, J. Gillis, W. Gillis, N. Goodrich, W. H. Groesbeck, Mrs. A. S. Gould, D. Gray, Mrs. L. Gray, W. Gray, S. G. Heath, Mrs. Hanson, E. Harris, H. A. Hill, D. J. Hannah, J. Hatch, G. and D. Hopkins, W. Hopkins, D. Hawley, A. Hill, D. Johnson, E. Johnson, J. and W. Jordan, A. Johnson, D. Law, J. Law, T. Law, A. B. and R. T. Law, W. Luddy, T. Liddle, Mrs. A. Liddle, G. Liddle, H. Lyle, T. Lowry, A. Lytle, J. Lawton, Mrs. C. McFarland, J. C. McMurray, J. McCabe, J. McNitt, E. and J. McCloughry, J. McDonald, W. McAllister, J. McKinney, jr., Mrs. McCurdy, W. McNish, D. McClerry, Mrs. McKil, W. McClerry, J. McMillan, E. McMillan, G. McMillan, J. McNaughton, D. McFarland, R. McFarland, J. McKeever, P. McDonald, A. McKinney, L. McMillan, W. McIntyre, J. McNish, J. McKinney, R. McClarty, S. McAllister, J. McArthur, W. J. McCollum, J. McGuire, L. J. Mattison, Mrs. Marresiec, T. Montgomery, C. Morey, C. Martin, J. Martin, Mrs. Mahaffie, A. More, J. More, M. Moneyhan, J. M. McFarland, M. Noonan, J. Nelson, J. Odbert, M. W. Orcutt, E. Orcutt, J. O. Partridge, H. and J. Perry, R. Pinkerton, Mrs J. Pinkerton, G. E. Porter, I. Pratt, W. A. Russell, L. Rodgers, W. Rose, W. H. Rodgers, E. Rich, I. Roberson, A. Rich, G. Roberson, S. Burrell, Mrs. T. Safford, S. and J. Shaw, R. Smith, W. Steele, steele and Norton, D. Scott, Misses Scott, C. Scott, W. Scott, O. Smith, W. J. Steele, A. Sweet, T. Steele, J. Steele, O. Shed, R. M. and F. Stevenson, J. B. Stevenson, W. H. Shields, E. Sutherland, F. Sweet, D. Standley, J. S. Sherman, A. Stevens, Mrs. W. H. Stewart, Mrs. S. Stewart, A. M. Sherman, G. F. Safford, J. H. Smart, J. Smart, E. S. Sherman, S. K. Sherman, Y. S. Stevenson, T. Stewart and Bros., J. Slatterly, B. A. Sherman, J. Sherman, J. Thompson, J. M. Thompson, H. J. Townsend, G. Tifford, J. Toohey, D. Tominum, J. H. Thomas, G. Vail,— Van Burkirk, T. E. Weir, E. Williams, W. White, G. White, D. Woodard, Mrs. J. Woodard, Mrs. A. Wright, J. Wright, J. and J. Winning, T. Whalley, A. S. Webb, W. Williams, — Willetts, Park, Williams and Co., J. M. Williams, S. W. Willson, F. Wilson, W. and J. Walker, L. Wallace, J. Wallace, M. Williams, A. Woodard, A. West, E. West, Mrs. R. West.

TOWN OF GRANVILLE, N. Y.—M. B. Allen, J. Andrus, L. Ayres. L. Averill, C. Aldons, N. Austin, D. Bulkley, E. and J. Beecher, R. Brayton, M. W. Blirm, H. Beckwith, G. Brown, W. Blossom, J. Barker, S. G. Barker, E. Bulkley, R. Backus, I. Baker, J. Bateman, Rev. D. Beecher, S. and E. D. Bullock, I. H. Bartlett. W. Baker, B. Baker, J. W. Baker, L. Burns, W. G. Brown, W. H. Boomer, W. P. Beecher, A. Bulkley, C. Brown, L. Brown, H. Bennett, J. S. Bartlett, B. E. Brown and Co., D. Brown, J. B. Brown, C. H. Bull, J. B. Brown jr., M. Bowler, A. V. Cook, T. Cratty, H. H. Carlton, N. R. Crippen, F. A. Chandler, T. Cree, G. Cook, S. Carlton, S. J. Carlton, S. Chapin, J. Carpenter, H. Carpenter, E. Clank, C. W. Carpenter, A. B. Cook, C. Chapin, S. Chapin, A. Conant, M. Cook, L. Crosby, W. Dennison, G. S. Dillingham, N. Day, Day and Herron, W. G. Day, M. Duel, S. Dibble, M. T. C. Day, Hiram Duel, Hosea Duel, Mrs. E. E. Duel, O. Dillingham, S. Dillingham, T. Dunn, C. G. Draper, J. Dillingham, Mrs. E. Dutcher, A. DeKalb, J. Davis, P. Donahue, Mrs. E. Doty, Mrs. E. Dunson, W. De Kalb, De Kalb and Reynolds, P. Donahue, R. G. Dayton, A. Dillingham, J. A. De Kalb, C. Ely, J. Eldred, J. A. Everts, F. Ensign, Empire Slate Co., P. Fanning, W. P. Frazer, W. B. Felch, B. F. Farwell, N. B. Folger, P. George, A. Grant, C. Grant, J. W. Gray, P. Harding, T. Hays, S. Hines, I. J. Hall, J. Hollister, G. Hollister, N. E. Hall, H. W. Hughes, W. Hurd, E. Hills, W. R. Hills, J. G. Hulett, P. Hogan, P. F. Hatch, T. Haley, M. Hulett, E. B. Hicks, S. Hall, Silas Holl, G. N. Hall, O. Hicks, J. Hicks, H. Ives, H. H. Ingalls, D. Ingalesby, I. W. Kenyon, E. S. Kincaid, J. and G. H. Lowell, E. Lee, J. La Gash, I. and E. N. Lee, N. Lee E. Lee, Mrs. I. Lewis, L. Lee, A. M. Lock, A. Lewis, D. K. Martin, O. J. Martin, L. and P. Martin, W. McCotton, F. Mason, L. R. and F. Mason. M. Maney, P. Matoouey, J. Middleton, M. McGavey, W. Marriam, A. H. Marriam, M. McGowan, C. R. Main, O. T. Mason, C. Mason, Middle Granville Slate Co., F. Man, I. Monroe, W. and M. McGan, S. Morrison, T. Murphy, M. Nealou, L. Northrop, G. Northrop jr., T. L. Northrop, J. H.

CARRIAGES! CARRIAGES! Joubert & White. (See page 14.)

**OVERCOATS from $5 to $30, at WAIT'S CASH STORE.
FROCK COAT SUITS Cheap at WAIT'S. (See page 81.)**

SEE INDEX, PAGE ELEVEN.   **181**

Northrop, E. Northrop, Mrs. E. Northrop, A. Norton, C. Norton, Chester Norton, W. Norton, M. Norton, W. Nelson, I. Norton, O. O'Brien, W. O'Brien, P. Pender, N. Parker, L. E. Prouty, G. Parker, W. Patten, A. G. Patten, A. Putney, H. Pepper, F. B. Potter, E. and F. Parker, J. M. Parker, W. J. Potter, Mrs. V. Potter, H. Palmer, F. Peets, J. W. Peets, R. Pauber, S. L. Potter, J. D. Potter, J. R. Potter, D. D. Peters, Penchyn Slate Co., P. Quinn, H. F. Qua, T. Ryan, R. C. Richardson, C. Rhodes, T. Reynolds, W. Rhodes, Mrs. E. J. Roberts, J. F. Ruggles, S. Reynolds, H. Smith, W. Sweet, S. Sweet, E. Smith, James Sheehan, J. Sheehan, M. Sheehan, E. Smith, D. Skelly, J. Stevens, R. Savage, G. W. Smith, S. Staples, S. Smith, C. E. Simons, S. Spaulding, J. Smith, W. W. Smith, C. A. Sweet, J. B. Shumway, C. Slehan, E. S Storrs, J. B. Shaw, R. Spring, E. Starks, A. Stoddard, L. Smith, E. Savage, S. Savage, H. Sennett, C. B. Stillson, J. R. Staples, J. Sykes, W. Thompson, S. Taylor, J. C. Tanner, F. Tanner, C. Taylor, J. Thompson, C. Thompson, O. F. Thompson, A. Temple, E. B. Temple, L. R. Temple, W. T. Travis, J. R. Tanner, J. C. Tanner, S. Van Guilder, N. Van Guilder, A. Van Guilder, Mrs. M. Vail, J. Van Schaick jr., L. Whitcomb, T. Williams, W. Ward, S. Wing, J. Wing, A. Willett, J. Willett, A. Wilson, W. Wilson, L. W. Wing, A. Willis, L. J. Webb, F. Wyman, G. B. Warren, F. A. W. Wyman, Wright, M. Whitcomb, G. Wooddell, S. B. Warren, M. K. Wait, C. E. Whitney, H. Warren, J. Williams, M. Whalen, E. J. Woodcock, T. B. Woodcock, D. Wood, D. Whitney, F. Wilson, L. Wheeler, J. Wilson, M. Whitcomb, H. and M. Waller, F. L. Wheeler.

TOWN OF POULTNEY, VT.—C. P. Austin, H. and L. Andrus, E. D. Andrus, H. Andrus, J. Angevine, H. Angevine, C. P. Austin, A.F.Adams, E. P. Andrews, H. Alix, Allard and Hotchkin, H. Ausment, B. Beamen, G. Brown, E. Butler, L. S. Bardwell, W. Bremen, E. Brayton, J. Benedict, J. B. Beamen, J. S. Benedict, Mrs. J. Beamen, G. H. Bessie, C. E. Bent, O. Bullock, P. Barker and Son, D. A. Barker, W. T. Bethel, L. Barber, C. L. Barber, W. F. Barber, O. R. Bateman, H. Ballard, H. Ballard, J. T. Ballard, D. Ballard, A. P. Babbit, R. Bliss, S. Bliss, A. Buckland, P. Beach, G. H. Boyce, J. N. and A. Clark, Clark and Mason, M. Chapin, Clark and Hooker, I. M Clark, O. Campbell, J. Canny, P. Carrigan, P. Connor, M. Carraway, F. Carpenter, H. R. Carpenter, Carpenter and Wesley, C. Carpenter, N. Carlton, A. B. Clark, J. W. Clark, R. E. and W. E. Clark, M. and P. Cassidy, H. Chandler, J. Cone, W. A. Cudman, J. Cone, E. Cone, C. Carpenter, S. Dean, S. Dean, R. Dalton, G. Dye, S. Dillingham, J. R. Derby, B. F. Derby, S. J. Derby, B. F. and J. R. Derby, J. O. Driscoll, J. Dogan, E. G. Dyer, J. Daly, W. Dayton, I. Davy, Davy and Jones, P. A. Davis, J. Engeam, B. Frisbee, W. L. Farnhan and Son, J. W. Fuller, W. W. Fuller, H. Fifield, H. W. French, A. D. French, N. C. Fenton, B. Fitch, Francis and Jones, F. Goodrich, B. Giddings, D. N. Giddings, J. Gibson, A. Gates, Mrs. E. Gates, J. Grady, W. Goodspead, J. Glidden, J. W. Gilmore, B. B Goodwin, H. Goram, T. Griffith, Gibson and Wells, M. Hyde, E. Hooker, N. Harris, H. Hall, W. M. Hall, J. Haugh, S. H Hastings, M. P. Hooker, N. C. Hyde, F. Hyde, C. Hydeville, H. Howe, A. Hosford, C. Hosford, P. Hosford, Mrs. H. Hosford, H. M. Hotchkiss, N. Hunter, A. Herrick, P. Hill, E. Hawes, J. Holland, A. Hawly, Igo and Hawley, M. Jackson, E. Jones, Jones and Lloyd, C. Johnson, A. Killbourn, Kelly and Ford, A. M. Knapp, W. H. Knapp, P. Kennedy, A. Hendrick, W. W. Kelly, J. Lewis, M. Lewis, R. Lewis, H. F. Lewis, Mrs. A. Lewis, D. Lewis, A. Lewis, C. Lynch, E. Lynch, S. H. Lampson, J. Lyons, P. Landry, A. Loveland, J. Lamont, C. C. Loomis, J. Larkin, J. Morse, E. Mallory, R. Marshall, H. Marshall, J. Marshall, A. Marshall, D. C. and E. A. Mears, J. F. Marie, R. E. Maranville, F. G. Martin, W. W. Martin, S. Mineberg, L. McWithy, W. McLeod, McCarthy and Kelly, T. McDowell, P. Mack, Mrs. Manogue, J. Mengher, C. W. Moseley, H. Mattison, J. A. and H. Morgan, T. Manchester, F. and A. Miller, R. E. Marandville, J. E. Manly, G. C. Martin, J. S. Norton, J. Newman, H. Nicholas, J. Obrien, P. Obrien, Parker and Ray, N. Raison, E. Pomeroy, A. Perry, S. Parks, J. S. Parks, J. E. Preston, J. Porter, Mrs. B. Porter, D. Paro, C. A. Parker, P. Phalon, E. Pepper, Parker and Mason, P. M. and S. D. Ross, E. Ross, H. Ransom, F. Ransom, B. G. Rice, A. Rice, R. F. Ray, R. Rowell, A. J. Rogers, W. Rowland, D. W. Robert, A. Rayder, S. Ross, Ray, Eli and Co., E. J. Roberts, O. Sherman, A. Sherman, J. Stowe, P. M. Scott, L. C. Spaulding, J. Spaulding, H. Spaulding, A. Smith, H. Smith, D. A. Smith, H. Smith, T. Streeter, F. and J. Thompson, L. Thrall, Mrs. A. Thornton, S. Thornton, A. Taft, O. Wood, Mrs. S. M. Willard, C. C. Ward, C. P. Ward, P. Wells, W. R. Williams, E. E. Williams, E. Whitcomb, A. Wheedon, M. Webster, R. B. Westover, J. Welch, Williams and Tuttle.

TOWN OF WHITE CREEK, N. Y.—I. Ashton, J. W. Ashton, D. G. Ashton, W. Ashton, J. Agin, J. Arnold, B. G. Allen, J. Q. Allen, W. Allen, J. Adams, D. Barber, D. Baldwin, A. Blakely, J. Bowers, R. Blaie, J. Brodie, M. Branagan, E. W. Briggs, J. Bennett, Joseph Bennett, A. Brayton, C. Bowen, G. S. Barton, S. Barker, J. H. Bennett, C. Burliet, M. Brownell, D. M. Buck, L. Bristol, Albert Burdict, L. Coulter, J. B. Curtis, T. Comstock, L. W. Crosby, L. Curtis, T. Chase, H. Coulter, B. P. and R. B. Crocker, S. Corbett, G. Coon, J. Chrisly, D. Callahan, B. Chase, S. Center, W. Center, G. F. Center, A Center, N. Cottrell, S. Cottrell, C. C. Cottrell, Mrs. P. Clark, L. Carpenter, A. W. Campbell, R. B. Dewey, F. Doan and Son, D. and M. Dwinnel, E. Dall, J. R. Dyer, J. Driscoll, A. Eldredge jr., W. Eldredge, I. Edie, S. A. Fuller, G. H. Flack, S. Fuller, W. P. Fisher, W. P. Fowler, W. A. Fowler, A. Fowler, L. Fowler, J. B. Fowler, D. Fowler, C. Fowler, A. Fish, B. F. Fowler, Fowler and Marshall, C. Frasier, A. J. Fowler, H. C. Gray, Mrs. C. Gilbert, R. C. Gifford, J. J. Gray, Mrs. R. C. Gifford, M. Gooding, P. Gilbert, M. Greene, J. Gay, M. D. Hubbard, I. M. Hodge, A. Harrington, M. Hurd, I. B. Hanna,

Custom Work done better at WILKINS' than elsewhere.

Go to **P. H. COREY'S, GLEN'S FALLS,** *for* **HOOP SKIRTS, CORSETS, GLOVES, HOSIERY, &c.**

Plain and Fancy INKSTANDS, PEN RACKS, SEGAR STANDS and CASES, and Unique WATCH SAFES, at BENDER'S, 73 State Street, Albany.

FARMERS' ALMANAC.

W. Horton, W. Hart, J. Harrington, J. S. Hutchings, S. Hoag, H. Haswell, D. Hitchcock, I. P. Hunt jr., I. P. Hunt, S. Hewett, J. Herrington, W. W. Johnson, H. Jones, W. H. King, J. King, B. Kenger, C. Kenger, P. Ketchim, J. Loomis, W. and W. Lawton, D. Lambert, Mrs. J. Lake, L. Lake, L. H. Lake, G. S. Lake, J. Larmon, J. Lay, G. W. Monroe, J. Mattison, T. McNish, N. Merrill, W. McRic, J. Mitchell, C. Mattison, E. Murray, J. Matthews, P. McDonald, P. Mahar, J. Mattison, T. McAllen, D. McMahon, J. McKeman, S. Morcley, Mrs. J. McCown, P. Monahan, D. and D. Mattison, R. Nicholson, W. Nelson, McD. Nelson, N. E. Niles, J. and D. Niles, E. Niles, H. Niles, J. H. Nichols, J. P. Noxon, D. Nagle, W. Olin, C. Poor, W. Pierce, H. Pierce, H. N. Pruyn, C. W. Pratt, S. Potter, W. N. Pruyn, W. I. Perry, I. B. Perry, S. Pratt, E. Pratt, U. N. Pratt, J. Pratt jr., D. A. Pratt, B. Pitney, J. C. Qua, A. Qua, J. H. Rice, G. Robertson, Mrs. S. Rice, G. Russell, H. Russell, T. Reed, C. Russell, J. Russell, G. Richards, N. P. Richards, R. Ransom, E. Russell, P. Russell and Co., D. Russell, B. Roolance, I. Rundell, H. and H. Rice, C. Reilhan, B. Shaw, S. Sweet, B. H. Sanderson, S. R. and G. Sweet, H. Starbuck, A. H. Sweet, L. Sisson, A. Smith, H. Sisson, Mrs. N. Simpson, G. Shanmahan, J. Sinnett jr., F. Sweet, S. Sharp W. H. Taber, S. Taber, H. Taber, J. Tinkhard, W. W. Thomas, W. Tierney, P. Tierney, W. Taylor, A. Vandenburg, J. Van Rensselaer, J. Woodworth, J. R. Warren, Warner, and Lovejoy, H. R. Wood, J. H. Wheeler, E. Wait, A. Wait, E. Whitcomb, M. Wallace, J. C. Wright, E. Wright, P. Ward, M. Wallace, M. D. Wallace.

TOWN OF NASSAU, N. Y.—E. Ambler, H. Allendorph, H. Adams, J. Adsit, J. M. G. Adsit, Mrs. N. S. Arms, J. H. Adams, E. S. Albertson, E. Atwater, L. Ayres, Mrs. Alexander, S. Ambler, A. Bink, J. Bink, C. M. Brown, J. G. Budd, W. H. Bedell, J. Brochny, C. Baker, E. S. Boyce, G. Bedell, P. Boyce, J. S. Bedele, C. Bextom, F. Basshold, J. Bullis, E. N. Ball, E. Bassett, A. Baily, A. Bailey, W. Brown, N. Bateman, G. Bateman, B. Budd, W. Baily, S. Bigelow, J. G. Bush, J. Bink, T. G. Brown, E. Boughton, J. Boughton, J. Brown, H. Bateman, J. P. Bateman, J. Belknapp, A. Carr, W. Conradt, D. Coons, A. Comes, J. Cummings, W. Cummings, J. W. Casey, L. Conant, L. Cole, W. Cole, E. S. Casey, J. Casey, C. Craw, E. Cumys, A. Casy, J. Curtis, A. D. Cumings, A. Cleveland, N. Clark, J. S. Cashan, G. Cleveland, J. Crane, M. Crane, S. Conant, B. Cook, R. Coleman, C. Cady, F. Dicham, E. Dusenbury, S. Dusenbury, J. N. Dusenbury, C. Davis, J. Davis, C. Drew, H. Dibble, L. O. Daboll, G. O. Daboll, W. J. Dunham, H. Dunham, E. Devreux, J. Dubois, N. Devreux, S. Devreux, P. Devreux, E. Devreux, H. Devreux, J. C. Enos, J. Eanning, S. Eanny, G. H. Fosmin, D. W. Fredenburgh, A. Fredenburgh, J. Fursman, P. Fike, M. Face, J. Face, P. Ferguson, R. Ferguson, F. Finger, J. Finch, S. Griffith, H. Germond, J. Germond, J. Gaffney, D. Gaffney, J. Gifford, J. Gavin, W. Gable, C. Green, H. Guih, B. F. Gardner, J. W. Gardiner, J. Gardiner, J. H. Gould, C. W. Herrick, J. Hemance, D. Hoy, N. Husted, S. Husted, F. Husted, C. Hicks, S. Husted, J. Harlton, W. Hall, L. Hunt, J. Hernold, J. F. Hayeboon, S. Hollis, Mrs. C. Hoag, N. Husted, P. W. Hicks, J. Hicks, E. Hovy, W. P. Hovy, E. P. Hopkins, B. Hopkins, J. S. Harris, S. G. Harris, W. L. Hays, H. Hays, G. Houghtalling, C. Hunt, E. Huester, Mrs. J. Hall, B. Jones, K. Johnson, I. Johnson, H. Kirby, G. Kirby, J. R. Knoppen, M. Knopp, H. Kelly, J. M. Kemp, A. Kelly, D. W. Kilner, B. H. Lane, J. H. Lane, J. Leyden, G. W. Larkins, T. C. Larkins, E. Larkins, C. Larkins, N. Mynders, J. Mills, J. McMurry, D. Morris, Mrs. L. Morris, J. Marks, W. McQuade, P. Meitenich, G. W. Mead, E. Mann, S. R. Mony, G. Memfield, G. Memfield, T. Miller, R. Mouy, C. Money, C. Ostrum, A. Pitts, J. Phillips, W. Pitts, W. F. Pitts, J. W. Pitts, L. Rowe, T. H. Reynolds, J. Rocherfelle, E. Rocherfelle, J. Roraback, F. Ruff, J. W. Rhodes, C. Richard, L. Roice, I. Smith, J. H. Smith, A. Seely, J. Schenck, D. Shamer, D. St. John, S. Stats, H. Schwarz, J. Saunders, S. Tenant, S. Tompkins, C. Tompkins, J. Turner, W. Turner, A. Turner, J. Tifft, S. Tifft, S. Tifft, Jeremiah and Tifft, J. Tifft, D. Tifft, J. T. Thompson, A. H. Tucker, P. Tifft, J. Upham, Mrs. T. Upham, C. Van Salisbury, P. Van Valkenburgh, E. Vichery, O. Vincent, J. Vanatler,—Vichery, H. Waterbury, S. Waterbury, S. Waterbury, D. Waterbury, C. H. Waterbury, S. P. Waterbury, J. E. Williams, J. Welch, J. Welch, A. Weidermix, S. Williams, G. Wood, J. Westfill, G. Westfall, B. Williams, J. Welch, jr., W. Weatherby, C. White, J. White, W. White, M. L. Woodward, J. Whitegoire, D. L. Wolcott, A. Wolcott, L. Wolcott, J. Wolcott, W. W. Williams, S. E. Williams, E. Williams.

TOWN OF BERLIN, N. Y.—J. D. Adams, C. Brown, D. Bentley, J. W. Burdick, A. S. Burdick, H. Babcock, D. Babcock, A. M. Brimmer, S. Burdick, C. Bentley, H. Brimmer, A. D. Brimmer, H. J. Brown, S. Coon, T. Collins, P. Canfield, F. M. Cowee, S. Church, J. H. Cranston, H. R. Cranston, J. Davis, A. Davis, T. Davis, J. Denison, D. Denison, G. W. Dodge, G. Daniels, U. J. Denison, G. T. Denison, L. Fuller, H. Grogan, S. Green, V. Green, R. W. Green, R. Green, H. Green, D. D. Green, O. W. Green, D. K. Green, W. P. Green, E. D. Green, H. Hull, H. D. Hull, D. P. Hull, O. G. Harris, S. Hull, D. Hull, P. Hull, A. Hull, A. P. Hull, H. P. Hull, E. Hull, D. J. Hull, J. Hakes, L. H. Jones, T. A. Jones, T. W. Jones, H. P. Jones, W. R. Jones, N. Jones, G. W. Kennedy, H. Lamphere, L. L. Lewis, R. Lamphere, S. C. Matteson, S. B. Maxou, J. McKay, J. McDonough, P. Manchester, A. Martin, A. C. Manchester, M. Mentor, D. W. Millarl, A. Millarl, J. Malone, A. J. Matteson, O. H. Merritt, D. O. Matteson, S. F. Matteson, J. Nichols, M. J. Niles, J. B. Niles, A. G. Niles, D. E. Potter, D. A. Rhodes, S. A. Rhodes, R. Smith, W. T. Smith, W. A. Smith, D. G. Satterice, W. R. sweet, R. Shaw, W. F. Satterlee, E. Sweet, W. N. Stillman, H. Smith, C. Saunders, R. H. Satterlee, H. Vars, D. Vars, E. Vielie, J. D. Wells, D. G. Whilford, R. Whitman, J. Young.

TOWN OF CALDWELL, N. Y.—N. R. Brown, L. B. Black, S. Burton, H. Benton, jr.,

GARRETT'S DENTAL ROOMS, Glen's Falls, N. Y.

White & Pearsall are Agents for the new Howe Machine, Glen's Falls.

The Place to buy Clothing Cheap is at WAIT'S.
The Latest Styles of HATS and CAPS at WAIT'S. (See page 81.)

SEE INDEX, PAGE ELEVEN. 183

Z. Bacon, J. Burton. T. Bendley, W. A. Brown, J. Bennet, W. H. Bradley. A. Brown, S. W. Crandal. A. Chapman. F. Coffin. G. H. Crane, C. Coulban, F. G. Crosby. J. Chambers, E. Dickenson, M. Davis. A. Eldredge, A. J. Eddy, R. Fielding, G. W. Fielding. D. Ferguson. W. Fuller. J. Griffing. C. Gates, K. Gates, J. Gleason, S. Hammond. R. Hammond, F. H. Hammond. B. Hall. E. Hood. H. Hall. R. Hall. C. Heath. A. How, F. B. Hubbell. J. Irish. S. Jones, A. B. Jones, L. Jenks. J. Larmis. H. Laplanch, R. Laudfire. C. D. Loyd, S. Loop, W. Lockhart. D. Mead, D. Moon. J. Martine, I. Marshal. J. Nickle. J. Orcott, O. Pember, E. L. Patrick. G. Pier. L. Pharmer, H. Russel, D. Russel. L. Ransom, J. H. Smith, O. Stanton. R. S. Stebbins, B. T. Stafford. P. Staats. T. J. Smith. J. I. Schermerhorn. C. Stewart. R. Shaw, N. Shaw, R. S. Shaw. S. Taylor. R. Varnum, Z. Van Deusen, J. Van Deusen. N. Wilcox. J. B. Wilcox, Dudley and Wilcox, W. J. Welkey, U. B. West

TOWN OF EDINBURGH. N. Y.—T. Allen, J. Rogers, R. Brewer. D. Bowdish, J. Partridge, W. Partridge. J. Lewis, E. F. Kise, V. Beaman. J. Ackley, M. Manning, D. McKay, W. Greenslet. R. Hewett. N. Burcalla. J. W. Cook. A. Olmsted, D. W. Partridge, A. I. Quimby. J. Wilbur. E. Wilbur, J. Burcalla. A. Scribner, A. G. Leford, J. B. Simpson, T. Edwards. W. Scribner. B. Burcalla, S. Scribner, J. Shaw, C. Bartlett. H. Wadsworth, E. Scribner. H. Savage, W. Allen, T. Olmsted. C. Olmsted, J. Blower, W. Jenkins. C. Rhodes. J. M. Robinson. I. Barker, N. Barker, S. Hayden, J. Tenant. Z. H. Madison. W. Hudson, R. Simpson, J. Kinnicutt. C. Scribner, N. S. Cairy, M. Slacknell, N. Brundage. H. Hamilton. S. H. Tarry, F. Noyes. B. Elithorp. E. G. King. D. Garden, L. Lion, O. T. Elithorp. J. H. Tenant, S. Tenant. P. Tenant. S. Tenant. J. O. Lion. C. J. Rice. E. Wilson, W. Van Vranken. L. Rhodes. J. Tenant. E. Bartlett. B. Springer, M. Vanevery. J. Vanevery. S. W. King. C. S. Edwards. B. Perry. A. White, H. Person, D. Renny. C. Edwards. J. Steel, G. Hunt, A. Armstrong, S. Brondage, S. and E. B. Elithorp, C. Sumner, H. Noyes. L. Kinnicutt, S. Noyes, N. Copeland. C. O. Butler, J. Ford. R. Smith, N. Brundage, J. and J. Wheeler, L. Frasure, J. King. T. Renn, J. Steers, M. Noyes, E. Edwards, L. Mires, S. Manning, S. W. Snow, J. E. King, H. Rhodes, F. Noyes, B. Booth. H. Harris, D. Stark, P. Gealon. J. M. Anderson. J. Anderson, S. Stark, O. White, O. Edwards, H. Person, E. Noyes, S. Batcheller, R. Batcheller, T. Edwards. H. M. Conkling, H. R. Colson, D. H. Yates. C. Edwards, L. Davenport, D. W. Jones. H Harvey, W. E. Snow, P. J. Noyes, M. Shealds. E. Fonda, C. J. Rice, G. Edwards, J. Bristoll, N. Youngs, J. Jenson, J. Wood, A. A. Clark, W. Edwards. A. Hunt, J. M. Dourny, W. Steers. J. McLane. C. Refreqne, S. Sumner. G, Huntoon. J. M. Elithorp, W. Vaughn, G. Wells, L. Partridge, R. Eglin, P. Sumner, W. Goethy, J. Jenkins, O. Greenfield, A. Dearn, S. Pulling, H. Tenant, J. Kinnicutt, J. G. Petit, A. Quimby.

TOWN OF GALWAY, N. Y.—W. R. Weld. R. Shaw, J. and W. Kelly, W. K. Chalmers. T. Ireland. P. and J. McKindley, J. Vines, J. L. Cramer, E. H. Vines, W. Ellis, S. E. Kidd, J. LeSeur, F. Shattuck, J. Mesmeallie, F. Moon. S. Vosburgh. J. P. Major, G. Davis. A. S. Whitlock, A. J. Grenell, A. P. Root. W. F. Cavert, J. Gibson. J. K. Ferguson, J. P. Luther, G. Turner. J. Anderson, W. Jackson, P. Preece, R. L. Paul. F. Sanders, J. T. Sanders, J. Serviss. W. Chalmers, C. Paul. A. Hartley, E. C. Durkee, T. B. Bartlett, W. Knox, A. Stewart. G. Mabon, J. A. Banta, W. L. C. Clark, F. Foss, J. Donnan, J. Crawford, J. H. Crane, A. Hoyt, J. H. Mead, J. H. Hays, B. E. Seabury, A. Stickle, M. West, J. P. Crouch, T. Jansen, J. P. Smith, A. Cook, J. Birch. J. Pemble, W. Grey, D, Fairweather, A. Ashley, J. Van Slyke. C. A. Cook. J. O'Brien, M. P. Welsh. W. H Mead, F. Hope, W. D. McCormick. L. Brown, T. A. Hays, P. Pettit. W. Scott. W. McConchie, N. Robinson. A. Bartlett. J. Bell. I. H. Plank. C. Sturgess. J. Burhans. A. N. Reynolds, H. Hall, H. Dennison, S. Stilwell, J Alexander, J. Moorhead, E. Chamberlin, D. Costigan. P. Clark. S. McChesney. E. S. Hermance. D. Pier, S. B. Pulling. W. Smith. I. Willer, M. Knights. A. N. Reynolds, P. Reynolds, W. B. Jaynes, M. Whiteside, S. Hudson, W. N. Mosher, W. Cornell, D. Inman, P. Burdick, J. N Hill. M. Harrington.M. Gifford, I. Hasbrook. E. Hinkle, P. Hart. D. T. Hart. R. Hall, L. Hastings. F. Hagedorn, W. Mabon, J. A. McMillen. H. Muddlebrook, M. Morrissey, T. Penny, I. S. Palmer. G. J. Palmatier. M. Pixley, I. Fuller, J. Shaw, E. Shipman. B. Blair. E. James. R. Orr, J. Riebeck. P. Doolin. P. Fitzgerald, J. Collins, T. Kirby, A. McDonald, J. Brown. P. Brown, M. Lee. E. P. Keeler. S. Hall, R. Hall. G. Wise, W. B Jaynes, D. J. Armatage, M. Armer, L. M Bullock, W. Beardsley, J. B. Brockett. S. Benson. P. Burdick, J. H. Bidwell. W. Burpick. J. Benson. W. Brigg, D. Goodfellow, G. Grey. L. Husted, W. J. Huyck, C. Ham. D. B. Ingerson, G. Lyon, O. Lansing. C. Mow. S. Mosher. S. McConchie, J. Meredith. J. Pettit, Z. Pulling, W. Pettit, J. Smith, H. Sleazer, J. C. Smith, H. Sweet. R. Rider. H. E. Shattuck, J. G. Savage, P. Smith, E. Brainard, M. Brosnahan, J. L. Bartlett, J. Blanch, W. Buckwell, M. T. Betts, J. Brown, J. Carter, T. Craig, D. W. Cook, J. H. Crane, T. Corning, H. L. Close. J. Davis. W. Demarandville. W. Foss. M. Fitzgerald. N. H. Gibbs, W. Snell, W. Tompkins, J. Tubbs. J. Tierney. B. Vedder, L. P. Vibbard, A. L. Stone. T. Mairs, C. Tompkins, J. McKenney. D. P. Wait. G. Willis, J. Warren, J. Whalen. W. J. Young, C. Preston, J. Moorhead, E. Chamberlin. W. Crouch

TOWN OF SHREWSBURY, VT—A. Pratt. D. Waterman. L. W. Dawson, H Huntoon, O. W. Lincoln, O. Holden. P. Wilkins, G. G. Aldrich, W. Caswell. W. Royce, O. G. Jones, W. G. Sawyer. M. Maloney, J. Riley, A. Barney. C. Webber, J. Huntoon. O. Dodge, E. W. Aldrich. A. Adams, L. Aldrich. E. Aldrich. A. F. Aldrich, A. W. Aldrich, E. O. Aldrich, T. Aldrich. J. Aldrich. L. Aldrich, S. Gould, J. H. Balch. D Balch. L. W. Beverstock. A. Bucklin. W. A. Colburn, H. Cook, E. B. Colburn. L. O. Colburn. H. Colburn, L. G. Fish, W. Guild, W. Gates, H. C. Gleason, J. Gilman, J. P. Gibson, L. Gibson,

PIANOS, ORGANS and MELODEONS, for sale by P. H. COREY, GLEN'S FALLS.

W. A. WILKINS' Cheap Clothing Store, established 1859.

BENDER will furnish you any Books Published; also, ENGINEERS' INSTRUMENTS, STATIONERY, FIELD BOOKS, &c., at 73 State Street, Albany.

184 FARMERS' ALMANAC.

The best Sewing Machine in the World is at White & Pearsall's, Glen's Falls.

L. G. Harris, V. Harris. H. G. Hewitt, C. C. Holden, E. B. Lord, N. Lord, W. Morse, L. I. B. Noyes, L. D. Olds, S. G. Parker, E. Pierce. F. M. Plumley, W. Phalen, W. H. Plumley, P. Russell, J. A. Russell, J. Rogers, E. Sanders, W. Smith, H. A. Starkey, C. Smalley, N. B. Smith, R. P. White, J. Wright, J. Wilmouth, H. A. Waterman, H. C. Johnson, C. Johnson, E. W. Johnson, P. Johnson, A. Johnson, J. Johnson, A. Knight, R. Lloyd, E. Lord, L. Lord, L. Moore, A. J. Noyes, J. Parker, N. R. Parker, A. Pierce, A. Plumley, W. Pierce, I. A. Russell, A. W. Russell, W. Russell, H. Sanders, S. F. Smith, W. Smith, N. Smith, W. Sanderson, E. P. Wilder, H. O. Wright, W. Roswell, H. W. Wilcox, T. Whitney.

TOWN OF BENSON, VT.—W. C. Dickinson, R. Sherwood, Mrs. P. Wilcox, I. Dickinson, L. N. Proctor, A. Walker, O. Goodrich. L. S. Noble, R. D. King, E. Strong, E. L. Barber, S. P. Sherwood, L. H. Kellogg, J. J. Bascom, D. Crofoot, R. P. Walker, J. Gibbs, A. R. Ladd, F. W. Walker, D. L. Osgood, D. Potter, W. Skeels. C. B. Goodrich, J. H. Goodrich, W. T. Nickerson, D. L. Stacy, S. W. Brown, A. J. Gibbs, A. Briggs, G. Scribner, T. Doane. S. Root, F. May, G. Root, S. M. Needham, H. Goodrich, A. L. Pitts, L. S. Haven, J. J. Howard, E. S. Howard, P. Goodrich, E. Norton, N. Adams, L. B. Cook, M. Bosworth, C. Walker, L. Payn, E. E. Smith, A. Smith, J. B. Stiles, H. Root, C. Hulburt, P. K. Hulburt, A. A. Orkens, W. Walker, A. Arnold, S. A. Arnold, M. C. Rice. H. White, J. Balis, J. H. and R. Gleason, H. J. Williams, C. Fay, Edgerton, G. Roberts, M. G. Barber, H. Barber, C. Boudrye, J. W. Williamson, H. King, W. C. Barber, H. E. Knapp, H. Hale, J. Scott, S. Bishop, R. W. Grinnell, H. Manley, E. Fish, W. Brown, J. H. and S. A. Aiken, W. J. Goodrich, N. N. Norton, M. F. King, A. S. Bartholomew, J. Falkenbury, J. D. King, M. Sisco, D. S. Belden, F. Higgins, J. Belden, C. Belden, A. Gibbs, A. Higgins, H. V. Downs, H. E. Hulett, J. E. Wright, N. F. Lee, I. Martin, Z. Hasbrook, J. Wilcox, R. Byram, H. B. Wilcox, A. Hall, W. Cowan, C. Perry, J. Carter, L. H. and H. Little, W. O. Higgins, J. S. Griswold, M. C. Peck, J. W. Adams, P. Meacham, H. E. Strong and Bro.

TOWN OF MOUNT TABOR, VT.—J. Canary, D. W. Lane, G. Marsh. J. P. Griffitt, S. M. Baker, H. P. Tabor, G. S. Tabor, E. A. Millard, M. Foley, H. Griffitt, P. T. Griffitt, S. Hestleton, C. Buffum, L. Nichols, P. H. Smith, J. F. Thompson, O. Greeley, J. B. Jenkins and Co., J. Barnard, R. Buffum, E. D. Sawyer, A. W. Tarbell, A. Kent, C. Smith, R. Smith, M. Cook, J. B. St. Mars, C. Hadley, E. Turner, L. Taylor.

TOWN OF STEPHENTOWN, N. Y.—E. Arnold, A. Atwater, H. Alderman, I. Adams, N. Allen, S. Arnold, A. Brockway, R. A. Brown, S. Brown, A. Bailey, R. M. Bull, W. Burke, J. S. Brockway. B. J. Briggs, B. F. Bull, E. Bailey, H. Bailey, J. Bennett, P. Beers, E. Beers, N. Beers, S. Boughton, D. Bardine, F. Brown, W. Bennett, G. Carpenter, S. Carpenter, L. Carr, H. Carr, J. H. Cranston, E. Cranston, H. Cranston, J. J. Carpenter, L. Cherevoy, W. Cherevoy, E. Carpenter, A. Chapman, J. Carrier, A. Carrier, M. G. Casey, J. Coleman, C. Crandall, J. Culver, A. Clefford, E. Crandall, D. Collins, S. Cole, B. Chase, M. Chase, S. Carr, E. Carr, R. Chase, T. G. Carpenter, P. Dean, P. Daniels, H. T. Douglas, L. Doty, S. Doball, T. Dwyer, W. Dimond, B. Doball, A. Doty, S. Doball, J. S. Eldridge, N. Eldridge, J. H. Eldridge, C. Eddy, N. Evans, A. Eldridge, L. Fellows, S. Finch, J. Freedenburgh. J. Fitzgerald, N. Gardner, J. Gleason, N. Goold, C. Gardner, R. Gardner, J. Greenman, D. B. Griffin, G. H. Hall, T. H. Horton, J. Hatch, P. Hatch, J. Holcomb, G. P. Holromb, A. Hemt. E. Huntington, J. Hunt, S. Harris, E. G. Hayes, G. Jenks, C. Jolls, R. Jolls, S. and R. Jolls, G. Jones, S. B. Kittel, S. Kittel, Jr., F. Kittel, W. J. Kennedy, H. Londsay, M. Londsay, T. McNealy, G. Moffitt, H. Moffitt, J. J. Moffitt, J. Moore, L. Moore, A. Mann, J. McGill, M. McDade, R. S. Odell, W. Odell, W. Pease, R. Palmer, S. Palmer, E. R. Potter, N. Parker, W. J. Potter, Q. Pomeroy, E. A. Rolla, D. C. V. Roberts, J. Reynolds, N. Reynolds, N. Rathbone, R. Rose, H. Rose, G. G. Rose, O. Rose, W. H. Russell, J. J. Sweet, R. Sweet, E. Sweet, L. Sheldon, A. Swan, B. Sherman, M. Sedgwick, A. Sedgwick, J. Smith, I. Tinby, B. Tayer, B. Tayer, J. Vary, B. Wiley, S. Wiley, J. Wilson, I. Whitman.

TOWN OF SANDLAKE, N. Y.—W. Rodgers, D. Shaver, J. L. Lape, P. Shaver, F. Shaver, T. Vanderzee, J. Coon. H. D. Uline, H. Mott, J. J. Lape, B. Taylor, A. Thomas, A. P. Thomas, D. H. Traver, P. M. Younghauts, R. S. Hastings, M. Roberson, A. Moul, J. W. Moul, G. Westfall, G. Miller, G. Garhardt, W. Cline, G. Cline, J. Shear, J. Wheeler, P. Young, J. Keller, P. J. Lown, T. Bullock, J. Cipperley, M. Cipperley, C. Cipperley, J. Minkler, G. Reichard, N. Castle, S. Whealer, W. Moul, J. Westfall, D. Westfall, S. Sagendorph, J. S. Reichard, I. Huntley, H. Finch, W. H. Dewit, A. R. Fox, M. Hoyle.

TOWN OF DAY, N. Y.—P. Colson, G. Baker, A. Lyon, W. A. Randall, A. R. Lawrence, G. Rockwell, A. Deming, J. S. Kinney, J. M. Young, J. Walsh, E. Colson, A. S. Fraker, J. Batcheller, J. Morris, H. Smith, W. Van Anery, E. Paul, C. Gray, L. Yates, W. A. Mosher, W. Mosher, W. Bonce, C. Mosher, A. Mosher, P. Flansburgh, S. Y. Rockwell, J. V. S. Havens, W. Greene, S. K. Lawrence, J. Fraker, J. F. Stimson, E. S. Delong, M. Turner, A. Delong, H. Sweers, H. S. Michaels, A. Graves, J. Dingnan, L. Ackerly, E. Herrick, J. Ross, I. J. Flansburgh, W. H. Marcellus, J. Yates, J. H. Mason, John Yates, W. Bloss, N. Bowe, J. Clute, J. Frasure, W. Yates, J. W. Guiles, B. F. Hildreth, P. Querney, J. Stead, J. Clute, A. Truax, E. Flansburgh, A. Guiles, S. N. Holden, A. Flansburgh, M. Darling, T. Kathan, T. Soloman, L. Goray, S. Houghton, N. Darling, S. Clark, C. E. Shiers, E. Person, A. Ogdeu, E. Bloss, T. Cook, H. Mosher, R. Kathen, O. Ellithorpe, H. Gray, L. Gray, W. Wait, L. Kathan.

TOWN OF HARTFORD, N. Y.—N. Allen, W. Atwood, R. Atwood, L. Arnold, R. Armstrong, R. Baker, W. Bump, J. Bump, R. Bump, J. H. Bump, B. Bell, D. Burke, I.

For three years Joubert & White have taken the First Premium.

HATS and CAPS can always be found at WAIT'S.
Get a HOWE MACHINE and be happy, at WAIT'S. (See page 81.)

SEE INDEX, PAGE ELEVEN. 185

Brayton, A. Brayton, S. Brayton, M. Brayton, S. Brayton, W. Brayton, T. A. Brayton, E. C. Brayton, A. Brayton, H. Brown, W. Brown, M. Bull, A. Briggs, G. Briggs, E. Brown, G. Bull, H. Burrell, W. Burrell, J. Brady, W. Brady, J. Bowen, C. Brayton, G. Bull, J. Bonshee, T. Brown, P. Burch, J. Brayton, G. R. Browne, M. Bourne, C. Brayton, H. Brayton, W. Brady, W. T. Brayton, W. Block, H. Cotton, W. V. Congdon, V. B. Congdon, W. M. Congdon, J. W. Chapman, M. Cooper, W. Coville, W. Casey, J. Conner, A. Cochran, O. Cambbell, J. Cooper, J. Conly, D. Casey, D. Cain, J. H. Deane, W. Davidson, H. Dixson, W. Davis, N. Durkee, O. Durkee, E. B. Dixson, E. Eldridge, T. Eldridge, L. Eli. R. Ellsworth, E. Elms, C. Felch, C. Felch, T. Flagler, J. Flagler, J. T. Goodell, J. D. Gates, L. Gates, H. Gates, N. Z. Gibbs, J. Graham, O. Griffin, T. Griffin, A. Gilchrist, W. Gilchrist, T. Gilchrist, R. H. Gilchrist, J. Graham, A. Gourley, W. Gibson, J. Gibson, J. E. Goodman, J. Guney, W. Grand, E. B. Harden, T. Harris, L. Harris, W. Hall, L. Hall, D. Hall, S. Hall, J. Higley, B. Hathaway, J. Hathaway, G. Hathaway, S. Huggins, L. H. Hills, S. Hall, L. Hatch, R. Holly, S. Harden, O. Heath, L. Ingalls, R. Ingalsbe, M. Ingalsbe, J. L. Ingalsbe, J. Ingalsbe, H. H. Ingalsbe, J. Jakway, T. H. Jakway, W. Johnston, J. Johnston, G. Johnson, M. W. Jones, S. D. Kidder, L. Lee, B. Lester, E. Labersier, J. T. Lytle, J. Luby, A. H. Maynard, J. Merrithen, J. McHughs, J. Magin, J. Martin, H. C. Maynard, J. W. Maynard, T. McDonald, J. McClarty, P. McCarty, A. McCoy, M. McCaughey, G. McCall, C. Marshall, W. Marshall, C. Marshall, Jr., R. Muller, F. McGouldrick, W. McCabe, W. J. McMullen, J. Moore, J. McCoy, J. Mason, R. Mullen, H. Martin, M. Murphy, M. Murry, M. B. McHughs, J. McHughs, J. M. Northup, G. Northup, W. B. Northut, G. H. Newton, M. V. B. Nelson, L. Norton, J. B. Norton, E. B. Norton, R. J. Nichols, H. B. Northup, J. E. Norton, J. Nichols, R. Nichols, O. B. Nelson, D. B. Nelson, P. Noonan, S. B. Oatman, C. Orcutt, S. Orcutt, T. Parks, H. Peets, O. F. Park, H. J. Qua, J. Qua, S. Rice, G. Rice, H. Reynolds, C. Ryerdon, H. Ramsey, D. Roach, A. Smith, J. Smith, R. Smith, G. Smith, P. Shine, D. Sill, R. Sill, Z. Sill, J. Shields, W. Shields, M. H. Slade, W. Slocum, B. Spray, J. Spears, J. Sullivan, W. Stoddard, J. Straight, D. Starks, H. C. Swain, C. B. Swain, J. J. Seeley, E. Townsend, C. Townsend, C. J. Townsend, W. Talman, D. B. Webster, J. F. Whittemore, P. Waller, M. K. Waller, S. Waller, S. M. Waller, T. Waller, W. H. Waller, D. Weer, G. Woddell, H. Woddell, C. Woddell, I. Warren, T. Washburne, W. Washburn, J. Wood, W. Wright, H. S. Wing, R. Wildes, B. S. Walling, C. Weare, M. Wilber.

TOWN OF SARATOGA SPRINGS, N. Y.—G. Algers, C. Ames, H. L. Aiken, Widow J. Black, J. Brown, T. R. Brown, C. Brown, S. Covill, E. Carrigan, J. F. Crawford, G. O. Chamberlain, Dr. Childs, H. D. Curtis, L. Curtis, J. Curtis, W. Cleveland, W. L. Chase, O. Colton, W. Carrigan, Crosby Joshua, T. B. Carroll, A. Cox, E. Davis, C. Davis, W. Dunning, M. Denton, J. Deyoe, A. R. Deyoe, M. Deyoe, J. Davis, J. W. Eddy, J. W. Esmond, M. French, S. Gilbert, O. Granger, Widow H. Granger, J. J. Gilbert, C. E. Gilbert, J. Gaylor, S. Green, G. Gisk, C. Hodgman, J. Ham, S. Hoyt, H. Haight, D. Hayes, C. Ham, Widow W. Hudson, A. Hall, B. Hutchens, E. Hodges, J. Johnson, D. D. Jones, T. Keith, K. Kelley, B. Leggett, C. Lasher, C. B. Moores, J. B. Murry, L. F. Noyce, J. Penrose, G. H. Patrick, B. F. Pryor, J. Pitney, J. Rowley, H. Robler, J. Rouse, L. Riley, J. Riley, R. Riley, J. Ramsdell, M. Ramsdell, C. A. Russell, J. A. Shouts, J. Saunders, W. Swart, R. Seaman, C. Slade, N. Slade, J. H. Shaver, J. Swanick, J. W. Smith, P. Smith, J. Steenburgh, G. Steenburgh, J. Sidmore, A. Tooley, W. Valentine, W. Verbeck, C. Vandenburgh, H. Wilson, F. Whitford, C. Whitford, J. Whitford, L. Warring, W. Warring, H. Weatherwax, C. Well, F. Winterfield, R. Winney, S. S. Wakeman, J. Wheeler.

TOWN OF WILTON, N. Y.—J. Bush, C. Bush, S. C. Green, F. Myres, A. Van Rensselaer, T. F. Comstock, P. Varney, Dr. J. H. Reynolds, J. Merrills, S. Washburn, D. M. Deyoe, H. Brown, J. F. W. Perry, O. Green, H. Woodard, W. Lincoln, J. Westfall, O. McCabe, W. Perry, C. Washburn, J. Goodale, J. Brisbin, J. Sprott, E. Hodges, Dr. T. B. Reynolds, A. J. See, A. Staple, R. E. Taylor, S. S. Carr, D. Carr, W. Comstock, E. Carpenter, J. Taylor, G. B. Hinkley, L. Emerson, C. Ellsworth, S. K. Chase, A. Chase, D. Chase, Mitchell, M. Williams, D. Sullivan, S. E. and H. Dimick, H. Deyoe, E. Sherman, A. Baker, A. B. Ferris, Z. Esmond, J. Esmond, T. Wandle, E. T. Golden, H. Davis, M. Kingsley, J. Sherman, W. Bunse, J. Bunce, J. Sadler, J. Wilkinson, W. L. Cooper, A. G. Cooper, D. Perry, W. Degarms, E. H. King, P. H. Deyo, J. Sherman, N. P. Stiles, P. Arnold, B. Durfee, W. Violie, W. S. Gilbert, B. Phillips, Z. Phillips, C. Holden, T. Ives, K. Perry, W. H. Perry, P. Esmond, J. Shook, J. Grey, P. Stiles, J. Slocum, J. Kathan, O. Hodges, C. Boyce, J. J. Brill, B. Williams, H. Martin, T. Pearsall, J. Miller, G. Ellworth, W. H. Taylor, D. M. Gailor, J. Pratt, I. Roods, G. H. Traver, O. F. Lockwood, D. A. Hunter, J. Delaker, — Sherman, J. Payne, A. D. Lord, P. Dimick, D. K. Taylor, G. Rosa, M. Hull, D. Hunter, M. Ide, H. Reed, J. S. Brackett, L. Howe, J. Ryan, N. Wagoner, J. P. Price, L. Boyce, W. A. Monroe, J. Butler, S. Ruggles, J. E. Quick, S. Petts, G. C. Vandenburgh, R. Milligan and Bros., A. Boyce, M. Miller, I. Boyce, T. Davis, G. Davis, C. Haviland, J. Freborn, D. McNeal, J. Hodges, R. Norman, L. A. Griffin, J. Santell, S. G. Allen, J. D. Stiles, J. McNeal, J. Stiles, D. Stiles, J. Butler, M. Ingersoll, J. Ingersoll, W. B. Collamore, J. Rich, P. C. Deyoe, J. Graves, G. D. Gown, W. Bradford, E. Wilcox, J. D. Perry, H. M. Hudson, L. Adams, I. P. Cookingham, J. Styles, J. Horace, N. Woolley, J. Crawburgh, J. Vandenburgh, S. W. Deyoe, C. C. Shaver, H. Ashley, T. Boyd, E. Boyce, J. H. Carr, A. Clute, J. Degraff, K. K. Deyal, J. Ellsworth, J. M. Gailor, M. W. Hillman, G. W. King, B. Norton, J. H. Norton, J. Patrick, J. Von Burren, N. H. Wicks.

Would you be happy? Buy your Clothing of WILKINS.

Latest styles Bonnets, Jockeys, and Boys' and Infants' Caps and Hoods, at COREY'S, Glen's Falls.

E. H. BENDER, Wholesale and Retail Dealer in every Variety of BOOKS, STATIONERY, &c., 73 State Street, Albany.

186   FARMERS' ALMANAC.

TOWN OF SUDBURY, VT.—J. M. Ketcham, L. Webster, D. L. Sawyer, E. Rich, M. E. Wallis, J. K. Foster, A. J. Ketcham, E. W. Sylvester, F. Holmes, D. Sanders, S. Sawyer, J. F. Goodell, G. and R. Smith, L. Hawkins, D. C. Kellehan, J. B. Hyde, D. W. Wheeler, W. P. J. Hyde, C. C. Sellick, R. Barber, J. K. and A. W. Hyde, C. A. Morton, N. A. Bucklin, J. T. Nichols, G. Harrington, H. Steel, A. and M. Burr, J. and S. Germond, D. H. and F. Landon, F. B. and J. Haff, J. M. Williams, A. Griffin, O. H. P. Ketcham, B Griffin, J. McKenna, T. J. Howard, A. S. Cool, E. Johnson and Bros., J. Spaulding, J. A. Griffin, A. Steel, M. C. Ketcham, F. B. Ketcham, P. Spooner, J. Mound, Z. Roberts, F. McIntyre, O. Downe, S. Young, E. L. Hall, S. Bresee, C. Smith, J. White.

TOWN OF RENSSELAERVILLE, N. Y.—L. Arnold, G. Arnold, A. Abrams, B. Alger, L. Burchard, P. Burhands, J. Bear, L. Burchard, C. Burchard, P. Bear, J. Borthwick, L. Barnes, P. Barrenger, L. Burhands, J. Bates, L. Barnes, jr., A. Benjamin, C. Burhans, J. Conchman, L. Craw, J. Conges, W. Conges, D. Conchman, A. Carl, J. W. Conchman, I. Drake, H. Davis, J. D. Drake, P. Edwards, M. B. Edwards, S. Ford, J. D. Frost, E. Fish, H. Fish, D. Fish, S. Ford, E. Goff, W. Goff, E. Humphrey, P. Hess, J. Hess, S. Hallenbeck, J. Kelsey, H. Kelsey, H. Lennon, R. Mackey, O. Mackey, R. Mackey, L. Mackey, H. Purrington, J. Rushmore, M. Smith, A. Snyder, H. Snyder, J. W. Tanner, I. Van Aken, L. Van Aken, W. Van Aken, S. White, B. White, J. White, C. White, W. S. White, D. White, J. Winters, J. Winters, P. Wicks, M. Watson.

TOWN OF POWNAL, VT.—T. H. Hall, E. A. Potter, B. Dunn, H. Dunn, M. A. Dunn, W. Burgess, J. M. Bacheldor, J. Bennett, P. Niles, D. Exford, L. D. Jepson, jr., O. Bates, A. Barber, C. Jewett, D. F. Bates, P. Wright, G. Montgomery, L. Haley, F. G. Pettibone, L. Burlingham, J. W. Wright, J. W. Hall, A. Ladd, M. Ladd, C. H. Barber, T. Ladd, J. Burrington, O. Niles, J. L. Mason, M. W. Potter, E. Barber, L. Welch, A. and L. Thompson, J. W. Service, S. Pratt, R. F. Parker, S. J. Gardner, A. Mattison, E. B. Mason, J. Myers, J. P. Myers, J. B. Myers, H. Myers, A. Barber, W. Morgan, B. Thompson, A. Fowler, B. G. Arnold, P. Lampman, W. Jackson, J. Barber, A. Morgan, H. R. Wood, O. Towslee, W. Towslee, S. Towslee, L. D Jepson, J. A. Barber, A. Morgan, jr., L. Barber, N. Thompson, A. Barber, P. Bushnell, J. J. Mattison, G. Brummer, J. Wilcox, E. Perkins, R. Stilman, J. W. Gardner, G. Bates, L. Goines, A. Gardner, F. Paddock, T. Brownell, M. Whipple, B. N. Foster, D. Carpenter, T. Paddock.

TOWN OF SUNDERLAND, VT.—G. W. Bradley, E. Bowen, M. Canfield, G. B. Bacon, E. H. Graves, E. G. Goldthwart, J. M. Gregory, J. J. Hill, L. G. King, H. Kenna, C. Parsons, S. Pike, A. R. Stilson, D. H. Andrew, J. Bacon, C. Webb, E. A. Graves, R. L. Graves, E. Hill, E. L. Lawrence, H. N. Shaw, J. Saygood, R. Wilkinson, R. Webb, A. R. Webb, W. A. Webb, A. Williams, A. Judson, F. L. Ames, J. Bowman, A. Elwell, G. W. Fowler, A. Knight, M. Knight, B. F. McLaughlin, D. Perry, W. S. Burt, J. Whitman, D. H. Hall, Milton Warner, C. S. Shaw, S. Henry.

TOWN OF PETERSBURGH, N. Y.—G. S. Odell, H. W. Wells, A. F. Babcock, A. P. Smith, J. G. W. Prosser, J. Coon, T. Buddington, E. Jones, E. P. Taylor, G. G. Allen, A. Hewit, B. F. Torrey, J. Cook, J. G. Phillips, W. Barber, J. S. Moon, S. T. Moon, H. A. Jones, G. C. Waite, C. T. Moon, J. H. Weaver, W. Steward, P. Steward, T. L. Nichols, W. B. Odell, P. Odell, A. Strait, J. G. Clark, J. B. Hewit, D. C. Maxon, N. Maxon, R. Moon, C. Macumber, D. G. Prosser, A. J. Prosser, W. Roach, O. P. Spence, S. L. Reynolds, R. Brimmer, L. Coon, E. S. Randall, G. Springer, N. R. Powel, O. D. Thurber, J. A. Wells, S. H. Eldred, G. Z. Scriven, A. Waterbury, J. H. Bonesteel, C. H. Babcock, D. Kellyer, W. H. Crandall, W. R. Scriven, H. Clark, B. S. Allen, J. H. Thrall, W. J. Pettit, J. Allen, D. Allen, E. J. Allen, J. Allen, J. N. Powers, P. G. Maxon, H. E. Stillman, C. Crandall, D. P. Hakes, Z. H. Scriven, L. Clark, N. Jones, A. Jones, W. R. Jones, S. Green, H. Hewit, C. Maxon, G. Powel, D. E. Welch, A. A. Moses, J. Welch, T. Livingston, W. Green, H. Steward, A. Jones, W. L. Griswold, D. S. Griswold, M. L. Powers, M. T. Brown, R. Brown, J. Lewis, E. R. Clark, S. Hewit, H. Moses, G. A. Sweet, D. E. Holmes, M. Taylor, B. F. Main, J. Odell, S. J. Hakes, A. C. Hakes, F. Hakes, Z. C. Wells, S. Babcock, A. Manchester, S. Green, S. Merithew, E. Thomas, S. C. Peckham, B. Avery, A. Y. Moses, N. Lewis, A. Kenyon, N. Church, J. M. Wells, D. L. Wells, G. Armsbury, J. T. Armsbury, S. Reynolds, H. L. Reynolds, W. W. Reynolds, G. Dennison, W. T. Reynolds, E. Comer, J. W. Tifft, C. H. Moses, A. H. Eldred, A. Brimmer, G. Brimmer, D. J. Brimmer, H. J. Brimmer, R. Crawford, W. Brimmer, M. Willcox, J. Brimmer, H. Babcock, S. Reynolds, J. Wenck, H. Green, D. M. Brimmer, B. B. Babcock.

TOWN OF BRUNSWICK, N. Y.—J. H. Allen, E. P. Abbott, D. V. Adams, J. V. Adams, R. Band, A. Buss, G. Boyles, P. Brust, G. Brust, W. P. Button, J. Brust, A. Bulson, J. H. Bornt, E. Bulson, C. H. Burbeck, M. S. Collyson, F. C. Collyson, W. Clark, J. Clum, H. A. Clum, S. H. Dater, C. W. Dater, H. Dater, G. Derrick, N. Derrick, E. C. Derrick, H. Ensign, W. H. Ensign, J. File, I. S. File, P. File, J. Grace, A. Haynor, A. Haynor, B. Hall, T. P. King, J. Kilmer, J. Link, E. Link, I. McChesney, E. McChesney, S. McChesney, H. McChesney, E. McChesney, T. Newbery, D. Philips, J. Rockenstyre, J. Smith, P. Smith, H. Smith, E. Smith, M. Lohnes, J. S. Eddy, J. Schermerhorn, J. Springer, P. Springer, J. H. Springer, G. M. Springer, C. Springer, B. P. Wagar, J. J. Wagar, A. Wagar, H. R. Conrad, E. Wagar, M. Hayner, G. A. Brust, W. Lape, A. Derrick, W. A. Derrick, J. B. Betts, T. H. Betts, J. L. Roberts, M. Coonrad, R. C. Collins, R. C. Derrick, S. H. Hull, A. S. Weatherway, W. J. Stillman, J. H. Coonrad, P. Haner, F. Groom, L. Brill, S. Simmons, M. Springer, R. McChesney, N. Dater, I. D. Hakes, B. B. Link.

Do your Teeth need Extracting?   Go to GARRETT'S.

White & Pearsall's Extensive Clothing Establishment, Glen's Falls.

For WINDOW SHADES, go to WAIT'S.
Kid, Buck and Calf GLOVES and MITTENS, at WAIT'S. (See page 81.)

SEE INDEX, PAGE ELEVEN. 187

Davis' Sewing Machine, best in market, on account of simplicity, durability, strength and perfection of work. For sale by COREY, Glen's Falls.

TOWN OF WARRENSBURGH, N. Y.—E. Wood, A. Scripter, G. Moulton, H. Moulton, A. L. Griswold, J. Moon, F. Woodward, B. Langworthy, L. Millington, J. A. McDonald, B. A. Potter, B. Graves, J. Norton, J. Woodward, L. Norton, J. J. Wood, J. Pelletier, J. P. West, S. Griffin 2d, P. Richards, P. McGan, A. Baker, J. Ripley, J. Beadville, E. G. Hall, R. Bennett, E. Cilley, E. Chadwick, L. Latham, N. Middleton, W. Middleton, E. Pratt, W. Farrington, A. Dodge, E. T. Sargent, O. Feathers, R. McKnight, B. M. Thompson, S. B. Noxon, M. Curdick, W. B. Farlin, S. Griffin, P. Stone, N. Burdick, J. Harrington, G. Weaver, G. Stone, S. D. Judd, J. Bennett, J. Woodward, T. Harrington, J. T. Harrington, W. Harrington, I. Harrington, B. Newton, H. M'Nutt, R. Gleason, C. Hill, R. O. Bryant, A. Viele, G. Lockwood, J.W. Harrington, J. McLarren, A. Aldrich, M. Burdick, C. Scribner, D. Varnum, H. K. Lewis, E. Chase, H. Wood, S. Bennett.

TOWN OF PITTSFIELD, VT.—C. A. Thomas, A. J. Ellis, J. N. Ranney, J. Ranney, A. Ellis, M. Tenney, W. Swift, J. Chandler, G. W. Sawyer, E. Martin, A. F. Guernsey, R. Guernsey, J. Ellis, J. Durkee, A. B. Lamb, J. G. Allen, C. C. Martin, J. Knight, I. Sherburn, I. Marrill, A. Allen, S. Warren, E. Segar, G. Segar, L. Breed, W. R. Blassom, O. Blassom, A. Thompson, S. Burr, J. Segar, A. Pinney, Rev. J. B. Clark, K. Brown, L. Patch, I. Holt, E. Twitchell, R. Ranney, O. Avery, J. Howe, M. Townsend, D. W. Long, R. Rice, B. A. Swan, I. Faggart, A. Pinney, S. Biship, E. Haner, A. Johnston, A. T. Boutwell, A. Pinney, L. Fuller, E. M. Rish, M. T. Parmenter, T. Parmenter, H. B. Call, D. W. Ranney, T. L. Parmenter, J. Case, L. Parmenter, A. Davis, W. Davis, C. Gibbs, H. O. Gibbs, R. Holt.

TOWN OF NORTHUMBERLAND, N. Y.—D. A. Bullard, J. Conery, P. Lennon, J. A. Wilson, A. E. Houseworth, W. D. Laing, E. W. Town, L. Suttalee, J. Billings jr., A. L. Finne, J. R. Fake, J. Mulquinn, J. Coffinger, F. Chapman, E. Hammond, J. Rourk, A. H. Pearsall, O. J. Bates, W. S. Deyoe, J. E. Bennett, J. H. Thompson, A. B. Bancus, D. Deyoe, J. C. Chapman, E. Woolley, S. Slocum, S. Winney, M. Comeskey, G. Reynolds, L. Vanderwerker, J. R. Vanderwerker, S. J. Burt, O. Burt, J. Burt, T. Fitzsimmons, J. H. Bullard, J. Rose, W. Leggett, S. Lewis, N. Sherman, G. Rouse, W. Hilton, C. Smith, G. Sutlin, W. H. Butcher, S. West, J. C. Harris, S. Vandenburgh, R. Hacket, D. De Garmo, E. Purinton, S. Thompson, L. Thompson, E. Strong, H. Ransom, N. Mory, J. B. Doty, W. Doty, J. W. Fuller, G. Hunter, C. Best, A. Smith, J. Snyder, L. Merchant, J. Merchant, J. Martin, G. Durkee, L. P. Burt, H. Snyder, H. Hall, J. Mulford, C. Mulford, J. M. Boice, D. Gahusha, A. Adams, W. Pettit, P. McGown, D. Willard, J. Brown, A. Brown, S. Clark, H. Ross, J. Fuller, E. J. Welch, E. B. Losee, H. Purinton, D. Purinton, S. Adams, W. Butcher, G. H. West, G. Lansing, D. West, S. Mott, J. Hanrahan, T. Hanrahan, P. Nevins, D. D. Mulford, S. B. Thompson, A. G. Deyoe, E. Petties, W. L. West, S. Holbrook, E. Whitford, G. Hartwell, A. S. Johnson, F. Winney, K. D. Winney, T. Williams, F. P. Rugg, W. J. Cook, R. D. Robins, E. Goodman, J. Sullivan, H. Cramer, J. H. Deyoe, T. W. Cramer, S. Chapman, J. Billings, G. Peek, J. Marshall, A. Marshall, J. R. Deyoe, W. H. Dodd, P. H. Lasher, F. Terhune, C. R. Burt, R. Burt, E. Mosher, D. Duncan, D. Duncan, J. Bancus, M. Lewis, F. Weil, J. Esmond, W. Ball, J. V. Snyder, H. Bishop, J. Bishop, L. Campbell, S. Gifford, A. Hall, S. Nelsey, M. J. Vanderwerker, J. Vanderwerker, J. Vanderwerker, J. S. Freeman, R. K. Thompson, J. Bickby, J. A. Palmer, R. White, W. Powel, D. Welch, J. Wagoner, T. Murphy, M. Gifford, E. Rice, H. Rice, H. Davis, W. Reddin, B. Collahan, D. Coffinger, A. De Garmo, C. H. Duel, G. M. Fields, S. Fuller, C. Green, O. Hilton, J. Mathis, D. Kingsley, E. Moran, N. Robinson, L. Robinson, E. Sweet, W. Vanderwerker, J. B. Winney, C. De Garmo, J. Mulford.

TOWN OF SUDBURY, VT.—H. Steel, G. Harrington, R. V. R. Horton, S. Breesa, E. L. Hall, S. Young, W. C. Haven, J. S. Haven, J. White, P. Smith, C. A. Morton, N. A. Bucklin, A. W. Hyde, R. Barber, C. C. Selleck, W. H. Sillir, H. J. Spencer, W. P. Abbott, A. C. Griffin, J. M. Williams, B. Morton, B. J. Haff, J. Germond, M. Clifford, F. F. Landon, P. Lester, A. Steel, J. Griffin, A. Horton, A. S. Cool, S. J. Howard, Johnson Bros., M. Ketchum, B. Griffin, C. E. Hewitt, W. Clark, J. F. Goodell, R. Smith, J. Smith, D. L. Sawyer, S. Sawyer, E. Rich, M. E. Wallace, J. K. Foster, A. J. Ketchum, E. W. Sylvester, F. Holmes, P. Holmes, L. Barrett, D. Sanders, Z. Roberts, A. C. Ackerman, P. Spooner, B. F. Ketcham, J. M. Ketcham, L. Webster, L. Hawkins, J. B. Hyde, C. Abbott, N. Knowlton, D. W. Wheeler, G. Rustutt, W. P. J. Hyde, P. Ketcham, S. Jones, C. Churchill, W. Brink, W. Blake, A. Burr.

TOWN OF MOREAU, N. Y.—W. Anderson, T. Abbot, M. Abbot, W. P. Angel, J. Allen, G. Burnham, B. Barker, L. Coffin, M. Buckbee, C. Betts, B. E. Bartlet, C. Bentley, J. Betts, W. Ball, D. Childs, B. F. Cornell, J. M. Cary, G. Cook, J. Cary, W. Carr, W. Cary, S. Crandell, C. Cronen, O. Carr, L. Cornell, W. Crandall, G. Comstock, H. L. Davis, R. Davenport, B. Durham, J. Davenport, D. Donahee, G. Degarmore, R. Denton, M. T. Dunnings, D. Devol, J. Devol, J. Edmonds, A. Ensign, D. H. Eddy, M. Fish, G. Griswold, W. Griswold, J. Hamilton, M. Henman, L. Hamlin, W. Hamilton, S. Hawley, W. Hayes, P. Hamilton, A. F. Hichcook, T. Hurley, A. Hacket, T. C. Howe, W. Hendly, J. Hodges, B. Inglasbee, W. Inglasbee, N. Jenkins, M. Jacobee, H. Jacobee, H. Jacobee, J. N. Jocobee, N. J. Jacobee, J. Jackson, P. Johnson, J. Johnson, P. Johnson, J. Kimpland, Mrs. A. Knapp, W. Knowland, J. Kingsley, T. King, H. Kenyon, N. B. Luther, B. Langdon, J. Lord, A. Laclaverack, B. Latimore, A. Lapoint, Mrs. J. La Barron, J. M. La Barron, J. McNamarra, H. Murray, S. Mott, W. Mott, R. Mott, S. Mott, J. W. Morgan, S. V. Mott, W. H. Miller, T. Newell, G. Bush, D. Newton, T. O'Brine, L. Olmstead, P. O'Brine, H. Parks, M. Parks, S. Ott, S. Olmstead, M. Parks, D. Parks, M.

Ding, dong, bell! **WILKINS is bound to sell.** (See p. 96.)

Fancy NOTE PAPER and ENVELOPES, Stamped with Initials or Monograms, at E. H. BENDER'S, 73 State Street, Albany.

188　　　　FARMERS' ALMANAC.

B. Parks, E. Pixley, J. Linchan, I. Palmer, J. Palmer, I Palmer, F. Palmer, W. Potter, G Rublin, N. Rice, P. Russel, A. L. Reynolds. S. Rhenbolton, M. D. Richards, T. Roach, C. H. Robinson, W. Ryalls, J. Rogers. J. W. snyder. W. Smith, C. Scovill, J. Skym, J. Smith, T. Smith, J. Sill, W. Stevens. A. Sprott, A. Sprott, J. Sprott, G. Sprott, O. Sweet, J. Sweet. T. Sweet, M. H. Sweet, S. Sweet, I. Slade, P. Stanton, J. Sprott, D. Sprott, T. Spicer, A. Schovill, E. Thompson, J. Thompson, A. M. Thompson, J. H. Thompson, Mrs. G. Tucker, G. Theyr, W. Theyr, N. Taylor, B, Vanwagoner, J. Varney, A. Varney, Z. Vandusen. S. Vandusen. A. Wyman, H. Washburn. D. Walker. P. Whigg, W. Waldren, G. H Wood, H. Wheeler. O. Woodward, A. Whipple, W. Williams. S. Whipple, A. Yates. G. Yates, J. Yardell.

TOWN OF CHARLTON. N. Y.—A Cox. J. Hedden. J. C. Smith. J. Watkins. H. Mead, D. W. Cook. P. Crane. J. Galager. J. W. Sherman. J. Brand, E. B. Sanders 2d, M. E. Myers. M. B. Bedding. F. D. Curtice. W. Y. K. Taylor. H. Folger, A. Laws, A. Davidson. G. L. Hall. E. B. Sanders 1st. M. Millard, L. Smith, Z. G. Crane, N. H. Sherman, A H. Hays. J. Harvey. A. Banta. W. L. Taylor. C. B. Murry. B. H. Knapp. A. Merchant, J. De Graff, W. H. Coon. J. M. Wells. C. Arnold. F. Curtiss. R. Taylor. J. Gardner, W. T. Williams. R. Ketchum. H. A. Smith, A. Y. Van Vorst. D. R. Holbrook, J. A. Parrent, J. Maxwell. W. K. Maxwell. J. L. South, E. Lard. D. L. Smith, J. Young, M. A. Van Vrankin, M Parrent. S. Barns. J. N. Budd, D. M. Watkins. T. Smith, J. N. La Rue, C. B. Janson. W. De Reaner, Peter Van Guyslin. M. L. R. Valatine, J. L. R. Valatine, J. C. Lane. J. Tower. W. A. Packer, T. Stag. J. Burns, G. Tibbitts, J. McConkie, R. V. Mynders, G. Crawford, H. Morehouse. J. E. McKnight, T. Alberts. G. A. Swart. J. Hays. D. L. Covert. N. Fisch. A. Devenport, W. O. Smith, P. Bann. I. C. Groot. T. Feeny. J. A. Sweetman, J. Gillen. N. Capin, J. F. Lerider. G. R. Beach, W. A. Cook. E. Weld, T. Hollnres. O, Tabar, T. H. Cunningham. M. H. Smith. J. B. Heaton. T. Wicks. G. M. Bell. J. H. Knapp, G. Bell. R. F. Alexander. R. H. Hallowel, J. Bell, B. Francisco, C. Robins. J. Mutlow. E. Weld. M. Panl, J. Covert, J. Davidson, E. Groot. J. H. Skinner. J. Sanders. E. Consulus. J. Anderson. W. R. Bunyan. R. Crothers. J. C. Gilchrist. J. Alexander. H. Ostrum. A. Lennon. T. McKindley, D. H. Ostrum. W. Watkins, D. A. Smith, E A. Wilkie. J. Mead. P. Toby, A. Gilchrist. E. T. Smith, R. H. Clark, W. Sneallie. R. Youngs. J. Morrow, J. B. Gilchrist. J. Glen. J. F. Bell, J. Prece, T. M. Gilchrist, A. De Graff. J. Conde. H. C. Hedden. G. C. Valatine.

TOWN OF CHITTENDEN, VT.—W. Osgood. J. A. Davis, N. Davis, B. B. Capron, W. Perkins, L. Edmunds. H. Eddy, H. and H. F. Baird. J. Baird. R K. Baird, S. Clark, M. L. Dow. D. Baird, H. Pratt, T. Hibbard. G. Hibbard. N. Hewett. R. Parish, A. Powell. C. Hewett. F. Bogue, C. Mills, H. Long. W. Edmunds. G. and L. Billings, T. Beebe, T. Borden. A. Durkee. A. Dodge. G. F, Durkee. T. E. Baird, D. D. Barnard, R. Harris. A. Ranney. J. Whetmore. A. Churchill. R. O. Dow, D. Whetmore. R. Morris, A. Mullin. M Fox. C. M. Wright. W. K. Baird, A. Collins. H. S. Alexander. H. Randall, P. and W. Shehy, J. Tarble. C. Manley. L. Bump. J. Cunningham, W. Mullin. E. Barnard and S. Tarble, Q. Churchill, J. Leonard. R. Woods. L. T. Winslow. S. W. Harrison, W. O. Harrison, P. Mullin. O. Monley. J. Condon. G. A. Bassett, E. Dowling, J. Halpin, T. Granger, A. L. Breed, J. Shaw. D. Noyes, H. Higgins.

TOWN OF FAIRHAVEN, VT.—Adams and Allen, J. Alard. S. H. Allard. A. Allen, Allen and Son. J. Adams, H. Alard. E. L. Allen. C. Austin. A. Briggs. A. Blanerhasset, H. Briggs. T. Boulger. H. Burk. L. Barber. M. Barber. J. Burnes. Widow Barnes, L. N. Collins. J. Campbell. R. M. Copeland and Co.. A. S. Cushman, Copeland and Williams, A. Dutton. I. Davey. I. Davey. S M. Dewey. Widow Dyer. Z. C. Ellis. E. Esty. W. B. Esty. O. Eddy. O. and J. W. Eddy. W. J. Esty. C. Eddy, L. Fish, J. T. Freeman. C. G. Fish. F. Farewell. M. and M. Fairhaven and Co., E. Gould, jr., T. Gilbert, C. Gardner, B. F. Gilbert. J. O. Gready. H. C. Gleason, Hughs and Owens. A. Hawley, T. Holloran, jr., O. Hamilton, H. Hamilton, A. W. Hyde, H. Hows, Widow Hosford, C. Inman, jr., R W. Jones, A. H. Kidder, W. C. Kitridge, W. Kinney, T. Miller, M. McNamara. Myers and Co., S. Miller, J. Morse. B. C. Naramore, M. O'Brine. D. Ormes. Owens and Hughs, O. Proctor. N. J. Proctor, J. Preston. W. Preston, C. B. Ramsey and Son, O. P. Ramsey, R. Richards, A. Richardson, R. Ray, H. Stanard. H. Sheldon, L. Sheldon, J. K. Sheldon, J. P. Sheldon, J. Sheldon, J. and J. Sheldon. J. J. Stow, J. Sheldon, P. Stair, L. Spaulding. Scotch Hill Slate Co., W. L. Town, J. Wilson, D. P. Wescott. J. Whitlock. S. Whitlock, J. D. Wood. C. E. Wood, J. P. Willard, A. Willard, H. Wescott, R. Wood, S. Wood. C. C. Whipple, J. J. Williams.

TOWN OF HADLEY, N. Y.—H. Aldrich, T. W. Austin, J. W. Allen. W. Aldrich. J. Brian, H. Blackwood, C. Blackwood. J. Bugsbee. J. Blowers, L. Bratt. A. Bovard, W. Blowers, C. Dayton, T Dayton, J. Dunn. G. H. Dingman, J. Dingman. J. Dorily, H. Dean, E..Ellis, E. A. Ellis, J. Everts, J. Elsworth, J. M. Flauders, J. Gilbert. S. Gray. E. Gray, B Gray, J. Gray, A. Graham. J. C. George, T. Goodnow, W. Goodnow. A. Hall, J. Holland, E. Hillman. O. S. Holden. A. Houghton. J. K. Houghton, T Harper, J. Huse, R. Johnson. J. Jeffers, M. Jeffers, H. S. Jenkins. T. Jones, M. Kellogg. A. Kennedy, C. Kennedy. D. Kennedy, D. Keef. J. Laughton. D. Martin, H. Moore, E. Newton, F. Odell. A. H. Palmer, J. C. Palmer, R. Parker, D. Parker. J. Parker, W. Parker, C. Rockwell, L. Rice, D. Swears. J. P. Salsbury, J. Smith, R. Scofield, J. Scovil, E. P. Smead, S. Varney, R. Woodcock, L. Wells. H. Wilcox. L. Woodard, H. Woodard, L. Wait and Co., D. A. Wheelock, J. H. Woodcock, R. Rollman.

TOWN OF WALLINGFORD, VT.—A. Hull. J. Anderson, R. Marsh, N. Hudson, E. Shomb, W. G. Marsh, P. Smith, B. Reilay, J. S. Emery, E. Crary, P. McInlear, O. Bal-

Joubert & White have a nice Chart in their office, Glen's Falls.

**Gents' FURNISHING GOODS, at WAIT'S One Price Store.
Ladies' FURS, in great variety, at WAIT'S. (See page 81.)**

SEE INDEX, PAGE ELEVEN. 189

lou, Wright and Phillips, J. Brown, G. Ramsbottom, J. Clemmons, H. Clemmons, H. Porter, O. Bump, J. Grover, L. Ainsworth jr., J. Monahan, W. Moors, L. Mann, H. Sherman, A. Adams, E. W. Kent, A. Warner, J. Randall, F. Miller, C. M. Townsend, H. H. Waldo, W. W. Kelly, D. Townsend, S. D. Townsend, P. G. Clark, L. Andrus, J. E White, W. F. Kelly, N. White, R. Hopkins, T. Edgerton, B. Perry, G. Hopkins, C. Button, H. Edgerton, S. Sherman, H. Edgerton 2d, I. Edmonds jr., D. Hagar, O. Hagar, E. Johnson, C. Buel, J. Hawkins, J. Dorson, C. Hagar, M. Shaw, I. Sweatland, M. Starky, L. Dorson, P. G. Hawkins, J. W. Gates, S. G. Gates, J. Gates, H. Patch, A. Barrons, J. C. Patch, D. Bucklim, L. French, A. Eddy, J. Colvin, W. L. Marsh, L. W. Congdon, J. H. Congdon, J. Culver, J. Dodge, M. Anderson, N. Anderson, I. Smith, E. H. Smith, H. Johnson, H. Pelsue, A. Chilson, A. Kent, S. Hemingway, W. Davenport, J. Wilmarth, J. Jackson, W. Kent, J. R. Fuller, W. B. Allen, E. Chilson, J. White, R. Earl, B. Gorton, I. Edmunds jr., W. Palmer, S. E. Rogers, J. Fuller, W. Fuller, J. Doty, W. Croft, J. Croft, B. Stafford, S. Hill, L. Ames, C. O. Stafford, D. Doty, C. Hall, N. Cook, L. E. Stafford, D. Hulett, L. Hulett, L. Brockway, G Earl, S. Aldrich, I. Aldrich, A. Stafford, A. M. Bruce, C Bruce, O. Carpenter, B. Stone, E. Ballou.
   TOWN OF JOHNSBURGH, N. Y.—H. Richards, R. Hodgson, R. Armstrong, H. Pennells, T. M. Somersville, W. Bates, R. G. Barney, E. Richards, E. O. Putnam, H. Waddell, J. M. Spoor, A. H. Pasko, R. Kenwill, D. F. Sheffer, D. H. Armstrong, A. Armstrong, A. Rexford, J. Eldridge, H. Liddle, J. Kenwill, L. Dunkler, T. Wakeley, O. Hitchcock, J. T. Smith, D. McCartha, S. Sheffields, J. Anderson, P. Glennon, T. Spain, Mrs. C. Dunn, H. B. Kenyon, R. Hack, T. A. Somerville, N. T. Eldridge, E. Morgan, S. Morgan, S. Somerville, J. A. Cole, J. Cooper, H. Hewitt, jr., W. Wakely, W. H. Davison, S. Armstrong, J. W. Armstrong, R. H. Armstrong, E. Dunklee, W. Lackey, M. Jipson, W. Moore, L. Girard, O. Bruno, J. McAvey, Mrs. D. Armstrong, J. Hodgson, R. Montgomery I. Morehouse, S. Morehouse, J. Ward, J. Wakeley, R. Whipple, A. Waddell, W, Pasko, J. Pope, T. W. Somerville, B. Harrington, T. J. Smith.
   TOWN OF MENDON, VT.—W. Buckley, A. Bissell, T. Buckley, T. Canty, P. Canty, H. S. Clark, J. and P. Cooney, Doyan and Murphy, T. Dunn, H. L. Eggleston, C. Eggleston, L. M. Gleason, A. Hatch, C. B. Hemenway, H. and J. Hawley, J. E. Johnson, M. Johnson, P. Kelly, J. Kelly, G. T. Kennerson, W. Kimball, L. Kelly, J. Lode, R. Magen, J. McLaughlin, D. McCarty, D. H. Orms, G. D. Petty, B. F. Harker, T. Pendergrass, E. Pike, A. Pike, jr., A. Pike, P. Prema, J. Blath, M. Pike, H. Pike, H. Pike, jr., F. Provost, P. Quirk, R Ranger, J. Ranger, R. F. Ranger, R. C. Richardson, J. Sawyer, I. P. Shaw, W. H. Shedd, H. Shedd, J. S. Seward, C. Stebbins, M. Shippee, O. Seargent, G. W. Sawyer, T. Spellman, O. Tenney, R. Thomas, H. F. Wilkins, G. A. Wilkins, H. Wood, E. R. Willis, L. Young.
   TOWN OF GRAFTON, N. Y.—I. B. Ford, A. B. Sweet, V. B. Jones, E. B. Howard, R. S. F.Waite, N. T. Burdick S. Allen, J. G Acoff, H. M. Arnsbury, I. Brock, A. M. Burdick, W. Church, S. Church, W. Steward, S. L. Corbin, H. Hassann, Reuben Hall, Silas Brock, T. Keller, H. A. Phillips, A Eldred, D. L. Scriven J. B. West, H. Banker, S. Hewitt, L. A. Hall, J. A. Phillips, W. J. Hakes, G. W. Scriven, P. R. Scriven, Rev H. L. S. Lewis, H. Feathers, W. C. Crandall, L. J. Agan, J. M. Brown, A. S. Brown, J. H. Bulson, G. H. Barnhart, W. B. Clark, P. Campbell, A. Clickner, G. H. Coonradt, G. W. Cotrell, W. Covey, G. Dumbleton, O. Dumbleton, J. Foster, A. Eldred, W. H. Grogan, B. Hayner, W. Hydorn, A. Hall, I. S. Howard, C. Johnson, R. Love, W. M. Lamphier, J. Keller, J. D. Martin, D. P. Martin, Dr. A. Maxon, A. C. Hunker, M. T. Brown, G. Warren, P. T. Hydorn, J. B. Durkee, R. P. West, D. E. Saunders, J. C. Hakes, N. L. Hakes, J. S. Saunders, A. H. Scriven, J. H. Scriven, W. W. Mateson, N. West, B. Dunham, H. B. Littlefield, J. M. Foster, W. Land, M. I. Barras, A. B. Burdick, R. Westervelt, J. L. West, L. P. Worthington, H. R. Worthington, A. D. Littlefield, H. W. Littlefield, A. W. Ford, A. I. Snyder, P. Hydorn, B. Bonesteel, A. Allen, P. S. Corbin, W. Odell, C. Osgood, D. I. Peckham, S. S. Peckham, W. W. Reynolds, J. H. Refenburgh, S. Stoel, E. Shaver, N. W. Simmons, D. L. Simmons, J. B. Slade, J. Snyder, M. Snyder, G. M. Arnsbury, H. Sweet, P. H. Jones, G. Tilley, F. P. West, S. V. R. Odell, W. Andrew, A. Wagar, W. Tilley, T. M. Tilley, A. Shaver, S. M. Steward, E. Steward, E. Snyder, G. W. Maxon.
   TOWN OF SHAFTSBURY, VT.—S. Ames, A. Ames, C. Andrew, G. C. Andrew, B. Andrew, H. and M. Barton, P. Bates, J. Bates, I. Bates, N. Bates, R. G. and A. Blackmer, E. M. Blakeley, W. P. Striker, J. Bowen, H. D. Bowen, L. Battum, L. R. Bowen, N, Battum, N. Battum, E. Buck, D. Buck, G. E. Buck, J. Bentley, S. Bottum, B. Solomon, J. Carpenter, E. V. Chase, M. Clark, H. Cole, P. Cole, N. Cross, J. N. Cross, T. Carpenter, C. Covey, J. Crahan, T. Darling, J. Dickinson, B. Dickinson, T. Draper, E. N. Dyer, G. W. Duncan, H. C. Elwell, T. Elwell, J. Elwell, jr., C. Elwell, M. Ellsworth, S. Elwell, P. and C. M. Fisk, A Fox. T. Fuller, N Fuller, M. Gidden, R F. Galusha, F. Galusha, M. Galusha, A. Galusha, Lyman and Seymour, Galusha, J. Galusha, A. Galusha, G. Green, H. Green, S Green, J. Hayward, A. Howard, S. Howard, M. F. Huntington, A. O. Huntington, L. Huntington, G. Huling, H. Hulet and Bros., P. Hulet, T. Horton, S. Hawkins, E. Hawkins, A. Hawkins, C. Harrington, S. Harrington, J. Harrington, J. Harrington and Sons, J. Hughs, W. Johnson, A. Johnson, F. Johnson, N. Kenson, M. L. Lane, C. C. Lane, G. Lane, B. Labouti. W. Loomis, A. Martin, O. Mattison, H. Mattison, M. and F. Mattison, R. Mattison, I. Mattison, J. B. Mattison, G. S. Mattison, R. Mattison, H. Mattison, J. T. Mattison, E. R. and S. E. Martin, C. S. Martin, E. McIntosh, N. Millington, G. P. Montgomery, J. and C. Morse, S. W. Monroe, T. Murray, D. Mattison, P S. Millington, D. Millington, C. M. Mattison, J. Montgomery, G. Montgomery, M. Murray, J. Niles, J. B.

Have your Clothing made at WILKINS'. (See page 96.)

P. H. COREY, dealer in MILLINERY and STRAW GOODS, GLEN'S FALLS.

E. H. BENDER, Wholesale and Retail Dealer in every Variety of
BOOKS, STATIONERY, &c., 73 State Street, Albany.

190 FARMERS' ALMANAC.

and J. S. Niles, W. W. Niles, D. S. Niles, J. A. P. Niles, M. N. Niles, S. W. Niles. H. D. Niles, A. Olin, A. Olin, jr., J. H. Olin, E. Olin, M. O'Kief, T. O'Council, H. Perkins, A. and A. Pierce, A. Pierce, L. Percey, J. S. Wait, W. Wait, J. Wait, T. Wait, G. Woodard, J. Rockwood, T. Robinson, S. Stockwell, C. D. Sweet, S. T. Surdam, D. Spencer, Darius Slocum, B. Stanley, E. and B. Smith, R. L. Strikle, E. Stone, R. Stone, C. Stone, Wm. Summers, M. Straiton, W. D. Taft, A. Taft, D. Tinkham, E. Tinkham, L. Tracey, H. Vaughan, A. Wheeler, J. H. Wheeler, M. Wheelock, D. C. Wheelock, H. D. Wood.

TOWN OF GREENBUSH, N. Y.—B. C. Akin, F. W. Akin, S. Allen, W. A. Austin, M. Bloomingdale, E. E. Brown, W. Bridger, L. L. Bagg, W. Blau, C. Bradbury, Q. Link, J. Best, W. R. Bedell, C. Crehan, W. Conse, J. A. Craver, J. Craver, A. W. Craver, J. T. Davis, W. R. Defreest, A. Dings, B. G. Dennison, D. Defreest, M. D. Defreest, J. K. Defreest, E. Davitt, G. Dunn, D. Defreest, C. Defreest, Dr. D. Elliott, E. Elliott, W. Elliott, J. Earing, E. J. Gennett, W. Goeweye, D. Green, B. Hoes, I. Hayes, P. R. Hogle, A. Hallenbeck, J. Hogle, J. Hall, W. P. Irwin, D. W. Irwin, M. O. Keefe, J. Keefe, N. Knowlton, P. Karner, J. C. Karner, T. Karner, C. Karner, G. Kimball, B. Kimmey, S. Kimball, A. Levingston, M. Lansing, W. Link, W. A. Lape, J. S. Link, W. L. Link, W. A. McCulloch, A. Morris, H. Mellius, D. S. Moore, S. Miller, M. Moulds, G. G. Ostrander, H. Ostrander, J. J. Ostrander, T. W. Olcott, M. Ostrander, W. Pratt, J. N. Porkman, D. Phillips, I. Polhamus, J. Proper, C. S. Payne, N. Proper, J. Phillips, A. Phillips, P. Reynolds, L. W. Ryesdorph, L. Ryesdorph, W. Ryesdorph, G. B. Rhodes, J. Ryter, W. Snook, G. Shehley, T. B. Simmons, A. H. Smith, E. A. Sliter, W. Sliter, P. Shaver, W. B. Schermerhorn, A. Slingerland, W. E. Scott, T. Teller, J. V. B. Teller, A. R. Traver, A. P. Traver, L. P. Traver, A. Traver, C. G. Vanrensselaer, C. Vaurensselaer, G. Vanrensselaer, J. Vandenburgh, I. Vanvalkenburgh, A. E. Vanallen, M. Vandenburgh, R. Vanburen, E. Wansyer, J. D. Whitbeck, A. L. Wetherwax, L. Wetherwax, M. Warner, A. Warner, S. Warner, J. Whitbeck, W. Witbeck, E. Wackerhagen, J. Yagle.

TOWN OF LANDGROVE, VT.—E. Abbott, J. Abbott, W. W. Abbott, W. K. Adams, A. Barber, J. Brown, H. Bolster, F. D. Bolster, D. Blood, A. Childs, D. Cooledge, D. A. Cooledge, A. Cary, J. Davis, jr., E. Davis, G. Davis, N. P. Davis D. G. Davis, S. Derby, J. Emerson, D. Eddy, H. Farnum, A. L. Fuller, A. Fenn, H. C. Fenn, D. Fisk, G. Fisk, E. Gilligan, D. Garfield, J. R. Haynes, C. Kingsbury, S. B. Kingsbury, J. Kidder, S. Kelley, T. J. Laikin, E. Moore, T. O. Moore, A. Nichols, S. Russel, A. Reynolds, F. shaw, L. Shaw, G. B. Shaw, J. Smith, J. Swallow, F. Shepherd, M. Thomson, J. S. Thomson, W. E. Tuttle, A. and H. Utley, W. W. Wiley, H. P. Warner, C. Woodward, A. Woodward, L. Woodward, H. Woodward, W. D. Wiggins.

TOWN OF GUILDERLAND, N. Y.—I. and T. Amsdell, L. Alright, E. Abrams, Geo. Allright, C. Armstrong, M. J. Blessing, M. L. G. Blessing, W. Birdsall, E. Bloomingdale, P. Ball, A. Bugger, M. F. Blessing, A. Bloomingdale, W. Becker, P. Bloomingdale, N. Beebe, J. P. Bloomingdale, C. Bloomingdale, J. H. Blessing, J. A. Blessing, T. Brennen, E. Becker, J. Becker, D. Becker, P. and J. Barkluff, P. Beebe, M. Beebe, B. Alvane, W. T. Beebe, N. Becker, J. H. Beebe, W. Blessing, E. Boughton, M. Y. Chesebro, John Cromme, J. Craver, S. Carhart, W. and T. Chesebro, R. D. Carhart, T. Clark, J. Carr, W. Crosby, J. Clay, J. J. Clute, H. Coon, R. C. Case, L. Crook, T. Carr, H. Carhart, J. W. Clute, H. C. Crounsey, J. Coon, G. F. Crounse, C. P. Crounse, A. Crounse, M. Crounse, W. P. Crounse, C. I. Crounse, F. L. Clikeman, J. Crounse, H. P. Crounse, J. P. Crounse, C. Chesebro, A. J. Crounse, J. F. Crounse, A. Cass, F. and J. Crounse, W. Clute, J. H. Clute, J. Cornick, D. Cass, J. Crounse, P. Dugan, C. M. Dennison, A. Dyer, G. Dutcher, A. Delmot, W. G. Davis, W. Davis, Widow Evens, J. Ellis, M. Fredendall, J. Fitzpatrick, John Fryer, P. Fryer, J. Fryer, A. Fryer, J. A. Fryer, J. Furguson, P. M. Frederick. D. and M. Frederick, H. Fredendall, C. Frederick, S. S. Fowler, J. J. Fryer, J. Frederick, C. Frederick, W. H. Furbeck, P. Fowler, W. Farley, G. H. Goodfellow, C. Goodfellow, P. Grant, S. D. Griffen, A. Groat, J. P. Griggs, J. H. Gardner, J. B. Grey, E. Grey, A. Gifford, R. Harris, W. Hallenbeck, C. Hein, A. Helme, J. Helme, J. H. Hewett, J. Hallenbeck, W. Henderson, C. Hartman, Widow Harris, W. Houghton, W. L. Van Auken, J. Van Auken, T. Van Auken, J. Van Etten, B. Van Auken, J. Vroman, A. Van Auken, F. Van Wie, J. Vroman, P. M. Veeder, F. P. Wormer, A. Wormer, J. C. Wormer, F. C. Wormer, P. Wormer, jr., D. F. Wormer, J. W. Waggoner, W. Woods, A. Wilkins, J. H. Wilsey, M. Wise, S. Westfall, J. Wormer, P. Welch, J. M. Williams, J. Weaver, A. Winnie, J. Wagner, G. Wagner, D. Wormer, L. Witherwax, A. Witherwax, A. Westfall, H. Witherwax, I. Walker, J. H. Waldron, C. Wood, S. Winn, P. Youngs, John Youngs, J. Snyder, W. Severson, S. Simpson, J. Salsbury, H. S. Smith, A. Sigsboy, John Sharp, G. Shafe, T. Shell, E. Spawn, J. J. Severson, J. H. Severson, C. Shandy, J. N. Severson, G. Severson, J. Stead, N. A. Severson, J. J. Smith, M. Sutphens, J. H. Sand, G. A. Sharp, A. Sharp, P. Sharp, P. Shaver, A. Scrafford, W. Scrafford, M. Shaver, M. Sitterly, J. M. Sitterly, W. P. Shulles, J. Spoore, P. Simmons, J. Tye, F. Tygert, Thos. Tree, F. Tygert, E. Traux, D. C. Thomas, C. Thornton, A. Tygert, G. Tygert, T. Tygert, J. Terry, A. Van Heusen, P. J. Veeder, J. P. Veeder, P. Veeder, A. Veeder, J. D. Verplank, T. Vandenburgh, A. Van Heusen, J. Van Heusen, H. and E. Vosburgh, D. Van Heusen, A. Van Heusen, J. H. Van Aernam, H. S. Van Auken, J. H. Van Aernam, C. and N. Van Aernam, R. Van Heusen, H. Van Aernam, J. Vanderpool, S. Van Auken, S. Hallenbeck, G. B. Houck, R. J. Hogan, A. Hallenbeck, J. D. Hart, I. A. Hart, G. Y. Hallenbeck, H. Hilton, A. Hilton, J. N. Hallenbeck, J. J. Hallenbeck, H. Hilton, S. Howard, J. Hallenbeck, jr., H. Hurst, M. Hendrickson, G. J. Hallenbeck, I. Hallenbeck, C. Jacobson, T. Jones, S. H. Jacobson, T. Jackson, H. and S. Jacobson, G. Y. and J.

GARRETT, Dentist, warrants every Filling, Glen's Falls, N. Y.

C. O. D. BOOTS and SHOES are the cheapest, at WAIT'S.
Boots and Shoes, every pair Warranted, at WAIT'S. (See page 81.)

SEE INDEX, PAGE ELEVEN. **191**

Johnson, S. Kelly, A. Kilmer, J. P. Kilmer, J. Keenholts, I. Knower, D. Keenholts, A. Keenholts, A. and H. Kaly, A. Landers, J. A. Lagrange, J. A. Lagrange, L. Lawson, J. Landers, J. Lagrange, N. Lagrange, N. Lagrange, H. and F. Lagrange, M. Livingston, M. Lagrange, H. J. Livingston, H. P. Livingston, J. Livingston, P. Livingston, F. Livingston, H. Livingston, H. S. and S. H. Lanchart, G. Lanehart, H. Lewis, A. Lagrange, P. J. Livingston, Widow J. Murray, A. Murray, J. and J. McKown, W. McKown, H. Mains, F. V. McKown, J. L. Main, L. Main, R. C. Main, S. S. Mapes, J. R. Main, Peter Machesney, A. and P. Meed, A. Moore, Widow Minekler, P. Martin, J. B. Nott, C. C. Nott, J. Ostrander, J. Oliver, J. Ogsbury, H. G. Ostrander, J. P. Ogsbury, J. Patterson, J. H. Payne, N. Pangburn, J. Pangburn, A. M. Pangburn, J. and L. Pike, J. Perry, P. Quinlan, P. Quackenbush, J. Quackenbush, J. Quackenbush, jr., A. Relyea, S. Rockefellow, D. Relyea, J. D. Relyea, L. Relyea, J. P. Relyea, J. D. Relyea, J. A. Reed, T. S. Relyea, J. Relyea, W. D. Relyea, A. Relyea, W. Robinson, Widow Radliff, C. Roll, J. Shoore, L. Spawn, M. Switzer, H. Sloan, J. Sitterly, J. Still, H. Schermerhorn, W. Siver, A. Spawn, C. Shafter, J. P. Siver, J. Smith, H. Spawn, G. W. Sigsby, C. Strape, A. Stall.
   TOWN OF WOODFORD, VT.—J. W. Hager, S. E. Gleason, G. Gleason, C. Wood, F. S. Gleason, C. M. Bliss, A. Fox, C. W. Cutler, E. A. Cutler, J. Bugbee, O. Eddy, J. Harbour, W. Wood.
   TOWN OF SEARSBURGH, VT.—A. Briggs, E. Briggs, G. Bond, A. Blanchard, D. Crosier, J. Crosier, S. Crosier, T. Crosier, D. Crosier, S. Crosier, T. Canedy, S. Doane, H. Fuller, G. Farrington, H. Farrington, F. Grousbeck, C. Grimes, L. Holt, O. Hall, J. Harvey, E. Harvey, S. Haskins, R. W. Irish, D. B. Leroy, W. B. Leroy, D. Morgan, W. O'Brien, J. B. Stevens, L. Stevens, W. Sumner, A. Tenny, F. Sprague, H. Wilson, G. Shipper, N. J. Wilson, G. Wheeler, H. Whitcomb.
   TOWN OF BALLSTON, N. Y.—S. Hides, J. Wakeman, M. Parmeston, H. C. Bryan, I. Harris, B. Hutchens, S. S. Baker, D. T. Lawton, T. Smith, H. Rowland, E. L. Yeomans, G. Slade, H. Cunningham, E. Westcot, J. Gorman, W. Grant, J. Gardiner, S. S. Hoyt, T. D. Pryor, T. Vail, S. Mowry, D. Boise, J. Rowland, P. Billenger, H. Vilscey, O. Whitbead, H. Benedict, I. Horton, H. Stover, P. Jones, G. S. Warring, J. Rowel, E. B. Cook, H. Perry, H. Koran, J. O. Bentley, W. N. King, J. Spicer, J. Fish, H. Traver, B. Hall, W. Cornell, G. W. Shepherd, H. Broughton, M. Youngs, W. Warring, C. Swan, M. James, J. E. Ladew, G. S. Moore, H. Benton, I. H. Johnson, J. M. Adams, M. Caulkins, S. Sherwood, C. Duboise, H. Van Ostrum, G. West, C. Kilmer, J. Leggett, J. Emoigh, I. Friuk, H. Grennell, I. Swan, R. Chatfield, I. K. Grinnell, J. Gifford, A. Hockritruser, C. R. Lewis, R. J. Arnold, N. Larkins, N. Walter, M. Jennings, S. Young, J. Watson, S. A. Parks, W. Wilson, W. Angle, W. Heacock, P. McPherson, J. P. Conde, L. J. Rogers, J. Zealing, J. Allison, J. Dixon, J. B. Smith, J. McKie, J. Pemble, L. Cole, O. Brown, A. S. Beach, H. Crippin, J. Richards, M. Corning, T. St. John, A. Wood, J. Ward, J. Clark, J. Blakeman, D. Capin, J. Hawkins, G. W. Taylor, A. Cipperly, L. Nash, H. Wood, E. Gleber, M. Kelly, R. Northrop, D. Stover, C. Wood, N. Mann, E. Settle, C. Cook, J. Thompson, I. W. Levisee, H. W. Wood, J. Whiting, W. Seeley, Wiswall, B. F. Baker, A. Hewitt.
   TOWN OF HAMPTON, N. Y.—H. Leonard, H. Phelps, I. E. Phelps, L. W. Manchester, J. Peck, W. H. Green, S. P. Miller, W. S. Miller, J. H. Miller, N. P. Churchill, J. Orms, F. Kilburn, B. E. Inman, Hon. R. Richards, C. E. Inman, E. Gould jr., F. Farewell, R. T. Ray, J. J. Stowe, J. O'Donald, N. Dady, J. Wilson, G. Warren, S. A. Warren, H. Hotchkiss, J. L. Clark, M. O. Stoddard, T. B. Clark, B. Merriams, L. Prouty, J. McCoon, H. Hotchkiss, D. Smith, L. Ostrander, L. J. Warren, M. P. Hooker, D. H. Fifield, S. Wilson.
   TOWN OF PROVIDENCE, N. Y.—R. W. Clark, T. Hughes, W. Y. Clark, P. Pallu, J. Hughes, A. C. Tabor, A. Manchester, P. Tabour, J. Clute, H. Cadmon, W. V. Price, A. Andrus, A. M Stone, R. Swan, T. Shaw, F. Shaw, E. Trump, S. Ginney, A. D. Kimball, J. C. Bogart, S. S. Hagedorn, S. Rockwell, H. Clute, W. Harris, N. E. Newell, G. Clauson, A. Curtis, J. Waite, E. Greenfield, P. Grant, W. Green, P. Flanagan, N Barton, I. Sly, W. N. Shaw, P. Shaw, R. B. Rosevelt, N. Evans, S. Woolsey, T. Wiley, J. Atkins, H. Terry, A. Ames, C. Buhannan, T. Hunter, H. McOmber, A. Waite, W. Briggs, S. Mosher, A. W Jewell, I. Mosher, W. Atkins, I. Colony, R. Hart, Z. Burdick, A. Eaton, R. Eaton, S. S. Smith, J. Wiley, J. Methober, J. J Shaw, J. Manchester, M. Chase, R. B. Waite, N. Case, J. W. Clarke, J. R. Tabour, G. A. McOmber, A. Bentley, T. Briggs, T. McGovern, H. N. Parker, R. Cornell, J. Conell, H. Shipman, P. C. Robertson, W. Binck, J. B. Soles, J. Marlow, J. Rosevelt, H. Sluzer, A. Bronson, S. Case, J. Smith, P. Van Pelt, M. Tobea, R. Tobea, H. Sanaford, P. S. Smith, T. S. James, J. Petit, W. Binck B. C. Bue, J. Benedict, H. Bentley, S. Bates, J. Briggs, G. Cassedy, J. Crannel, E. Cadmon, J. W. Clarke, H. W. Carpenter, W. Conklin, H. Devon, A. W. Duel, G. A. Evans, Finch and Co., J. Frilas, Green and Enos, J. Shew, J. Holland, N Thomas, J. Nonewell, D. Niekock, S. Heart, H. Kilmer, H. Lyons, T. McOrme, J. Mosher, A. Meeker, J. McOrmlee, A. McCoy, J. Mullen, E. Orey, J. L. Pearse, N. Packer, J. Palmer, W. N. Parker, N. Pulling, N. Schermerhorn, W. N. Smith, E. Seism, R. Sherwood, J. B. Sales, S. Tabour, E. S. Trout, D. Tohea, M. Tohea, P. Van Pelt, I. Woodard, H. Whitney, S. Woolsey, H. T. Trovelt.
   TOWN OF PUTNAM, N. Y.—W. Anderson, jr., T. Anderson, J. Best, jr., J. M. Blair, J. Blanchard, R. Belden, G. G. Burrnell, J. D. Burrnell, J. Backus, Rev. S. Bigger, Rev. H. Belden, W. M. Cunnings, W. A. Cunnings, J. L. Cummings, T. W. Cummings, D. Cummings, S. Crammond, R. W. Crammond J. M. Crammond, H. Congdon, F. Craig, S. Campbell, H. Dedrick, A. Dedrick, J. A. Easton, W. M. Easton, D. Easton, G. Easton,

Go to **COREY'S, GLEN'S FALLS,** for **RIBBONS, TRIMMINGS, FANCY GOODS,** &c.

WILKINS sells Clothing 15 per cent cheaper than others.

BIBLES, PRAYER and HYMN BOOKS, SUNDAY SCHOOL BOOKS,
Merit Cards, &c., at E. H. BENDER'S, 73 State Street, Albany.

192   FARMERS' ALMANAC.

W. French, N. Flannery, J. Graham, I. Graham, J. Gourlie, D. Graham, J. Graham, jr., A. Hulett, P. W. Hutton, R. R. Hutton, T. G. Graham, W. Graham, A. C. Gourlie, W. Hulton, H. Hill, J. Hennesey, N. King, T. Lidgerwood, J. Lidgerwood, J. A. Lidgerwood, D. Lillie, T. Lillie, W. Lillie, C. R. Lyons, D. Loigh, R. S. Lillie, R. Maxwell, T. B. Maxwell, I. Maxwell, W. McArthur, A. G. Meiklejohn, W. McLaughlin, J. McLaughlin, J. McLaughlin, jr., W. Moore, H. Moore, R. Patterson, R. H. Patterson, E. Roberts, M. Ricket, E. H. Sears, J. Shear, J. Shear, J. Smith, R. Simpson, R. E. Simpson, J. Simpson, J. Shear, L. Smith, G. W. Thompson, D. Williamson, D. Williamson, A. Williamson, R. Williamson, D. R. Williamson, R. C. Willey, J. Wright, W. J. Wright, C. W. Williamson, C. Webster, R. P. Graham, H. Easton, S. Haynes, J. Lillie, F. D. Sheperdson, A. Smith, T. B. Patterson, W. Gourlie, L. Dedrick.

TOWN OF WESTERLO, N. Y.—L. A. Holmes, C. Bentley, A. Fox, W. Requa, T. Petrie, S. H. Smith, N. Laupaugh, H. A. Ford, C. P. Laupaugh, H. Hempstead, G. Adriance, W. Conger, G. Flood, M. Brato, H. K. Jones, M. Brainon, P. R. Vineyard, S. B. Pond, J. M. Moak, J. Castle, J. Troutner, A. Kingsley, J. Flagler, J. Brato, J. Wideman, E. B. Reynolds, J. Hitson, G. Weinburger, C. Weinburger, E. Cole, O. H. Hunt, J. G. Cole, S. M. Cole, Z. L. Babcock, I. Gale, J. Hempstead, L. Bates, G. Smith, A. Gage, R. Apple, L. Stanton, E. Gibbons, A. Garret, A. Miller, U. J. Huyck, W. Bates, C. Cole, U. G. Myers, R. Swartnout, J. Vineyard, G. Dempster, T. Dobbs, J. R. Snyder, R. Rone, J. Hallenbeck, R. Ward, E. Gibbons, N. White, H. Shear, J. Gibbons, G. S. Goewey, H. Weaver, J. Selick, H. Boomhower, I. Van Leuben, P. Van Leuben, B. Swartnout, S. V. Brewster, J. Haslet, H. Wilsey, A. Barber, L. Barber, A. Weber, U. V. L. Laupaugh, F. Groesbeck, G. Van Leuben, R. Haight, E. Haight, W. Knowles, P. Mabey, D. Maybe, J. Green, W. Campbell, D. Peck, D. Gould, E. Snyder, E. Tompkins, P. Knowles, P. S. Wickhem, J. Udell, N. Youmans, H. Wilkins, A. Smith, R. Stewart, H. R. Petrie, L. Lockwood, H. Atkins, H. Snyder, J. E. Jones jr., L. Preston, D. H. Snyder, M. Galup, J. Sherwood, C. H. Cole, J. Cari, H. Abrams, E. Hilton, J. Swartnout, J. Swartnout, P. A. Myers, W. P. Rosecrans, J. H. Snyder, S. B. Martin, W. J. Lawrence, J. Burger, Sir W. Udell, R. Winston, L. Chamberlain, G. Hogaboom, D. Stanton, J. R. Stanton, W. Vineyard, W. H. Vineyard, R. Winston, S. Green, E. Haines, R. Swartnout, L. C. Lockwood, A. Thayer, S. Winston, L. Haines, J. Haines, D. H. Haines, O. Winston, G. Haines, E. Hopkins, J. Slade, F. Brato, G. Wheeler, J. N. Mabey, S. Maybe, T. S. Ramsdell, E. Snyder, D. P. Shepherd, S. Lockwood, J. Shoat, R. D. Stanton, C. Morse, J. H. Myers, M. D. Dernett, B. Tripp, P. Lobdell, O. Bryan, A. Bryan, D. Bundell, R. Myers, A. Green, N. Pond, E. Spalding, O. D. Gifford, T. Ingalls, J. Mabey, D. Terloss, C. Husted, J. N. Reynolds, J. Snyder, J. B. Taets, C. Van Buren, A. Bryan, J. S. Rundell, E. Whitford, D. M. Wooster, A. Spalding, J. F. Green, W. Huyck, N. Holmes, A. Vineyard, A. Seaman, T. H. Dyer, C. Stone, L. St. John, J. M. Dernett, W. D. Calder, W. A. St. John, E. R. St. John, W. St. John, L. C. Ingalls, G. Lockwood, J. A. Bishop, R. W. Stanton, J. Van Buren, A. Stanton, M. Hartenstein, W. W. Dyer, C. Dyer, G. E. Bishop, C. Hinkley, McC. Terboss, L. Hinkley, L. Bishop, W. Sherwood, R. L. Simpkins, D. H. Bishop, D. J. Bishop, J. S. Lockwood, G. C. Knowles, J. Simpkins, S. Davis, J. W. Prosser, H. Simpkins, A. D. Hannay, O. Hunt, C. S. Lobdell, E. Stone, S. Green, N. N. Knowles, H. H. Rundell, J. W. Conel, J. Huyck, J. T. Mackey, W. E. Dernett, D. Stanton, D. Stanton, C. Hinckley, L. De La Mater, P. M. Knowles, E. Mabey, W. Swartnout, E. Haines, W. M. Norton, A. N. Blossom, L. Woodruff, G. Peck, A. Lockwood, J. H. Welch, D. Arnold, Z. Lockwood, J. M. Hannay, J. E. Dedrick, C. Bishop, R. P. Simpkins, E. Baker, J. S. Baker, J. Rundall, D. Green, A. Green, A. W. Baker, J. Reynolds, R. Helley, L. Lape, H. R. Lockwood, J. Bedell, R. W. Schofield, A. Garret, E. Bishop, D. Lockwood, J. E. Schofield, J. Hunt, J. H. Lamb, D. J. Rundell, J. Rulend, J. Lobdell.

TOWN OF IRA, VT.—V. Carpenter, A. Ellis, L. Fish, B. Fish, P. Fish, A. Fish, L. Mason, J. B. Stevens, P. P. Clark, L. W. Fish, L. Fish, E. C. Fish, E. C. Fish jr., H. Flagg, A. Gates, G. Gillhoan, H. Gillmore, C. Lincoln, I. Mann, I. Wilkinson, W. Wilkinson, M. Greene, M. Flanagan, A. Farrell, C. Geddings and Sons, G, Mumford, C. Mumford, N. Clifford, E. Howard, J. Hudson, L. Mann, T. Monday, C. Perry, O. F. Johnson and Smith, B. Lincoln, J. Logan, J. Lynch, Wheeden and Wireman, A. Tower, M. Kelley, A. E. Day and W. Leonard, N. Clifford, J. Anderson, J Wetmore, A. J. W. Thornton, J. Thornton, W. Tailor, A. Wetmore, M. Morrin, B. Wool, S. Beach, Thornton and Mullenville, J. Goodspeed, T. Burk, J. B. Spencer, A. J. and C. Spencer, J. Brown, W. Curtis, J. Lincoln, C. M. Lincoln, S. Peck, L. Peck, L. Tower, J. Collins, H. White, I. Weaver, M. Curtiss, E. and H. Collins.

TOWN OF WEST HAVEN, VT.—S. Adams, E. Adams 2d, H. J. Adams, R. C. Abell, B. Adams, E. F. Barnes, S. C. Barber, W. J. Billings, D. D. Bixby, J. J. Briggs, I. Cook, T. Clark, J. Carty, D. Downs, Mrs. N. Fish, Miss H. M. Fish, C. C. Forbes, V. N. Forbes, R. Field, N. Fish, F. S. Foot, J. Francisco, E. Field, F. Goodol, W. E. Gibbs, T. G. Hunt, H. R. Hunt, R. Hitchcock, Mrs. A. W. Hitchcock, W. L. Hitchcock, A. Humiston, S. W. Horton, W. Ingalls, H. Ingalls, T. Jakeway jr., Mrs. G. A. Jakway, W. Jakway, F. Kelly, J. Kelly, H. Kelly, P. Lana, J. S. Moon, M. McDonald, J. C. Norton, P. Norton, J. Offensend, G. Offensend, J. O'Reilly, W. Preston, J. R. Roberts, W. H. Sisco, S. W. Tryon, T. Wilsey, A. Whitt, H. A. Wyman.

TOWN OF HORICON, N. Y.—P. Smith, R. P. Smith, N. Pratt, P. A. Hastings, P. Haskins, W. Bennet, W. H. Davis, I. G. Frasier, A. Whittaker, J. Hastings, G. Waters, S. Waters, G. B. Green, C. Streeter, I. Hill, R. Boyd, R. Z. Bennett, H. S. Waters, R. Dred,

For a nice Top-Buggy go to JOUBERT & WHITE'S, Glen's Falls.

E. H. BENDER,
BOOKSELLER, STATIONER,
PRINTER & BINDER,
73 State St., Albany, N. Y.

BLANK BOOKS, MEMORANDUM & PASS BOOKS,
On hand and Made to Order.

Gold Pens, Pencils, Diaries, School Books, Photograph Albums, Stereoscopic Views, Writing Desks in Rosewood, Paper-Mache, Plain or Beautifully Inlaid with Pearl; Plain and Fancy Inkstands, Pen Racks, Segar Stands and Cases, and Unique Watch Safes.

BENDER WILL FURNISH YOU ANY BOOK PUBLISHED.
Also, Engineers' Instruments, Stationery, Field Books, &c.

FANCY NOTE PAPER and ENVELOPES,
Stamped with Initials or Monograms, at E. H. BENDER'S.

BIBLES, PRAYER & HYMN BOOKS, SUNDAY SCHOOL BOOKS, MERIT CARDS, &c.

The Largest, the Cheapest and Best
BOOK AND STATIONERY STORE IN ALBANY,
IS BENDER'S, 73 STATE STREET.

The Stationery Department Replete with every variety of Stationer's Articles. Competition Defied in Quality, Quantity and Prices of Stationery. The Trade Supplied with Stationery and Every Article Used in the Counting Room, at Manufacturer's Prices. Paper of all kinds, by the Case, Ream or Quire.

PRICES OF BOOKS, STATIONERY, FANCY GOODS, &c., &c., REDUCED.

LITHOGRAPHING AND PRINTING
Executed in every style.

Banks, Insurance Companies, and all other Companies Supplied at
BENDER'S, 73 STATE STREET, ALBANY, N. Y.

Scrip, Certificates, Drafts, Checks, &c., &c., gotten up in All Styles. Law Blanks of Every Form, by the Single Sheet, Quire or Ream, and Attorney's Stationery, County Clerk's Record and Deed Books, &c., Made after Special Forms; Surrogate's Blanks and Blank Books Prepared, Engineer's Instruments, Stationery, Field Books, &c.,

AT BENDER'S 73 STATE STREET.

☞ $450 PIANO FOR $325.

The undersigned has an order on a Piano maker in New York City, calling for a **NEW PIANO** valued at $450, which he will sell for $325 cash, *and will go with the person to New York to pick out the piano and pay his (or her) expenses there and back.*

Address E. A. BEEBE, Room 14,
396 Broadway, Albany, N. Y.

Latest Novelties in Ladies' Boots, at WAIT'S.
Romeo and Juliet Walking Boots, at WAIT'S. (See page 81.)

SEE INDEX, PAGE ELEVEN. 193

G. Smith, E. R. Smith, J. F. Smith, J. West, A. J. Barton, J. W. Barton, C. E. Hart, W. Kanavan, J. F. Pritchard, J. Rising, B. Hays, Ziba Remington, E. M. Sexton, T. Bentley, A. A. Ross, H. Stammard, J. H. Leach, C. Griffin, L. Hemenway, S. T. Harrington, G. Dorset, L. O. Wood, G. Ross, S. Ross, A. Streeter, W. Smith, H. Hays, L. Hays, J. McKinstry, J. H. Smith, C. P. Hill, S. Pritchard, C. Mattison, C. Bates, N. Kingsbury, W. S. Warner, Z. T. Hawkins, W. P. Smith, M. Ingram, C. Ingram, J. M. Stone, W. Wilson, O. Smith, G. Norton, P. Brown, E. Brown, A. Nichols, B. T. Wells, J. Willson, R. Nichols, S. B. Carpenter, J. F. Underwood, R. Johnson, W. Johnson, G. Halley, D. C. Prouty, J. Hays, C. Dorset, V. H. Paige, H. Kimble, R. Bolton, T. E. Bolton, A. B. Davis, M. Tripp, L. Tripp, N. F. Dred, G. Bartlett.

TOWN OF POESTENKILL. N. Y.—S. Blewer, L. Lynd, G. W. Davitt, D. Place, L. Castle, J. Springer, D. Barrenger, J. Cottrell, W. Colchammer, J. Maul, P. Castle, P. Defriest, G. Moul, F. Moul, G. Campbel, G. Wotherwax, J. Dingman, H. Kilmer, Philip Kilmer, G. Link, G. Kilmer, J. Bristol, H. Keon, M. Link, S. Link, G. Link, J. J. Miller, J. Minie, G. Kilmer, P. Fasburg, J. Fasburg, J. M. Miller, J. Litight, G. Litight, Henry Becker, J. Hulser, P. Strunk, C. Read, W. H. Whyland, W. Slouter, J. Slouter, Peter Snyder, B. Snyder, J. B. Weaver, J. Clickner, T. Lape, L. R. Hoag, J. Smith, J. Bredages, B. Ebbings, G. Ives, W. Cottrell, G. Ostrander, A. Whyland, J. Whyland, J. Miller, M. Moody, W. Clark, G. W. Ives, O. Ives, H. Weaver, G. Cooper, L. Whyland, Wm. Whyland, N. Kats, I. Barber, A. Strunk, G. Cottrell, H. Fisher, F. Fissure, J. A. Polock, J. Ives, S. Carwright, J. Barber, J. Olt, M. Dustern, A. Dustern, B. Randal, H. Mose, W. Cottrell, H. Belinger, J. Babcock, K. Bailey, C. Able, W. C. Cooper, R. Cornmings, B. Cooper, M. Engert, W. Furgerson, J. F. Hayner, G. Hayner, J. A. Hull, H. Herington, G. Henderson, W. Henry, B. Horten, P. G. Hayner.

TOWN OF LANSINGBURGH. N. Y.—D. Aldrich, I. Allen, J. L. Button, L. D. Button, S. Bucklyn, P. A. Brewster, W. H. Clapper, H. Derrick, N. Derrick, C. W. Derrick, M. H. Haynor, G. H. Haynor, S. Haynor, B. Hunter, L. Leversee, J. Louck, C. Leversee, J. Mosher, B. Nutting, N. Overaker, G. W. Pitney, W. D. Perry, W. D. Perry, M. V. Perry, Mrs. G. Perry, J. Roberts, J. Ryan, J. Ryan, E. Sherman, J. A. Snyder, J. A. Snyder, M. Sipperly, H. Vanarnum, P. C. Wager, S. Wager, J. A. Snyder, J. A. Snyder, D. V. Leversee.

TOWN OF EASTON. N. Y.—J. B. Allen, E. S. Anthony, T. Almy, E. D. Allen, D. W. Abeel, R. Abeel, W. V. S. Allen, L. Austin, F. K. Brownell, H. Brownell, E. W. Brownell, T. Bennett, Z. W. Beadle, J. F. Beadle, A. Brownell, B. Beadle, E. Brownell, H. Brownell, J. H. Brownell, S. Brownell, H. Bigalow, S. Benson, J. V. S. Becker, R. S. Borden, B. Barker, D. Baker, I. Borden, A. Briggs, G. L. Baker, A. C. Briggs, W. Booth, B. N. Becker, W. Briggs, T. W. Brayton, M. Butler, T. D. Beadle, M. C. Burch, S. A. Buckley, H. T. Borden, S. Battle, J. and J. Battle, H. Britton, G. Bulson, D. Bratt, W. H. Barton, H. Bannus, T. Barry, C. J. Button, D. Burdick, D. Becker, E. Burdick, H. K. Becker, J. H. Becker, W. Burdick, L. Barber, L. Barber, J. Burch, R. Baker, R. Buel, C. Babcock, I. A. Burton, H. Burch, H. Burch jr., J. S. Bulson, J. Cass, A. K. Coggeshall, W. J. Chase, P. Coggeshall, S. Clark, S. Chase, J. E. Crandell, M. M. Crandell, W. Crandell, D. Crandell, J. R. Crandell, A. Crandell, C. P. Coy, W. S. Chapin, A. G. Cochran, W. Crow, J. Conkhite, N. Corliss, T. Corliss, A. Cottrell, H. Cottrell, Crandell, T. Conner, A. Crandell, D. Conklin, C. A. Cornell, C. A. Cornell, S. Cornell, W. F. Adams, A. Darrow, S. C. Diver, J. Duffy, D. Donavan, W. Droyer, G. W. Deud L., Dorsey, D. Delvert, W. Dunphy, M. Dunphy, J. Dilevergne, D. D. Denais, I. Dilevergne, P. M. Devoe, A. D. Ridder, E. English, P. English, O. J. Ensign, J. G. Edmondson, R. Eddy, Z. Eddy, T. Eddy, J. B. Eldridge, J. Eldridge, Hill and English, W. Fryar, J. Fryar, J. B. Fursman, S. Fort, J. W. Fort, V. Fryer, P. Farrell, W. Fryar, F. Fowler, M. Flatley, H. Flatley, P. Gannon, D. Green, J. Griffin, W. Gates, J. H. Garrison, R. T. Gifford, E. Gifford, S. W. Gifford, H. Gifford, J. A. Groesbeck, E. Harrington, C. Harrington, W. H. Harrington, A. J. Harrington, E. Harrington, R. Harrington, H. Harrington, W. Harrington, A. Harrington, S. Harrington, E. Harrington, M. Hoag, S. P. and T. W. Handy, W. N. Handy, S. H. Houghtaling, H. Hill, J. Hogan, W. Hoxie, J. E. Hoag, S. D. Hoag, W. Hogan, J. L. Hills, E. Hayden, T. Hayes, R. Hoag, J. Higgins, A. Hill, L. Hagerman, I. Hall, J. H. Hillman, Z. Hathaway, E. Harrington, E. W. Hollister, F. O. Ives, M. Joice, D. Kenyon, B. Lynch, J. Laddy, A. Luther, E. Sooker, H. Leslie, W. Murray, E. Mulligan, F. W. Marshall, J. McMullen, P. McCarty, J. Metgowan, W. McDermott, T. McGowan, J. McFarlane, W. Moore, W. G. Maine, E. McCrady, A. Montgomery, S. McArthur, H. Northrup, H. Norcross, J. Nolty, B. V. Niver, P. O'Neil, L. Potter, A. Pratt, J. Pratt, J. W. Smith, Asahel Perry, M. C. Perry, J. W. Peckham, LeR. Potter, J. D. Pettys, E. Pettys, S. Rich, L. Rathbun, H. Rathbun, P. Rathbun, R. Robinson, J. Robinson, O. K. Rice, H. Reynolds, W. C. Reynolds, L. Remington, G. Remington, A. Reynolds, N. Rattell, A. Rogers, R. K. Robertson, C. V. Slocum, F. A. Slocum, C. Snell, J. S. Snell, L. Slocum, H. Stevens, E. Sheham, T. B. Stafford, A. Slocum, T. Schuyler, I. Shade, R. Sarle, J. A. Starbuck, H. Smith, J. Salter, P. Smith, S. W. Smith, S. Sheldon, J. F. Skiff, J. Safford, J. U. Skiff, J. Silvey, J. H. Sheldon, S. Sheldon, C. B. Taber, W. Travis, J. H. Teff, H. Tubbs, H. Taber, S. Teff, F. Teff, F. C. Tobey, T. Smith, A. Thompson, G. G. Vandenburgh, I. Vauvechten, W. H. Vanburen, H. Vanburen, P. A. Van Wie, W. Weltech, R. Wilson, H. Waters, W. Waters, F. G. Wheldon, E. Wright, D. Waite, M. Welch, J. Wells, A. C. White, A. Wood, W. P. C. Waldron, S. W. Winton, J. W. Warner, W. F. Winton, S. S. Witbeck, C. Whitaker, A. A. E. Wilbur, P. Wilbur, J. Wilbur jr., S. Wilbur, G. Wilbur, P. Wilbur, F. Wilbur, T.

Ladies' Undergarments and Gored Tucked Skirts, at P. H. COREY'S, GLEN'S FALLS.

W. A. Wilkins' Cheap Cash Clothing Store, Whitehall, N.Y.

E. H. BENDER, BINDER and PRINTER, and Wholesale and Retail
BOOKSELLER and STATIONER, 73 State Street, Albany.

194 FARMERS' ALMANAC.

Wilbur, J. Wilbur. J. Wood, S. B. Williams, J. Williams, D. B. Wheldon, H. and J. P. Wilcox, W. Whipple, A. Young.
TOWN OF DORSET. VT—E. Danforth, H. A. Williams, H. Farwell, W. M. Kellogg, A. P. Chapman, G. W. Farwell, R. Sykes, O. C. Gilbert, H. West, A. Kinnie, A. S. Sheldon, C. E. Sheldon, O. Sykes, C. Lathrop, U. S. Kent, J. Holly, I. N. Sykes, D. Sykes, P. B. Farwell, A. C. Roberts, W. D. Clemonds, W. A. Martindale, J. Sykes, N. J. Wilson, Hiram Holley, Harvey Holley, Ira Batchelder, C. Field, H. B. Kent, C. Baldwin, I. Barrows, N. Sykes, W. Williams, J. McBride, E. Maniey, J. Touhey, E. Holton, D. Barton, D. Wade, M. Sheridan, D. Blackman, S. Wilkins, C. W. Phelps, A. Hilliard, A. B. Armstrong, E. Farwell, F. Paddock, Z. Paddock, P. Barrows, R. Dunning, P. Kelley, T. Dalton, J. Roberts, H. G. Harwood, A. Richardson, T. A. Ridout, J. H. C. Hodge, W. Robinson, B. Sexton, A. Ladd, H. Bebee, A. Bowen, J. Andrus F. G. Harwood, W. Ames, J. Jexton, J. Holchan, J. Paff, G. Baldwin, O. Nichols, A. Lanfire, H. Thompson, J. W. Kelley, H. Benson, B. A. Rogers, H Buffum, R. P. Bloomer, E. P. Luther.
TOWN OF LUZERNE, N. Y.—T. Coman, T. Coman, H. Coman, E. Coman, S. Morton, M Putner, J. Hovy, E Haw, P. Chowan, C. Wogar, J. Millier, W. Ramsy, A. Newcomb, J. Garley, A. Thomas, E. Richardson, R. Ramsey, J. H. Gailey, T. Wilcox, J. Wilcox, J. Dean, H. Ston, P. S. Scovil, W. H. St, John, J. Towner, A. Porteous, W. Scofield, H. Beach, H. Pulver, I. Millan, W. Ston, J. B. Wellar, L. Oharrow, D. Richardson, John Crannell, S. Garly, A. Garly, J. Garly, A. Hemstrat, W. Hall, S. Johnson, O. Dean, W. Wilcox, J. Ives, C. Ston, E. Wicks, O. Moors, W. H. Ives, S. Lapray, W. Smeed, D. B. Jones, J. Stevenson, E. Taylor, R. Lindsy, S. How, C. How, M. How, S. How, S. Moors, E Clements, C. Stewart, M. Thompson, S. Rice, G. Taylor, H. Hall, A. Twist, A. Orlan, H. Levins, C. Brare, J. Hart, W. S. Taylor, V. Hoyle, C. Bullard, J. Firguson, N. Gage, C. Balding, E. Wilcox, H. McMaster, J. Saben, F. Gustin, G. T. Rockwell, B. C. Butler, J. Taylor, Dr. J. G. Porteous, J. Rockwell, J. Woodruff, A. Bovard, A. Moors, L. How, J. N. How, J. How, H. Clemments, J. Moors, J. Stewart, J. Stewart, J. Foaly, J. Taylor, E. Kerr, A. Twist, G. Hill, E. Rose, T. Levins, W Morse, L. Lindsy, W. Taylor, B. Rolph, J. Firguson, W. Girard, T. Balding, M. Chadwicks, C. McMaster, W. Eli H. P. Guiness, J. McEwen, L. Rockwell, P. Clear, D. Stewart, J. B. Bunnson, E. J. P. Wilcox.
TOWN OF KNOX, N. Y.—J. M. Chesebro, E. Champion, M. Champion, J. Thousand, J. Quay, H. Barckley, J. G. Crary, G. Gallup, G. Gallup, J. Gallup, S. Allen, A. Crounse, D. Saddlemire, S. Sand, A. Sand, W. sand, J. Bassler, C. Saddlemire, C. Saddlemire, N. Chesebro, J. Saddlemire, J. Allen, J. Torry, R. Wolford, A. Merselis, C. McDermott, J. Pitcher, D. Pitcher, A. Barkley, C. Chute, H. Truax, W. M. Truax, P. Schoonmaker, P. Schoonmaker, J. Osterhont, A. White, J. Clickman, J. Armstrong, M. Aelsas, C. Gaige, J. Van Auken, C Sturgis, W. McDonald, P. C. Sand, J. Armstrong.
TOWN OF FORT ANN, N. Y.—D. Griffin, P. Barker, L. Meeker, M. B. Colman, L. Z. Wait, E. Huestis, E. H. Colman, D. Nicols, G. H Briggs, O. G. Burnham, L. Hall, S. Barrett, J. T. Mason, J. Graham, B. F. Bailey, L. Barnard, W. H. Root, G. P. Moore, L. Bailey, J. Monahan, A. C. Brown, A. S. Clark, E. Nicolson, S. Beecher, B. Badger, C. Farr, S. Woodruff, L. Andruss, M. Vaun, R. W. Baker, M. Harris, E. Chase, M. J. Farr, N. Sheldon, J. Barnett, J. Gilmore, C. Van Wormer, C. Winegar, S. Haskins, T. N. Dewey, A. Benton, H. Bailey, A. A. Hulet, J. Pierce, J. Wood, G. Johnson, W. Woodruff, B. F. Brewster, G. Stevens, J. H. Thompson, C. Finten, H. Vaun, J. H. Skinner, S. Adams, L. Vaun, G. Washburn, J Crandall, L. Washburn, J. H. Finten, G. L. Stevens, A. Vaun, Z. Washburn, D. Washburn, J. Main, E. Thelms, M. V. B. Washburn, D. Nielson, J. Cutter, G. Bull, J. Sunderland, E. Crandall, J. O. Brown, S. D. Wyman, G. Ashley, A. Baker, J. Rice, J. Ryan, L. Weller, A. White, J. White, L. Rowel.
TOWN OF HEBRON, N. Y.—J. Punish, D. Punish, J. Cole, C. Cole, E. D. Hannibal, J. Darrow, S. Root, C. Boynton, W. P. Lincoln, J. M. Moore, W. Moore, S. Mahuffy, J. H. Moore, T. Gregory, A. Shehlen, M. Purcell, R. Shaw, J. Wright, S. M. Ingersoll, C. H. Wilson, W. S. White, C. Wilson, J. Wilshn, J. Jenkins, S. K. Sherman, L. Punish, E. G. Wilson, N. W. Ameeden, W. B. Sweet, A. E. Munsson, J. Munsson, S. Boynton, J. Hatch, H. F. Nelson, J. Allen, M. Clark, T. Brattie, J. Craig, W. Ingalls, B. Andrews, S. Ayres, J. Glasin, C. Glasin, H. Smith, S. Hannibal, M. Brown, D. Hick, W. Royo, T. Laing, E. West, D. Mullan, G. Holmes, W. Shaw, F. Rogers, L. Wright, J. Murtha, S. Rogers, D. Andrews, S. Smith, D. McCotter, D. Hanna, R. Hanna, J. Ayres, J. Braynar, H. Braynar, M. McFadden, R. Dunkan, D. Braynar, A. Braynar, J. Smith, W. D. Ely, S. Nelson, D. Nelson, J. Gould, H. Nelson, J. Reed, L. Nelson, J. E Pratt, J. Braynar, J. Bute, S. Button, J. Wouland, A. Swift, J. Foster, M. Temple, C. Getty, D. Allen, D. Nelson, H. Laing, D. Durham, W. C. White, J. Welch, E. Smith, W. smith, L. Welsh, L. Smith, C. Hewitt, E. Dud, R. Ely, J. Dudd, W. Dudd, A. James, J. H. Getty, J. Hannibal, J. Durham, W. Hill, J. J. Nelson, J. McCarter, C. Webster, A. McMillan, J. Bell, W. Burridge, J. M. Connel, J. Davenport, H. Dennison, E. Woodard, C. Woodard, J. Lee, W. J. McClellan, J. T. McClellan, G. McKnight, D. McClellan, A. McClellan, W. Howard, L. Chamberlin, E. Howard, H. Howard, J. Chamberlin, G. Rogers, L. S. Anterlin, S. E. Spur, C. Rogers, J. Fraser, J. J. Johnson, J. J. Rogers, J. C. Getty, J. McKnight, T. Moraffy, G. Montgomery, E. Dixon, C. Sheldon, J. Mullen, M. Mullen, W. Ferguson, G. Wilson, M. McCloy, W. McGill, D. McCloy, A. Carson, K. McEnchron, D. Guthrie, J. McEnchron, R. Hague, J. R. Hull, G. Rea, R. McDonell, T. White, S. Irwin, G. Gibson, W. W. Shaw, W. F. Getty, T. Murphy, R. Copeland, M. Dugan, J. S. McClellan, A. Johnston, J. M. Rogers, D. Rogers, A. Foster, A. Gourlay, N. Reynolds, G. Qua, F. Russell, S. Burke, L. Warwick, A. Gillis, A. Copeland, A. Ponell, J. Huggent, B. Outman,

GARRETT, DENTIST, Glen's Falls, N. Y.

Rubber Boots and Overshoes, at WAIT'S.
Mens' and Womens' Artic Overshoes, at WAIT'S. (See page 81.)

SEE INDEX, PAGE ELEVEN. 195

H Head, G. W. White, P. Flack, H. Lundy, W. Montgomery, J. Kenyon, A Bradford, G. Waterman, F. Day, J. Day, J. Hand, S. Ingalls, D. W. Getty, L. Copeland, J. Randle, J. Johnson, W. Wilson, C. Donaldson, S. Burridge, D. Burridge, J. McKnight, N. H. Williamson, W. N. McClellan, A. Coy, E. L. Coy, J. Beattie, B. Reynolds, S. Huggins, E. Getty, J. Randles, J. Mitchell, C. Waller, J. Hall, J. E. Wilson, G Chapman, L. Clough, J. Carey, J. Crosier, S. Adams, M. Purcell, J. Smalley, O. Smith, J. C. Smith, J. Moffitt, E. Wood, S. Raymond, A. Patrick, W. J. Bentley, J. Bentley, J. Pattison, H. Pattison.
TOWN OF STONY CREEK, N. Y.—J. A. Combs, F. Holmes, L. Whealor, G. Wicken, S. Simons, F. J. Dean, P. Brannon, D. Kathan, A. Tucker, W. Gamby, S. Simons, S. R. Baker, W. Hack, P. Gray, R. Hack, E. Baker, M. Van Auken, D. Van Auken, A. Holmes, M. Coon, E. E. Moses, A. McDonald, N. Nolton, C. Smith, J. McDonald, S. Swears, B. A. Inlay, J. Nolton, E. Steavens, C. Van Dusen, E. Inlay, J. O'Neal, G. H. Van Dusen, N. White, W. W. Scofield, W. Glassbrooks, J. C. Fuller, J. Q. Adams, J. McDonald, W. Swears, A. Murray, B. J. Hall, E. Van Auken, E. Black, E. Swears, W. H. Walsh, G. W. Baker, J. Ormsby, J. E. Fuller, A. Winslow, J. J. Winslow, J. Perkins, W. Hernstreet, D. C. Perkins, J. Hull, J. B. Dean, J. W. Gilbert, J. Riley, D. M. Cameron, L. Harris, J. J. Flanders, J. H. Cameron, J. Robison, W. A. McDonald, S. Fuller, E. Goodnow, L. K. Burt, A. Tripp, J. S. Irwin, J. White, J. White, W. Thompson, I. C. Weaver, J. L. Fuller, G. Murray D. M. Dunlop, H. J. Fuller, S. Harris, L. Robison, C. Clute, J. C. Willis, C. G. Rhodes, E. Wait, J. Harris, S. Harris jr., F. Cameron, A. B. Fuller, A. Cadney, W. W. Cameron.
TOWN OF PAWLET, VT.—J. Leach, J. Smith, S. Weed, H. Winchester, A. Goodspeed, J. N. Mason, D. Hulett, A. S. Whitcomb, J. H. Sheldon, A. Grinnell, J. M. Andrus, F. A. Bromley, M. Robinson, E. Pratt, F. Blakeley, N. Winchester, A. Willard, W. Blakeley, D. Blakeley, F. Andrus, G. Douglass, F. Viets, O. Loomis, A. Boynton, H. Allen, D. McGrath, J. R. Sherman, C. Hulett, O. Parris, H. Lathe, G. F. Hammond, G. W. Burt, H. Hollister, O. H. Simonds, S. Wilcox, J. M. Shaw, D. C. Blossom, S. Culver, S. Hitt, S. Brown, J. Wiseman, A. Goodspeed, J. A. Orr, D. Folger, F. Stearns, C. Philips, A. Whedon, S. Wood, Q. A. Pratt, H. Kelly, C. E. Reed, J. Hulett, H. E. Hulett, W. White, A. A. Monroe, G. W. Knight, A. Smith, C. J. Monroe, H. Hosford.
TOWN OF RUPERT, VT.—T. L. Sheldon, L. A. Bibbins, Elisha Hawley, S. H. Rising, A. P. Sheldon, J. Bonneville, J. Boynton, C. A. Sherman, G. Hopkins, L. D. Hopkins, F. Howlet, H. W. Stoddard, J. Parker, O. J. Beebe, D. Parish, J. P. Youlin, E. Flower, E. Hurd, L. Flower, A. T. Hurd, J. E. and H. H. Hadaway, J. J. Jenkins, S. Moore, W. A. Stearns, E. Burton, I. F. Sheldon, C. F. Sheldon, C. M. Sheldon, G. Harmon, E. Roberts, H. Barden, T. J. Prescott, W. Sheldon, D. Smith, L. Sheldon, E. Sheldon, G. Burton, J. L. McCall, W. Scott, P. W. Youlen, P. E. Youlen, W. Moncrief, E. Hibbard, C. Gookiers, A. Mawhinney, O. Clark, S. Moore, E. C. Fonda, C. Moore, H. O. Moore, S. Harwood, R. Stone, N. McMain, C. A. Roberts, H. Higgins, A. J. R. Danforth, E. Danforth, O. Brewster, H. J. Moore, G. Jenks, H. Eastman, W. Root, W. Phelps, H. Sykes, E. Sykes, G. C. Leach, J. Leach, W. B. Denio, A. H. Denio, S. Philips, C. Philips, D. Taylor, M. Jykes, D. F. Sykes, J. Farrar, S. H. Taylor, A. Trumbull, H. S. Smith, S. Barden, E. P. Sheldon, H. Sheldon, A. Monroe.
TOWN OF NORTH GREENBUSH, N. Y.—J. E. Bishop, M. Van Alstyne, G. N. Sharpe, J. E. Van Allen, C. Veeder, D. W. C. De Forest, J. S. Sharpe, J. G. Sharpe, D. M. Haywood, S. Craver, J. Fonda, D. Phillips, J. Phillips, D. L. De Freest, I. C. Manville, J. Manville, Z. Bass, W. Bass, L. J. De Freest, D. P. De Freest, G. De Freest, W. Bloomingdale, J. Wendell, G. H. Manville, C. Vandenburgh, R. Vandenburgh, G. Vandenburgh, E. Proudfit, J. De Freest, P. A. Allendorph, J. J. Fonda, E. Cole, C. C. Philips, J. Mesick, D. D. Schermerhorn, I. H. De Freest, G. De Graff, H. Pfeiffen, H. J. Pitcher, D. B. Williams, G. Shaver, E. De Freest, F. M. Traver, D. Traver, D. Strope, M. B. Wetherwax, P. Shaver, A. Thomas, R. M. De Freest, H. A. Downs, H. Van Allen.
TOWN OF CAMBRIDGE, N. Y.—H. Abbott, J. Austin, W. Austin, L. Bartlett, E. B. Becker, J. Bennett, P. Brady, P. Butler, J. Burnett, J. M. Baldwin, M. Conway, R. Coulter, H. Coulter, A. Coggshall, A. S. Crandall, W. Curtis, T. F. Cornell, J. W. Conkey, J. Curtis, T. Culver, J. Comesby, R. Comesby, H. R. Coulter, B. Cavanaugh, P. Conway, H. Darrow, M. Duel, J. Darrow, L. Donehue, P. Dimpsey, R. Edie, P. Edie, J. P. Fowler, N. Fowler, F. Fowler, W. Fowler, S. J. Farr, H. Greene, T. P. Greene, H. Greene, T. Greene, S. Greene, W. Greene, J. Greene, J. P. Greene, J. W. Greene, S. Greene, J. Greene jr., W. Greene, M. Gilmore, C. N. Grover, C. Graham, P. Graves, J. W. Greene, K. A. Haxton, J. S. Hall, W. S. Hall, J. L. Hunt, R. Hilman, W. Hamilton, J. Haxton, J. L. Haxton, E. Judson, N. Kenyon, H. King, J. King, E. Kenedy, W. C. Larmon, B. Long, N. S. B. Loomis, B. F. Lockrow, P. Lyons, J. Mitchell, K. McNemary, T. McNemary, M. McEnry, R. Miller, G. Miller, W. Miller, T. McNerney, T. McNerny jr., T. McNerny, D. S. Pratt, A. N. Pruyn, B. Potter, H. Potter, O. S. Pratt, A. Pratt, J. Pendy, D. Robertson, D. Robertson jr., J. Robertson, G. Russell, J. Skiff, C. Skinner, J. Stevenson, N. Sherman, W. Skillie, W. R. Stuart, J. E. Small, J. Shiland, A. Skiff, T. Skellie, Z. Sherman, A. M. Sherman, A. M. Stevenson, W. J. Stevenson, A. Skillie, C. Shaw, W. Shiland, L. Sherman, C. A. Skinner, T. E. Skillie, R. P. Twist, H. Weir, E. Weir, P. Welch, M. L. Wright, W. W. Wright, A. P. Wiatt, M. Welch.
TOWN OF HOOSICK, N. Y.—A. Boughton, L. J. Burgess, H. Burgess, A. Brown, N. P. Brown, J. S. Bancus, P. Brown, R. D. Bratt, H. Bovie, W. J. Bovie, I. Bovie, M. Barnett, G. Chace, J. W. Clark, P. Carpenter, R. Ames, H. Andrews, C. Austin, J. Armitage, R. Agan, J. P. Armstrong, S. Bovie, J. Bratt, S. Bratt, R. Boughton, J. Boughton, J.

SASH and BONNET RIBBONS, in great variety, at COREY'S, GLEN'S FALLS.

Buy your Clothing of W. A. Wilkins, Whitehall, N. Y.

25

BENDER will furnish you any Books Published; also, ENGINEERS' INSTRUMENTS, STATIONERY, FIELD BOOKS, &c., at 73 State Street, Albany.

196   FARMERS' ALMANAC.

Boughton. W. Babcock. A. Breece, G. S. Burgess, G. W. Brown, P. Baker, D. Baldwin, J. H. Brownell, W. H. Brownell. T. Baker, S. Baker, P. Bosworth, W. P. Chace, J. Case, J. B. Case, N. Carpenter, W. Carpenter, G. Cox, F. Carpenter, A. Crawford, J. Danforth, N. Eyclesnymer, P. Eldridge, L. Flinn, A. G. Joslin, J. O. Joslin, J. James. R. James, jr., A. Keech, G. B. Keech, W. F. Kellyn, L. Le Banon, C. Lanton, I. B. Le Bannon, M. and F. Mosley, C. Mosley, P. Mosley, S. J. Mosley, H. Macumber, J. Maynerd, Caleb Nicholus, G. W. Ostrander, A. Osborn, H. Osborn, S. Percy, D. W. Percy, J. Pierce, L. Pierce, E. Percy, R. Quackenbush, P. W. Richmond, M. B. Royce, A. E. Reynolds, G. Reynolds, D. Richmond, T. Shivers, E. Spaulding, K. Sedam, B. G. Sweet, P. Sweet, C. Sweet, T. Sweet, J. T. Sweet, A. Sweet, T. T. Sweet, T. Sissin, R. Smith, J. Shoulters, P. Slade, H. Spicer, A. Spicer, G. Stockwell, A. H. Webster, L. Wilder, W. A. Wood, J. Warren, L. Willson, E. C. Wait, J. B. White, J. A. Fonda, S. Goodin, S. Goodin, Roger Guile, R. Gardner, C. Gardner, V. W. Gardner, T. A. Gardner, T. Graves, J. D. Helling, H. H. Hains, A. Houghton, H. H. Herrington, P. Herrington, N. Herrington, J. G. Haverland, D. Hartin, T. Hill, J. W. Herrington, H. Hill, G. Hallenbeck, A. Hoag, P. Haswell, L. Herrington, J. Hallenbeck, R. L. Harrison, A. J. Hains, B. Joy, D. Jones, A. Johnson, O. Johnson, W. Johnson, C. Johnson.

TOWN OF CLARENDON, VT.—A. Aldrich, W. W. Arnold, H. Bishop, P. Benson, W. Benson, T. J. Briggs, H. F. Button, T. Brown, J. Butler, E. B. Holden, B. Colvin, L. F. Colvin, B. Chapman, H. Chapman, B. Chapman, J. H. Chapman, J C. Colvin, L. Congdon J Congdon, E. Congdon, D. Cavanaugh, E. Cook, M. S. Clark, D. C. Combs, G. W. Congdon, W. R. Crossman, G. W. Crossman, G. R. Davis, F. A. Davis, J. A. E. Ewing, D. P. Eddy, W. S. Eddy, H. H. Eddy, P. A. Eddy, J. Eastman, E. Eastman, H. P. Everest, J. D. Everest, D. S. Everest, B. Fisk, M. Fisk, J. Fuller, M. Farrell, C. H. Gleason, J. J. Hayes, H. Hill, M. Harvey, E. H. Horton, O. Hewitt, A. C. Hayward, H. Hodges, H. Hitchcock, E. L. Holden, J. W. Lincoln, H. L. Jones, E. Kelley, E. S. Kelley, M. W. Kelley, S. and E. Kelley, S. T. Kingsley, H. Kingsley, H. Kingsley, J. Kelly, D. Kimball, J. F. Learned, A. Moore, B. Murray, W. D. Marsh, J. McCann, M. E. Marshall, J. S. Holden, A. Newton, A. Newton, A. J. Newton, J. E. Nelson, A. Pratt, T. Pierce, J. N. Pierce, C. C. Pierce, D. Platt, N. Potter, W. Potter, N. M. Powers, E. Peck, T. Quincy, G. M. Ridlon, J. Rhoades, B. Riley, L. Round, E. P. Seamans, Stafford and Seamans, E. D. Sherman, L. Smith, E. and A. D. Smith, D. Smith, Smith and Shaw, Smith and Hayes, L. P. Smith, H. Smith, N. J. Smith, J Q. Steward, D. S. Squier, H. B. Spafford, W. Wetmore, J. D. and H. C. Tubbs, H. C. Tower, L. Tiernan, A. Westcott, A. W. Westcott, L. M. Walker and Sons, W. L. Wylie, J. Weeks, H. Webb, F. Weeks, W. S. Weeks, H. K. White, E. W. Wilson, J. Wilmarth, J. L. Marsh, D. Tubbs.

TOWN OF BRANDON, VT.—H. Alden, E. Avery, H. M. Buckland, D. Blackmer, E. N. Briggs, B. Barnard, A. Brownell, H. A. Banes, H. P. Brown, G. Bliss, A. S. Cook, J. W. Cheney, C. Capron, J. L. Cahee, T. Cary, C. W. Conant, J. A. Conant, A. Dyer, H. Ellis, O Ford, E. Fuller, B. F. Field, E. French, F. Farrington, E. Goodnow, D. Goodnow, L. Goodnow, J. Gill, S. Goldsfrink, S. L. Goodell, A. W. Goss and Tatl, D. F. Goodrich, N. Hack, S. W. Harrison, E. D. Hood, R. Hull, J. Howlton, P A. Hatch, S. J. Hall, S. J. R. Hack, O. B. Howland, E. H. Hubbard, A. Homlon, J. V. Ives, S. V. June, D. M. June, J. Jackson, M. P. June, B. W. Johnson, D. E. Jackson, A. H. P. Ketcham, E. Keeler, J. Knolton and Sons, H. L. Leonard, W. Lillid, L. Langwan, R. V. Marsh, S. Morehouse, O. T. Morgan, E. McDonald, H. McDonald, L. Merriam, H. S. McCollom, C. Merrill, C. Merriam, T. McKeon, F. Mayeo, R. Mankton, H. H. Merritt, Z. Neuring, R. Noes, J. Noyes, H. F. Noyes, H. Noyes, H. T. Nott, C. P. Ormsbee, N. W. Patch, J. Paine, S. Patch, G. W. Parmenter, W. Phillips, D. L. Phelps, D. T. Packard, H. W. Patch, H. and D. E. Kent, J. Rogers, M. Riley, H. Roberts, J. C. Rich, J. Rosseler, G. A. and S. E. Segar, S. Smith, E. D. Selden, T. B. Smith, N. T. Sprague jr., W. B. and F. Sanderson, J. H. Smith, W. W. Severy, D. C. Smith, C. Spooner, O. F. Smith, H. A. Temener, R. E. Toper, J. Townsend, N. Thomas, F. W. Tait, F. J. Thomas, E. Willis, F. Winslow, E. R. Wood, J. Walker, H. Winslow, C. M. Winslow P. Werner.

TOWN OF WHITEHALL, N. Y.—Mrs. A. Adams, E. Adams, S. D. Adams, J. P. Adams, W. J. Allen, W. Allen, H. Bartholomew, H. A. Bartholomew, A. Bartholomew, F. Bartholomew, A. Bartholomew, W. Bartholomew, J. Beckweth, W. C. Brocknay, P. Burke, E. Benjamin, E. Benjamin, J. Bartholomew, P. Benjamin, D. Beckwith, A. Bartholomew, S. Benjamin, O. Bascom, Blin and Vaughan, J. Barnes, Mrs. M. C. Bourdman, G. H. Buel, B. Brown, J. Buel, L. Cook, W. Clark, J. L. Clark, Mrs. C. Chapman, N. Collins, O. Collins, J. Collins, M. W. Cook, T. Conner, J. Campfield, R. Coleman, J. Collins, E. Davis, E. E. Davis, M. Denbusher, E. Doogless, A. Doogless, H. Doogless, O. F. Davis, R. Doig, P. Fish, A. G. Foster, F. E. Fish, H. Finch, H. Finch, B. Gilbert, G. S. Griswold, A. H. Griswold, H. Gipson, L. Gass, E. Giddins, De Wett German, A. Havley, R. D. Halester, A. Harlow, J. R. Harlow, A. Hall, R. W. Hurbert, H. and S. Hurbert, M. Harris, J. Harris, B. Hatch, J. Haley, S. Halcomb, S. Halcomb, G. and C. Hall, S. T. Jillson, S. W. Jackway, R. Jacket, D. Jacket, R. Johnson, J. Jillson, M. Johnson, M. Johnson, J. Johnson, De Wight Johnson, A. Jackson, G. W. Jackson, N. Jackson, M. Jackson, Mrs. D. A. Martin, S. Mitchell, J. Menens, S. McFarren, J. McFarlan, T. Murry, T. Melvin, J. G. Martlin, D. McFerren, J. McFerren, jr., S. Mariom, M. Maison, F. Murrey, Eben Murrey, J. Nolan, C. Nickols, J. Osgood, P. O'Donnal, L. O'Conner, J. F. Peters, Henry Parkes, F. Pangman, C. Perry, H. Perry, J. J. Pangman, A. S. Polly, J. Potter, A. S. Polly, J. Rourke, J. F. Rogers, M. J. Reonolds, L. Rooker, J. Ryran, Samuel Renolds, M. Rooker, J. Rodgers, D. Riley, Rathbone, W. Rathbone, A. Rathbone, H. Renolds, Isaac

For durability in a Carriage go to Joubert & White's, Glen's Falls.

The best Custom Cutter at White & Pearsall's, Glen's Falls.

**Fine and Coarse BOOTS, at WAIT'S One Price Store.
Boys' and Youths' Boots, at WAIT'S One Price Store.** (See page 81.)

SEE INDEX, PAGE ELEVEN. 197

Spink. N. Smith. S. G. Skeels. H. Skeels. J. Sears, P. Sweet. A. Spince. H. Stephens. G. Staten. H. Spring, E. Tanner, I. Virge. Virge. E. P. Wood. W. J. Wood, John White. S. Wood. H. R. and W. F. Wait. L. White. O. White. W. Wright. R. Wright, W. White. L. Wells. L. Willson. Mrs. O. Watkins. W. Washburn. J. Welsh, I. Wood. J. W. Wood, I. N. Wood. L. Wells. A. Whiting. J. Wilson, E. Warren, C. Brown, M. Brown, P. Beckwith, J. Brown. M. Beckett, J. Burns, T. Brown, J. Brown, jr., H. Bartholomew. N. Beckwith, F. Kingsley, G. Kingsley, L. Kingsley. W. Lyon. L. Law. A. Lumas. H. Lumas. W. Kinner.

TOWN OF DRESDEN N. Y.—P. Adams, R. Barber jr., I. Barber, M. Barber, R. Barber. S. Barrett, T. Bartholomew, J. Beebe, J. Barrett. H. Bulles. C. Bartholomew. R. Beebe, J. Belden, J. Bartholomew, J. Bartholomew, P. Bartley, L. Belden. G. Belden, M. Belden. C. Belden, B. Benjamin. W. Baccie, D. B. Barrett. S. Barrett. J. Barrett. J. Bartholomew. D. Barrett. P. Babour, W. Carter, J. W. Carter, F. Carter. A. H. Chubb, A. Clemons. J. D. Clemons. C. Coats, P. Crockwell. M. Dann, E. Dedrick. J. Traush. H. T. Foster. J. Gibberd. E. Gregory, D. Gregory, O. F. Gillett. C. Holcomb. P. Halett. R. J. Hurlbert. D. Huntington, E. Huntington, H. Hopkins. A. Hathaway. M. Jones, M. Lewis. J. Losau, L. Loogar, J. Megourty, T. McDonnell, J. McDonnell, C. Martindale, C. Mellon, J. Noole, C. Noble. R. N. Phillips, C. Pease, L. Roberts. H. Rice. J. Ripley. R. W. Steele, J. Snody, J. Slavin, R. Shattuck. D. Stockwell. W. Snody, R. Sutherland. A. Stockwell. O. L. Steere. A. Sleight. S. Subtle, I. Woodcock, W. S. Weatherbee, J. Wilsey. W. Wilson, A. Waters. H. Walace, J. Walace. R. Walker, A. Walker, A. Winn, L. Wilsey.

TOWN OF HAGUE. N. Y.—T. C. Ward. E. Ward, W. Baldwin. R. Potter. S. Norton, B. Clark, J. G. Ward, D. Phillips. E. Fish. A. Durkee. S. Wesburn, N. Wright, E. Fish. B. Van Buren, J. Brewster, S. Stark. J. B. Foot. L. Newman, J. Jenkins, G. Lane, H. Spaulding. E. Moss, O. Burt, T. B. Crossman, A. A. L. Tuttle, A. Davis, W. Orcutt, E. L. Davis, H. Sexton, J. A. Balcom, H. Jenkins, A. Shattuck, J. H. Shattuck, W. Eviss. H. Tunney, H. Fish, H. Stark, N. Holeman, J. M. Clewathon, I. Decker, P. Foot, P. Foot jr., J. C. Richmond, G. E. Foot, S. Balcom, R. Gleason, L. Brenin, E. T. Ackerman, S. R. Ackerman, P. Irish, A. Putnam, A. Bryan, S. Robbins, R. Robbins, A. Bevvins, M. Balcom, J. W. Rising, C. Balcom, J. H. Doollen, R. Spencer, S. Hays, R. Resey jr., O. Garfield. W. Bryan, A. Elethorh, G. F. Elethorh, C. Dolbeck, W. Bevins, J. Brown, E. C. Rand, W. Tuffen, O. Yow. L. Burnett, W. Cook, L. S. Phelps, S. Roberts, A. Philips, C. Ostyce, J. C. Walker, S. Shattuck, J. Wood, J. Riches. H. Remington.

TOWN OF CASTLETON, VT.—B. F. Adams, B. F. and J. Adams, H. Ainsworth. H. Armstrong, C. Baxter, H. G. Bassett. C. L. Barber, A. P. Babet, A. W. Barker, G. Barber, D. Babet, W. F. Barber, Barrows and Graves, J. E. Barnes, H. R. Beals, S. F. Beach, J. S. Benedict, C. Beach, L. and S. Bishop, S. Bidwell, D. E. Bibbins. E. A. Billings, S. Bliss, E. Bliss, M. Brewster, A. J. Brown, H. O. Brown, C. Bromley, E. Burns, M. Burns, O. C. Burritt, L. S. Bardwell, M. B. Brown, M. Callahan, S. Cauch, M. Cotter, S. B. Clark, N. Clark, T. Coffer, R. M. Copeland, W. Cook, J. Culver, P. Crowly, J. Crowly, W. A. Clark, Cedar Mountain Slate Co., Curtis and Williams, Castleton Town farm, B. Carver, G. Coutire, I. Davey, M. Denmison, P. Dickerman, P. Dwire, J. Doyle, W. H. Drake, A. P. Drake, J. Duffey, R. O. Dorman, E. E. Eaton, M. Eaton, J. F. Eaton, C. C. Farwell, Field and Donnelly, P. Fitzpatrick, J. and A. W. Flagg, J. F. Freeman, L. Francis, E. Gorham, S. B. Goodwin, T. D. Goodwin, S. Gorham, A. H. Griswold, P. D. Griswold, H. Griswold and Sons, A. Griswold, Mrs. J. D. Gaines, E. Gleason, H. Hall, F. S. Heath, E. Higly, T. N. Hooker, Mrs. H. Hait, A. M. Hait, T. G. Hunt, E. Hughes, A. W. and P. W. Hyde, A. W. Hyde, Hydeville Co., M. Jackson, L. Johnson, Wm. and W. Jones, J. J. Jones, O. Jones, S. H. Langdon, H. Langdon, C. Langion, D. S. Lincoln, J. Learned, G. W. Mason, D. C. Atwood, Mrs. E. Morgan, R. E. Moore, R. Morris, G. W. Moore, J. Mulvey, P. C. Mooney, J. E. Manley, J. Manogue, J. Morgan, J. P. Manogue, B. McKean, S. W. Northrop, N. N. Northrop, C. L. Northrop, S. W. Nelson, A. Ostrander, T. Oconners, J. C. Parsons, F. Parsons, N. Parsons, S. Parsons, A. F. Parsons, A. Palmer, F. Parker, T. Parkhurst, A. Pease, L. O. Perkins, B. Perry, J. Perkins, H. Peck, R. M. Phillips, H. A. Pond, P. Pond, A. Pond, C. E. Porter, L. W. Preston, D. C. Potter, L. S. Pruty, M. Price, F. Post, A. A. Ranson, J. H. Ranson, J. H. Remington, T. W. Rice, S. Ross, H. R. Roberts, C. S. Rumsey, J. Ryan, C. S. Sanford, J. Sheriden, J. Sheriden jr., B. D. Sherman, T. M. Sherman, A. C. Shaw, C. S. Sherman and B. F. Adams, C. S. Sherman, A. G. W. Smith, O. C. Smith, O. Smith, J. Smith, H. Spencer, C. Stevens, C. Stanard, L. B. Smith, P. Sloan, J. Stevenson, E. Teborlo, J. Thornton, A. Thornton, A. P. Thornton, A. Tomlinson, H. Tomlinson, S. Tomlinson, J. D. Woodward, H. Westover, West Castleton Railroad and Slate Co., C. H. Whillock, L. D. Whillock, F. J. Williams, J. Williams, J. Williams, J. Winters, S. D. Williams, J. Williams, J. H. Wilson, J. B. H. Woodbury, J. P. Wood, C. W. Wood, O. Wood, Mrs. E. Wyatt, Western Vt. Slate Co.

TOWN OF SHERBURNE, VT.—J. Johnson, R. N. Taylor, L. E. Wood, L. H. Hodgman, S. W. Adams, C. W. Adams, M. A. Ballard, H. J. Colton, B. Maxham, W. Bates, D. W. Taylor, G. Colton, S. Colton, G. Estabrooks, E. Estabrooks, E. Colton, Alphonso Estabrooks, E. West, 3d, A. F. Estabrooks, A. T. Eastabrooks, M. Hackel, T. S. Chamberlain, R. D. Estabrooks, J. H. Pinney, J. Colton, J. A. Morse, Lewis Hawkins, O. D. Wilson, D. Wilson, C. N. Adams, I. Wheeler, E. Z. Dutton, J. L. Ordway, G. Hutchins, L. H. Willard, G. Kent, H. O'Neil, N. Bates, R. Maxham, J. P. Turner, S. F. Sawyer, E. Orcutt, J. Ide, W. Manly, A. Chase, E. Williams, O. W. Bates, L. H. Rood, W. Sawyer.

Bie yer Cloze ov W. A. WILKINS. (See page 96.)

The Largest, the Cheapest and Best BOOK and STATIONERY STORE in Albany is BENDER'S, 73 State Street, Albany.

198 FARMERS' ALMANAC.

A. Quimby, A. Wyman. L. O. West, J. Ayres, J. H. Ayres, S. Ayres, E. S. Madden, G. G. Spaulding, D. D. Spaulding, L. Johnson, J. C. Taylor, J. F. Hadley, A. C Foster, Hosea Spaulding, S. Newton, J. E. Chapman, J. Davis, P. E. Lewis, P. L. Hammon, E. West, jr., C. Solga, E. W. Merrill, Z. H. Russ, J. Webb, W. Webb, R. Tracy, H. Growe, W. H. Grandy.

TOWN OF MIDDLETOWN, VT.—S. W. Southworth, J. Atwater, S. Kelly, A. Haynes, J. P. Taylor, E. R. Buxton, G. Taylor, E. Streeter, S. Wait, J. Lewis, H. Haskins, A. J. Leonard, A. Barker, H. H. Hutchens, J. Carens. A. Hyde, F. Barrett, D. Cook, E. Cook, C. Crosby, L. Parker, J. Richardson, L. B. Adams, E. Copeland, A. Spaulding, H. Spaulding, R. Spaulding, C. Clift, M. Paul, G. Gardner, H. Clift, E. P. Harrington, M. Wiseman, R. Mehurin, H. Headley, M. Smith, L. Copeland, J. L. Gardner, W. Dudley, J. Powers, P. L. Whitmer, J. B. Louis, A. W. Gillman, H. Youngs, E. Woodward, J. Haynes, O. Lobdill, G. Spaulding, D. Morgan, M. Coy.

TOWN OF SANDGATE, VT.—E. Bentley, R. Bentley, W. Bentley, R. Bentley, H. Bentley, W. Bentley, D. Bentley, A. E. Beebe, I. and I. jr. Bristol, A. Botsford, R. P. Barber, J. F. Barber, J. E. Brush, L. A. Bennett, H. Bowen, G. Barber, J. B. Covey, M. J. Covey, S. J. Covey, P. Creamer, G. and H. Draper, P. Dooley, H. Dunton, J. J. Dunlap, E. Enos, J. H. Fop, A. Gray, J. Gale, D. Geary, W. G. Hamilton, M. Hamilton, A. M. Hamilton, J. Hamilton, C. Hamilton, B. Hamilton, E. L. Hamilton, W. J. Hamilton, W. R. Hoyt, M. Hoyt, P. Hoyt, M. Hoyt, E. F. Hoyt, E. Hoyt, J. Hurd, B. Hurd, I. W. Hurd, E. L. Hurd, E. B. and R. S. Hurd, J. Hurd, C. J. Hurd, T. Hays, A. D. Kent, C. H. King, W. Lewis and Son, H. Moffit, H. Moffit, A. Morey, J. McLenithan, T. McDaniel, N. Mears, D. Murphy, J. W. F. Newsome, G. H. Perkins, D. Prindle, Z. Prindle, A. Prindle, L. Peck, S. Peck, W. J. Pierce, J. M. Provan, R. M. Provan, W. B. Randall, R. Randall, A. Richards, D. and W. Richards, J. Reynolds, M. and F. Robinson, W. Sweet, C. V. Smith, C. Snow, C. Squires, W. Skidmore, D. Snyder, J. Santiss, J. Sage, W. Turner, J. Turner, A. V. Turner, T. Tellier, A. J. Torrance, A. W. Wheldon, A. J. Woodard, C. R. Woodard, G. Woodard, H. Woodcock, W. Mattus, A. Wilcox, J. F. Wilcox, J. and J. Wyman, J. Wyman, H. Whitlow, T. Wright.

TOWN OF GLASTENBURG, N. Y.—T. T. Elwell, J. Elwell, M. Beels, J. W. McDonald, J. H. Matteson, E. A. McDonald, D. McDonald, A. Twitchell, F. Twitchell, G. Harrington.

TOWN OF PERU, VT.—J. Q. Adams, S. Aldrich, J. Burt, C. Batchelder, A. Batchelder, Edmund Batchelder, D. Batchelder, Edward Batchelder, J. G. Batchelder, G. K. Davis, H. O. Davis, H. Griswold, M. Granger, J. J. Hapgood, L. Howard, J. Hapgood, J. C. Lakin, J. P. Long, R. Lampson, Z. Lathrop, N. Lillie, M. B. Lyon, J. Lyon, J. Lincoln, A. C. Nourse, C. Phillips, J. D. Priest, I. Russell, S. J. Robbins, M. Raby, J. H. and A. J. Simonds, W. B. Simonds, S. A. Sawyer, F. K. and S. Stiles, Harvey and Hezekiah Stone, F. B. Smith, E. H. Tuttle, J. R. Utley, W. Woodard, I. K. Walker, S. Walker, P. J. Walker, M. G. Walker, J. Whitny, L. S. Wait, P. I. Wyman, B. Williams, A. I. Byand, N. H. Cresman, A. D. Corbet, H. Gould, M. Cook, Jesse Brown, Justin Brown, J. Farnum, J. W. Farnum, C. R. Bryant, C. I. Brown, C. Jinkins, A. C. Sloan, Harley and C. Cooledge.

TOWN OF WINHALL, VT.—W. J. Allen, F. Ameden, C. Ameden, S. S. Axtell, Wm. Brooks, C. Benson, V. Benson, L. Benson, I. Bailey, O. Bailey, J. C. Bolster, J. Barnard, J. G. Barnard, G. W. Barnard, O. Benson, A. K. Burbank, F. B. Baldwin, D. K. Burbu, G. P. Burbu, W. H. H. Burbu, B. C. Benson, C. Burchard, Lewis Brooks, M. Benson, E. Briggs, W. W. Benson, N. Brown, C. Bush, E. Barney, A. W. Clayton, Z. K. Cone, A. Corbit, M. M. Cressy, E. A. Cochran, A. C. Chamberlain, C. Chamberlain, J. Capen, E. S. Chapin, W. F. Colman, A. O. Cohman, J. M. Colman, G. L. Colman, A. Cummings, G. A. Cummings, W. Cudworth, J. L. Capen, C. Capen, P. Chamberlain, S. S. Colburn, W. F. Chaflin, W. P. Clayton, C. Dean, P. Duane, L. Dean, J. Dunn, H. M. Dean, C. E. Dunbar, H. C. Dean, J. Douglass, O. G. Eddy, S. Eddy, J. A. Emery, O. Elmore, S. Foster, H. Gale, J. G. Gale, D. Gale, W. Gordon, A. P. Graham, J. Gordon, C. Green, T. Gordon, H. P. Gould, J. N. Hunting, O. C. Harwood, J. Hayward, Z. Hayward, D. Hayward, Frank Hayward, H. C. Holden, J. Hill, D. C. Hosley, J. How, H. Hubbard, N. W. Hill, D. H. Hews, O. C. Hall, R. Hews, J. Johnson, S. Johnson, Chas. C. Johnson, L. Johnson, L. J. Johnson, W. F. Judd, F. Kedder, R. S. Kendall, J. Kendall, H. J. Kendall, J. Kelley, I. Kelley, W. Kirkwood, W. D. Leonard, A. Lenson, F. Lyon, H. J. Lackey, J. H. Lackey, F. G. Lackey, P. T. Lawrence, J. Larabee, C. L. Leonmore, C. N. Leonmore, J. Leonard, H. McCoy, J. Martin, F. Morgan, C. N. Morgan, A. W. Prouly, A. S. Phillips, J. S. Parsons, W. J. Percy, J. Perry, E. W. Perry, C. L. Puffer, L. Picard, Paul Robbins, C. B. Robbins, E. Rugg, N. H. Robinson, C. Rona, S. A Shattuck, D. Shattuck, F. A. Shattuck, F. W. Sheldon, J. Smith, O. Slade, W. A. Slade, G. W. Sessions, J. C. Skenner, W. S. Syles, H. B. Stephens, H. Slade, G. F. Slade, W. H. Sanders, C. Stone, C. Taft, D. Taft, L. Taylor, G. Taylor, G. J. Thompson, E. D. Valle, H. Valle, H. Wright, N. Wright, E. V. Wilder, R. T. Wood, C. Williams, W. Williams, C. R. Williams, C. B. Williams, Jas. Williams, H. L. Williams, C. C. Wheeler, A. L. Wetherell, J. W. Woodcock, J. H. Woodard, R. Winship, E. Winship, W. G. Williams, G. A. Williams, A. E. Wetherell, J. T. Wilder, J. Wilder, H. Wheeler.

TOWN OF TINMOUTH, VT.—J. Aldis, N. Brown, D. Baxter, J. T. Ballard, G. Brown, D. Clark, N. Clark, T. Clark, B. R. Clark, E. Crosby, C. Cramton, A. N. Cramton, R. Cook, G. Capron. D. G. Hathaway, L. Campbell, L. Cobb, L. Cobb, H. Corey, J. Currie, T. Battle, A. Doty, D. Doty, C. Egeston, J. Eusign, B. Farry, H. S. Grey, J. P. Grover,

Buy your Clothing at White & Pearsall's, Glen's Falls, and save money.

Garrett, Glen's Falls, makes Tooth Filling a Speciality.

Ready-made Clothing at bargains, at WAIT'S.
For your WEDDING SUITS, go to WAITS. (See page 81.)

SEE INDEX, PAGE ELEVEN. 199

W. Grover, L. Grover, J. Grover, S. Green, D. Gilbert, E. Hoadley, C. Hoadley, H. Hopkins, R. Hopkins, O. Ives, E. Ives, D. Lewis, A. Lewis, A. Lewis, J. Norton, M. Norton, C. Norton, W. W. Norton, J. W. Noble, H. D. Noble, J. B. Noble, A. Noble, P. C. Paul, S. Phillips, I. Phillips, W. Preston, A. Packard, I. Rogers, L. Rice, J. R. Round, H. M. Scott, W. Scott, T. Stafford, B. Stafford, D. L. Strange, L. Tooley, A. Valentine, E. Valentine, J. E. Wood, T. Youngs, C. Youngs.

TOWN OF PITTSFORD, VT.—A. G. Allen, E. T. Adams, L. J. Andrews, F. Burditt, R. Burditt, B. Burditt, D. M. Burditt, M. Burditt, R. F. and C. Burditt, N. I. C. Barns, B. F. Barns, J. R. Barns, M. C. Bogue, J. D. Butler, J. F. Bresee, W. E. Bresee, H. and O. T. Bates, Mrs. D. Bates, Mrs. E. Booth, E. M. Bailey, O. C. Bowon, O. Cooley, A. F. Cooley, W. Chaffee, D. Chaffee, E. Connell, W. Creed, B. J. Douglass, P. Doolon, A. B. Dickerman, M. and M. Duffey, A. A. Dickerman, C. Dike, G. N. Eayres, S. Eckley, J. F. Eggleston, S. T. Fenton, M. Fitzpatrick, D. Fitzpatrick, J. M. Goodhough, D. J. Griffith, D. Gould, J. P. Giddings, Mrs. E. T. Hall, R. Dan, T. D. Hall, R. Hall, W. E. Hall, E. J. Hitchcock, C. Hitchcock, N. H. Hand, G. and L. Hendee, E. H. and E. R. Hendee, C. J. Hendee, C. R. and G. G. Hendee, D. T. Holden, H. S. Hewitt, M. J. Murphy and Son, — Howland, J. W. Hudson, H. Hurt, W. P. Hatch, H. Jackson, G. D. Jackson, S. H. Kellogg, A. C. Kellogg, H. F. Lathrop, S. B. Loveland, A. N. Loveland, M. Landon, M. Leonard, J. Leonard and Son, E. Luddibush, J. Lowth and Son, D. L. Mills, D. E. Milis, A. Mills, A. Morgan, B. D. Morgan, J. Manly, B. Manly, S. Manly, F. Manly, C. Murthur, C. Mahan, W. Mitchell, C. Mussey, J. McCale, W. Nichols, A. Nomse, M. O'Donald, S. Parmelee, O. W. Phillips, J. C. Powers, A. C. Powers, A. Potter, E. E. Paine, A. T. Reynolds, G. Reed, E. Randall, D. A. and J. Richardson, O. and R. C. Smith, C. Smith, Mrs. E. Smith, S. F. Smith, B. Stevens, J. Sergeants, C. R. Spencer, C. A. Stiles, A. Thomas, C. G. Thomas, J. Thomas, M. Thomas, E. R. Thomas, M. J. Wood, W. P. Ward, J. Ward, N. Willis, G. D. Wheaton, E. C. Wheaton, R. Woodcock, I. B. Worden, A. S. Whipple, J. Wolcott, L. White, S. D. Winslow, E. C. Warner, J. Warner, W. A. Wing, C. W. Wheeler.

TOWN OF CLIFTON PARK, N. Y.—J. T. Davis, G. Tifft, M. Sampson, W. Hicks, G. Morse, W. Jones, I. Rogers, G. Jones, G. Taylor, T. Nixon, W. Van Voorheise, S. Taylor, W. Reynolds, D. Hegerman, C. Hawley, G. Clement, D. Rosekrans, W. V. Woodin, J. Taylor, S. Clapper, D. Hegerman jr., John N. Craver, F. S. Parks, H. Blanchard, E. G. Morse.

TOWN OF RENSSELAERVILLE, N. Y.—C. Hughs, J. Hughs, C. Hand, I. Hoag, R. Hulbert, W. Ingraham, J. Jennings, R. Jennings, S. Kingsley, O. Lounsbery, Daniel Lounsbery, W. Lounsbery, N. Lounsbery, M. Lee, E. Lee, J. Lee, A. W. Mackey, G. Mackey, E. Mackey, H. Mackey, W. B. Mackey, W. L. Mackey, A. Mackey, A. Mackey jr., J. C. Mackey, A. K. Mackey, G. Merritt, P. Miller, A. Mackey, S. Niles, L. Niles, E. Osborn, E. Pratt, J. Pullman, A. Palmer, F. Palmer, D. Rugg, F. Rugg, E. Snyder, G. Slawson, J. Sayre, H. Sayre, P. Snyder, W. R. Tanner, John Tanner, J. Tanner, W. Tompkins, S. Taliman, A. Woodruff, Lewis G. Woodruff, A. P. Yauman, E. W. Andrus, J. Alverson E. Benn, W. Benn, E. Benn, J. Benn, J. Benn, G. W. Barrett, I. Barrett, A. Bryant, F. Bryant, D. Bush, O. Bonton, J. Burnett, A. Campbell, E. H. Chadwick, J. Cole, N. Cole, W. Crandall, E. Cook, A. Cartwright, Walter Doolittle, T. F. Doolittle, D. Doolittle, C. Davis, L. Delamater, G. Delamater, Z. Delamater, J. Demanch, W. Davis, C. Delamater, E. Edwards, I. Frost, C. Frost, E. Frost, A. Felter, J. Felter, H. Felter, B. Fullington, D. Fish, J. G. Felter, A. Giffard, J. H. Giffard, G. Giffard, F. Giffard, W. Giffard, I. Giffard, J. Gardner, M. Goodrich, W. P. Giffard, N. Gifford, S. Griffin, B. Z. Howe, J. Hagadorn, T. Hagadorn, J. Hagadorn, L. Kenyon, W. King, L. Lincoln, R. Lounsbery, H. Lincoln, R. Lounsbery, J. Lobdell, W. Lee, A. Lee, R. H. H. Mare, R. Mackey, W. Mackey, A. Mare, S. Pullman, S. Pullman, G. Pullman, W. Pullman, J. Prosser, H. Post, E. Ramsdell, R. Sandford, G. Sandford, J. Shulter, John Sweet, W. Sawdy, A. Shufult, M. Sheldon, R. Sherman, L. Sanford, J. Sherman, Lewis Sherman, W. Southard, G. St. John, J. B. Shulters, G. Snyder, E. Terbush, O. Terbush, R. Townsend, E. Teter, T. Thorne, M. Teter, John Turner, N. Teel, A. Townsend, N. Traver, W. Van Aken, J. Wood, H. Wood, W. Watson, N. Wood, R. Washborn, jr, B. Yaumans, A. Yaumans, W. Aley, C. Almy, S. Alger, D. Aley, F. Abrams, N. Abrams, G. L. Bouton, A. Borthwick, S. V. H. Bouton, W. Bouton, N. Borthwick, H. J. Bouton, J. Bell, A. Bouton, J. Bouton, E. Bouton, O. Bryant, A. Bouton, A. Bouton, R. Bouton, L. Barthwick, D. Conner, L. Conklin, J. T. Conklin, A. L. Cross, I. Cross, A. Crocker, D. Conklin, T. B. Chadwick, S. S. Cartwright, R. Cole, E. Cole, E. Cole, J. Demond, Rufus G. Dean, S. Demond, H. Dayton, W. Decker, I. R. Finch, N. H. Ford, M. Frink, R. Finch, J. Fairley, C. Fruit, F. Slurman, T. Gould, A. Green, J. Gusmon, S. Green, H. Gould, R. Garvey, T. Haight, D. Howland, P. S. Kenyon, D. R. Knowles.

TOWN OF SEARSBURGH, VT.—A. E. Briggs, E. Briggs, G. Bond, D. Crosier, J. Crosier, S. Crosier, T. G. Crosier, T. Canedy, S. Doane, W. M. O'Brien, J. B. Stevens, W. Shinner, F. Sprague, S. Wilson, G. Shippee, N. J. Wilson, H. Fuller, G. Farrington, H. Farrington, F. Gronsbeck, C. Grimes, L. Holt, E. Harvey, S. Haskins, M. Jollivette, D. C. Leray, W. Leray, D. Morgan, G. Wheeler.

TOWN OF DANBY, VT—A. Brown, D. C. Bromly, H. Bromly, A. N. Baker, O. Baker, A. S. Baker, S. Baker, N. L. Baker, O. G. Baker, F. Bromly, J. Green, R. Edgerton, A. N. Colvin, C. H. and A. Colvin, A. T. Colvin, N. Colvin, C. H. Congdon, H. Dillingham, I. Edmonds, L. R. Fisk, H. Fisk jr., O. Fisk, J. Fletcher, I. Sweat, G. Gilmore, E. T. Green, J. T. Griffith, J. B. Griffith, P. Hill, F. R. Hawley, J. Hadwin, L. Harrington, H.

W. A. Wilkins sells Bully Cloze Cheaper nor anybody elts.

FRINGES, GIMPS and DRESS TRIMMINGS, of every description, at COREY'S, GLEN'S FALLS.

B. Harrington, O. B. Hulett, S. Harrington, D. Harrington, A. Haly, C. G. Herrick, H. S. Herrick, M. C. Hulett, H. O. Herrick, S. Hulett, A. B. Herrick, J. H. Hilliard, O. R. Hadwin, P. W. Johnson, P. G. Knights, S. Kelly, I. W. Kelly, H. B. Kelly, T. Lyon, H. A. Lillie, A. A. Mathewson, I. Nichols, T. Nichols, J. E. Nichols, W. Otis, J. S. Parris, L. G. Parris, W. Parris, J. N. Phillips, W. L. Phillips, L. Palmer, D. W. Rogers, E. J. Reed, C. T. Reed, R. Sherman, H. Sherman, E. Sherman, J. Sowle, A. D. Smith, Wm. Southwick, E. Staples, E. A. Smith, W. H. Vail, I. H. Vail, W. Vaughn, D. Wetherby, D. Fish, G. Rawls, G. W. Phillips 2d, E. Holton, I. Cook, A. Buckline, G. Hadwin.

TOWN OF MOUNT HOLLY, VT.—J. Archer, N. A. Holton, I. Jackson, W. Jackson, I. Clark, S. Patrick, S. George, W. James, A. Allen, S. H. Ackley, C. Burton, B. B. Bixby, W. Billings, L. Barrett, L. C. Cook, M. Dickerman, D. Dawley, I. French, M. D. Harrington, F. Holden, M. Hammond, H. Holden, R. Hemenway, L. Hammond, W. Holden, D. Horton, A. Holden, S. Holden, L. A. Ives, T. Kenedy, P. Lovel, W. Lovel, I. D. Martin, D. Packer, S. Perkins, D. Priest, A. C. Randall, J. Trask, S. Thompson, M. H. Benson, C. Barrett, G. Carlton, A. Cook, P. Carlton, T. Dana, I. S. Dickerman, J. M. Davenport, J. Davenport, D. E. Eddy, A. Flanders, D. W. Fuller, F. L. Frost, S. D. Graves, H. N. Goodell, H. E. Goodell, L. Graves, A. Gibson, A. Hill, G. P. Hammond, A. Ives, I. Jaquith, H. A. Jaquith, E. Jaquith, G. S. Mead, D. H. Parker, E. Priest, Fred. Parmenter, R. Puffer, S. Pillsbury, E. Pillsbury, D. Priest, H. Proctor, N. Smith, J. W. Thomas, C. N. Tucker, S. Tucker, A. Tucker, P. Tier, S. Tucker, W. A. Underwood, N. Zuel, L. Barnett, A. Bixby, C. Burgwell, A. Crowley, N. C. Earl, B. M. Goodrich, D. P. Gibson, C. Hemenway, T. Hastings, L. Hammond, W. C. Knight, R. L. Lawrence, C. O. Lovell R. R. Parker, Amos Sawyer, Asa Sawyer, O. F. Wheeler, J. C. Wood.

TOWN OF DUANESBURGH, N. Y.—J. Abbey, L. Avery, Col. H. P. Allen, M. C. Avery, I. E. Avery, N. Abrams, G. Allen, W. R. Bard, W. Y. Bronk, A. Bronk, J. O. Becker, J. Buckley, B. F. Blythe, D. Britton, G. Baumis, G. Becker, S. Brown, Gen. J. S. Brown, C. Beebe, J. Blanchard, W. W. Bender, Peter Brothers, R. Briggs, J. Brewer, M. Bradt, E. A. Brewster, T. B. Briggs, W. Briggs, C. Briggs, D. Campbell, L. Chapman, S. P. Curtis, W. Conklin, G. W. Conover, C. Cramer, S. M. Cheeny, J. Cullings, B. Clute, E. Chatman, C. P. Curtis, W. H. Curtis, E. G. Crounse, J. F. Clogston, J. Chisholm, J. E. Cullings, J. A. Cullings, C. B. Carpenter, J. B. Carpenter, E. Carpenter, S. Christman, J. Christy, D. R. Coulter, J. Case, H. Clapper, W. B. Dorn, C. Dennison, J. Dennison, G. Denuison, T. Dougal, A. Dorn, T. O. Dorn, J. Donnan, P. De Forest, S. G. De La Mater, Col. J. J. De Forest, E. Davis, J. Y. R. Durfee, D. G. Durfee, J. Davidson, D. Davenport, S. Dare, D. P. Durfee, A. H. Delavan, J. Donahoe, B. M. Duane, J. W. Fidler, E. Frisbee, M. E. Foot, E. A. Frisbee, L. Fairchild, J. Ferguson, R. A. Fryer, J. A. Ferguson, D. Ferguson, A. Goodspeed, S. W. Gardinier, J. M. Green, J. Green, C. Gardiner, D. G. Griffeth, P. Gaige, D. Griffeth, J. L. Gaige, S. Gallup, A. N. Gaige, S. Hill, L. Herrick, N. Heilegus, J. Hotaling, H. Hansett, G. W. Howard, J. B. Humphrey, H. G. Herrick, L. Hawes, J. Hawes, H. G. Hoag, W. Harden, C. D. Hoag, M. E. Hoag, S. Hoag, E. E. Hare, R. Hunter, J. Hunter, A. Hunter, J. K. Jones, A. D. Jones, J. L. Jones, J. H. Jones, B. Jones, G. Jeffers, J. Johnson, J. Jeffers, N. C. Jenkins, J. D. Jones, W. Koons, J. W. Koons, W. S. Knight, R. W. Kline, G. Ketchum, T. R. Liddle, J. Ladd, M. Levey, E. Lester, R. J. Liddle, G. W. Lester, P. Leroy, G. A. Love, G. La Villa, T. Ludlum, E. Ladd, C. Ladd, J. Liddle, R. Liddle, T. G. Liddle, W. Liddle, A. Liddle, A. J. Liddle, J. Liddle jr., W. H. Liddle, C. Liddle, A. S. Liddle, B. T. Lake, J. L. Markly, A. Macomber, I. Morse, A. K. Mosher, J. McClure, N. N. Markle, E. B. Morse, I. Marsh, T. R. McClew, G. T. McFarlan, J. McMillan, H. H. McMillan, W. A. McMillan, J. A. McMillan, L. Mott, A. McDougall, H. McDougall, R. W. McDougall, R. Munger, S. Munger, J. Moore, T. Moore, E. Mackey, J. McDougall, A. Markle, J. Montancy, A. Montancy, J. McGovern, J. McQuade, G. H. Maxwell, W. Malloch, H. Mickel, G. Mathews, J. Mark, I. Mayer, R. W. Macy, A. McMillan, W. McKinney, G. Newkirk, J. Netherway, P. J. Onderkirk, J. J. Ostrander, S. Perry, C. M. Patterson, C. C. Patterson, J. Petit, J. Passage, H. Pulver, J. S. Pulver, J. Pulver, J. M. Paughurn, J. H. Patterson, M. Quant, H. Quick, S. Quimby, J. Rogers, H. Reagles, J. Rockwell, M. H. Rector, A. Rector, S. Rector, R. Rector, R. Rector, L. Rector, A. Rockwell, G. Reynolds, Z. Smith, J. Steward, J. D. Stilwell, S. Slawson, N. Smith, E. Shoots, W. Swart, J. N. Schermerhorn, J. J. Smith, E. G. Smith, J. Sheldon, B. Sheldon, J. Sheldon, M. T. Sheldon, C. Scrum, M. H. Smith, C. Schoonmaker, J. Shute, J. Slawson, S. S. Slawson, G. Schrade, P. Smith, S. Scace, H. Shaffer, J. Skiff, T. K. Stevens, T. W. Saunders, J. Staley, J. Turnbull, P. R. Turnbull, S. Tripp, J. H. Titus, J. Tiffany, W. Turnbull, J. L. Turnbull, P. Tiffany, W. Tiffany, G. J. Turnbull, J. Tedball, M. R. Victory, A. Van Pelt, N. Van Patten, T. Van Beuscoten, V. Van Rensselaer, A. M. Vanderpool, C. Van Wormer, J. Wiltsie, W. Wells, J. W. Waddell, G. Wilkinson, G. Weed, W. Wright, E. G. Wilber, D. Wiggins, W. Weaver, J. White, R. B. White, J. V. Wemple, J. H. Wilkins, W. Waddell, H. Wright, Col. J. D. Wood, A. L. Wilber, I. R. T. Wood, B. Wiltsie, G. Westfall, B. Wilber, H. Wilber, J. Wainwright, J. C. Wright, M. Westfall, T. Westfall, J. Leudrum, J. McGuire, D. Young, W. Young, D. S. Yeomans, S. Young, W. Young, H. Zeh, J. H. Zeh.

TOWN OF COEYMANS, N. Y.—A. Ackerman, Van Ackerman, J. Armstroug, M. Adams, J. Allen, G. Buggs, W. S. Briggs, H. Brown, L. and A. Blaisdell, J. Bugbee, T. T. Bedell, E. Blodgett, W. Blodget, D. W. Blossom, B. Brate, G. Bleecker, John Babcock, S. Bannus, G. Cronk, L. Coonley, P. Coonley, D. P. Coonley, J. Cary, S. Coonley, D. S. Carhart, G. and T. E. Cronk, J. W. Cook, J. Carr, T. Crum, Jas. H. Cutler, G. H.

Heavy SHIRTS and DRAWERS for 62 Cents, at WAIT'S.
For a nice-fitting suit of CLOTHES, go to WAIT'S. (See page 81.)

SATINS, SILKS, VELVETS, FLOWERS and FEATHERS, in variety, at COREY'S, GLEN'S FALLS.

SEE INDEX, PAGE ELEVEN. 201

Cutler, J. Cary, C. Carr, G. Coonley, J. Coonley, W. S. Cole, H. Callanan, L. A. Carhart, E. Carhart, M. Dwyer, J. Derbyshire, J. Davis, A. B. Foreman, W. C. Falkner, Joshua Gedney, B. Gedney, M. Griffin, A. Green, G. Groesbeck, P. Grogan, J. D. Hotaling, J. Hotaling, J. H. Hotaling, E. Hotaling, S. H. Haslet, A. Hallenbeck, L. Huyck, J. Hunt, C. Hotaling, H. B. Joslin, J. W. Jolley, J. E. Jones, E. Jaycox, P. Keefer, H. Keefer, W. Kniffin, H. Klinhanns, S. Lawson, I. Lawson, H. Lott, F. N. Loucks, K. Litchfield, J. Lameraux, W. J. Lameraux, J. Lameraux, J. H. Lasher, G. C. Lamereaux, E. Lawson, W. Laly, F. Leedings, D. McCarty, W. C. McCullough, M. Merritt, Z. Mead, J. Mead, M. S. Merritt, I. Mosher, H. Mosher, J. J. Mull, B. T. Mull, J. P. Montross, R. McCarthy, W. Millbanks, I. Martin, S. Norris, F. Nodine, M. Nickerson, S. Nickerson, J. Nodine, F. Onderdonk, J. Opell, E. Osterhout, J. Powell, A. Powell, J. W. Powell, J. H. Powell, W. Palmer, A. Palmer, N. Palmer, J. Pelton, E. Powell, A. Pelton, W. Riley, I. Richardson, A. M. Robinson, J. Robinson, J. J. Radcliff, P. Rowe, M. Rarrick, H. Rarrick, D. Reynolds, C. Reynolds, D. Robinson, W. Robinson, DeWitt Stephens, F. Slater, A. Schoonmaker, J. Schoonmaker, J. J. Schoonmaker, E. Shear, C. A. Shear, P. Shear, J. Shear, D. Slack, G. Spaulding, T. G. Stanton, W. Sickle, N. Serls, H. Springsted, C. Snyder, J. Sickler, G. W. Sickler, N. Schermerhorn, W. Schoonmaker, F. Smith, T. E. Seamen, L. Swarthout, T. E. Swarthout, P. Seabridge, J. S. Smith, J. P. Sickler, C. Slingerland, P. Sickler, J. Stephenson, E. Sweet, J. Stewart, P. Shear, H. Strevell, G. Terry, Wm. Tuttle, W. Terry, A. J. TenEyck, J. Thorn, D. C. Tompkins, A. Tompkins, F. Tompkins, H. Tompkins, P. A. TenEyck, B. TenEyck, R. Townsend, P. B. TenEyck, J. A. Ten Eyck, R. Thorn, W. Tompkins, C. Vanderzee, C. H. Vanderzee, W. T. Vincent, L. R. Vincent, D. Vincent, S. Vincent, H. Vrooman, D. Vrooman, C. Vrooman, J. Vrooman, P. Van Buren, R. K. Vincent, R. Vanderbilt, Martin Vanderpool, S. Vanderhuyden, P. Vanderpool, J. Vandusen, A. Whitbeck, V. A. Whitbeck, A. Whitbeck, A. Whitbeck, J. T. Whitbeck, W. J. Whitbeck, J. A. Whitbeck, T. Whitbeck, W. Whitbeck, J. Whitbeck, jr., W. J. Whitbeck, D. Wiltsey, P. Wiltsey, E. Wiltsey, H. Wiltsey, I. Whitbeck, D. Whitbeck, I. T. Whitbeck, A. E. Willis, T. T. E. Waldron, B. Waldron, H. Waldron, W. Wagoner, J. D. Winne, A. Wiltsey, G. Wagoner, G. Whipple.

TOWN OF CORINTH, N. Y.—J. Andrew, T. Andrew, Thos. Andrew, P. Andrew, C. L. Allen, G. W. Allen, E. Ambler, J. Ambler, J. Angell, A. Angell, Alfred Angell, E. Angell, G. Brooks, S. E. Burnham, D. Barrett, E. A. Bailey, J. Barrett, L. R. Burch, J. C. Barrass, H. W. Barrett, A. A. Brackett, A. W. Brown, W. W. Carlton, J. Carlton, B. Carlton, H. E. Cowles, M. L. Clother, T. Crooker, W. M. Clother, L. Clother, B. P. Clother, C. J. Clother, H. N. Clother, S. Clother, A. N. Clother, F. Carpenter, T. G. Carpenter, T. D Carpenter, D. Carpenter, W. A. Comstock, W. Comstock, G. G. Cole, Isaac Carpenter, L. B. Deuell, J. Deuell, John Eggleston, Jared Eggleston, R. H. Eggleston, J. Eggleston jr., S. Eggleston, H. Eggleston, A. A. Eddy, D. C. Eggleston, E. Edwards, G. W. Edwards, E. Earls, H. Eddy, J. Early, E. Early, J. Freeman, D. Fenton, W. Flansburg, H. R. Grippen, N. W. Grippen, W. Greenfield, B. Guiles, E. E. Hickok, L. Herrick, S. Hoyt, I. Handy, A. D. Holden, O. Herrick, H. Howard, J. Herrick, E. M. Haines, J. N. Hodges, A. Hawley, G. Howe, A. G. Hodges, S. Heath, R. Heath, O. Heath, T. Hayes, P. C. Hayes, J. S. Haynes, B. Hickey, N. M. Houghton, Wm. Ide, S. Jones, R. Kendall, S. D. Kelsey, J. Kilbharn, C. P. Kingsley, D. Kingsley, D. Long, J. Loveland, P. Lincoln, H. Lindsey, A. Mallory, J. Merritt, P. B. Murry, J. Manning, C. Martin, A. Miner, E. L. Miner, C. Morrison, J. Nims, P. Purqua, W. Raymond, J. Redmond, D. Reeves, A. Robbins, P. J. Randall, O. J. Randall, Wm. Riley, Wm. Race, D. C. Randall, H. Reynolds, J. G. Stearns, J. Stearns, J. Steadman, J. St. John, J. H. Steadman, S. Simpson, D. Steadman, J. St. John, A. Showers, A. Saxton, I. Turner, T. Tiffany, W. I. Traver, E. Varney, L. Wells, G. White, H. Wilson, B. Woodard, L. Wandall, A. H. Woodcock, A. P. Young, L. Yack.

TOWN OF ROTTERDAM, N. Y.—J. Akin, E. Akin, W. Akin, N. W. Akin, Mrs. J. Allen, J. B. Austin, A. Appley, P. Acker, J. Backus, S. L. R. Buchanan, Mrs. J. W. Bradshaw, F. Bradt, N. Bradt, L. Basa, A. N. Bradt, G. K. Bradshaw, J. Bennet, L. Burdick, T. Bullock, F. Plato, G. Brougham, A. Brougham, A. A. Bradt, D. Bradt, C. Burk, D. C. Bradt, G. B. Brown, Burk and Slats, J. W. Buys, M. Brown, H Brown, N. Bigelow, A. Betts, F. Baringer, S. Bradshaw, B. Boink, Mrs. J. Buys, J. Bakeman, W. Brougham, J. Babcock, T. Barker, P. Becker, M. A. Blessing, J. Brush, J. Baringer, W. Bouts, A. Crawford, S. Crawford, J. T. Clute, H. C. Cady, W. A. Cromee, P. Vandyck, D. D. Cambell, D. Crouch, J. N. Clute, J. H. Chambers, A. Cullings, Mrs. J. M. Crawford, W. Chism, J. Chrisler, S. Chrisler, J. Crouch, N. Clute jr., S. Caikins, M. O'Connor, N. M. F. Clute, P. Carr, M. Chism, J. M. Chism, H. Clumminayer, R. Carr, H. M. Crane, J. Enos, J. Deforest, A. H. Delmont, H. Darrow, F. Dandenburgh, J. Ditch, H. Ellers, J. Fisher jr., W. W. Fisher, J. Fisher, G. Fisher, J. Furbeck, P. Furbeck, C. Finchout, J. Furley, P. Furley, J. Funstone, P. Flynn, H. Lurman, P. Flanagan, N. Fryer, J. Gregg, J. Gardinier, G. Gordin, J. Gordin, D. Gordin, J. and J. Gregg, M. Gregg, A. T. Gifford, Mrs. E. Gordin, M. Gents, A. Gregg, J. M. Gardiner, J. E. Green, J. Galvin, W. A. Ham, H. W. Herrick, T. W. Houghtaling, H. Hammilton, M. Ham, P. W. Ham, L. W. Herrick, G. S. Hunt, J. Hunt, W. Hotaling, J. C. Holton, J. Hines, M. Hount, E. Hanson, E. Hurly, J. Hilman, G. S. Harmons, J. S. Hogg, F. Herk, G. Ives, J. Jackson, C. Jeffers, J. Jeffers, J. B. Kline, S. Kerns, C. Kellerhous, W. Lyons, M. J. Levy, J. Levy, J. Lambert, J. Lambert jr., W. Lambert, P. A. Livingston, J. Lenard, C. Long, Mrs. S. McCan, S. J. McMillen, W. J. Mudge, J. Mudge, N. Maybee, J. J. McCue, S. Maybee, A. McMillen, M. McNelly, P. Miller, J. H. Miller, R. McMichael, J. Myres' estate, J. McMillen, J. S. Mc-

Custom Work done better at WILKINS' than elsewhere.

Competition Defied in Quality, Quantity and Prices of STATIONERY, at BENDER'S, 73 State Street, Albany.

202 FARMERS' ALMANAC.

Cue, W. H. Miller. W. Miller. I. McDaniel, J. Mitten. C. Miller, A. Mason. C. Mires, C. McCaffery. S. Moore. W. Mark. D. Murch. C. Newhouse. B. Ostrander, J. Openhauser, S. Patterson. J. C. Peck S. Putnam. A. Y. Putnam. A. Putnam, A. Pangburn. A. Platoe. F. B. Penny. J. Phillips. F. T. Pierson, R. J. Peck. J. M. Philips. J. Peter. Mrs. E. Pangburn, O. Pulman. J. C. Perry. T. Page, J. C. Peck. D. Peck. Mrs. H. Peck, Mrs. M. Quick J. H. Quackinbush. A. Quackinbush. C. D. Rynex. E. Rynex. E. W. Rynex, W. Rinkle. Mrs. E. Robinson. D. Row. M. Rigly. G. Wren. N. Reinheart, Mrs. A. Ratcliff. S. Richmond. J. F. Swart. J. Staly. A. Sharkey. R. Schermerhorn. A. A. Schermerhorn. W. Shannon. A. B. Schermerhorn. E. Schermerhorn. J. Sitterly, P. Shufelt, M. Sitterly, B. Snyder. G. Shufelt. O. Squires. A. V. Schermerhorn. N. J. Schermerhorn. Mrs. E. Vandyck. J. R. Sitterly. W. Scrafford. S. J. Schermerhorn. S. J. Schermerhorn. J. J. Schermerhorn. J. J. A. Schermerhorn. J. J. and S. J. Schermerhorn. J. Schermerhorn, J. B. Schermerhorn. J. B. Schermerhorn. Mrs. J. Schermerhorn. S. Schermerhorn. D. C. Schermerhorn. M. Shewer. B. T. F. Schermerhorn. W. Williams. J. Sayer. B. Schermerhorn. J. B. Smith. A. Sibell. P. Stevis. Mrs. J. Strong. P. Shannon, G. Shaver, J. Snyder, J. Sinner. S. Swits. J. Stephens. W. Stephens. J. W. Shannon. D. V. Stimpson, Mrs. N. Stassey. M. Sinnot. T. Turnbull, J. Turnbull. J. J. Turnbull, I. Trunex. J. Thomas. M. Veeder. N. Veeder. N. Van Yost. N. Van Patten. J. Van Valkenburgh. J. J. Valkinburgh. J. P. Vine, J. Van Valkinburgh. H. G. Veeder. W. Van Dyck. J. Van Patten. J. W. Van Patten. J. V. Van Patten. H. Vedder. J. G. Veeder. H. W. Veeder. G. Veeder. S. Valk. A. H. Veeder. A. Valk. J. C. Perry, J. Van Patten. A. P. Van Dyck. W. Veeder. E. Van Wormer. P. Vine. J. S. Van Slyke. N. Van Patten. A. Van Eps. J. M. Veeder. H. Van Lake. J. M. Vedder. H. Vermilya. J. B. Van Zant. N. Veeder. E. Vine. C. G. Weaver. A. B. Wemple. S. Wescoatt. J. D. Wemple. A. Warren. Mrs. J. Waggoner, J. Wright. S. A. Weart. S. Wands. A. Walrout. G. White. E. K. Williams. P. Willey, J. Werts. T. Welch. C. Wormer. J. Willey. J. Wolford, H. Peck. J. Pangburn.

TOWN OF BERNE, N. Y.—J. M. Allen. G. Adriance. J. Brownell. H. Brownell. W. Brownell. C. Banner. H. Brownell. J. H. Bronk. T. Batcher. I. Brate. I. Boyington. J. Cummings. H. Cornell. H. Conger. D. Conger. P. H. Devoe. D. S. Dyer, J. Dyer, R. Davis. J. Davis. I. H. Devoe. A. B. Davis. J. Dyer, J. D. Flansburg. S. Flansburg. G. Flansburg. J. T. Flansburg. D. Flansburg. G. Filkins. G. W. Filkins. D. C. Filkins. H. R. Filkins. C. A. Filkins. C. O. Filkins. J. Fowler, J. D. Gardner. D. S. Gardner, N. Gallup, G. Gallup. A. Hempstead. A. C. Hempstead. A. R. Hungerford. A. Hungerford. I. Hungerford. G. Hotaling. T. A. Hungerford. J. Joslin. J. Kendall. S. Lagrange. G. Lawson, A. D. Lamb. I. Lobdell. P. Long. F. Lagrange. M. Livingston. R. Miller. J. McNab. M. Maher. J. Flansburg. J. H. Moak. S. Miller. H. McCumber. A. J. Northrop. M. O'Brien, J. Osterhout. J. O'Brien. W. Pitcher. S. Picher. S. Palmer. W. Pier, L. Quay. R. Reamer. J. Ryan. H. A. Stalker. H. Strevell. R. Strevell. A. Shultes. L. st. John. A. K. Slade, E. Schermerhorn. C. Secor. J. Schermerhorn, J. Stalker, I. Strevell. F. D. Secor. M. Shaffer. A. A. Smith. S. Tompson. D. S. Van Dusen. J. Van Dusen. A. Van Schaack. E. B. Vincent. G. B. Vincent. T. Vincent. W. C. Vincent. N. Van Schaack. C. Warner. A. J. Warner. E. Warner. H. Warner. P. Warner. J. N. Warner. E. Warner. A. A. Warner. F. Ward. I. White. N. Weedman. G. S. Waggoner. B. Winne. J. H. Weedman. W. Waggoner. J. B. White. S. P. Winne. T. Williams. P. Youngs. S. P. Youngs, D. Barber. P. Barber. H. Barkman. L. Bolster. M. Becker. P. Baker, P. L. Bradt. W. Bradt. R. Boughton. E. Bogardus. A. M. Bogardus. B. Bogardus. P. Bull 2d. R. Barkman, G. Baker, P. Baker, P. Bower. H. C. Ball. A. Becker. P. Becker, J. Barber, J. Boomhauver. G. I. Barber, R. Ball. D. Ball, P. S. Ball, P. Ball. J. Ball, F. Bolster, J. N. Bogardus. S. R. Cowen. E. Carl. W. Carl. M. Crocker. P. I. Deitz. C. Deitz. I. Deitz. J. M. Deitz. A. I. Deitz. S. Dixon. B. B. Dyer. M. Freidendoll. E. W. Fowler. N. Gifford. P. Hochstraper, P. I. Hochstraper. J. Hochstraper. J. C. Haverly. H. Willsey. J. S. Hays. J. Hillon. J. Hays, J. Joslin. P. King. B. Kirkpatrick. J. Lawson. H. Luckey. J. Luckey. H. Moak, A. Miller, C. Nelson. M. Nelson. C. Nelson. A. Onderdonk. L. Onderdonk. D. D. Palmer, J. Patten. P. H. Powell. N. Palmer. C. Reynolds. C. Renhart. D. H. Reinhart, P. Simons, J. R. Shufeldt. I. Shufeldt. J. Stalker. J. I. Shultes, H. J. Smith, L. Swartout. J. Sickles, J. P. Shaffer. D. St. John. W. Shultes, J. Sherman. R. Sisson. S. Sweet, L. Swart. W. Sherman, P. Shultes, J. Shultes, J. N. Shaffer. E. St. John. I. V. Shultes. C. Swart. H. Smith. P. Shultes. N. Shelden. R. Smith. E. M. Sheltes. J. Shultes, J. Starkwether. A. J. Sweet. M. Saddlemire. I. Watson. W. B. Tompkins, E. Tompkins. S. Van Vranken, J. F. Weidman. W. A. Willsey. J. B. Wilcox. J. Wright. M. Wright. Morgan Wright. I. Willsey. A. Wright. J. Willsey. G. G. Waggoner. G. Wright. A. S. Willsey. J. P. Warner, E. S. Wright. J. J. Wright. E. Wright. A. Willsey, J. R. Wright. C. W. Wright. S. S. Wright, A. Wright. T. J. Wood. P. Weidman. S. S. Youngs. J. Youngs, C. P. Zeh. W. Zeh, C. Zeh. P. Zeh. F. Zeh. P. W. Zeh. P. Alverson. C. Alger, C. C. Cook. T. Cook. E. Crippen, jr., J. Crosby. P. Cambell. H. Cline. J. Cambell, A. Crocker. I. Denison. H. L. Dearstine, J. L. Delamarter. A. Delamarter, D. Durfee. A. Deitz. S. Damond. J. Deitz. C. Esmyer. Jas. Farquer. Joseph Farquer, S. Finch. R. Finch. J. Furman. W. Furman, I. T. Garvey, H. Gifford. J. Gifford. M. Gathen. W. Gifford, A. Gifford, E. Hall. H. H. Harris, M. Hess. R. Hontaling. W. Kniskerne, A. Cline. S. Legget. L. Mair. M. Miller, A. Messer. J. Miller. D. Merrihew. J. Mackey, J. Norton. A. Noel, J. Owen, O. Pearly, J. Post, D. E. Post, J. Piter, S. Youngs. W. Young, A. A. Youmans.

TOWN OF RUTLAND, VT.—G. Allen. J. Allen, J. and E. Allen. H. W. Aldrich, A. Ames. M. Ames. J. Atwell. E. L. Bailey, A. Barnes. W. F. Barnes, J. E. Barnes, Barnes and Van Allstine, H. H. Baxter, Henry L. Blanchard, B. F. Blanchard and Son H. H.

All of Garrett's Dental Work is WARRANTED. Glen's Falls.

For CARPETS and OIL CLOTHS, go to WAIT'S.
For FINE READY-MADE CLOTHING, go to WAIT'S. (See page 81.)

SEE INDEX. PAGE ELEVEN. **203**

Blakley, C. Bebee. L. A. Bebee, J. Brewster, L. A. Billings. F. Billings. J. L. Billings. G.
A. R. Buessell. E. S. Briggs. M. B. and A. M. Brown. E. Bourdman and Son, S. Bourdman, C. G. Bourdman, M. Bowen, J. S. Billings, J. Cain, E. Campbell, A. Capron, A. S. and J. W. Crampton, H. L. Cherry, J. W. Crampton, H. Clark, jr., M. Clark, H. S. Clark, A. W. Clark, J. A. Cheney, B. Cheney, G. Cheney, A. Cleveland, C. Clement. Clement and Son, A. Crippin, B. Collins, P. Cornnell, G. W. Chaplin. N. B. Congdon, B. Conners, M. L. Curtiss, S. W. Curtiss, S. Clemons, L. Capron, B. Capron, W. T. and H. E. Capron, L. Carpenter, E. G. Chatterton, E. L. Chatterton. J. M. Chatterton, W. Chatterton, R. Chatterton, F. Chaffee, J. A. Davis, W. C. Davis, S. L. Daniels, O. G. Danforth, B. Demick, J. A. Deland, J. M. Dewey, W. Dreinwater. Warren Dickerman, F. Dewey, W. J. Dunckley, H. H. Dyer, F. Eastman. L. Eastman. J. Eyers, F. Edgerton, M. G. Everts, J. Engrem. M. A. Edgerton, A. H. Farmer, J. Fitzgerald, B. J. Fisk, W. G. Fisk, N. Fournier, G. Graves, J. Graham, M. E. Gate, S. Green, W. Green, J. B. Gleason, L. Gleason, P. E. Gleason, A. A. and B. R. Green, T. George. W. Gilmore, M. Gilmore, W. and J. S. Gilmore, N. Griswold, F. Griswold, E. Griswold, S. J. Griggs, J. G. Griggs, W. Goodhin, L. F. Goodrich, J. M. Goodnow, C. F. Graham, J. Graham, M. Goldsmith, L. Gould, S. Hayward, H. Hayward, M. Hayward, D. Hart, F. S. Hale, C. Hall, J. Hall, J. M. Hall, H. Hall, J. Hanley, A. Hawley, W. Hastings, M. Hilliard, M. Hitchcock, L. Hosford, Forter Harvey. J. Howland, Hulet and H. L. Gleason, D. B. and R. S. Humphrey, L. Hulbert, A. F. Johnson, Z. Johnson, C. L. Johnson, N. Johnson, S. F. Kelley, Kelley and Davis, J. Kelley, A. D. Ladd. T. Lampson, D. Lapael, M. Lester and Sons, A. Lester, M. W. Lester. J. K. Larned, W. Lincoln. L. M. Lircomb, T. Londergin, L. Long, J. Long, S. Loveland. J. E. Manley, M. S. Mauley, M. and J. Moran, E. Mead, J. Mead, H. Mead, J. M. Mead, R. C. Mead, W. Mills, D. Morgan, B. Morgan, P. H. Munford, G. Munford, W. Murdock, G. Mussey, H. Massey, J. McConnel, McLaughlin and P. Gillian, J. McGuin, P. and M. McLaughlin, T. J. Omsber, P. K. Osgood, J. O'Brine and Son, D. O'Enark, P. and J. O'Roark, J. B. Page, R. E. Patterson, S. Parker, W. Parsons, A. Pratt, J. Pratt, A. Palmer, F. M. Pennock, B. Perkins, M. Perkins, L. Perkins, A. Parry, J. Persons, J. H. Patch, R. Pierpomp, E. Pierpomp, C. N. Phillips, M. Pike, A. H. Post, B. W. Pond, C. Porter, H. W. Porter, J. B. Porter, J. W. Poaler, R. Proctor, H. C. Richards, J. M. Reed, E. A. Reed, D. Reed, A. B. Reynolds, M. Reynolds, I. C. and S. Reynolds, W. G. Ripley, Ripley and sons, J. Ross, P. Robertson, A. E. Russell, S. and P. Robertson, R. Sharp, W. Shangro, C. E. Stratton, L. Sargents, J. Seward, W. H. Seward, F. H. Shedd, C. H. Sheldon, Sheldon and Slason, L. Sheldon, T. Spelman, J. H. Smith, F. and C. E. Spencer, L. and A. Spencer, A. Simouds, N. P. and P. Simonds, D. Smith and Son, G. L. Smith, E. Smith, D. H. Smith, E. Smith, L. B. Smith, H. Strong, Sutherland Falls Mar. Co., S. Sargent, Sheldon and Gilmore, A. B. Thayer, G. C. and M. Thrall, C. and R. C. Thrall, R. Todd, J. Tower and Son, J. C. Thompson, O. Thomas A. W. Thornton, J. S. Tuttle, L. Vaughu, D. Verder, L. M. Walker, L. Ward, H. Ward, A. J. and C. E. Ware, M. Warner, L. Watkins, A. Watkins, J. C. and E. Wells, M. Welch, J. and A. Wetmore, D. Wing, D. Wing, T. Wilson, Williams, C. L. Williams, J. Williams, J. White, E. Wright, E. Wright, W. S. Wright, C. F. Wright, W. H. Wright, H. Woodruff, Oscar D. Young.

TOWN OF STILLWATER. N. Y.—J. V. Arnold, T. D. Arnold, O. Bathuck, S. Badgely, C. Denton, C. Denton, R. Eldridge, W. Eldridge, R. Moore, L. Teal, E. Abel, B. Baker, W. Baker, R. O. Baker, J. T. Baker, P. Baker, R. Bullis, A. Bidwill, C. Blood, C. Blasdell, A. Bortwell, Mrs. J. A. Betts, R. Baker, M. Butler, P. K. Best, S. Clever, T. Clemants, C. Cooper, J. Cleveland, W. Clark, S. H. Carlton, R. Ciperly, B. Conners, P. Dalton, L. Deyoe, W. A. Dunn, W. Dyer, L. Dwight, H. Ewing, J. Edmonds, G. Edmonds, J. Elmer, J. A. Flagler, J. Farley, A. Fellows, H. Fullerton, P. Farrell, J. Farrell, J. Flinn, G. P. Rowley, J. Foley, P. Gailor, C. E. Gallett, C. Gilbert, B. Gilbert, C. Golden, S. Hall, Mrs. S. Hunter, J. C. Holmes, D. B. Holmes, E. Holmes, J. Holmes, J. Humphrey, E. Humphrey, E. and B. Haskins, W. Hall, J. H. Huff, D. Hickey, E. Hulihan, T. Hulihan, J. Hulihan, Mrs. Knapp, M. Kilby, O. Lawrence, J. N. Lockrow, R. Megat, Mrs. H. Marshal, A. C. Marshal, M. Mahon, J. Wiley, J. Pink, W. Parks, N. Ostrander, R. Rogers, T. Sweeney, M. Sweeney, W. Taylor, J. Thompson, G. Vanderwerken, W. Vanderwerken, S. Wood, E. Wool, N. B. Arnold, F. B. Arnold, T. Arnold, J. Arnold, C. Abel, G. W. Nilson, R. H. Barber, G. Bush, C. Barber, A. Bunce, T. D. Brightman, T. Dunham, J. Brightman, W. Coons, Mrs. Coons, A. Dodd, H. Duel, J. Flin, J. Ferris, D. Flagler, S. Flagler, S. G. Flagler, W. Flagler, J. Hart, A. M. Hart, A. Perkins, L. Perkins, L. Barber, H. Putnam, M. Robbins, H. D. Rogers, F. strang, I. strang, S. Strang, E. Strang, D. Sullivan, S. Searls, W. Turner, E. Hunt, T. Huestis, W. Huestis, E. K. Homer, B. Hart, H. Ingram, T. M. Myers, I. Meyers, H. Myers, E. Vandenburgh jr., J. B. Wright, T. Woodworth, C. D. Bull, W. Barrett, D. Baldwin, C. Bloomingdale, J. Becker, W. H. Blood, A. Britt, J. L. Baker, J. A. Currin, M. Corkins, S. Carden, H. M. Clark, Mrs. M. Dickinson, W. Denison, C. Edmonds, A. Edmonds, G. Edmonds, S. Edmonds, T. Fordham, M. Ford, W. B. Fuller, T. E. Fellows, B. Flinn, C. Flike, R. Gardner, A. Gallop, I. T. Gleason, S. Gleason, I. Hicks, S. Hewitt, J. Holterin, S. Hewit, L. Hodgeman, E. N Hart, D. Clark, E. Handy, J. J. Lansing, G. F. Lamb, S. Dunham, J. Lynch, G. V. Lansing, J. Lee, R. Moore, B. Moore, D. Mulherrin, R. Merchant, G. W. Mancius, M. Noland, J. B. Newland, M. O'Neal, W. Osgood, S. Post, P. Tombs, M. Post, Mrs. E. Parker, J. Pendergast, J. Quackenbush, L. Rowley, T. Sherman, O. Secor, H. Sisson, S. Stratton, F. Stratton, J. W. Smith, W. Taylor, S. Tompkins, E. Vandenburgh, C. Vandenburgh, A. Van Wie, Clark, Wood and Co., J. F. Wetsel, P. V. Wetsel, P. Wil-

P. H. COREY, dealer in MILLINERY and STRAW GOODS, GLEN'S FALLS.

WILKINS sells Clothing 15 per cent cheaper than others.
26

E. H. BENDER, Wholesale and Retail Dealer in every Variety of
BOOKS, STATIONERY, &c., 73 State Street, Albany.

FARMERS' ALMANAC.

liams, A. Brightman, O. V. Bishop, W. P. Curtis, R. Coffin, Phillip Co., Cotton and Co., J. Dalton, W. L. Denison, W. Dean, C. Ensign, A. Brigs, Mrs. I. Freeman, J. Farnam. H. Osgood, E. Hewit, N. Hill, E. K. Heustis, J. V. N. Houghtaling, C. Oliver, E. Leggett, S. Tomson. E. Larington, E. Munger, Mrs. M Munger, W. Nielson, R. Newland. P. Nolan, Mrs. J. Nolan, R. Oliver, B. W. Osgood, D. Pangburn, J. L. Pangburn, H. Bradt. G. Riley, S. Rowley, G. Rowley, J. Rogers, L. Salsbury, D. Smith, A. Smith. J. Thomson, E. Smith, H. A. Van Wie, D. Wie, J. Walker, E. Smith, Mrs. A. Wiley. S. Wing, G. Wing, E. Wilber, B Searls, V. Searls. P. Tracey.

TOWN OF NEW SCOTLAND, N. Y.—J. Albright, P. Albright, I. Albright, F. Albright, W. Alkenbrack. F. Allbright. G. Boyd, D. Bennett, A. J. Blessing, G. Becker, J. Bueannan, J. Bell. H. Bell. J. Bender. H. Crounse, E. Cranfield, H. Earls, D. Earls, D. Fisher, W. Flansburgh, J. H. Flansburgh, E. Fitch, J. Fert, H. Felter, C. Frederick, R. H. Fossman, J. H. Hotaling, N. Hotaling, A. F. Hallenbeck, P. F. Hase, A. Johnson, C. Jacobson, J. F. Bullick, G. L. Bartin, S. Cook, G. W. Bender, A. Becker, H. F. Blessing, Mrs. Beebe, J. H. Becker, D. Bradt, S. H. Butler, A. Cook, E. Comstock, A. Coughtry, W. J. Coughtry, P. R. Fubeck, P. Gifford, W. Ferguson, C. Frier, A. Frier, J. Frier, L. Hess, O. Hotaling, R. Herst. H. Hotaling, J. Hilton, A. Hallenbeck, J. Hendrick, P. C. Haverly, F. L. Joshlin, A. A. Johnson. P. H. Radley, D. Calanan, H. Creble, C. J. Rowe, W. Plant, W. Van Allen, H. H. Van Derzee, J. Haight, N. B. Houck, R. B. Hotaling, A. Hallenbeck, H. Terguhan, F. Ingraham. J. D. Johnson, E. Jones, G. Kruffen, DeW. C. Lawrence, H. B. Mead, W. McCulloch, H. B. Mead. A. McHineh, G. L. Mitchel, E. B. Mitchel, C. Mucke, P. Micle, C. Mosher, W. W. McCullen, E. Mathias, S. Mosher, J. McFab, J. D. McCulloch, P. O. Sterhout, S. Sterhout, S. C. Rowe. H. Perry, J. C. Radcliffe, W. H. Keeguay, F. Sager, N. Crawford, R. Vanderbelt, P. Van Allen, E. Jones. P. N. Johnson, F. Johnson, A. Johnson, S. Koonz, J F. Koonz, C. Luke, P. Luke, J. McElroy, J. H. Martin, A. McHarg, H. McHarg, J. McCollum. C. Mathias, J. Miller, S. Martin, A. McMillin, J. McMillin, J. Mathias, D. Martin, J. T. Moak, J. W. Moak, J. McCulloch, R. Markle. C. Mart, S. Marsham, P. S. Markle, R. Moak, J. S. Moak, W. McMullen, J. Oliver, F. L. Joshlin, A. Lagrange, A. Lagrange, O. Lagrange, F. Lagrange, J. C. Lagrange, P. Livingston, P. Livingston, W. McClaskey, W. Martin, J McBride, J. E. Oliver, A. K. Oliver, N. Oliver, A. E. Oliver, G. G. Oliver, J. Reid, A. Reasc, A. Sager, H. Schermerhorn, J. Allen, A. Allen. D. Allen, C. Bammas. W. Britton, R. Bennett, C. Beaman, R. W. Bates C. J. Crounse, I. Cass, G. Countryman, D. Anthony, N. A. Delong, J. Delong, D. Deitz, R. D. Flagler, C. Finkle, D. Flansburgh, G. Fuller, P. H. Flansburgh, J. Flansburgh, M. Flansburgh, F. Fuller, P. Hotaling, T. Hotaling. W. J. Hough ton, J. Honck, J. T. Houck, P. J. Houck, A. Booth, W. H. Conger, M. Flansburgh, J. Hartman, J. P. Hotaling, J. Lenard. R. Long, H. Pangborn, J. K. Radley, D. Radley. A. Slingerland, W. T. Spore, J. Van Atten, J. B. Van Atten, T. Van Atten, M. Van Atten, W. B. Van Atten, J. Van Atten, I. H. Van Wie, P. Waldeerman, M. J. Witheck, J. Arnold, G. Britton. H. P. Bradt, H. P. Beate, P. A. Bradt, W. N. Beate, P. W. Beate, B. Beate, J. V. and H. Bradt, J. H. Coughtry, J. L. Dunbar, P. L. Houck, I. Johnson. H. Joshlin, H. Seedings. J. L. Loucks, P. Moak, J. N. Moak, F. Rilyea, J. Vadney, H. Wilsey, J. Sensly, M. Slingerland, M. Slingerland, P. Slingerland, J. Slingerland, T. Slingerland, C. Slingerleret, J. Scutt, J. Shear, E. Statt, J. Snyder, S. P. Simmons, W. simmons, J. Salsbury, Z. Smith, J. Thomas, W. Van Astel, D. Van Dyke. J. H. Van Dyke. S. Winston, B. Winston, N. J. Waldeermar, G. Wagems. J. J. Waldeermar, L. Winile, G. White, J. Patterson, R. Patten, A. Pangborn. W. J. Regleod, W. Reid, J. A. Reid. D. V. S. Boynsford. J. A. Reamer, S. Sager, G. W. Schermerhorn, H. Schermerhorn, H. Smith, A. N. Smith. J. Smith, A. J. Smith, J. S. Secor, P. C. Sigsby. W. Swift, A. H. Schermerhorn, W. Talar, R B Taylor, J. Tygert, W. Tygert. C. Terwilligor, J. E. Taylor, J. Taylor. F. C. Van Wormer, P. Van Schack, J. Van Olinda, J. Van Guislen, A. Van Auken, I. Van Auken. N. N. Ward, J. F. Ward. P. Winnie, A. Winnie. H. J. Winnie, Z. Winnie, W. D. Wands. J. C. Wands. T. Wands. W. H. Winnie, S. Woodworth, C. Woodworth, E. E. Wands, J. Wayne, A. Wayne, J. Whitbeck, J. Waidman Jr., J. H. Wayne, A. Wood, E. Wood, J. Warner, F. Warner, E. Wood, R. Wood, A. Wright, J. Young, W. Young. W. P. Young.

TOWN OF WATERFORD, N. Y.—J. Anderson, J. Anker, D. Brewster, J. H. Brewster, M. Bedell, C. Boughton, J. Bailey, J. Bedell, F. Lawrence, J. B. Clute, S. Cheever, J. C. Cramer, G. Cooper, H. Campbell, R. D. Davis. G. Levitt, J. B. Enos, Barner and J. Evers. D. Gregg. jr., G. Gillett, A. and M B. Griffin, J. Higgins, S. Hemstreet, J. Higgins, D. T. Lamb, P. Lavery, H. Lape, C. Moat, J. B. Palmer, J. F. Pruyn, J. Roe, V. Reddish, J. B. Morrell, W. Shires, B. Slade, R. Sanders. W. H. sanders. Titcomb and Waldron, G. Travis, N. Taylor, M. Traver, R. Tannard, H. H. Tenbrook. M. C. Vanderworken, J. Vanvorhees, C. and M. F. Vanderken. H. Vanvorhees, J. Vanderken, W. C. Vannees, H. S. Vanorman, W. H. Weaver, I. S. Wolcott, H. White.

TOWN OF BOLTON, N. Y.—O. Cotton, J. Smith, G. R. Fish, C. Doolittle. I. Streeten, J. Gates, E. Reynolds. J. Coolidge, J. Putney, R. Putney, G. Roberson, S. Roberson, O. Anderson, C. French, D. Barton, L. Wells, L. Davis. R. Davis. O. Person, D. Griffin, B. Griffin, W. Goodman, G. Bentley, A. Lane. L. Dalrymple, M. Granger, P. Norton, A. Randall, W. Bentley, L. Sherman, S. S. Whealer, E. S. Brown, S. Fuller, J. Varnum, M. Wells, J. Maxham, W. Pratt, S. Veeley, W. Griffin, J. Van Denburgh, S. Stanton, W. Brown, G. Reynolds, G. W. Seaman, A. Lenox, M. O. Brown, M. Fish, W. George, S. Burton, S. Trusdale, W. Taylor, W. Barber, C. Storey, A. A. Tanner, J. Lamb, J. B. Coolidge, J. Fordan, W. Thomas, W. Barton.

CARRIAGES! CARRIAGES! Joubert & White. (See page 14.)

OVERCOATS from $5 to $30, at WAIT'S CASH STORE.
FROCK COAT SUITS Cheap at WAIT'S. (See page 81.)

SEE INDEX, PAGE ELEVEN. 205

TOWN OF SHUSHAN, N. Y.—T. S. Cleaveland, J. Cleaveland, W. Orcutt, G. Arnott, A. Shaler, J. M. McFarland, H. Hedges, J. McClay, A. M. Collins, J. Collins, J. Ackley, A. McLean, A. McLean, H. Dunham, J. McGeoneh, J. Hill, J. Deebe, D. C. Beebe, R. Haskie, C. Randles, E. Stevens, S. Smith, S. Valentine, J. C. Simpson, A. Bowker, T. D. Oviatt, A. Dobin, J. Cowan, J. L. McFarland, D. Weir, J. Beverage, J. Shelle, Wm. H. Martin, J. Coulter, J. Small, J. Green, A. Rea, S. M. Arnott, G. Telford, T. McMorris, J. Maxwell, A. Shellie, A. Maxwell, A. Green, J. E. Robertson, J. Sinawll, J. Hill, Wm. Green, J. Green, T. B. Lonsie, G. M. Arnott, P. McArthur, J. R. McArthur, C. Brown, G. Coulter, C. B. Carter, H. Weir, W. G. Maxwell, J. Rouse, W. McFarland, Jas. Maxwell, L. Cole, J. Collins, R. Stewart, W. Vance, C. Weir.
TOWN OF CHESTER, N. Y.—A. Alger, S. Austin, G. Adams, A. Agard, J. B. Braley, F. H. Barrett, H. Bartlett, W. O'Baldwin, D. Burker, S. Bates, H. Batch, N. L. Bailey, L. Burdett, F. F. Bans, W. J. Bans, T. Bans, P. Byrne, M. L. Byrne, Wm. Byrne, George Braley, G. Bibby, T. Bibby, W. Beadnell, J. Braley, C. Burge, N. Church, O. Collins, P. Cohan, D. Cooper, T. J. Carpenter, A. Carey, A. B. Carr, D. Carr, S. G. Carpenter, Geo. Chandler, C. Cowles, F. Clipper, E. Carpenter, J. Donley, D. Donahy, M. Duell, Jas. L. Dunn, W. Dunn, E. Dunn, J. W. Dorris, L. Duell, J. Duell, H. Eastman, H. Ferriss, S. Ferriss, E. Force, F. Force, R. A. Foster, M. Fish, G. Fish, A. Fish, R. P. Fish, D. Fish, W. F. Ferriss, W. J. Ferriss, F. Ferriss, L. C. Ferriss, F. Force, C. E. Fish, W. Fish, S. Fish, N. A. Foster, I. W. Fish, I. Fish, J. W. Fish, J. P. Graves, H. C. Graves, Wm. F. Gould, R. H. Green, T. M. Hill, S. Hill, M. Hedges, D. Howe, W. Humes, S. Higgins, S. Howe, S. F. Howe, T. Johnson, D. J. Jones, A. W. Jenks, J. Kipp, J. L. Kipp, C. Kipp. C. Leggett, J. Lavery, E. Lavery, M. Mead, T. Murphy, R. Murphy, T. Mahony, P. McAvigh, A. May, A. Mead, L. Mead, B. D. Middleton, J. McKinstry, Jas. Metcalf, P. McPhillips, L. F. Mead, F. May, E. Mitchell, L. Mead, E. B. Mead, R. P. Mead, T. Mead, H. Mead, S. Mead, W. T. Mead, J. E. Mead, S. Mead, A. Mead, G. Mosey, J. R. Mills, T. Mills, I Mills, O. B. Mead. M. Nelson, C. Noxon, S. Newberg, A. S. Oliver, J. H. Parcells, C. Prouty, J. R. Perry, S. Perry, J. Peersons, W. S. Perry, N. Perry, D. Pitkin, W. H. Roberts, C. Reynolds, A. Robinson, J. Reynolds, J. H. Remington. E. Runnells, Nathan Rounds, R. Richard, J. Rawlins. D. Sullivan, S. Sherman, S. C. Starbuck, G. Swan, J. A. J. Smith, L. Southwick. T. J. Smith, P. Smith, A. A. Southwick. A. Scott, B. Smith, W. Shields, J. H. Smith, J. D. Smith, W. B. Tripp, S. Thurston, J. L. Tripp, A. Tabor, T. Taylor, A. Thurston, S. Thurston, H. Thompson, L. Thurston, G. H. Tabor, S. M. Tyrrell, C. Tyrrell, S. Thompson, C. Underwood, J. Underwood, M. Vosburgh, W. Vandeworker, D. Vandeworker, M. Vandeworker, A. Van Benthuysen, P. Van Benthuysen, R. Wood, J. Wood, J. Wallace, F. Wallace, R. Wallace, C. Wikes, S. C. Willis, S. A. Winslow, A. Wilcox, R. Wallace, J. Wallace. A. Whitney.
TOWN OF NISKAYUNA, N. Y.—U. V. Burk, I. N. Benedict, J. Bevis, L. Brewer, A. J. Bradt, J. Champion, I. F. Cregier, L. V. Clute, J. J. Carpenter, G. Chambers. M. T. Green, N. Griffith, W. Green, J. F. Hogle, E. Ham. C. Ham, C. Ham, P. L. Hilton, J. B. Keehum, J. C. Keehum, B. C. Lansing, E. Lichfield, I. N. Linly, H. Lamp, J. Milbanks. F. McCann, T. Mesick, T. V. Milmine, N. Pearso, L. Pepper, J. C. Pepper, J. H. Putnam, P. Palmer, C. Reynolds, F. Rankin, H. Rankin, C. Stanford, W. N. Stanford, J. Scarff, W. Steers, P. Snell, M. Siver, J. J. Spor, E. C. Tymeson, J. Van Vranken, C. Van Vranken, J. J. Vroman, J. B. Van Vranken, R. Van Vranken, G. Van Vranken, J. M. Van Vranken, J. P. Van Vranken, J. F. Vedder, P. Vandenburgh, J. A. Vedder, A. Van Vranken, J. Van Antwerp, J. Van Vranken, N. J. Van Vranken, A. Vedder. C. Vedder, W. Van Vranken, J. J. Vroman jr., J. Vanderbilt, M. Van Heuson, S. H. Vedder, M. Winne, J. Winne, G. L. Whitbeck, J. H. Warner, F. Wessels. J. Bonk. M. Barnt, M. Crawford, H. Lamp. J. P. Miller.
TOWN OF PRINCETOWN, N. Y.—W. J. Staley, J. Gresson. Marlett and Schuyler, A. Tuaing, J. Tuaing, J. Marlett. T. S. Marlett, E. Stack, J. Samson. A. Smealie, J. Donnon, W. Donnon, D. Elele, S. Donnon, J. and D. Taus, R. Smealie, J. Smealie, G. Dugall, R. B. Jeffers, R. B. Jeffers jr., J. Kelley, F. Winder, J. Conning, J. Mohr, T. Ennis, J. Ennis, J. Ennis, J. Countermine, T. Young, S. Houghton, J. Hardenburgh, A, Miller, C. Ruggles, R. Anghempack, J. M. Wear, J. Walker, E. Dougal, F. Rhoda, P. Fifabeck. W. Patten P. Brumaghim, I. Dorn. P. Levey, W. Liddle. W. Bird. D. Maybe, A. Robison, A. Liddle, R. J. Kelley, S. Kelly, R. Van Valkenburgh. W. Maxwell, C. Springer, J. C. Murray. C. Slater, J. Miverman, K. McGine. D. Ferguson. A. Wingate. J. F. Martin. J. Claston. J. C. Flansburgh, R. J. Wingate, R. Rynex, C. Grote, J. B. Bradshaw, H. Burbanks, J. Rynex, F. Lemmon, H. Weast, P. C. Connor, M. Van Vranken, W. C. Hanna. R. Bradshaw, H. Tenpenny, G. Trumbull, W. W. Rynex, J. J. Bradshaw, G. B. Gifford. F. Bradshaw, J. B. Bradshaw, C. Bullock, A. Griffene, W. Bradshaw, C. Robbins. J. Temple. J. Weart, J. W. Grifford, D. M. Rodgers. A. P. Wingate, J. H. Weart, J. Liddle, J. Weart jr., A. Tullock, J. Morrison, J. Kaley, A. Blessing, C. Kaley, A. A. Kaley, J. Van Derpool, W. Blessing. A. Mellarg, P. Van Buren, J. Miller. M. Broughain, S. Brown, A. T. Young, S. Gordon, W. Young, Morgan, A. Collins, J. Broughain, J. Kaley, F. Myndirse, F. Blessing. W. McMillen, A. Darrow, J. Tygert, A. McDonald, J. Weller, A. Kelley, T. Passigo, F. Gifford, M. Scrofferd, W. Brewer, M. Van Wormer.
TOWN OF MALTA, N. Y.—D. Allen, S. Arnold, D. Arnold, J. Arnold, W. Arnold, H. Allen, M. Butler, J. Black, W. Burtis, B. Bendon, G. Burr, G. W. Burr, J. Brehin, J. Brown, H. Brown, J. L. Brownell, D. Bidwell, J. H. Buck, I. Benedict, J. Baker, J. Barnhart, C. Corp, H. B. Corp. J. Coon, M. Conners, S. D. Caldwell, David N. Collamer, J. Chase, W. A. Collamer, P. Crowley, S. Corp, W. Denton, J. D. Deyoe, H. Doolittle, S.

Go to COREY'S, GLEN'S FALLS, for RIBBONS, TRIMMINGS, FANCY GOODS, &c.

W. A. Wilkins' Cheap Cash Clothing Store, Whitehall, N.Y.

Fancy NOTE PAPER and ENVELOPES, Stamped with Initials or Monograms, at E. H. BENDER'S, 73 State Street, Albany.

206 FARMERS' ALMANAC.

Davey, E. Dunning, S. Deyoe, W. Doharty, M. Y. Dunning, M. Devine, H. K. Doolittle, C. Denton, G. E. Denton, C. Davis, W. W. Emigh, J. Eldridge, T. Eldridge, J. E. Foster, L. J. Fish, B. Freeman, A. Fellows, A. C. Face, A. Fellows, T. R. Fish, L. Gage, W. German, I. Gifford, W. Haight, T. Hallion, R. S. Hall, H. Hegeman, D. Hennessy, J. Higgins, J. Hall, DeW. C. Harris, D. W. Hall, R. Hall, B. B. Hall, A. H. Hemphill, B. Hill, W. B. Hill, J. Johnson, T. J. Johnson, I. Knapp, L. Knapp, T. Kenny, B. Kerley, W. Kelly, H. Lansing, L. Landon, C. Lindley, J. R. Lockrow, D. R. Leggett, M. Lynch, E. D. Miller, D. Miller, J. Moore, E. Millard, C. McCrada, S. Morrissy, S. M. Morehouse, I. Millard, W. D. Marvin, J. Mohan, T. Mohan, M. Noonin, M. Noonin, D. Noonin, P. Noonin, R. A. Ogden, P. Parks, J. C. Payne, J. Phillips, J. S. Phillips, S. Phillips, H. Phillips, H. Patric, W. Ryan, G. Rogers, C. Rogers, S. N. Rowel, J. D. Raymond, I. Rowley, G. Rowley, J. Rowley, S. Rowley, J. C. Ramsdale, S. Ramsdale, P. Resley, G. N. Riley, J. Riley, C. Riley, J. O. Riley, S. Reno, E. Roarback, J. Southard, I. Southard, E. Sweet, I. Sickler, P. Sickler, C. D. Sickler, A. Stilwell, W. W. Stillwell, S.Sevathing, W. Selch, G. Speck, J. Shohe, J. Story, J. Shine, M. Smith, P. Sullivan, J. Tripp, C. Thompson, W. Tompkins, R. Tompkins, S. Van Hyning, H. Van Hyning jr., T. Van Hyning, J. Van Hyning, L. Van Hyning, H. Van Hyning, E. Van Hyning, G. H. Van Hyning, L. Van Aernem, A. J. Van Aernem, B. Vail, M. R. Vincent, D. Van Hyning, P. Vincent, W. Vanbenchoten, O. D. Vaughn, D. Van Wagoner, J. B. Weeks, K. L. Weeks, C. D. Worden, B. White, J. Wiggins, J. B. Wiggins, D. Wiggins, P. C. Wiggins, A. Weed.

TOWN OF WELLS, VT.—J. Norton, W. Lamb, W. Lamb, O. Goodrich, M. Cullen, I. Goodspeed, H. McFadden, H. E. Paul, H. Clark. O. Sprague, M. Williard, H. Show, R. Costello. A. Mitchell, I. Mitchell, T. Howe, E. Cone, W. Ronee, N. Francis, M. Francis, G. Gibbons, A. Borden, J. Borden, Nelson Lewis, H. B. Carpenter, C. Farrer, T. Morrills, A. Lewis, R. Lamb, B. T. Hadoway, N. Poul, J. F. Reed, J. Clemens, H. Francis, Theson Howe, J. Howe, P. Howe. J. Willlard, I. George, W. Cooper. A. Youngs, P. O'Brien, R. Pember, D. S. Parks, M. Parks, W. Goodspeed, S. Clark, J. H. Parks, Levi Lewis, A. C. Grover, M. D. Grover, L. Grover, W. Goodrich. J. W. Potter, J. S. Hulitt, E. Lewis, B. Lewis, C. Spaulding, C. A. Parker, H. Burton, J. C. Hopson, N. W. Ceondall, A. Hopsan, S. Buxton.

TOWN OF READSBORO', VT.—T. Greenslit, M. Brown, Dexter Bishop, N. Pitre, C. Bishop, A. Bishop, H. Martin, S. Hicks, A. Hicks, D. J. Hicks, H. D. Oakes, W. Yates, L. Bowen, O. M. Bowen, E. A. Pearson, Daniel Goodell, J. Gifford, H. L. Sheldon, C. S. Bryant, M. S. Bryant, P. W. Rice, A. Rice, S. Rathbone, W. Carpenter, D. Carpenter, S. Carpenter, D. C. Carpenter, A. Carpenter, E. Carpenter, G. Brown, M. Stafford, S. L. Stafford, S. Baily, D. N. Baily, E. K. Carpenter E. Tyler, T. Lenard, J. Stowe, A. Bishop, F. Fisk, A. Ballock, J. Ballock, T. S. Walker, R. Amidan, F. Hortau, N. Sprague, jr., L. Blanchard, W. T. Blanchard, J. P. Lord, J. B. Howe, E. A. Blanchard, E. W. Blanchard.

TOWN OF MANCHESTER, VT.—G. G. Burton, Z. Ward. W. Wilson, D. E. Purdy, S. N. Walker, B. McLean, J. C. Walker, S. Seaver, C. B. Munson, H. Lathrop, E. Lathrop, M. Purdy, J. S. Pettibone, D. H. Dyer, J. W. Bowen. J. D. Purdy. W. A. Purdy, N. S. Purdy, E. H. Graves, L. Lampson, M. Cook, D. P. Walker, J. Bell. J. Green, J. H. Phelps, J. Williams, D. B. Smith, J. I. sheldon, S. Boynton, J. Hawley, W. Brownson. A. L. Miner, E. J. Hawley, H. K. Fowler, B. S. Vanderlip, B. Munson, P. Dudley, L. Munson, J. W. Burnham, E. L. Way, N. J. Pusay, M. W. Hall, A. B. Way, J. Slocum, A. Renlo, A. Wyman, H. Reed, W. Reynolds, M. Reynolds, M. Wait, J. Seaver, M. Logan. M. Whitten, M. Burkirk, A. Eddy, H. Botsford, J. Perry, D. Busher, J. Elliott, L. and M. Pettibone, J. R. and J. Burnett, D. Phillips, W. Taylor, S. Boston, E. Mattison, A. Lawrence, J. Wicks, S. W. Bourn, C. Pond, H. Taylor, G. W. Utley, D. Eddy, J. B. Hollister, M. Wicks, G. Taylor, S. Dean, C. A. Roberts, E. A. Jameson, W. N. Dean, F. A. Baker, E. J. McNaughton, S. Benedict, F. A. Benedict. E. Hollister, R. A. Roberts, J. Weatherbee, A. Richardson, J. D. Wait, J. Battis, E. smith, F. Sykes, J. W. Kelley, O, McNebo, G. Wilson, J. B. Nichols, B. Jameson, C. F. Long, Wm. Chellis, S. B. Young, A. Briggs, A. G. Clark, G. Wilson, J. Howe.

TOWN OF STAMFORD, VT.—J. W. Millard, R. D. Brown, W. Bratton, A. F. Bratton, J. Houghton, S. C. Millard, W. S. Brooks, J. O. Sanford, A. W. Willmarth, A. F. Bratton jr., G. Lamb, W. B. Cook, O. Harris, T. P. Goodrich, F. R. Hannan, J. Stroud, D. Morey, D. Blood, J. C. Stafford, M. Cudworth, N. W. Smith, R. Parker, P. Morrissey, S. W. Webster, I. Roberts, J. White, J. Sullivan, P. Sullivan, G. Bridges, J. Bridges, A. Lee, O. Clough, J. E. Oaks, H. Barber.

TOWN OF GREENFIELD, N. Y.—N. C. Allard, H. L. Akin, D. M. Angel, G. C. Alger, A. C. Allard, C. E. Ambler, S. B. Alcot, E. Angel, C. Allen, A. Allen, R. Allen, N. Allen, J. Allen, J. Ashton, L. Adams, S. Archer, P. Bennet. D. Bullard, W. Bently, C. Brigham, J. C. Bowen, J. Boll, M. Barret, C. Butler, S. C. Barber, J. A. Briant, G. Briggs, A. Baily, C. E. Benedict. S. Baily, J. Billings, W. Bockes, T. Burdict, A. M. Bracket, A. Bracket, D. Ballou, C. Bullard, J. C. Brinen, G. B. Bixby. J. Byrne, G. R. Barber, G. Bishop, A. Bently, E. Brown, W. Bell. N. Baker, A. Baker, F. Rowland, F. O. Conklin, R. Clokie, J. Clark, J. Clayton, D. Cornell, W. R. Colamer, J. Cary, R. Conkhite, J. Conkhite. T. Canty. J. V. Conklite, S. Calkins, S. A. Conkhite, L. S. Coper, I. Carpenter. H. Cramer, G. Comstock, T. Comstock, A. S. Conkhite. C. Chamberlin, T. B. Carrol, J. Chapman, R. R. Cole, C. M. Clark, B. Croton, M. Cady, J. Conly, L. Cady, W. Cole, J. Cory, P. Coury. D. C. Cary, N. Cary, B. S. Carman, V. Chatfield, C. Cole, J. Carman, S. Craig, G. Corp, W. Camfield, J. J. Craig, S. Covell jr., I. Crawford, N. Corp. S. Carman, A. Cary, J. H. Crator, W. Dunning, J Denton, E. Duel, J. Delany, W. C. Donan, B. W.

GARRETT'S TOOTH PASTE Preserves the Teeth from decay.

The Place to buy Clothing Cheap is at WAIT'S.
The Latest Styles of HATS and CAPS at WAIT'S. (See page 81.)

SEE INDEX, PAGE ELEVEN. 207

Dyre, J. Dillon, P. Duel, Z. Daniels, J. T. Daniels, P. P. Deyoe, E. Danon, I. Dewit, A. Day, B. C. Dake, W. Dake, C. Dake, A. J. Dorman, P. H. Dorman, A. Dake, C. W. Dake, S. S. Easton, J. Ehrenbrack, E. Edwards, D. W. Eldridge, C. Foote, I. Frink, J. D. Ford, W. Fisher, M. C. Facon, L. Green, D. D. A. Green, J. Green, J. Gifford, E. T. Green, G. A. Goodwin, J. B. Gardner, H. L. Gardner, S. Gregory, D. Harvey, G. Hawkins, R. Hewit, H. Hill, A. H. Hewit, C. Harris, L. Harris, W. Harris, D. C. Hoit, M. Hecock, J. Hays, A. D. Hewit, C. Hewit, E. Hays, H. Humes, I. Harris, J. Herritage, O. Hathorn, B. H. Ingham, S. B. Ingham, E. H. Johnson, J. G. Johnson, J. P. Jesup, H. King, L. King, D. Kane, H. C. King, E. S. Ketcham, T. Kelly, W. King, C. B. Kasson, P. H. Killmer, H. T. Lawton, J. Lockwood, H. Lockwood, H. Lincoln, Z. Lawrence, T. Lyman, H. Kingsly, S. S. Lewis, J. S. Lincoln, A. Martin, L. Mosher, W. Canty, J. A. Miller, T. Butcher, E. T. Miller, W. A. Medberry, L. Mills, N. Medberry, W. Middlebrooks, M. D. Morehouse, T. Morehouse, P. Mullen, S. Mitchel, J. Morehouse, J. Newell, J. O'Farrell, R. M. Ormsby, A. Overbagh, C. G. Petit, S. Pearsal, O. Peacock, J. S. Peacock, B. T. Prior, J. Quivey, K. H. Ross, E. Rood, W. F. Rowland, J. L. Rowland, A. Russel, W. Smith, E. Smith, J. V. Smith, B. Standish, E. Standish, G. Spaulding, J. Seamons, L. Scot, I. Scofield, J. G. Smith, J. L. Scot, A. H. Scot, R. Scofield, O. Sears, D. F. Scot, W. Shoemaker, J. B. Spence, S. Scouton, W. Shields, N. Shaul, A. J. Spring, D. J. Shaul, J. Gouie, J. H. Smith, T. H. Tompkins, W. H. Warring, W. H. Ring, J. H. White, W. H. Rood, C. L. Williams, J. B. Wing, G. G. Woodward, D. Wheeler, S. D. Williams, N. Williams, H. Whipple, S. H. Wiley, J. Wheeler, E. R. Youngs, C. Hewit, E. Hodges, B. Hill.

Ladies' Undergarments and Gored Tucked Skirts, at P. H. COREY'S, GLEN'S FALLS.

Buy your Clothing of W. A. Wilkins, Whitehall, N. Y.

SPECIAL CIRCULAR
To Beginners and Amateurs in Music.

At the beginning of the Winter Term, January 5th, 1870,

RIPLEY FEMALE COLLEGE,
POULTNEY VT.,

Will commence a regular COURSE in Music, such as is pursued at the best Conservatories, consisting of Theory, Vocalization, Piano or Organ. Those finishing the prescribed Course in these three studies (Piano or Organ being optional with the student) will receive a Diploma, after passing a satisfactory examination.

The class system will be pursued, and lessons given every day instead of twice a week. The advantages of the class system over private instruction are—

1st. Students, by reciting every day, avoid rendering mistakes habitual, and will have them easily corrected.

2d. They accustom themselves to playing before others, thus overcoming a great portion of that timidity and nervousness so unfavorable to good execution.

3d. By observation, criticism and comparison—by hearing the different suggestions to other students, they not only learn to criticise their own playing, but also that of others, thus fitting themselves in a much shorter time for practical and successful teachers and performers.

Instruction given on all the smaller instruments when desired.

Sheet music sent on receipt of marked price.

Teachers supplied with music at a discount.

Further information can be had by addressing

REV. J. NEWMAN, D. D., President.
or H. C. TREAT, Prof. of Music, R. F. C.,

Poultney, Vt.

EXPENSES.

Tuition in the Full Course,	$60 1st Term.
" " "	50 2d "
" " "	40 3d "
" one branch "	20 per "
Use of Piano for Practice, 1 div. daily,	8 per year.
Board in Institution, including Furnished Room, Lights and Washing,	234 per Year.
Fuel (when used) per Week,	50 cents.

For information in regard to the Literary Department address

REV. J. NEWMAN, D. D., President.

☞ Open as a Summer Resort July, August and September.

www.ingramcontent.com/pod-product-compliance
Lightning Source LLC
Chambersburg PA
CBHW032136160426
43197CB00008B/668